The Future of Pensions
in the United States

Pension Research Council Publications

A complete listing of PRC publications appears at the back of this volume.

The Future of Pensions in the United States

Edited by Ray Schmitt

Published by

The Pension Research Council
Wharton School of the University of Pennsylvania

Distributed by the
University of Pennsylvania Press
Philadelphia

The chapters in this volume are based on papers presented at the Pension Research Council Symposium, "The Future of Pensions in the United States," Philadelphia, Pennsylvania, May 7–8, 1992.

Copyright © 1993 by the Pension Research Council of the Wharton School of the University of Pennsylvania

Printed in the United States of America

Library of Congress Cataloging-in-Publication Data
The Future of pensions in the United States / edited by Ray Schmitt.
    p.   cm.
  Includes bibliographical references and index.
  ISBN 0-8122-3239-9
  1. Pensions—United States.   2. Pension trusts—United States.   3. Retirement income—United States.   I. Schmitt, Ray.
HD7125.F879   1994
331.25′2′0973—dc20   93-21092
                                 CIP

Structure and Role of the Council

Founded in 1952, the Pension Research Council is one of several research organizations within the Wharton School of the University of Pennsylvania. As part of the nation's first school of business, the Council functions in a bracing environment of academic freedom and objectivity. The basic purpose of the Council is to undertake research that will have the effect of strengthening those arrangements designed to provide the financial resources needed for a secure and dignified old age. It seeks to broaden public understanding of these complex arrangements through basic research into their social, economic, legal, actuarial, and financial foundations. Although geared to the long view of the employee benefits institution, projects undertaken by the Council are always relevant to real world concerns and frequently focus on issues under current debate.

The Council is composed of individuals with career experience with large corporate plan sponsors, organized labor, actuarial consulting firms, the accounting profession, the legal profession, investment counselors, banks, insurance companies, not-for-profit organizations, and several academic disciplines. The Council does not speak with one voice and espouses no particular point of view. The members do share a general desire to encourage and strengthen private sector approaches to old age economic security, while recognizing the essential role of Social Security and other income maintenance programs in the public sector.

The members of the Council are appointed by the Dean of the Wharton School and serve indeterminate terms. The Council reviews the findings of current research projects, acts to generate new research proposals, and reviews external proposals. In performing these functions, the members identify areas in which additional research is needed, consider the general form the research should take, and then evaluate the qualifications of persons deemed capable of carrying out the approved projects.

The research projects are carried out by persons commissioned under individually designed ad hoc arrangements. The researchers are normally academic scholars, but nonacademic experts with special qualifications for the tasks involved may be used. The research findings are reviewed by members of the Council who may offer criticism as to both the substance of the report and the inferences drawn from the studies. The author of any manuscript is free to accept or reject the criticisms of the Council members, but the latter have the privilege of recording in the published document their dissent from any interpretive statements or points of view expressed by the author. Whether or not written dissents are included, publication should not be interpreted to indicate either agreement or disagreement by the Council or its individual members with the substance of the document or its inferences.

The Future of Pensions in the United States

Introduction   xi
Ray Schmitt

1. Gaps in Retirement Income Adequacy   **1**
Emily S. Andrews
Comments by Donald S. Grubbs, Jr.   32
Comments by Gary D. Hendricks   40
Comments by Bruce D. Schobel   45

**2. Innovations and Trends in Pension Plan
Coverage, Type, and Design**   **53**
Olivia S. Mitchell and Anna M. Rappaport
Comments by Alan L. Gustman   92
Comments by Marc M. Twinney, Jr.   98

**3. Roundtable Discussion: Defined Benefit/Defined
Contribution Trends**   **102**
Ray Schmitt (Moderator), Angela Chang,
Robert L. Clark, Edwin C. Hustead
The Trend Away from Defined Benefit Pension Plans   111
Angela Chang
Firm Choice of Type of Pension Plan: Trends and
Determinants   115
Robert L. Clark, Ann A. McDermed, and
Michelle White Trawick

4. Death and Taxes: Can We Fund for Retirement Between Them?   **126**
Gordon P. Goodfellow and Sylvester J. Schieber
Comments by David C. Lindeman   180
Comments by Alicia H. Munnell   187

5. Pension Benefit Guarantees in the United States: A Functional Analysis   **194**
Zvi Bodie and Robert C. Merton
Comments by James B. Lockhart III   235

6. Estimating the Current Exposure of the Pension Benefit Guaranty Corporation to Single-Employer Pension Plan Terminations   **247**
Christopher M. Lewis and Richard L. Cooperstein

7. Panel Discussion: The Role of Regulation in Pension Policy   **277**
Dallas Salisbury (Moderator), Evelyn A. Petschek, Meredith Miller, James A. Klein, Phyllis C. Borzi, Edwin C. Hustead, Richard Hinz

Contributors   297
Index   307

Introduction

Ray Schmitt

Well documented demographic changes have caused many experts to express concern about the nation's capacity to provide retirement income and medical care to the future elderly at levels comparable to today's, while simultaneously meeting other needs of society. If economic growth rates do not mirror historical averages, the elderly may have to choose whether to retire with a lower standard of living than they would have achieved under more favorable economic conditions, or to work longer. Furthermore, pockets of poverty are likely to remain among older Americans, particularly for minorities and nonmarried women.

In the current economic environment of large and growing federal deficits, Congress is faced with painful choices in achieving policy goals: raise taxes, reduce spending, or some combination of both. As the federal deficit has mounted, so too has the clamor to cut back on some of the direct and preferential treatment woven into our tax system. One target is the estimated $50 billion tax expenditure related to tax-favored pension plans—the largest tax expenditure in the federal budget. Indeed, steps have already been taken to reduce pension largesse and to ensure that tax-favored plans are broadly based and nondiscriminatory. But what effect will further actions have on the future of pensions in the United States?

Our private pension system is undergoing gradual change in the type of pension plan commonly offered. This may be the result of a number of factors: changing business structure, with new jobs coming primarily in small firms; changes in workers' preferences; and a reaction to the considerable and complex regulation of pension plans—particularly the traditional defined benefit plan. The effects of job mobility on pension accumulations, and vice versa, may become a source of greater policy scrutiny as the consequences of the integration of the United States into a larger global economy become more apparent. The need for more flexible and less job-dependent retirement savings may increase the demand for defined contribution plans in the context of employer-sponsored pensions and for more purely individual savings. These possibilities may reinforce Government involvement in assuring that defined contribution account balances are saved for retirement, and may arouse renewed interest in proposals like inflation-indexed Government bonds.

Employer-sponsored pensions and other retirement savings are tax-favored, but the efficacy and distribution of those tax advantages is a matter of tax policy debate. The fact that only half the work force are covered by an employer-sponsored pension plan raises concerns about both equity and adequacy of the private pension system. Critics cite the low pension plan participation rates for lower income earners and higher rates for higher income earners. They claim that distributions of this sort are inequitable in a tax subsidized system paid for by all taxpayers. This has led to a call from some analysts to reconsider the tax preferences accorded employer-sponsored retirement plans. Others counter that these considerations may be distracting policy analysts and policy makers from focusing on a more comprehensive evaluation of our nation's retirement income security system.

A recurrent theme in the papers presented in this volume is that there is a conflict between retirement income policy and tax policy, with the latter seemingly gaining the upper hand. Some say that this conflict has led to distortions in public policy. Critics charge that the host of legislative changes enacted during the 1980s was only outdone by the number of complex and onerous rules issued by the regulatory agencies to implement the new laws. Some of these changes appear to have been designed to raise revenues without increasing tax rates or reducing spending, rather than to enhance retirement income security.

American workers and retirees have come to expect that their pensions will be protected. However, the financial problems of the Pension Benefit Guaranty Corporation (PBGC) and future economic conditions in certain sectors of the economy may put this guarantee to a test. Coming on the heels of the savings and loan association (S&L) collapse and the massive taxpayer bailout, the situation causes alarm. Unless significant changes are made in the way pension insurance is priced and benefits funded, it may be necessary either to curtail the portion of the pension promise that Government can guarantee or to expand taxpayer liability.

I. Gaps in Retirement Income Adequacy

Evaluating the successes and failures of our retirement income system is a daunting task both because of the presence of complex technical issues and because personal value judgments must invariably be involved. Emily Andrews draws on a broad spectrum of research to establish a framework for discussing retirement income adequacy.

Andrews first evaluates the current status of the elderly based on her review of empirical measures of retirement income and retirement income adequacy. Her review suggests that poverty is disproportionately found among nonmarried individuals and minorities. Furthermore, while the income of the aged is generally similar to that of the working-age population, she states that the retirement income of many may still not be sufficient for them to maintain their preretirement living standards. According to Andrews, this reality may reflect the relatively higher degree of income inequality found among retirees. But she finds it more troublesome that pockets of relative poverty are likely to remain.

Andrews's paper lays out three different measures that can be used to assess the adequacy of retirement income. The standards examined compare retirement income to (1) preretirement income, (2) income of younger persons, and (3) poverty levels. All the methods examined by Andrews show that retirees do not need to replace their full preretirement income to maintain their standard of living, at least at the time of retirement.

With regard to the first method, Andrews cites various replacement ratios developed over the years that compare retirement and preretirement income. These studies make adjustments for changes in work related expenses, taxes, and savings that occur before and after retirement. For example, a study by Bruce Palmer indicates that married couples earning $30,000 or more need about 68 percent of their preretirement income replaced in order to maintain their preretirement standard of living. This needed replacement percentage is larger for those earning less than $30,000, increasing to 82 percent for those earning $15,000.

Andrews discusses techniques in comparing retirement income to income of younger persons. At the same time, she makes the reader aware of the difficulty in making such comparisons. Nonetheless, she reports that, taken as a whole, the aged population generally enjoy a standard of living comparable to the working-age population.

But Andrews notes that median retirement income replacement rates for various segments of the retired population reported in studies by other researchers are generally well below the various measures of retirement income adequacy discussed in her paper. Andrews attributes this difference partly to the fact that the calculations examined were limited to Social Security and pensions. Moreover, she says that hypothetical replacement rates may overestimate the income needs of retirees.

Andrews discusses two computer models for projecting retirement income levels in the twenty-first century. One set of projections is derived from the PRISM model developed by ICF/Lewin. The other set is derived from the DYNASIM model developed by researchers at the Urban Institute. But, she points out, projection models are only as accurate as the assumptions that go into them. Even though pension coverage rates are not expected to increase, both models project higher real levels of retirement income in the future. In particular, private pension income is expected to be more prevalent with pension recipiency for married couples projected to be over 85 percent. Nonetheless, Andrews stresses that serious pockets of poverty are likely to remain, particularly among minorities and nonmarried women.

When members of the baby boom start to retire, Andrews speculates that many women will be entitled to higher Social Security benefits on their own account and to pension payments from employer-sponsored plans. Consequently, some of the gaps in retirement income adequacy observed today may not be an issue 20 years from now. But she cautions that many retirees may be forced to reduce their living standards in retirement and may face greater discrepancies in purchasing power than earlier generations.

Andrews maintains that the maintenance of middle-class living standards will require increased lifetime savings, but a significant restructuring of employer-sponsored pension plans does not appear to be the most efficient means of increasing retirement savings. Moreover, requiring small employers to provide pension plans along the lines of a Minimum Universal Pension System (MUPS) advocated by President Carter's Commission on Pension Policy during the early 1980s, would not, in her opinion, be the best remedy. This conclusion is based on the disemployment effects that she argues would be caused by such a mandate.

Andrews offers several options for improving retirement income adequacy. For instance, the Social Security benefit formula could be modified to further increase replacement rates for lower earners. If this were done, she says, the 50 percent Social Security spousal benefit could be reduced and Supplementary Security Income (SSI) benefits increased. At the same time greater efforts could be made to seek out those who are eligible for SSI but who do not apply for benefits because of lack of knowledge or the stigma associated with "welfare" benefits. Of course, improvements in Social Security and SSI could increase the cost of the current system. But Andrews notes that, if Social Security benefits were all subject to tax (with the exception of the return of employee contributions), additional revenue would be available to reduce poverty among the elderly.

Even if legislators seek new policies to encourage savings and undertake greater regulation of the financial sector, Andrews concludes that inequality of income and poverty will continue. Nonetheless, she thinks retirement income policy should be targeted toward the maintenance of preretirement living standards and the eradication of pockets of poverty among the aged.

The paper's first discussant, Donald Grubbs, concurs with Andrews's policy goals and suggestions. But he emphasizes that retirement income adequacy cannot be thoroughly addressed without considering the separate needs for a regular flow of income to meet recurring expenses and for resources available to meet health care costs when they occur. Grubbs notes that the lack of adequate health insurance for the elderly is not essentially different from the lack of coverage for younger people, many of whom have no health insurance at all. What he strongly stresses, however, is the enormous unpredictability of health care costs for retirees and what effect that could have on maintaining preretirement living standards.

Grubbs questions the significant increase in the proportion of retirees projected to receive pensions in the next century. While Andrews finds these microsimulation projections "baffling," Grubbs calls them "unlikely." This opinion is based on a number of factors. Grubbs reasons that it is unlikely that the proportion of employees covered under employer plans will significantly increase. He also points out that defined benefit plans are being replaced by defined contribution arrangements. Defined-contribution plans usually make payments in the form of lump sum distributions that are often consumed before retirement. Increased labor mobility also makes it less likely that employees will continue employment long enough to receive a significant life annuity. All these factors, he concludes, bode ill for improvement in the number of persons receiving pensions.

Both models adopt the Social Security Administration's assumptions regarding future growth in real wages (that is, wages in excess of inflation). Grubbs notes that these projections result in real wage increases of 43 percent over the next thirty years. While a "rising tide raises all ships," he emphasizes that different wage growth assumptions would lead to very different results from those indicated by these models. Grubbs tells us there are only three ways both to eradicate poverty among the elderly and to enable all Americans more nearly to maintain preretirement living standards. The first is to increase Social Security so that Social Security by itself provides an adequate minimum retirement income for all retirees. The second would require every employer to provide a minimum pension. The third would be a combination of the first two.

Grubbs comments that comparing retirees with the working age population serves no useful purpose because it ignores the fact that older workers earn substantially more than younger workers. He thinks a more appropriate comparison would be to look at workers between ages 50 and 60. He claims that such an analysis would show that retirees have substantially less income than those a few years younger who have not yet retired.

Gary Hendricks, the paper's second discussant, stresses that it is not so important that a model avoid systematically overstating or understating an income component, but that the distribution and the covariance of the components of income for individuals be correct. Given his reservations concerning the limitations of microsimulation modeling, he seriously questions the conclusions Andrews suggests based on the projections she reviewed. To be specific, he says that, although only 46 percent of the full-time workforce are presently covered by private pensions, 85 percent of workers in the model end up with one. Yet there may be a high correlation between pension coverage on the old job and pension coverage on the new job.

Hendricks is also distressed by the real wage growth assumptions used in the models reviewed by Andrews, and points out that real wage rates, on average, have grown more slowly over the past twenty years. There is nothing in the discussion of the simulations to convince him that, for the next generation of retirees, many of those in the income groups with the greatest need will find their situation greatly improved. Since even a modest amount of income from assets can make a large difference in determining whether one is near-poor during retirement, Hendricks surmises that even a small mandated employer contribution to a defined contribution plan could ease the stress of retirement for many who otherwise become near-poor when they leave the labor force.

Bruce Schobel, the paper's third discussant, echoes concern over the reliability of projections made many years into the future and emphasizes that they have to be regarded with considerable skepticism. He feels, however, that we can probably start from the premise that levels of Social Security (but not Medicare) benefits will remain basically the same as today for several decades.

Schobel points out that the present-law Social Security Old-Age,

Survivors, and Disability Insurance (OASDI) benefit formula produces absolutely stable and predictable replacement rates under any economic condition. Thus Social Security's contribution to future retirement income can probably be predicted with greater confidence than that of any other source. But, as he points out, normal retirement age for full Social Security benefits rises for workers born in 1938 and later. This amounts to a benefit reduction.

Workers born after 1959 will have to work until age 67 to get the same Social Security replacement rate that a worker gets today at age 65. Schobel says that unless retirement behavior changes Social Security will contribute less toward the adequacy of retirement income in the future than it does today. Of course with Americans living longer, he says, we might anticipate that some of this extra longevity will be reflected in longer working lives, rather than going entirely to longer periods of leisure.

While Social Security law may not change very much in the next thirty to forty years, Schobel observes that changes already scheduled in the law and the way that they function in the context of changing family situations and other circumstances will cause the level of benefits to fall substantially relative to previous earnings. Thus, everything else being equal, Schobel predicts that retirement income can be expected to be less adequate in the future than it is today.

Although the appropriate response to this prediction would be to increase savings of various kinds, Schobel says that Americans seem to be doing exactly the opposite. As a result, he is much less confident that "retirement income will improve in the future," as Andrews predicts. In fact, he cautions us that the reverse might be true.

II. Innovations and Trends in Pension Plan Coverage, Type, and Design

Olivia Mitchell and Anna Rappaport outline pension trends and identify key factors, including changes in business conditions and career patterns, that will shape employer-sponsored pensions of tomorrow. According to the authors, it appears unlikely that the nation will return to an era like the 1970s and early 1980s when pension plans flourished. Growth of pension plans generally, and of defined benefit and defined contribution plans specifically, will depend on a number of factors including demographic trends, the business environment, human resource policy, and public policy and federal regulation. They say the big unknown for the future is how strong large businesses will be and how strong the traditionally unionized manufacturing component of the economy will be.

The authors outline forces that would either depress or support pension coverage. Forces that would *depress* coverage are lower real pay levels and marginal tax rates; more competitive labor and product markets causing buyouts and corporate downsizing; reduced profits, pay, worker-firm attachment, unionization, and firm size; increased administrative costs and complexity resulting from pension regulation on top of which rising health care costs are superimposed; and extensive and complex pension regulation, including nondiscrimination requirements, premiums charged for pension insurance, and fees reducing employer's ability to offer pension plans.

Forces that would *support* pension coverage and defined benefit plans are the aging of the workforce, which will probably heighten awareness of retirement income needs; increasing desires to retire early, which raise the need for pension income; the tax preferences accorded qualified plans; employer need to reduce turnover for younger employees while increasing retirement rates among older workers; and increasing concerns over the long-term level of both Social Security and Medicare benefits.

Health benefits for both active and retired workers will have an important effect on retirement offerings. Mitchell and Rappaport point out that workers' decisions to retire are increasingly being conditioned not only by their pensions but by the health insurance they will have during retirement. It is possible that retiree health insurance cost pressures may force more employers to reconsider the entire cost, structure, and contents of their retirement package. Moreover, they maintain that any national health insurance plan will exert severe cost pressures on employers not currently offering pensions and could come at the expense of a further reduction in pension coverage.

According to the authors the bottom line is that a more rational, stable, and coherent retirement income policy is needed, and that pension legislation should fit into this policy rather than being formulated in deficit reduction terms. They feel that public policy should preserve a central role for pensions and both defined benefit and defined contribution plans should be available to meet the diverse needs of business and workers.

Alan Gustman, the first discussant of the Mitchell/Rappaport paper, stresses that economists do not know enough about the importance of the various forces shaping workers' demands for pensions, and the firm's willingness to supply them, to determine the size of the effect of each on the motivations for pensions and the pension related outcomes observed in the labor market. Moreover, there are no direct attempts to estimate econometrically the relationships between pension policy, compensation, labor inputs, and output produced. He states that as a result, Mitchell and Rappaport have good reason for limiting much of their discussion to *qualitative* effects and the direction of the impact of specific causal factors, rather than proposing *quantitative* answers to the questions they address. Rather than commenting extensively on the paper, he outlines what is needed to provide better quantitative measures.

Gustman tells us that economists have a better idea of the forces shaping the *workers' demand* for pensions than they do of the forces shaping the *firms' willingness* to supply them. But he states that we have no reliable estimates of the importance of each of the separate effects operating on either side of the market. An appropriately specified model would tell us about the forces shaping the demand for pensions and would provide enough information to gauge the likely effects of changes in public policy on the workers' demands. But while the empirical models we have available generate results with appropriate signs—that special tax treatment of pensions increases demand for pensions and that higher incomes are associated with higher demand—Gustman considers the models relatively crude.

Because of the foregoing factors, Gustman states that there are many questions that we are in no position to answer quantitatively. How big are the effects of regulations? What would be the effects of relaxing these regulations? Gustman says we know the directions of these effects, that is, the qualitative answers. But we do not know their quantitative importance.

Marc Twinney, the paper's second discussant, brings the perspective of a manager of a large industrial pension plan. Twinney holds that the primary reason larger, international manufacturing firms provide pensions is to remove older, less efficient employees from the workforce in a socially responsible way. He declares that firms do not provide pensions to recruit and hire employees or to tie employees to the workforce and avoid recruiting or training costs—reasons cited by economists as concurrent functions served by defined benefit plans. The fact that this occurs is incidental to the primary goal. These secondary effects, according to Twinney, result from controlling the costs of providing retirement income and are acceptable to the firm and to employees.

Twinney states that large firms prefer the defined benefit form for their retirement objectives not only because of cost but also because of the effectiveness of this type of pension arrangement. Defined benefit plans allocate more of the pension contributions to those persons who retire than to those who depart before retirement age. Moreover, the sponsors' assumption of investment risk (and reward) has driven direct employer cost down compared with defined contribution plans, according to Twinney. Since the defined benefit plan can be focused at a selected retirement age or maximized at a specific period of service, orderly retirement can be encouraged that is not dependent on high market values (that affect defined contribution account balances) or subjective factors. He declares that any one of these advantages of the defined benefit form of providing pensions could be compelling; collectively they are overwhelming.

Twinney asserts that the web of law and regulations designed to ensure that lower paid workers accrue adequate benefits under tax-favored plans is one of the consequences of the failure of the nation to mandate a minimum private pension as recommended in 1980. He points out that in the United Kingdom the regulation of private pension plans is made less complex because of the requirement that employers provide a second level of Social Security benefits unless they "contract out" by providing supplemental private benefits. However, just as other paper presenters and discussants point out, Twinney considers it doubtful that the United States could now solve the pension coverage issue by requiring a minimum private benefit when mandated coverage is probably key to any solution on the health care coverage issue our nation is facing.

III. Roundtable Discussion: Defined Benefit/Defined Contribution Trends

The trend away from defined benefit plans and toward defined contribution plans is the subject of much debate. Between 1975 and 1988 the proportion of pension participants covered by a primary defined benefit pension plan fell from 87 percent to 66 percent. There are differences of opinion as to what is causing this movement and what the implications are for future retirement income security.

Angela Chang sets an analytical framework for a roundtable discussion on the topic. She does this by reviewing three economic studies that focus on two competing explanations of the declining prevalence of primary defined benefit plans: a shift in the preferences of firms and a shift in employment. The first emphasizes the effects of pension regulations, which have become very complex and have raised the cost of sponsoring defined benefit plans relative to defined contribution plans. The second focuses on the shift in employment in the U.S. labor market away from manufacturing jobs, where defined benefit plans are typically offered, toward more service-oriented industries, where defined contribution plans predominate.

Chang emphasizes that how we choose to define a trend is quite important. If we define a trend in terms of the number of firms that offer defined benefit plans, we would conclude that the decline results primarily from a shift in firms' preferences. If we define the trend in terms of the numbers of workers who are covered by defined benefit plans, it would suggest that the trend primarily results from a shift in employment across sectors and that the shift in firms' preferences accounts for less than half the decline. Although she says a shift in the firms' preferences does seem to be a significant factor, none of the studies examine the specific reasons for the diminished popularity of defined benefit plans, such as whether regulations have really raised the cost and reduced the advantages of defined benefit plans or whether the changes in the U.S. labor and product markets have made employers more reluctant to bear the investment risk associated with defined benefit plans.

Robert Clark presents an update of his earlier work on trends and determinants in pension plan choice. Clark estimates that structural changes in the economy account for less than 18 percent of the total decline in the relative use of defined benefit plans. He shows that not only is there a change in the total distribution of the percentage of firms in each size category that is part of a structural change in the economy, there is also a change in the percentage of firms in each size category that have a defined benefit plan. Even among the largest plans with 10,000 or more participants, he reports that the proportion of firms with defined benefit plans declined by 5 percentage points. While it is clear that a larger proportion of the decline in defined benefit plans is among small firms, Clark says it is incorrect to say there is no change in the distribution of pension plans among large firms. He also points out that there is a time trend away from defined benefit plans, so that even the larger firms starting new plans are much more likely to set up defined contribution plans.

Edwin Hustead underscores Clark's observations by showing that the percentage of medium and large employers sponsoring defined benefit plans has declined over the last decade from around 90 percent to 69 percent according to the Hay/Huggins benefits survey. At the same time defined contribution plans are now offered by 95 percent of the surveyed firms. While most larger employers have both kinds of plans, small employers choose a defined contribution arrangement if they adopt a plan at all. Hustead says we lose sight of the fact that small employers become medium employers and medium employers become large employers. As a benefits consultant, he says that an employer's choice of plan is driven largely by the expense in establishing and maintaining the plan. Because compliance with the laws and regulations is particularly costly for defined benefit plans, he predicts that ten years from now perhaps only governments and large firms will have such plans.

IV. Death and Taxes: Can We Fund for Retirement Between Them?

Gordon Goodfellow and Sylvester Schieber outline the evolution of the government's commitment to retirement security and evaluate equity considerations related to various elements of the retirement system. Their paper points out that government commitments to retirement income security are coming under increasing scrutiny and criticism because of the relative burden they place on the current level of government finance, and because they pose an even larger burden in the future. They argue that, before striking off piecemeal to fix any part of the retirement system, policy makers should carefully consider how they might coordinate policy adjustments to achieve long-term goals. They develop an analytical framework to assess the extent of the federal government's commitment to individual retirement accruals under various programs and how these interact.

The federal government's earliest and longest ongoing commitment to retirement security has been to its own workers through the direct provision of pensions. Its largest current commitment to retirement income security is through Social Security, which today touches the lives of almost every worker and retiree in the country. The commitment that has been least understood, and in many ways most controversial, has been the provision of tax incentives for employers to establish and maintain pension programs for their own workers. The authors discuss the nature of the government's commitments to each of these programs and the public policy concerns that are being voiced about them.

The authors describe the redistributional aspects of Social Security benefits and how early retirees under the program almost always benefited from a program that paid out more in benefits to successive cohorts of workers than generally would have been paid out under an actuarially fair retirement program. But they discuss present value calculations that show that many of today's younger and higher-paid workers will not receive Social Security benefits commensurate with the taxes they pay, an equity concern that has been raised by some critics of the program. Troublesome, too, is the long-term viability of the cash benefits provided by Social Security. Notwithstanding the historic 1983 Social Security Amendments, which did much to restore confidence in that program, they note that the estimated day when the system will be unable to meet its benefit obligations under its current structure is coming closer. Correcting this problem by either raising taxes on workers or slowing the growth of benefits paid to retirees will exacerbate the problem of people getting a fair economic return from their participation in Social Security. The discussion about the fairness of Social Security sets the stage for the authors' defense of the continued tax-favored treatment of employer-sponsored pension plans.

Goodfellow and Schieber outline the nature of the tax incentives accorded pensions and discuss the concept of the "tax expenditure" associated with them. The concept of tax expenditures is spelled out in the Congressional Budget Act of 1974. In the case of pensions, the tax expenditure is the amount of tax revenue that the government forgoes currently because taxes are deferred on pension accumulations until benefits are actually received. The Treasury Department estimates the taxes that would be collected on pension fund contributions and earnings in the absence of preferential treatment and subtracts the estimated taxes paid by current beneficiaries. For fiscal year 1993, the department estimates that tax preferences related to employer-sponsored retirement plans will result in $51.2 billion lower tax collections than if the preferences did not exist.

The authors contend that the underlying theoretical basis for defining tax expenditures related to pensions is flawed. The tax expenditure for pensions assumes that, if pensions did not benefit from the existing preferences in the law, contributions would be taxed when made to the plan and annual plan earnings would be taxable in the year earned. The authors show that under this model the taxation of the inflationary return on assets amounts to double taxation of earnings because some portion is not consumed in the period in which it is earned. In other words, the current measurement of the tax expenditure overlooks the fact that some portion of the return on assets is not a real economic return for deferring consumption because the purchasing power of the money decreases from price inflation.

The authors argue that it does not make sense for the government to profess widespread commitment to retirement income security on the one hand, and on the other hand to estimate tax expenditures related to pensions on the basis of a model that would penalize workers for saving for their own retirement. In support of their position, the authors cite the fiscal 1993 Federal Budget submitted by the Bush administration to the U.S. Congress, which indicates that failure to take account of inflation in measuring interest income should be regarded as a negative tax expenditure (i.e., a tax penalty). The authors estimate that, if the inflationary returns to pension assets in the total pension system had not been considered for purposes of the tax expenditure calculations, the Treasury estimates would have been halved over the last four years.

Goodfellow and Schieber maintain that the actual measurement used by the Treasury Department to estimate the tax expenditure exaggerates its size for several reasons. First demographically, offsetting high levels of pension contributions for today's workers against relatively low taxable pension benefits of today's retirees underestimates the taxes that will ultimately be recouped. Second, the methodology does not take account of the combined effects of pensions *and* Social Security, which also receives preferential tax treatment (although this will decline in the future). Third, the estimate includes pension plans of governmental and tax-exempt employers, even though there are no deductibility issues raised when nontaxable employers contribute to pension plans. While the authors acknowledge the beneficial effect of tax incentives for pensions, they feel the estimated revenue losses associated with employer-sponsored plans are currently greatly exaggerated.

While most analysts agree that pension participation has fallen below half the U.S. workforce, Goodfellow and Schieber argue that considering the full workforce at a point in time misrepresents the true effectiveness of the pension system. At one point in time a particular worker may have a low probability of being in a pension plan because he or she is young, or working part-time, or at a low wage level that leaves little room for deferring consumption until later. But many workers in these situations will find themselves in other situations later in life where there is a much greater likelihood of their being included in a pension plan. The authors look at the baby boomers' pension participation rates in 1980, 1985, and 1990. Indeed, they find that the participation rates for various age groups consistently increased over the decade. The authors explain and document that the lowest levels of pension participation tend to occur in the youngest age cohorts, and note that these people have to pass through middle age to get to retirement.

The authors assert that the true effectiveness of the pension system can only be judged by looking at the extent to which current workers can expect to receive benefits from the system during their lifetime. While they do not attempt to estimate the future expectations of all current workers, they do look at the pension participation rates of a group of people approaching the threshold of retirement. This analysis focuses on the total population in 1990 in the ages 45 to 59. Looking at everyone within this age bracket, the authors find that 61.3 percent were participating in some form of employer-sponsored pension or saving program or were married to someone who was. When individuals are excluded who had not had any attachment to the work force during 1990, more than 70 percent of the remaining individuals were receiving a benefit, actively participating in a pension plan, or married to someone who was. They stress that these levels of coverage far surpass those generally cited by critics who simply look at the lower pension participation rates of the entire population.

Goodfellow and Schieber develop an analytical framework showing the combined tax effects of pensions and Social Security to provide a perspective on how the overall federal tax structure treats hypothetical individuals. They first use present value analysis to compute the lump sum amounts that would accrue under two deferred taxation schemes—one based on *nominal* interest returns and one based on *real* interest returns. They then compare these amounts with amounts that would be accumulated in a regular savings account where contributions and earnings are taxed as they accrue. The difference in values represents the gross tax benefits for qualified plans. When the authors examine the tax benefits on the basis of real interest returns (which reflects the decreased purchasing power of the deferred compensation), they find that the net tax benefits are only about one-third the level of those estimated using nominal interest returns. Still, higher-paid workers and long-term workers received greater tax benefits than lower-paid or short-service workers.

But the authors believe that juxtaposing the tax benefits that accrue to various individuals participating in employer-sponsored plans with Social Security gains and losses gives a more complete picture of the net tax effects of the payroll and income tax systems. Although the analysis focuses on single individuals and thus does not take into account the value of Social Security dependent and survivor benefits to workers with dependents, the essence of their findings is that for those workers with above middle earnings levels, the negative rates of return on their Social Security contributions overwhelm the tax benefits provided through a relatively generous pension plan.

Goodfellow and Schieber advise that, given the long-term planning horizons required for retirement preparations, now is the best time to begin to address revisions in our national retirement policy that are necessary to deal with the demands baby boomers will pose as they move into retirement. They suggest that one policy option would be to reduce Social Security benefits for higher earners on a prospective basis, coupled with a clear message that these individuals will need to fill in the gap created by prospective benefit reductions. They would use these net savings to further subsidize Social Security cash benefits to lower earners and to reduce future underfunding of Social Security. While the authors recognize that this would bring added criticism to the Social Security "money's worth" argument, they state that it could be countered with the argument that higher earners are given tax incentives to save for retirement outside Social Security. Because private plans are not fully indexed, the authors suggest that higher earners could be permitted to "buy back" some indexed Social Security benefits or, alternatively, that the government could provide indexed securities which could serve as a funding basis behind an indexed annuity.

David Lindeman, the paper's first discussant, offers a number of suggestions regarding how the analysis could be improved or undertaken differently. While Lindeman has advocated analysis along the lines of that tackled by Goodfellow and Schieber, he comes to the conclusion that a less consistent and more qualitative analysis would be more helpful. He says what emerges from the paper confirms what we already know: pensions are a middle-class benefit to workers in good jobs for people with stable work histories, in firms and occupations that have been relatively successful in coping with the structural changes in the economy.

Lindeman notes that Congress has indirectly limited the tax preferences accorded pension plans through tighter limits on maximum pension contributions and benefits, limits on plan funding levels, and excise taxes on distributions that exceed certain limits. Congress has also established tighter and more rigorous coverage and nondiscrimination rules. Lindeman considers these responses by policy makers to be motivated in part by the drive to accelerate budgetary receipts over the short term because of a general unwillingness to raise taxes on current consumption. Another reason is an equal reluctance to tamper very much with the structure of social spending on the aged. Consequently, he says we try to achieve our social ends through more tax code regulation.

Lindeman tells us that, even if we continue the current muddle of a tax structure, eventually we are going to have to ask what we are getting for regulation relative to the costs. If our concerns are solely ones of tax equity, we could deal with them at the individual taxpayer level rather than at the plan level. In short, he believes that we are "pushing on a string" by trying to shape retirement outcomes in what is, after all, a voluntary system.

Alicia Munnell, the paper's second discussant, disagrees strongly with the policy conclusion flowing from the Goodfellow/Schieber paper. Specifically, she does not agree with the suggestion of the authors that benefits under Social Security be reduced for highly paid workers with the net savings used to further subsidize the benefits for lower-paid workers, at the same time letting higher-paid workers rely more on private pensions to fill the gap created by prospective benefit reductions. She states that Social Security has two unique advantages over even the best pension plan: it allows workers to take the full value of accrued benefits with them as they move from job to job, and it provides a fully indexed annuity after retirement. Munnell's solution is not to alter the basic structure of Social Security but rather to include pension accruals in the personal income tax base, as suggested by the theory of comprehensive income taxation.

First, Munnell contends that in the absence of wealth transfer taxes, an income tax is more equitable than a consumption tax. Second, she says taxing pensions on a deferred basis can be justified only if such favorable treatment achieves desirable social goals—that pension plans provide rank and file employees with retirement benefits they would not have accumulated on their own or, failing that test, that they increase saving of those who are covered so that national saving and capital accumulation are greater than they would have been otherwise. Munnell contends that the evidence does not conclusively support these justifications.

Munnell asserts that pension benefits are a trivial source of income for retirees in the bottom two-fifths of the income distribution. Only 46 percent of private full-time workers are covered, and both coverage and payments tend to be concentrated among higher-paid employees. She also asserts that the assets of pension plans do not represent a net increment to national capital accumulation. Given that the revenue loss associated with tax-qualified plans does not appear to be achieving major social goals, she declares that the taxation of benefit accruals should be shifted to a current basis.

Munnell challenges a number of points made in the Goodfellow/ Schieber paper. While she agrees that eliminating the inflation component of the return to capital is clearly desirable on theoretical grounds, inflation indexing is not currently part of our tax law nor likely to be so in the foreseeable future. Thus, she says, it makes little sense to apply such an adjustment in the area of pensions when it is not applicable to any other part of the economy.

Munnell agrees that the cash-flow approach to measuring the tax expenditure associated with tax-qualified plans may not be the best, but she says the reason has little to do with systematic overestimates of the revenue forgone. Munnell says a better estimate of the annual revenue loss would be the difference between (1) the present discounted value of the revenue from current taxation of pensions as they accrue over the employee's working life, and (2) the present discounted value of the taxes collected when benefits are received by the employee after retirement. Munnell's calculations suggest that the current treatment of pensions reduces tax revenues between $40 billion and $69 billion in present value terms. Thus she concludes that the revenue loss associated with the favorable treatment of pension contributions and earnings under the personal income tax is substantial regardless whether it is measured in the traditional way or by her proposed alternative.

V. Pension Benefit Guarantees in the United States: A Functional Analysis

Zvi Bodie and Robert Merton explore how the PBGC system for guaranteeing pension benefits may be improved using "functional analysis." They lay out a number of economic justifications for having the government directly involved in retirement benefit arrangements and explain the difference between government and private-sector obligations.

Their analysis begins with a brief description of the functions served by the pension system and a determination of how they are currently performed in the United States. They then explore the roles of government and the private sector in providing retirement income security and the complex interaction between them. The paper then focuses on the federal system for insuring defined benefit plans in the private sector against default risk. Finally, they consider how pension benefits might be adjusted for changes in both the cost of living and the standard of living.

Bodie and Merton outline two methods of computing pension liabilities—one based on accumulated benefit obligations (ABO) and the other on projected benefit obligations (PBO). The primary difference between the two methods is that the first does not take salary projections for future service into consideration, while the second does.

The authors note that the plan sponsor is under no legal obligation to pay more than the amount promised explicitly under the plan's benefit formula. Because private plans generally do not offer formal cost-of-living increases to retirees, or index wages up to the age of retirement for former employees with deferred vested benefits in pay-related plans, Bodie and Merton find it difficult to see either the accounting or economic logic for using projected pension liabilities. PBGC's exposure is limited to ABO if the plan were to end (that is, nominal benefits unadjusted for inflation).

One of the major advantages of a defined benefit plan over a defined contribution plan is that it protects the employee against investment risk. The economic efficiency of this protection is enhanced by the provision of PBGC guarantees against default risk. The authors state that to understand the efficiency gains from guarantees of pension benefits it is critical to distinguish between employees and investors (stock- and bondholders) in firms that provide pensions. Unlike the firm's investors, the employees holding the sponsor's pension liabilities prefer to have the payoffs on their contracts as insensitive as possible to the default risk of the firm itself. Employees, they say, are like investors who are constrained to hold a large fraction of their wealth in the form of long-term bonds issued by a single firm, which is also their employer. The PBGC provides assurances to plan participants and beneficiaries against default risk.

Bodie and Merton state that every guarantor, regardless whether it is a private sector or governmental entity, must employ some feasible combination of monitoring, asset restrictions, and risk-based premiums if it is to maintain economic viability without creating unintended and undesirable side effects. They then provide an analogy between the PBGC and the failed system for insuring savings and loan associations (S&Ls).

In the case of S&Ls, the authors say that poorly structured public policies and regulatory "forbearance" eventually led to misallocation of economic resources and an unintended and undesirable redistribution of wealth. In the case of the PBGC, they think there is a growing body of evidence that current public policy is leading us in a similar direction. They caution that there are significant similarities between pension insurance and deposit insurance, including multiple and conflicting goals of the guarantee program; failure on the part of many in the legislative and executive branches of government to fully recognize or disclose the true costs, benefits, and incentives of the guarantee program; a tendency to interpret losses to the guarantee fund as the result of abuse or incompetence rather than as a predictable response to the incentives built into the system; and failure to act promptly to limit losses because of fragmentation and conflict of interest within the government regulatory apparatus.

The paper notes the fragmentation of regulatory authority among three government agencies—the Department of Labor, the Department of the Treasury/Internal Revenue Service (IRS), and the PBGC—and points out that the objectives of the agencies can conflict with one another. For instance, the IRS guards against pension overfunding to prevent loss of tax revenue but also grants funding waivers to firms in financial distress.

Bodie and Merton present alternatives for reforming the PBGC that go beyond the legislative changes sought by the executive branch. One option is to increase the monitoring of pension plans and seize assets of the plan sponsor if the funding ratio drops below a certain level. A tradeoff to frequent surveillance could be an increase in the funding cushion. However, they say, increased reliance on monitoring would require better accounting data and the ability and willingness of the PBGC to terminate plans and seize collateral assets of sponsors that violate funding standards.

The paper sets forth other options for insuring defined benefit plans that would be based on asset restrictions and risk-related premiums. The authors assert that the PBGC has ignored the impact of pension plan asset mix on its exposure. When there is a mismatch between assets and liabilities, they show that the economic value of the guarantee can be quite significant. For a fixed premium, Bodie and Merton contend that the PBGC must restrict variability between assets and promised benefits. Plan sponsors could hedge all of the guaranteed benefits by investing in default-free fixed-income securities with the same cash flow pattern as the pension benefits—a practice known as "immunization."

An alternative is to charge risk-related premiums. While the PBGC already has a variable-rate premium structure that takes underfunding into account, premiums are unrelated to asset-liability mismatch. Bodie and Merton state that the risk-related premium must be related to the variability of the difference between the value of the pension assets (excluding the value of the guarantee) and the present value of guaranteed benefits.

Bodie and Merton construct a hypothetical system that differs from the current PBGC structure in that: (1) premiums are charged on the basis of the present value of the guaranteed benefits rather than on a per capita basis; (2) premiums reflect the volatility of pension fund net worth; (3) pension assets include collateral assets of the plan sponsor; (4) there is no maximum premium; and (5) the plan is terminated if premiums are not paid. The authors then develop tables and figures showing risk-based premiums as a function of the immunized fraction and the funding ratio. They find that a risk-based premium varies the most when the plan is fully funded, depending on the fraction of the benefits immunized. When the plan is underfunded, the risk-based premium is by far the largest, but it is less sensitive to the composition of the pension asset portfolio.

The scheme just described relies primarily on adjusting the risk-based premium at the end of each insurance period. But if the PBGC were constrained to charge a fixed premium, Bodie and Merton say that the PBGC would have to rely exclusively on monitoring and asset restrictions. If full funding were required together with 100 percent immunization, minimal premiums could be set so as to cover the operating costs of PBGC's monitoring compliance with the rules. But if 100 percent immunization is deemed undesirable PBGC can allow a trade-off between the funding ratio and the fraction of benefits immunized.

Bodie and Merton arrive at the following conclusions. First, while they see a positive role for government to play as a guarantor against pension default risk, they believe the PBGC guarantee should not encourage defined benefit plans over defined contribution plans. Both plan types have advantages and disadvantages, and there is no clear economic reason to favor one type over the other. Second, they believe that pension guarantees should not subsidize firms or workers in distressed industries, by charging premiums significantly lower than the risk of default. Subsidies provided by underpriced guarantees are less visible to the public than other subsidies and can lead to large and unintended distortions in resource allocation and to socially undesirable redistribution of income. Finally, they remind us that the words "deposit insurance" underscore the enormous costs that can be generated by the mismanagement of government liability guarantee programs.

In discussing the paper by Bodie and Merton, James Lockhart, the PBGC's Executive Director, concurs with the authors that the pension guarantee subsidies of PBGC insurance are less visible to the public than other subsidies and can lead to serious economic distortions. He agrees that overcharging the sponsors of well-funded plans in order to subsidize underfunded plans or financially distressed firms might cause financially healthy sponsors to terminate their defined benefit plans. Lockhart concurs with the authors that ultimately the United States could be left with bankrupt defined benefit plans with benefits financed directly by taxpayers.

While Lockhart concurs with the authors that the PBGC shares some of the similarities with the failed FSLIC, he takes exception to some of the points mentioned in the paper. While some of these similarities are legislated, he says others are within PBGC control and he outlines steps being taken to lessen their impact. Yet, despite these steps and some of the differences with FSLIC, Lockhart agrees that PBGC is at risk.

Lockhart does not entirely agree with the authors that the PBGC is subject to multiple and conflicting goals or that there has been a failure to fully recognize or disclose the true costs, benefits, and incentives of the pension insurance program. For instance, he points out that PBGC has "booked" several large probable losses even though the underfunded plans have not yet ended, and that PBGC includes footnotes in its financial statements showing "reasonably possible" losses ($12–20 billion in 1992). In addition, Lockhart emphasizes not only that PBGC reports projected potential losses over a ten-year time horizon, but that staff are working with the Office of Management and Budget on improving their modeling capabilities. The goal of PBGC's legislative proposals, he says, is to build the proper incentives into the pension insurance system to encourage companies to fund rather than terminate their plans.

Lockhart discounts the charge made by Bodie and Merton that there are conflicting interests within the government's regulatory apparatus. He considers these regulatory conflicts as more theoretical than real. Besides coordinating closely with the Department of Labor, Lockhart says PBGC and IRS work closely, particularly with regard to funding waivers. He asserts that very few waivers are granted now and those that are granted are secured. However, Lockhart concedes that there is a very real tension between higher pension funding to protect the PBGC and the resulting loss of tax revenues from higher corporate deductions.

The PBGC does take a proactive role in monitoring companies, according to Lockhart. But PBGC concentrates on the financial health of the plan sponsor and the pension liabilities, rather than on the assets of the pension plan, which, he says, seem to be the main concern of the authors. However, he says that PBGC's ability to be proactive is constrained by the legislative framework setting up the termination insurance program. PBGC must be concerned that a pension termination may force a company into bankruptcy and potentially into liquidation, potentially harming the very people that the program is designed to help.

Lockhart contends that PBGC has used functional analysis as a methodology for improving the termination insurance program as suggested by the authors, but along the lines of a property and casualty insurance model rather than that of a lender. He takes issue with how Bodie's and Merton's analysis is applied to PBGC. Lockhart states that there is an overemphasis in the authors' model on the pension plan itself and an underemphasis on the financial health of the plan sponsor. While the functional analysis used by PBGC is similar in certain respects to that used by the authors, it produces different legislative solutions because of a different emphasis. Nonetheless, Lockhart maintains that the objective of both approaches is to produce the right incentives to reduce the risk and the size of losses from terminations.

Lockhart disagrees with a requirement that pension plans immunize their liabilities. Such a practice could have a negative impact on equity markets and cause sponsors to abandon defined benefit plans if they could no longer benefit from the higher returns that are usually earned on equities. While Lockhart declares that PBGC must refine its risk-based premium structure in the future, it must include corporate risk as well as asset mix and the amount of underfunding. He concludes his discussion by outlining various ways to strengthen the insurance program through stricter funding rules, restricting the growth in benefit guarantees, and increasing PBGC's recoveries in bankruptcy.

VI. Estimating the Current Exposure of the Pension Benefit Guaranty Corporation to Single-Employer Pension Plan Terminations

A central feature of President Bush's FY 1993 budget proposal was the change in the budgetary treatment of PBGC's operations from a cash to an accrual basis of accounting. This proposed shift in accounting treatment served to focus attention on the widening exposure of the PBGC to future pension termination claims, as well as the need to recognize this exposure as it accrues.

In their paper, Christopher Lewis and Richard Cooperstein describe how they applied the theory of options pricing to construct the initial estimates of the PBGC's contingent claims exposure to pension terminations in the FY 1993 budget. Options pricing methods have been used in the past to estimate the value of expected claims in other areas such as deposit insurance, mortgages, and international interest guarantees.

In an options pricing framework, the authors say that pension insurance is analogous to an indefinite maturity put option, with the value of the pension assets representing the underlying asset and the value of pension liabilities representing the exercise or strike price. They say that expressing pension insurance as an option is complicated by the legal constraint that permits firms to exercise their "put option" only in the case of firm bankruptcy. Thus the central problem in assessing the value (option price) of pension insurance is determining the probability that the sponsoring firm will fail and with what level of pension underfunding.

Lewis and Cooperstein use a simplified closed-form options pricing model in conjunction with a Monte Carlo simulation to estimate PBGC's contingent liabilities. The paper demonstrates the important relationships between pension funding, pension benefit growth, and firm equity and the options value of pension insurance. According to their analysis, PBGC's exposure to future pension claims is almost $35 billion from current guarantees and an additional $8 billion from future guarantees.

Lewis and Cooperstein make the case for the federal government to budget for contingent liabilities as they accrue, instead of as the cash outlays come due. By acknowledging these accruing costs in the federal budget, they say, contingent claims pricing provides policy makers with time and the correct incentives to enact reforms to reduce the contingent liability before the option is exercised.

VII. Panel Discussion: The Role of Regulation in Pension Policy

A panel discussion led by Dallas Salisbury discusses what should be the appropriate role of regulation in pension policy. Representatives of government agencies, congressional committees, organized labor, and the employee benefit community present their views on this question.

Evelyn Petschek, with the Treasury Department, focuses on the pension nondiscrimination rules that had their origin in the Revenue Act of 1942. In order to be considered tax-qualified, a plan cannot discriminate in favor of the owners, officers, or highly compensated employees of the firm. The nondiscrimination rules are designed to ensure that pension plans are broadly based and cover rank-and-file workers.

Petschek says these rules were initially very simple and broad. But starting with the Employee Retirement Income Security Act (ERISA) in 1974 and, more recently, the Tax Reform Act of 1986, Congress expressed, both in the legislative history and in the way in which some of the provisions were formulated, a concern with the subjectivity that existed in the preexisting nondiscrimination rules. Prior to this time, Petschek says, subjective rules allowed employers basically to negotiate with the various IRS district offices across the country as to what was or was not discriminatory in a pension plan.

According to Petschek, the Treasury Department interprets the 1986 Act as having mandated a move toward the use of objective rather than subjective nondiscrimination testing. However, she says, it has become clear that there is necessarily an important balance to be struck between purely objective rules on the one hand, and subjective rules on the other. She emphasizes that much of the underlying importance of the nondiscrimination standards is to insure that the tax expenditure associated with qualified plans is well spent and that the distributional effects of the scheme set up in the tax code is broad based.

Meredith Miller, with the AFL-CIO, believes that the role of government regulation and legislation should be an activist one that furthers specific pension goals, such as preservation, security, and enhancement, but also one that would have the government an equalizer. Organized labor expects the government to take into consideration the multiple roles that workers and funds have in the pension area. The AFL-CIO defines the long-term best economic interests of plan participants to include a balancing of such factors as appropriate financial

rate of return relative to risk, continuous employment of plan participants, promotion of long term and local economic growth, corporate
responsibility, and job creation. Miller believes we are at the crossroads
where tough decisions are surfacing about whether we are going to
maintain and build upon an employment based system or, instead,
improve Social Security.

James Klein, representing the benefits community, states that, for
both good and bad reasons, Congress often leaves to the regulatory
agencies the difficult task of filling in the gaps of what are generally
vague or sometimes structurally complex legislative provisions. Moreover, the legislation is typically the product of a number of different
committees with different agendas. Notwithstanding the difficult task
facing the regulatory agencies, he is baffled that it takes several hundred pages of regulations to implement a few lines in the tax law
concerning nondiscrimination rules. He feels that this is the result of a
misconception of policy makers that the principal objective of many
plan sponsors is somehow to cheat plan participants and not provide
them with adequate benefits. Klein says that it would be an ironic and
bitter twist if in the name of greater equity we end up diminishing
employers' support for tax qualified pension plans.

Phyllis Borzi, with the House Subcommittee on Labor-Management
Relations, remarks that ERISA was initially developed as a labor statute. Labor laws are written in a fundamentally different way than tax
laws in that they establish broad-brush principles. Gaps in those principles are filled in, not by regulatory agencies, but by the courts. Broad-
brush principles set out goals, objectives, and some rules. Since ERISA
was passed, she says, we have moved away from broad-brush labor
principles to a tax statute. To a great extent, the complexity of ERISA is
caused by its taking on the aura of a tax statute. Borzi claims this has
occurred, in part, because the legislative changes that have occurred
over the last decade have been deficit driven rather than driven by
retirement income policy. She says what needs to be done from a
Congressional viewpoint is to go back to first principles and figure out a
way to let participants enforce their rights while the regulatory agencies deal with global issues.

Edwin Hustead, representing the actuarial profession, decries the
trend away from defined benefit plans. After a flurry of regulations,
laws, accounting rules, and court decisions beginning in the 1980s,
he says, defined benefit plans among medium and large employers
dropped precipitously. Because a typical 401(k) plan does not generally provide as much retirement income as a traditional defined benefit
plan, Hustead claims the trend away from defined benefit plans could
lead to a generation of retirees with less income. He cautions that it

may be too late then for Congress to reinvent the present system. While he says the legislative focus over the next few years will be very much on health care, he believes that at some point a conscious decision must be made on what direction our private pension system should take and what the relative roles of each type of plan should be.

Richard Hinz, with the Department of Labor, believes that the role of regulation is a balancing act between equity and efficiency. He thinks the role of the Department of Labor is to fulfill this function while at the same time representing the participant where he or she cannot be represented adequately. Hinz says that the Department is concerned with the equity of discrimination testing, but realizes that this needs to be balanced against the efficiency of broader incentives for sponsors to provide plans. Moreover, the Department of Labor is concerned both with compassion and equity in providing broad insurance coverage to all defined benefit participants and with the efficiency problems of distortions in capital markets caused by the moral hazard associated with insuring pension liabilities.

Dallas Salisbury concludes the panel discussion by making several observations. First, while in 1978 only 25 percent of defined benefit plans were sufficiently funded if they were to terminate, about three-fourths of them now have enough assets to meet benefit commitments. Second, increasing numbers of Fortune 500 firms are implementing cash balance plans rather than getting completely out of defined benefit arrangements. These plans must still pay insurance premiums to PBGC. Third, in discussing the tax expenditure associated with tax-qualified plans, Salisbury points out that half of the revenue loss as calculated by the government is associated with public employee plans, including the federal government's. While he firmly believes that the private pension system will continue to grow and that PBGC will not need a taxpayer bailout, he predicts that the private pension system will remain regulated because it will continue to have tax preferences.

This volume comes at a time when our policy makers are being called upon to formulate a coherent and well-defined retirement income policy to guide our nation into the twenty-first century. The papers and discussions that follow provide a comprehensive backdrop for assessing the future of private pensions in the United States.

Chapter 1
Gaps in Retirement Income Adequacy

Emily S. Andrews

Evaluating the success and failure of our retirement income system is daunting both because of the presence of complex technical issues and because personal value judgments must invariably be involved. Nonetheless, a broad spectrum of research can be drawn on that establishes a framework for discussion. This paper starts from basics and proceeds to a set of policy recommendations that could be implemented in the future to fill in the gaps in retirement income adequacy.

A workable definition of retirement income needs to be developed to proceed with such an evaluation. Several alternatives are available, including the income of retirees and the income of the elderly. Measures of adequacy need to be defined as well. A number of measures are considered, such as the poverty rate, the relationship of income in retirement to income at other stages of life, and the distribution of retirement income. Definitions for each of these measures are explored.

A considerable body of research has been conducted on these issues. First, empirical measures of retirement income and retirement income adequacy are reviewed. The review suggests that poverty is disproportionately found among nonmarried individuals and minorities. Furthermore, while the income of the aged is generally similar to that of the working-age population, the retirement income of many may still not be sufficient to maintain preretirement living standards. This reality may reflect the relatively higher degree of income inequality found among retirees.

Two sets of income projections are reviewed, based on well-regarded microsimulation models. One set is derived from the PRISM model developed by ICF/Lewin. The other set is derived from the DYNASIM model developed by researchers at the Urban Institute. Both models project higher real levels of retirement income in the twenty-first century. In particular, private pension income is expected to become more prevalent. Nonetheless, pockets of relative poverty are likely to remain and living standards may not be equal to those enjoyed prior to retirement.

Observed gaps in retirement income adequacy suggest two policy solutions. First, relative poverty can be addressed through a restructuring and realignment of federal retirement, disability, and welfare programs. The maintenance of middle-class living standards will also require increased lifetime savings. Policies to achieve this end are not clearcut. Nonetheless, a significant restructuring of employer-sponsored pensions does not appear to be the most efficient means.

I. Defining Retirement Income Adequacy

A number of concepts must be defined before undertaking an assessment of economic well-being in retirement, particularly because the terms "retirement income adequacy" and "gaps in adequacy" depend on the values of society and those of the observer. To start, a definition of retirement income must be established. Only then can measures be developed to evaluate economic well-being. Such measures are related to three issues. Is retirement income adequate relative to desired or actual living standards? Is the distribution of income satisfactory given society's expectations? And is poverty too prevalent?

A. Defining Retirement Income

Retirement income is not a simple concept. In fact, several different definitions are often used. Retirement income may include all sources of income received by retirees or all sources of income received by persons of retirement age. While individuals retire at different ages, retirement age is often defined as the age at which Social Security benefits become available, whether or not they are collected.[1] Retirement income regarded from the standpoint of the aged includes all individuals of a specified age and older and enumerates income from all sources.

In some instances, retirement income is directly linked to the elusive concept of retirement. Retirement may be narrowly defined to be the complete cessation of labor-force activity. Broader definitions include workers who have terminated their career jobs but who have secondary jobs or work part-time schedules. Other definitions are three-pronged, encompassing work, partial retirement, and full retirement.

When retirement income is linked to the actual status of retirement, two sources of income may be considered—Social Security and employer-sponsored pensions. When the replacement of earnings is the focus of analysis, the definition of retirement income is often restricted in this manner. In other circumstances, the full spectrum of non-wage income is considered, from asset income to means-tested welfare payments. If retirement is broadly defined, earnings from part-time or non-career jobs are added as well.

The definition of retirement income is sometimes expanded to include the implicit consumption of the services from owner-occupied housing. Income may also be imputed for the annuity value of non-financial assets, including primary residences and vacation homes. Asset availability is particularly important when evaluating the resources held by the elderly that could be used to pay for long-term care.[2] Non-cash benefits may also be added to the income of the elderly. Health insurance is the most important non-cash benefit, including Medicare and retiree health insurance financed by employers.

B. Income Equivalence

The simplest measure of relative well-being is mean or median income. If the income of retirees is substantially below that of the working population, retirement income adequacy may be questioned. Two types of comparisons can be made: (1) the income of retirees can be compared to that of younger age groups at a point in time, and (2) the income of retirees can be compared to their own income at an earlier point in time. Complex technical adjustments are required, however, to equate the income needs of younger families to those of retirees. A variety of scales have been developed to make these comparisons possible.

Compared to the Nonelderly

Income is most often related to the family. While earnings are tied to the individual employee, other income sources, such as asset income, may be jointly owned. Furthermore, families consisting of married couples and families with children pool and spend their income together. Based on family income, the income of the elderly falls short. This shortfall is deceptive, however, as fewer family members share resources in elderly families than in nonelderly units.

At the other extreme, per capita income is used to make welfare comparisons. Per person measures, however, tend to understate the relative well-being of larger households. While two cannot live as cheaply as one, two persons can share their income and live together more economically than two persons living alone. Economies of scale are apparent in housing and in other consumption items.

Differences in family composition also affect economic well being. A three-person family composed of a mother and two children may have different income needs from those of a family with two adults and one child. An infant does not consume the same resources as a hungry teenager. Thus indexes have to be developed to adjust family income for differences in size and composition.

The best-known index used to make such comparisons is the poverty line developed by Orshansky (1965) for families of different types and sizes. The poverty-line index was developed based on the Department of Agriculture's minimum food consumption standards and on the share of expenditures accounted for by food in family budgets. The poverty index also makes adjustments for family size and age. The family-size adjustment suggests considerable economies of scale, with the consumption needs of a couple weighted only 26 percent higher than the needs of an elderly man living alone.

Many have criticized the poverty index because of its ad hoc adjustments for scale economies and for its rigid relationship to food consumption. It has been suggested that changes in the prices and availability of other basic nonfood commodities, such as housing, should also directly affect the poverty line.

Over the years, equivalence scales have been developed with different theoretical foundations. Researchers such as van der Gaag and Smolensky (1982) estimate equivalence scales based on variations in actual patterns of consumer demand (budget shares) associated with differences in family size and composition. Criticism of their work, however, notes that consumer consumption patterns are constrained by income rather than need. Other scales, developed by researchers such as Danziger et al. (1984) and Vaughan (1984), are based on "subjective" responses about income adequacy.

Income equivalence among the elderly and nonelderly based on any of these indexes depends upon the relative scaling used for age and family size. For instance, the economic well-being of an elderly couple with income of $15,000 per year can be compared to that of a working age family of four with income of $30,000. Without adjustment, the elderly family has 50 percent of the resources of the nonelderly family. On a per person basis, the elderly family is as well off as the nonelderly family. Ruggles (1990) presents information for an array of other equivalence scales (Table 1). Based on the poverty-line scale, the hypothetical elderly family described above is 65 percent as well off as the nonelderly family. The van der Gaag and Smolensky measure places the elderly household at 87 percent of the younger family's living standard, while the scale developed by Danziger et al. fixes their well being at 96 percent. No one "right" answer emerges from this collection of work.

TABLE 1   Equivalence Values Under Alternative Scales

Family size		Official poverty line	Van der Gaag and Smolensky	Danziger et al.
1	Elderly	0.94	0.63	0.65
1	Nonelderly	1.02	1.00	1.00
2	Elderly	1.19	0.89	0.80
2	Nonelderly	1.32	1.28	1.25
3		1.57	1.27	1.40
4		2.01	1.56	1.54
5		2.38	1.66	1.65
6		2.69		1.74
7		3.05		

Source: Based on Ruggles (1990, p. 74) using calculations from van der Gaag and Smolensky (1982) and Danziger et al. (1984).

From the perspective of subjective response, the elderly express fewer income needs than the nonelderly. Nonetheless, their desires reflect the experiences of a cohort that has lived through substantial economic change. Thus, the elderly's expectations may, in part, reflect living standards appropriate to earlier days. Comparisons between the elderly and nonelderly are also difficult to make because the consumption items needed by the elderly are likely to be quite different from those of the working age population. Moreover, equivalence scales designed for poverty populations may not reflect equivalence among other income groups.

Compared to Prior Earnings

Some of the equivalence scales developed over the past few decades are based on the judgments of experts about consumption needs. The poverty index follows this approach with respect to food, making ad hoc adjustments for other consumption items.

Within the context of retirement, a methodologically similar equivalency concept is that of the "hypothetical" replacement rate. In this case, expert opinion is used to relate the needs of persons in retirement to the living standards enjoyed while they were working. The Social Security Administration has historically provided information on typical earnings replacement rates that could be expected from Social Security. Employers offering defined benefit plans often calculate representative replacement rates that "full-career" workers could expect to receive from Social Security and private pension payments combined.

Hypothetical replacement rates generally adjust post-retirement

TABLE 2   Hypothetical Replacement Rates

Preretirement salary	Dexter	President's Commission	Palmer
$6,500		0.86	
$10,000	0.82	0.78	
$15,000		0.71	0.82
$20,000		0.66	0.75
$25,000	0.72		0.71
$30,000		0.60	0.68
$40,000			0.68
$50,000		0.55	0.66
$60,000	0.58		0.66
$75,000			
$80,000			0.68

Source: Based on Palmer (1989, p. 723) using calculations from Dexter (1984) and the President's Commission on Pension Policy (1981).

consumption needs downward for factors such as work-related expenses, taxes, and savings. The assumption is made that expenditures for items such as work-related clothing and transportation will no longer be needed in retirement. Retirees are frequently assumed to have no further need to continue saving. Upward adjustments for consumption expenditures to compensate for activity limitations are not generally included.

The most recent study of this type is by Palmer (1989), who critiqued earlier analysis by the President's Commission on Pension Policy (1981) and by Dexter (1984). Palmer specifically considers the impact of the Tax Reform Act of 1986 using data on consumption patterns from the 1984 Bureau of Labor Statistics (BLS) Consumer Expenditure Survey. He compares the expenditure patterns of married couples for each of eight salary levels based on two groups of consumer units—retirees and workers. Using a model that takes account of taxes, expenditures, and savings, he finds that couples with preretirement earnings of $15,000 require a replacement rate of 82 percent to maintain living standards, while those with preretirement earnings of $80,000 need a rate of 68 percent. These replacement rates are generally higher than those of earlier studies (Table 2). For instance, replacement rates for couples in both the President's Commission and Dexter studies were 55 percent and 58 percent respectively for couples with incomes above $50,000.

While Palmer presents more carefully constructed "hypothetical" replacement rates, the concept of a replacement rate itself remains elusive. For one thing, Palmer did not investigate the income needs of single persons in retirement. Furthermore, his sample of workers and retirees may not reflect the vicissitudes of actual working life. Replacement rates might be different if based on longitudinal lifetime consumption patterns. Nonetheless, the replacement rate concept provides a useful measure to evaluate whether older workers face significant declines in their economic well-being after retirement.

C. The Distribution of Income

Another indicator of retirement income adequacy can be developed by comparing the income distribution of individuals aged 65 and over to that of the working-age population. Greater income inequality may indicate that a higher proportion of older families have inadequate financial resources. The Gini coefficient is the standard measure used to evaluate income inequality. A Gini coefficient of 1 indicates complete income equality. The smaller the Gini coefficient, the less equal the distribution of income.

Changes in the distribution of income over time may reflect improvements in retirement income adequacy. For instance, if retirement income becomes more equal across elderly family units, poverty may be declining and income adequacy improving (particularly when mean or median income is rising as well). Similarly, if the degree of income inequality among the aged is reduced relative to the non-aged, retirement income adequacy may be improving relative to the rest of the population. Thus an aggregate indicator such as the Gini coefficient provides another tool with which to evaluate retirement income adequacy.

D. The Poverty Rate

Retirement income adequacy has often focused on the issue of poverty rather than on the economic status of the elderly as a whole. The official poverty line measures the cash income of families. Nonmarried elderly persons living with other family members are not included among the poor even if their own resources place them below the poverty line. While family resources are generally shared, elderly persons with income below the poverty line may not meet standards of retirement income adequacy as their limited resources preclude them from living independently. Independent living has become one of our society's goals in retirement.

Alternative poverty measures have been constructed that add non-cash benefits such as Medicare and food stamps. In general, the inclusion of these items reduces poverty among the elderly. While it is relatively straightforward to provide a cash value for food stamps, the monetization of other in-kind transfers, such as Medicare, is prone to greater difficulty. Because the elderly poor would be unlikely to spend the full cash market value of per capita Medicare expenditures on health insurance on their own, estimates have been made of the expenditures recipients would have made themselves if their income were higher. Using these recipient values raises the poverty rate relative to market value estimates.

Other adjustments include the annuitization of financial and nonfinancial wealth. Federal eligibility for welfare benefits through the Supplemental Security Income (SSI) program is predicated on no more than a minimum level of assets. Similarly, eligibility for the Medicaid program, which often finances long-term care, requires that assets be spent down. Yet, in terms of poverty, both the technical methods used to annuitize assets and the appropriateness of doing so have created considerable controversy.

While the Census Bureau provides information on a number of alternative poverty rates, the official rate remains the standard precisely because of the conceptual and valuation issues described above. Nonetheless, the trend in poverty appears to be similar no matter the definition used (Ruggles, 1990).

II. Gaps in Retirement Income Adequacy

The concepts described above can be used to investigate the presence of gaps in retirement income adequacy. But accurate measures of retirement income are required. The retirement income system can be evaluated using a number of studies. The measures surveyed, however, are constrained by measurement problems, data limitations, and conceptual choices.

A. Measuring Retirement Income

The most comprehensive and timely information on the income of the aged is provided by Grad (1990a) for 1988. Her findings are reported for married couples and nonmarried persons age 65 and older by age and sex.[3]

In 1988, married couples received income from a variety of sources. Of these, 35 percent had income from earnings; 96 percent received traditional retirement benefits from Social Security and employer-sponsored pensions; 40 percent received private pensions; and another 17 percent received pensions from civilian government employment. Asset income was also widespread, with 76 percent of all couples receiving some income from assets. SSI was received by a scant 3 percent.

Individuals aged 65 and over who were not married had a somewhat different distribution of income by source.[4] Only 13 percent had earnings. While 94 percent received retirement benefits, only 22 percent had private pensions[5] and 11 percent pensions from civilian government employment. In marked contrast to married couples, 10 percent of all persons who were not married received SSI.

The median annual income of elderly married couples was $20,305 in 1988. Their median income from earnings was $9,534. Median pension income (from all sources) was $16,303. Among recipients, Social Security and private pension payments amounted to $9,751 and $4,374 respectively. Couples receiving asset income enjoyed $3,319 annually.

Persons who were not married had median annual incomes of only $7,928. Earnings provided $5,271 to those who worked. Median retirement income payments to nonmarried persons were $8,134. Social Security furnished $5,589 and private pensions provided $2,616. Median asset income was just $1,517.

Several facts stand out. First, median incomes from any specific retirement or nonretirement source are not high. Second, total median incomes are not high. Third, unmarried individuals have less than half the income of married couples. Given economies of scale in two-person households, individuals without spouses are financially worse off.

B. Relative Living Standards

Two comparisons can provide benchmark estimates about the overall income adequacy of the aged. First, do the elderly have living standards similar to the nonelderly? Second, have the elderly been able to maintain preretirement living standards? Although several studies have addressed these issues, their findings do not provide an entirely consistent conclusion about pervasiveness of retirement income adequacy.

Compared to the Nonelderly

Hurd (1990) presents a series of measures for 1979 that compare the income of the elderly to that of the nonelderly. Based on reported income, the income of aged households was 52 percent of that of working age households.[6] The figure increased to 66 percent when income was adjusted for underreporting (Table 3).

By contrast, the per capita income of aged households (adjusted for

TABLE 3   Income of the Aged Relative to the Nonaged, 1979

Ratios	Household	Poverty	Budget	Per capita
Money income	0.52	0.64	0.84	0.90
Money income (adjusted for underreporting)	0.66	0.82	1.07	1.16

Source: Based on Hurd (1990, p. 577) using calculations from Smeeding (1989).

underreporting), was 116 percent of that of nonaged households, suggesting that aged households are better off. The poverty index equivalency measure (in conjunction with adjusted income) placed that ratio at 82 percent and the budget-share (demand-based) index developed by van der Gaag and Smolensky found the income of the aged to be 107 percent of that of the nonaged. Many would agree with Hurd that, based on the work by van der Gaag and Smolensky, the income of the aged is largely similar to that of the nonaged. Nonetheless, such comparisons are known to be vulnerable to the relative weights assigned to large and small families.

Hurd's data are for 1979—a single point in time. Radner (1991) tracks the relationship between the income of the elderly and that of the working age population over several decades.[7] He concentrates on family income. He finds that the aged/nonaged income ratio fell from 67 percent in 1947 to 50 percent in 1967. From 1967 to 1979, the median income of the aged rose from 50 to 54 percent of that of the nonaged. Between 1979 and 1984, that ratio increased even more, from 54 percent to 65 percent. This dramatic shift suggests that by 1984 elderly households maintained a living standard comparable to that of the working-age population. While the aged/nonaged income ratio edged off to 63 percent by 1989, the income of the aged would probably compare favorably. Nonetheless, since all sources of income are included, retirement income alone (excluding earnings) may not meet overall standards of adequacy.

Compared to Prior Earnings

The replacement rate is the best tool with which to compare the retirement income of actual retirees to their own preretirement living standards. Grad (1990a) calculates earnings replacement rates for a sample of workers applying for Social Security benefits in 1983 using the New Beneficiary Survey (NBS). She tests two separate definitions of earnings—the average of the five highest years of earnings over the worker's career (highest) and average earnings during the last five years before benefit recipiency (last earnings). Median replacement rates for men receiving pensions and Social Security reached 42 percent of their highest earnings and 56 percent of their last earnings. Similar median replacement rates for women reached 48 percent of their highest earnings and 59 percent of their last earnings. Men without pensions had median highest-earnings replacement rates of 27 percent and last-earnings replacement rates of 43 percent. Women without pensions had median highest-earnings replacement rates of 30 percent and last-earnings replacement rates of 48 percent.

Several peculiarities stand out. First, replacement rates differ significantly according to the definition of preretirement earnings. Furthermore, according to Grad, replacement rates based on last earnings increase with preretirement earnings, whereas replacement rates based on highest earnings remain relatively flat. With regard to highest earnings, Grad discovered that the work histories of many survey respondents were atypical compared to our economic priors. For many retirees, some or all of their highest-earnings years occurred prior to 1971 rather than during their last years on the job. In addition, many retirees had gaps in their Social Security coverage or reported part-time earnings.

Hypothetical replacement rates have been estimated at 55 to 85 percent of preretirement earnings. Calculated replacement rates, even rates based on last earnings, do not reach those goals. This may, in part, be because Grad's calculations are limited to Social Security and pensions.

An earlier study by Fox (1982) using data for 1976 found somewhat higher replacement rates. Fox calculates rates based on Social Security benefits and employer-sponsored pensions as a percent of earnings selected from the last ten years immediately before retirement. In one calculation, he computes replacement rates based on four years of earnings out of the last ten. He excludes the highest and lowest three years of earnings and keeps the middle four. After adjusting these earnings for inflation, he calculates after-tax replacement rates. These rates average 66 percent for married couples, 57 percent for men without wives, and 62 percent for women without husbands.

Fox also computes replacement rates based on total income, that is, including asset income and postretirement earnings. This income is compared to income reported in the survey year closest to retirement. Retired workers are defined as those who began receiving Social Security benefits by 1976. Median total-income replacement rates computed by Fox are 62 percent for married couples, 69 percent for nonmarried men, and 77 percent for nonmarried women. Contrary to theoretical replacement rate constructs, those with higher preretirement incomes have higher total-income replacement rates, suggesting that more affluent retirees enjoy relatively higher standards of living in retirement, while less affluent retirees are less well off.

Even if Grad's findings were closer to those of Fox, a puzzle remains, as neither study finds replacement rates fully consistent with hypothetical rates developed to represent comparable pre- and post-retirement living standards.[8] Of course, hypothetical replacement rates may overestimate the income needs of retirees. Nonetheless, both the budget-share equivalency scale of van der Gaag and Smolensky and the subjective measure of Danziger et al. suggest that a one-person elderly household needs about 65 percent of the income of a one-person non-elderly household.[9] In any event, both the Grad and the Fox studies cast some doubt on the conclusion that income is generally adequate in retirement.

C. Trends in Income Inequality

Even if the median income of the elderly has improved over time, the income distribution of the aged may have become less equal. Radner (1991) provides a wealth of data tracking trends in income inequality. He reports that income inequality, as measured by the Gini coefficient, rose from 0.416 to 0.426 for aged units between 1979 and 1984.

In addition, Radner shows that the income of the aged has been, and continues to be, less equally distributed than that of the non-aged. Greater income inequality among the aged would be expected because the elderly have had a lifetime to build up their earnings-related pensions and assets. Over a lifetime some individuals will be more successful than others. Similarly, over a lifetime more successful individuals will be able to place more funds in savings. Differences in the savings rates of families will also develop, even among those with similar income. As a consequence, those who have been more financially successful and those who have been more thrifty will tend to have greater retirement income by the time they reach age 65. Their success takes nothing away from other retirees. By contrast, if greater income inequality reflects greater poverty, retirement income adequacy is threatened.

D. Below the Poverty Line

Despite the shortcomings of the official poverty index, no agreement has been reached about a substitute. Similar patterns of poverty emerge, however, under most alternatives. Overall, poverty is no more prevalent among the aged than among the nonaged. Nonetheless, concentrations of poverty are found among particular subgroups of the elderly population. Furthermore, a higher proportion of elderly in poverty-prone groups also subsist on income relatively close to the poverty level.

The Unmarried Elderly

Poverty rates among the nonmarried elderly (single, widowed, and divorced) have been higher than the poverty rates among married couples. In fact, aged poverty is frequently considered a women's issue because women make up the vast majority of nonmarried persons aged 65 and older. Nevertheless, poverty among men without spouses is extremely high as well. While the income of 18 percent of all aged units (couples and single persons), based on their own income and not on the income of other extended family members, fell below the poverty line in 1988, that figure increased to 28 percent for nonmarried women and 20 percent for nonmarried men (Grad, 1990). The poverty rate for aged married couples, based on their own income, is only 5 percent.

These figures are higher than those reported if other family income is taken into account under official rates, which take into account other family income. In this case, the poverty rate for nonmarried women aged 65 and older is reduced to 21 percent and that for nonmarried men is reduced to 16 percent. Nonetheless, based on Grad's figures, over 70 percent of nonmarried women do not live with other family members. One quarter of those women are in poverty.

Another aspect of poverty among the aged is the bunching of individuals and couples with income close to the poverty line. Twenty-six percent of nonmarried men and 34 percent of nonmarried women have income within 125 percent of the poverty line. This compares to 10 percent of married couples. This 125 percent cut-off is often referred to as the near-poverty line. For women living on their own, the near-poverty rate rises to 41 percent. For men on their own, that rate reaches 32 percent.

Poverty rates among nonmarried persons also tend to increase with age. For nonmarried men, the own-income poverty rate is 17 percent for those aged 65 to 74, and 24 percent for those aged 75 and over. A similar pattern is found for nonmarried women. Their rates increase from 25 percent for the young elderly to 30 percent for those aged 75 and over.

Several economists have studied the dynamics of poverty for widowed women. Burkhauser, Holden, and Feaster (1988) found that the death of a husband dramatically alters the risk and pattern of poverty in retirement. The group that fare worst are widows whose husbands did not have income from employer-sponsored pensions. Based on findings from the Retirement History Survey, Hurd and Wise (1989) suggest that a large proportion of a couple's wealth is lost when the husband dies. They also suggest that husbands in poor families may die earlier than husbands in families with greater financial resources. Hurd (1990) also notes that the formula for survivor's benefits in Social Security may also contribute to increased poverty rates. He indicates that the typical benefit reduction for widows is about 33 percent of the couple's benefit, but that the poverty line for a single elderly person is 21 percent below the poverty line for an elderly couple. In combination, these findings suggest that changes in the Social Security benefit formula, increases in pension eligibility, and purchases of life insurance could materially affect the economic losses of the transition to widowhood.

Minorities

Poverty rates among minorities are greater than those among white families aged 65 and over. The median income of black elderly units (couples and nonmarried persons) combined was $6,303. Elderly couples and nonmarried persons of Hispanic origin had median incomes of $7,266. By comparison, the income of white elderly couples and unmarried persons was $13,117. It is not surprising, given these medians, that the income of many minority couples and unmarried persons age 65 and older falls below the poverty line. Overall, the poverty rate for black elderly units is 46 percent and the near-poverty rate is 61 percent. Among those of Hispanic origin, the poverty rate is 39 percent and the near-poverty rate is 53 percent. Over half of all nonmarried elderly minority persons are in poverty and over two-thirds are in near poverty.

Differences in income sources reflect the poverty status of the minority aged. Social Security alone is a much more important source of income for minority aged than it is for the white elderly. Social Security Administration tabulations indicate that poverty rates climb steeply for those elderly who receive the majority of their income from Social Security. Whereas 31 percent of white elderly receive private pensions, only 17 percent of black elderly and 19 percent of elderly of Hispanic origin have pension income. Similarly, while 72 percent of white elderly have income from assets, only 25 percent of black elderly and 37 percent of elderly of Spanish origin report asset income. By contrast, while only 5 percent of white elderly receive public assistance, that figure climbs to 22 percent of elderly blacks and persons of Hispanic origin. Minority elderly also tend to be fully retired as fewer continue to earn wage and salary income. While little analysis has been done on the paths leading to poverty among the minority aged, patterns of lifetime poverty or near-poverty status are likely to be more important determinants than in the case of aged widows.

E. Income Sources and Income Adequacy

Retirement income adequacy necessitates more than one source of income in retirement. Many have cited the traditional three pillars of retirement income—Social Security, employer pensions, and savings. These three pillars appear to be the key to adequacy. Over four-fifths of those with all their own income from Social Security are poor or near-poor. Nearly half of those with 75 to 100 percent of their own income from Social Security are poor or near-poor. Having more than one retirement benefit reduces the incidence of poverty significantly for both married couples and nonmarried persons. The variety of income sources increases among elderly couples and persons with higher incomes.

The impact of earnings and income from assets on retirement income adequacy is striking, particularly among the nonmarried elderly.[10] Among married persons, 7 percent of those without earnings are in poverty compared to 3 percent of those with earnings. Among nonmarried persons, the impact of earnings is much stronger. Only 7 percent of nonmarried persons are in poverty (based on their own income) if they receive earnings, compared to 32 percent of those without earnings.

The difference in poverty among the elderly based on asset income recipiency is even greater. Among married couples, only 2 percent of those with asset income are in poverty, compared to 16 percent of those without assets. Among nonmarried persons, 10 percent of those with asset income are in poverty, compared to 36 percent of those without assets. The receipt of asset income, of course, is a result of life-cycle circumstances tied to earnings, savings behavior, and inherited wealth. Nonetheless, even the median asset income reported by nonmarried persons, at $1,517 annually, may ward off poverty.

III. Future Retirement Income Adequacy

The situation of retirees may not be the same in the future. Perhaps the most obvious change in circumstances is related to the increased labor force participation of women. When the baby boom start to retire, many women will be entitled to higher Social Security benefits on their own account and to pension payments from employer-sponsored plans. Furthermore, legislative changes such as five-year vesting are likely to raise the retirement income of women. Consequently, some of the gaps in adequacy observed today may not be an issue twenty years hence.

Two microsimulation models provide forecasts of retirement income in the future. The first, DYNASIM (Zedlewski et al., 1990), was developed at the Urban Institute. The second, PRISM, was developed by Lewin/ICF (1991) and updated for the Advisory Council on Social Security. The two models differ in a number of ways, although both age an initial population throughout their work lives and calculate pension and Social Security benefits based on forecast work histories and marital status changes.

A. Projections of Retirement Income

DYNASIM and PRISM both forecast the median income of married couples and nonmarried men and women (Table 4). PRISM provides a projection for the year 2018 and baseline estimates for 1988. DYNA-SIM provides a baseline projection for 1990 and forecasts for 2010 and 2030. Both the PRISM baseline figure for 1988 and the DYNASIM figure for 1990 are lower than actual median incomes for couples for 1988 reported by Grad. By contrast, PRISM overestimates the median income of nonmarried men and women while DYNASIM underestimates it.

In terms of income recipiency, the two models perform rather differently, with PRISM tracking actual 1988 recipiency rates more closely. DYNASIM's 1990 pension recipiency rates may be too high for married couples (60 percent for couples in 1990 compared to an actual recipiency rate of 55 percent in 1988). Both PRISM and DYNASIM underestimate pension recipiency for nonmarried women, but DYNA-SIM's underestimate is greater. DYNASIM overestimates the receipt of earnings by married couples, and both models underestimate the percentage of nonmarried persons with earnings. Finally, DYNASIM overestimates the presence of asset income for nonmarried individuals and for couples alike.

PRISM provides more accurate estimates of the share of income provided by different income sources. The DYNASIM simulations are extremely weak in a number of areas, showing relatively low baseline estimates for the share of income from pensions and assets for both couples and nonmarried men and a relatively high proportion of income from earnings. Both models misjudge the income sources of nonmarried women. For that group, PRISM underestimates the importance of asset income and overestimates the importance of Social

TABLE 4 Projections of Retirement Income

Study year	Grad 1988	Lewin/ICF— PRISM 1988	Lewin/ICF— PRISM 2018	Zedlewski et al.— DYNASIM 1990	Zedlewski et al.— DYNASIM 2010	Zedlewski et al.— DYNASIM 2030
Married couples						
Median income	$22,063	$19,755	$31,513	$15,500	$24,400	$36,700
(1988 dollars)						
Recipiency (%)						
Total income	100	100	100	100	100	100
Social Security	93	95	98	93	96	96
Pension income	55	53	88	60	86	93
Earnings	35	34	32	43	44	45
Asset income	78	81	89	96	97	96
Share of income (%)*						
Total income	100.00	100.00	100.00	100.00	100.00	100.00
Social Security	34.20	36.00	34.80	42.00	37.00	37.00
Pension income	18.60	18.00	25.20	11.00	18.00	21.00
Earnings	21.40	21.50	18.50	33.00	28.00	30.00
Asset income	23.90	24.20	18.40	14.00	16.00	11.00
Nonmarried men						
Median income	$8,586	$9,856	$17,482	$7,200	$10,900	$16,900
(1988 dollars)						
Recipiency (%)						
Total income	100	100	100	100	100	100
Social Security	91	92	97	87	91	94
Pension income	40	39	73	43	70	85
Earnings	17	13	13	15	15	16
Asset income	57	70	83	86	88	87
Share of income (%)						
Total income	100.00	100.00	100.00	100.00	100.00	100.00
Social Security	37.90	40.30	38.90	57.00	48.00	49.00
Pension income	19.60	21.80	30.80	14.00	23.00	29.00
Earnings	14.90	13.50	11.60	20.00	20.00	16.00
Asset income	23.60	23.00	14.90	6.00	8.00	4.00
Nonmarried women						
Median income	$7,555	$7,760	$10,935	$6,000	$8,100	$12,900
(1988 dollars)						
Recipiency (%)						
Total income	100	100	100	100	100	100
Social security	91	99	97	85	93	96
Pension income	31	28	67	26	50	73
Earnings	11	9	9	9	8	7
Asset income	62	66	74	89	88	87
Share of income (%)						
Total income	100.00	100.00	100.00	100.00	100.00	100.00
Social security	45.90	52.40	48.30	71.00	69.00	68.00
Pension income	13.30	14.40	21.20	7.00	13.00	20.00
Earnings	8.50	7.80	7.30	10.00	8.00	8.00
Asset income	28.20	22.00	20.70	3.00	7.00	3.00

Source: Based on Grad (1990a), Lewin/ICF (1991), and Zedlewski et al. (1990).
*Percentages do not add to 100% because of other sources of income not included in table.

Security. DYNASIM misrepresents the share of all sources of income by overstating the importance of Social Security.

Because knowledge about the income of retired women is of critical importance in view of the higher poverty and near-poverty rates among that group, accurate modeling is particularly important. A model that presents more pessimistic estimates in the present may perpetuate that pessimism in the future. Unfortunately, groups at greater financial risk are probably harder to model.

Both models project significant gains in median real income in the future. For married couples, the estimates provided by PRISM and DYNASIM are extremely consistent, with the PRISM figure for 2010 falling between the DYNASIM estimates for 2010 and 2030. The projections for nonmarried women are also consistent with incomes increasing over the projection years. Somewhat perversely, however, PRISM projects higher levels of retirement income for nonmarried men in 2018 ($17,482) than DYNASIM projects for 2030 ($16,900).

The biggest gains in income recipiency stem from pension income. Both models project pension recipiency for married couples to be over 85 percent. Similarly, rates of 70 percent or more are projected for nonmarried men and rates of 50 to 73 percent are projected for nonmarried women. This group shows the strongest continued increase in recipiency over the projection period according to both models. By contrast, the percentage of couples and nonmarried persons receiving income from other sources is relatively stable.

Coupled with the growth in pension recipiency is an increase in the share of income accounted for by pensions. These increases are relatively modest, however, in the case of married couples and nonmarried men, particularly in contrast to the substantial gains in recipiency. Presumably lower-wage, shorter-tenure workers will be the beneficiaries of the recipiency gains. As a consequence, the pension entitlement of these workers will tend to be less generous than the entitlements of current pension recipients. The gain in the share of income accounted for by pensions among nonmarried women is greater.[11]

Both sets of projections indicate a significant increase in the real income of retirees in the twenty-first century. The extent to which these projections are believable is related to the ability of each model to project current year values, to the validity of the modeling of lifetime outcomes, and to the reasonableness of the economic assumptions incorporated in each model. The difference between the DYNASIM projections and Census Bureau data suggest that DYNASIM projections may be less reliable. Nevertheless, the key findings of the DYNASIM and PRISM projections are similar: gains in real income and gains in pension recipiency.

B. Assumptions Embedded in the Projections

Projections of the future are only as accurate as the assumptions used to develop them. In particular, forecasting accuracy is tied to assumptions about the growth of the economy and developments in the labor market, including the prevalence of public and private pension plans. In addition, assumptions about life-cycle savings and consumption critically affect forecasting accuracy. In many areas, the assumptions used in PRISM and DYNASIM models differ.

Wage Growth

Retirement income growth is more rapid according to DYNASIM projections compared to PRISM. In particular, the retirement income of married couples is projected to grow at an average annual rate of 1.6 percent between 1988 and 2018 according to PRISM, compared to an average annual rate of 2.9 percent between 1990 and 2010 and 2.5 percent betwen 2010 and 2030 according to DYNASIM.

Differences in retirement income growth are partly related to differences in wage growth, because pension income is earnings related. PRISM uses wage growth assumptions based on Alternative II of the 1991 Social Security Trustees Report. Average wages are assumed to grow by 1.1 to 1.5 percentage points in excess of the inflation rate with a long run wage growth rate of 1.1 percent. Real wage growth in the DYNASIM model (developed earlier) is based on the 1986 II.B Social Security Trustees Report. Over time, the Trustees Reports have become more conservative about prospects for economic growth.

Labor Force Participation

One of the differences in the two sets of retirement-income projections is related to earnings. Earnings generally play a greater role according to DYNASIM. Earnings, of course, stem from labor market activity. Based on DYNASIM, 34 percent of men age 65 to 69 and 21 percent of women will be in the labor force in 2010. PRISM labor force participation rates are considerably lower, at 25 percent for men aged 65 to 69 and 17 percent for women by the year 2000.

Pension Recipiency

Both microsimulation models predict that most future retirees will receive income from employer-sponsored pension plans. The size of these gains compared to current recipiency rates are somewhat baffling, because pension coverage is not projected to increase. Consequently, increased recipiency must stem from the effects of shorter vesting (under the 1986 Tax Reform Act), a greater incidence of full career coverage, and the increased labor force participation of women. Presumably, recipiency gains are also dependent on each model's assumptions about the likelihood of pension coverage on job change.

Microsimulation models attach probabilities to labor force participation, job change, and pension coverage for individuals as they age. Past research has provided a stock of information on the determinants of labor force participation and job mobility. Even a relatively simple assignment of probabilities ought to lead to reasonable patterns of labor force activity. Virtually no research has been conducted on the likelihood of pension coverage on job change, however.[12] Assumptions made on this point may bias the probability of pension recipiency upward.

Investment Income

Over the past 20 years, the elderly have increasingly supplemented their pension income with income from investments. The receipt of investment income in the future is probably the hardest income component to predict. Economic research provides scant guidance on the determinants of savings. Furthermore, the savings rate in the United States has been lower than that in most other industrialized nations. Nonetheless, the demographics of the population imply that the baby boom cohort, as it reaches maturity, will increase savings in order to prepare for retirement.

DYNASIM simulations use findings from the 1983 Survey of Consumer Finances (SCF) to assign asset values in the future. Only income from financial assets is reported. Zedlewski et al. (1990) indicate that little is known about the determinants of saving. Possibly as a consequence, little change in recipiency is reported. The share of asset income is projected to increase by 2010 and decrease thereafter in response to trends in other income sources.

PRISM projections of financial income are also made on a relatively ad hoc basis compared to the rest of the model. Assets are assigned to family units based on an analysis of the 1984 Survey of Income and Program Participation (SIPP), according to initial levels reported for specific subgroups of the population. The PRISM model adjusts the assets of the elderly over time for future saving and dissaving in retirement. If an individual dies, the spouse is assumed to receive all the couple's assets.

Based on these assumptions, PRISM projects some growth in the recipiency of asset income among nonmarried persons. Nonetheless, because of the growth of other sources of income—private pensions, in particular—the share of total income provided by asset income is projected to decline among the elderly by 2018 relative to 1988.

Projections of asset income are extremely sensitive to a host of factors. Both models assume growth rates keyed to intermediate assumptions about GNP growth based on Social Security Trustees Reports. Only financial assets are considered in the projections. Yet housing is the most important asset held by most families. Housing prices have sharply declined in many areas of the country in recent years. These shifts could affect other components of household saving for better or for worse. While asset income is the most highly skewed source of income among the elderly, for those elderly in the upper deciles of the income distribution, asset income is an important supplement to Social Security and pension income. Our inability to project asset income with confidence means that the future retirement income adequacy of much of the middle class will be difficult to evaluate.

C. Issues Needing Further Consideration

Published findings from these well-regarded microsimulation models do not address several issues key to evaluating continued gaps in retirement-income adequacy. In particular, neither study reports replacement rates, either for pension income alone or for the combination of income from pensions and assets. Yet this is a key measure of retirement-income adequacy and could have easily been derived. Similarly, neither model provides sufficient information on the incidence of poverty among the most vulnerable groups—nonmarried persons and minorities. While the use of the current poverty level standard may be conceptually difficult to justify when projecting income into the future, some indication of the situation of the poorest elderly groups is needed for any thoughtful reevaluation of retirement income policy.

Replacement Rates

In work based on an earlier version of PRISM, replacement rates for retired baby boom couples[13] averaged 45 percent of preretirement income based on Social Security benefits and employer-sponsored pensions (Andrews and Chollet, 1988). Common sense suggests that current version PRISM pension replacement rates are likely to be similar. A 45-percent replacement rate does not diverge greatly from the 1988 calculations made by Grad. However, it lies below replacement rates suggested by Palmer or others based on needs assessments and below rates implicit in many of the income equivalency measures.

No published data compare projections of future retirement income to projections of income of the working-age population. Such comparisons would also be feasible using assumptions about wage growth, demographic factors, and labor force participation. Without comparative information across age groups or over the life cycle, the economic well-being of future cohorts of retirees cannot be fully analyzed. Comparisons across age groups at a point in time indicate comparative standards of living within the context of current standards of living. Replacement rates indicate comparative standards of living over a lifetime. Because these assessments have not been made, current forecasts provide an incomplete assessment of future retirement income adequacy.

Income Distribution and the Poverty Rate

Measures used to evaluate retirement income adequacy and retirement income gaps also consider the distribution of income and the incidence of poverty and near poverty. Zedlewski et al. (1990) have considered the distribution of cash income among elderly families. In their work the percentage of married couples with income less than $10,000 per year is projected to decrease from 18.4 percent in 1990 to 0.5 percent in 2030. The percentage of nonmarried men with incomes of less than $5,000 is projected to decline from 20.9 percent in 1990 to 1.7 percent in 2030. Similar percentages for nonmarried women fall from 34.9 percent to 4.0 percent. Nonetheless, no DYNASIM projections are presented in terms of poverty rates or Gini coefficients.

Lewin/ICF (1991) present distributional information from PRISM in yet another way. Their tabulations indicate that the median income of the bottom one-fifth of the income distribution will increase from $11,971 for married couples over the 1986–1990 period to $19,272 in 2016–2020. Median incomes of nonmarried men in the bottom quintile are projected to increase from $5,743 to $9,972 over the same period, those of nonmarried women from $4,783 to $6,878. Lewin/ICF further indicate that total median incomes of married couples rise from 276 percent of the poverty line in 1988 to 441 percent in 2018. Median incomes of nonmarried men and women increase from 174 percent and 137 percent of the poverty line in 1988 to 308 and 193 percent respectively. Nonetheless, while these figures also suggest that fewer elderly will be in poverty or near poverty in the future, direct measures of income inequality and poverty rates are not provided.

Earlier work using PRISM indicates that the percentage of married baby boom couples[14] below 125 percent of poverty will fall from 11.2 percent to 1.6 percent for current retirees (Andrews and Chollet, 1988). The percent of nonmarried baby boom men within 125 percent of the poverty line is projected to fall from 31.5 percent to 5.4 percent for current retirees. Nonetheless, nonmarried baby boom women with income within 125 percent of poverty remains extremely high at 43.3 percent (but reduced from 64.9 percent). Thus many women will continue to have inadequate retirement income despite significant increases in lifetime labor force participation and in pension recipiency.

Our knowledge about the distribution of retirement income in the future remains incomplete. In particular, recent studies have not considered the distribution of retirement income among minorities. Poverty and near-poverty rates among black retirees are likely to remain high, and the distribution of income in retirement is likely to become less equal.

More broadly speaking, estimates of income inequality for the population as a whole are not available. Some increase in the inequality of income among the aged may be expected after the year 2000. Even though pension income is projected to become more universal, the recent trend toward greater income inequality among the working-age population will necessarily translate into greater in retirement income inequality in the future. Furthermore, a less equal distribution of assets among the baby boom cohort will also increase the Gini coefficient.

IV. Policies to Improve Retirement Income Adequacy

Retirement income adequacy should be reviewed from three dimensions. First, does retirement income meet society's expectations? Second, are poverty rates acceptable? Third, is income inequality too great? Empirical evidence suggests that the income of the aged today is, on average, comparable to that of the nonaged. By contrast, current retirement income does not appear to maintain living standards achieved immediately prior to retirement. Projections suggest that retirement income will improve in the future, although not necessarily as fast as that of the working-age population.

While poverty among the elderly is no greater than among the nonelderly, serious pockets of poverty persist, particularly among minorities and nonmarried women. Projections of income into the twenty-first century indicate that, although poverty is expected to decline, near-poverty rates among nonmarried women will remain high.

Because society has taken pride in historic reductions in income inequality, recent evidence of a shift toward greater inequality has been met with concern. Increasing inequality tends to be most disturbing if it signals a greater concentration of households at the bottom of the income distribution.

Depending on trends in the distribution of wages, future cohorts of retirees may face greater discrepancies in purchasing power than earlier generations.

A. Retirement Income and Living Standards

The issue of relative living standards is complex because no consensus exists about the standard our society seeks to achieve. Preserving the consumption patterns of individuals in retirement appears to be an appropriate goal. Furthermore, living standards in retirement probably should be linked to economy-wide productivity gains. In other words, retirees today should not have to live as they did in the 1950s, and retirees tomorrow probably should not live as they do today. Nonetheless, theoretical replacement rates, according to current calculations, may actually overstate income needs. That supposition notwithstanding, many people may be forced to reduce their living standards in retirement.

For instance, in the case of many nonmarried elderly persons, adequate income appears to be predicated on a continued pattern of work. The issue of work in retirement continues to be a sensitive one. On the one hand, an extended debate has taken place about the work-disincentive effect of the Social Security earnings test.[15] By contrast, the phased-in increase in the normal retirement age under the 1983 Social Security amendments has been criticized for penalizing persons unable to work. In view of both concerns, a serious reassessment of the integration of the Social Security Disability Insurance program with the Old Age and Survivors Insurance program ought to be undertaken. These programs should be reviewed (and potentially redesigned) to encourage continued labor force participation without placing those who can no longer work in financial jeopardy.

Recent interest in encouraging more portable employer-sponsored pensions is also tied to the notion of an adequate replacement rate. Theoretically, a worker who stays on one job until retirement will tend to have higher benefit payments under a defined benefit pension plan[16] than a worker who changes jobs and has similar final-pay plans on each. Portability losses result from gains in productivity and prices that are not captured in the benefit formula calculation for pensions earned on prior preretirement jobs. As a consequence, even with similar lifetime wages, the one-job worker will have higher pension benefits than the retiree who had greater lifetime job mobility.

Unfortunately, issues of pension portability and equity are not simple. When job change is voluntary, workers presumably make welfare-enhancing decisions. Furthermore, pensions are used by employers to implement personnel policy. Presumably, employers use pensions, in part, to restrict job mobility, perhaps to capture returns from training and skills tied to the firm. While research on pensions and job change has proved inconclusive, breaking that link could have unforeseen labor market consequences. Furthermore, there appears to be little political will to force employers into providing pensions that could be easily transferred. Even the most straightforward remedy, the indexing of past vested pensions for inflation, is not being seriously considered.

Nonetheless, with multiple sources of income, retirement income adequacy seems assured. For middle-income workers, adequacy is as dependent upon individual efforts as on the government. Replacement rates based on pension income alone (from both Social Security and employer-sponsored pensions) do not appear to maintain living standards. Public policy has not determined how to encourage saving, however. While tax incentives through IRAs were regarded as a means to this end, even when IRAs were universally available on a tax-deferred basis only a relatively small percentage of the population found them attractive. Nonetheless, based on that experience, more research on their effectiveness could be undertaken. An analysis of the Canadian experience might prove fruitful. IRAs could supplement retirement income in a meaningful way even if they were predominantly used by older, middle-class workers.

Recent concerns about retirement income supplementation have also arisen in view of the changes in the pension system that have taken place over the past decade. In particular, the primary point of growth in the system has been in the use of defined contribution plans in general and 401(k) plans in particular. These plans raise certain concerns that were not considered important when defined benefit plans predominated. First, defined contribution plans (including 401(k) plans) are more likely to provide lump sum cash distributions on job change equal to the value of the vested benefits in the plan.[17] These distributions are frequently used for consumption purposes despite a 10-percent excise tax on their use. Consequently, funds make their way out of the pension system, reducing retirement income streams. Legislation has been called for to prevent the expenditure of these funds prior to retirement. No study has evaluated the impact of these outflows on future retirement income, however, nor whether their restriction would improve retirement income adequacy.

Another concern stems from the voluntary nature of 401(k) plan participation. Although voluntary plan participation rates are high, encouraged by employer matching, not all employees offered the choice of contributing to a plan on a tax-deferred basis take the opportunity to participate. While the tax code has rather stringent participation standards to guard against the disproportionate use of 401(k) plans by highly compensated workers (who can more easily afford to save), plan participation is correlated with earnings. Once again, the ultimate impact of plan participation on future retirement income has not been evaluated. Consequently, no measures can be developed to evaluate whether some shift toward voluntary contributions will jeopardize retirement income adequacy for a segment of the population.

B. Poverty in Retirement

The issue of poverty (and near poverty) in retirement is a serious one for nonmarried individuals and minorities. While the nation can be proud of the progress made in improving the living conditions of the elderly since the 1950s, the poverty rates experienced by widows over age 65 are not acceptable. Although this situation will improve over time, limited projections suggest that many nonmarried elderly women will still face inadequate living standards in the twenty-first century.

Low retirement income results, in part, from low lifetime earnings because of limited labor force participation, low wages, or both. Obviously measures to increase earnings (particularly to combat discrimination) and to encourage labor force participation will lead to higher retirement income. But such measures may not necessarily be effective if individuals choose to remain out of the labor force or do not have the education and skills to qualify for higher-paid jobs.

Consequently, three other tools are available to improve retirement income—employer sponsored pensions, Social Security, and Supplemental Security Income (SSI).[18] The 1981 President's Commission on Pension Policy proposed mandated employer-sponsored pensions, in part to address the issue of income adequacy in retirement. The potential disemployment effects of mandating plans for small employers reduces the attractiveness of this proposal.

A more focused approach would look to federally provided retirement programs to reduce poverty among the aged. Several changes could be contemplated. First, the benefit formula could be modified, increasing replacement rates for workers with lower monthly earnings. If replacement rates at lower earnings levels were boosted, the 50-percent spouse's supplement could also be reduced. This would simultaneously raise benefits and reduce the reduction in benefits experienced by widows under the current system.

Furthermore, SSI could be closely integrated into the Social Security system with either an automatic minimum benefit provided or means-tested benefits continued. In addition SSI benefit levels should be reevaluated to ensure that minimum federal benefits are ensured. This could involve a significant, and difficult, realignment of federal-state responsibility and authority on welfare payment issues.

An additional policy challenge, however, relates to the fact that a large proportion of elderly persons who are eligible for SSI benefits never apply. A variety of explanations have been suggested for this situation including lack of information about the program and a continued fear of the stigma of welfare. Other explanations for low participation hinge on the fact that those elderly who do not apply are probably eligible for only minimal supplements. Nonetheless, if minimums were realigned toward the poverty line, more poor elderly could reap substantial benefits from the program.

To this purpose, the experience of other industrial nations should be consulted with an eye toward system redesign. Of course, universal minimums would raise the current cost of the national retirement income system. These benefits could be paid for directly, however, through greater use of the income tax. If Social Security benefits were all subject to taxation (with the exception of the return of employee contributions),[19] additional revenue would be forthcoming to reduce poverty among the elderly.

C. The Distribution of Income

The full taxation of benefits would maintain the concept of social insurance, provide a base of protection for all retirees, increase revenue, and remove intergenerational tax advantages. If Social Security benefits were taxed like other pensions, few could argue that individuals not in need of government revenues were being subsidized by the federal government, in particular since implicit lifetime real rates of return to upper income retirees will be extremely low or negative.[20] In other words, although Social Security contribution rates are not progressive, lower wage workers receive a far higher real rate of return on their contributions from a lifetime perspective because the Social Security *benefit formula* is progressive. That is, the formula is designed to replace a far higher percentage of the monthly earnings of low-wage workers.

Further increases in the inequality of income among the aged, however, cannot be addressed by changes in the structure of federally provided benefits or by changes in tax policy. Inequality at retirement age is a result of lifetime labor market outcomes and differences in savings behavior (skill, work, and luck). By retirement age these forces have had a lasting impact. They continue to operate, however, with some older persons supplementing their income through work, others choosing greater leisure, and a third group finding their activities limited despite themselves. Similarly, at every income level, some persons will be thrifty and fortunate in their investment decisions, while others will consume their assets and make unwise or unlucky investments.

These factors touch upon issues that are broader than those related to retirement income policy. As such, policy makers may affect the income distribution of workers by promoting equal opportunity and job training programs to meet the skill needs of the twenty-first century. Similarly, legislators may seek new policies to encourage saving. Finally, greater regulation of the financial sector may be called for to improve the stability of our institutions. Nonetheless, even with these changes, inequality of income will continue to be greater among the elderly than among the working age population. Consequently, the most effective retirement income policy ought to be targeted toward the maintenance of preretirement living standards and toward the eradication of pockets of poverty among the aged.

The views expressed in this paper are those of the author and do not necessarily reflect the opinions of Mathematica Policy Research, Inc. or any of its clients.

Notes

1. Currently, persons must reach age 65 for full benefit eligibility and age 62 for partial benefits.
2. Long-term care issues, in particular, and health care costs, in general, are not considered in this paper.
3. Grad's study also reports on income of those between age 55 and 64.
4. The data from which these figures are drawn suggest that over three-quarters of the nonmarried elderly are women. Over four-fifths of nonmarried aged women are widows. Over half of all nonmarried aged men are widowers.
5. Unmarried women were less likely to receive private pensions than unmarried men, with a 19-percent recipiency rate posted for women compared to a 28 percent rate for men.
6. Aged households and working-age households are defined as follows. Aged households are headed by a person aged 65 and over. Working-age households are headed by a person under age 65.
7. Radner indicates that adjustment for family composition would have little effect on the trends presented.
8. Boskin and Shoven (1987) use the Retirement Income Survey to calculate replacement rates that actually exceed hypothetical rates by some margin. To do so, they use career average indexed earnings and make a series of other adjustments that increase their rates even higher. While these calculations raise some important issues about appropriate income comparisons, the authors

appear determined to prove that the elderly receive consumption windfalls in retirement. Perhaps the key policy issue raised by their use of the data is whether the living standards of earlier decades are sufficient in retirement or whether the gains of economic growth should be shared as well.

9. Only the official poverty rate scale suggests that an elderly person needs 92 percent of the income of a nonelderly person to meet minimum living standard needs.

10. Some 35 percent of married couples report earnings compared to 13 percent of nonmarried persons. Some 78 percent of married persons report asset income, as do 61 percent of nonmarried persons.

11. The DYNASIM projections, however, take until the year 2010 before the share of pension income received by nonmarried women equals the actual share of income provided to them by pensions in 1988.

12. Some recent research on pension portability has considered the probabilities of pension coverage on job change using the Survey of Income and Program Participation. Gustman and Steinmeier (forthcoming) found that 13.8 percent of workers without pensions who changed jobs in 1984 had a pension on their 1985 job. By contrast, 35.8 percent of workers with a pension who changed jobs in 1984 also had a pension on their 1985 job.

13. These are individuals born between 1945 and 1954.

14. Once again, these are individuals born between 1945 and 1954.

15. The earnings test reduces immediate Social Security benefits among younger recipients who earn over a specified amount each year.

16. Defined benefit plans provide for monthly annuities in retirement frequently based on final pay and years of service.

17. Cashouts include vested employer contributions and employee contributions to the plan.

18. The SSI program is the welfare component of the Social Security Act providing means-tested benefits to the elderly, blind, and disabled.

19. Presumably the nontaxable share of benefits would be allocated over time rather than having payments presented tax-free for a period immediately following retirement.

20. Rates of return on Social Security contributions can be calculated for different groups of retirees by comparing the sum of contributions paid to the present discounted value of future benefits payments.

Bibliography

Advisory Council on Social Security. 1991. *Social Security and the Future Financial Security of Women*. Washington, DC: Advisory Council on Social Security.

Andrews, Emily S. 1987. "Changing Pension Policy and the Aging of America. *Contemporary Policy Issues* (September): 84–97.

Andrews, Emily S. and Deborah J. Chollet. 1988. "Future Sources of Retirement Income: Whither the Baby Boom." In *Social Security and Private Pensions: Providing for Retirement in the Twenty-First Century*, ed. Susan M. Wachter. Lexington, MA: Lexington Books: 71–95.

Andrews, Emily S. and Michael D. Hurd. 1992. "Employee Benefits and Retirement Income Adequacy: Data, Research, and Policy Issues." In *Pensions and the Economy: Sources, Uses, and Limitations of Data*, ed. Zvi Bodie and Alicia H. Munnell. Philadelphia: University of Pennsylvania Press: 1–30.

Boskin, Michael J. and John B. Shoven. 1987. "Concepts and Measures of Earnings Replacement During Retirement." In *Issues in Pension Economics,* ed. Zvi Bodie, John B. Shoven, and David A. Wise. Chicago: University of Chicago Press: 113–46.

Burkhauser, Richard V., Karen C. Holden, and Daniel Feaster. 1988. "Incidence, Timing, and Events Associated with Poverty: A Dynamic View of Poverty in Retirement." *Journal of Gerontology* 43, 2:S46–S52.

Danziger, Sheldon, Jacques van der Gaag, Michael K. Taussig, and Eugene Smolensky. 1984. "The Direct Measurement of Welfare Levels: How Much Does It Cost to Make Ends Meet?" *Review of Economics and Statistics* 66,3:500–505.

Dexter, Michael K. 1984. *Replacement Ratios: A Major Issue in Employee Pension Systems.* Washington, DC: Public Employee Pension System.

Fox, Alan. 1982. "Earnings Replacement Rates and Total Income: Findings from the Retirement History Study." *Social Security Bulletin* 45, 10 (October): 3–23, 53.

Grad, Susan. 1990a. *Income of the population 55 or Older, 1988.* Washington, DC: U.S. Department of Health and Human Services, Social Security Administration.

———. 1990b. "Earnings Replacement Rates of New Retired Workers." *Social Security Bulletin* 53, 10 (October): 2–19.

Gustman, Alan L. and Thomas L. Steinmeier. Forthcoming. "Pension Portability and Labor Mobility: Evidence from the Survey of Income and Program Participation." *Journal of Public Economics.*

Hurd, Michael D. 1989. "Poverty of Widows: Future Prospects." In *The Economics of Aging,* ed. David A. Wise. Chicago: University of Chicago Press: 201–22.

———. 1990. "Research on the Elderly: Economic Status, Retirement, and Consumption and Savings." *Journal of Economic Literature* XXVII, 2 (June): 564–637.

Hurd, Michael D. and David A. Wise. 1989. "The Wealth and Poverty of Widows: Assets Before and After the Husband's Death." In *The Economics of Aging,* ed. David A. Wise. Chicago: University of Chicago Press: 177–99.

Lewin/ICF. 1991. *Future Financial Resources of the Elderly: A View of Pensions, Savings, Social Security, and Earnings in the 21st Century.* Washington, DC: Social Security Advisory Council.

Orshansky, Mollie. 1965. "Counting the Poor: Another Look at the Poverty Profile." *Social Security Bulletin* 28 (January): 3–29.

Palmer, Bruce A. 1989. "Tax Reform and Retirement Income Replacement Ratios." *Journal of Risk and Insurance:* 702–25.

Palmer, John L., Timothy Smeeding, and Barbara Boyle Torrey, eds. 1988. *The Vulnerable.* Washington, DC: Urban Institute Press.

President's Commission on Pension Policy. 1981. *Coming of Age: Toward a National Retirement Income Policy.* Washington DC: U.S. Government Printing Office.

Radner, Daniel. 1983. "Adjusted Estimates of the Size Distribution of Family Money Income." *Journal of Business and Economic Statistics* I,2 (April): 135–46.

———. 1991. "Changes in the Incomes of Age Groups, 1984–1989." Social Security Administration, Office of Research and Statistics, ORS Working Paper Series 51 (September).

Ruggles, Patricia. 1990. *Drawing the Line: Alternative Poverty Measures and Their Implications for Public Policy.* Washington,DC: Urban Institute Press.

Smeeding, Timothy M. 1989. "Full Income Estimates of the Relative Well-Being of the Elderly and the Nonelderly." In *Research in Economic Inequality.* Vol. 1, ed. D. Bloom and D. Slottje. Greenwich CT: JAI Press: 83–122.

Van der Gaag, Jacques and Eugene Smolensky. 1982. "True Household Equivalence Scales and Characteristics of the Poor in the United States." *Review of Income and Wealth* 28 (March): 17–28.

Vaughan, Denton R. 1989. "Using Subjective Assessments of Income to Estimate Family Equivalence Scales: A Report on Work in Progress." In *U.S. Bureau of the Census, Survey of Income and Program Participation and Related Longitudinal Surveys: 1984* (selected papers from the 1984 Annual Meeting of the American Statistical Association). Washington, DC: U.S. Department of Commerce, Bureau of the Census.

Zedlewski, Sheila R., Roberta O. Barnes, Martha R. Burt, Timothy D. McBride, and Jack A. Meyer. 1990. *The Needs of the Elderly in the 21st Century.* Urban Institute Report 90-5. Washington, DC: Urban Institute Press.

Comments by Donald S. Grubbs, Jr.

Emily Andrews stimulates us to think more carefully about what we mean by retirement income adequacy, how to measure it, and how to solve the problems of inadequacy.

Defining Retirement Income Adequacy

Retirees need economic resources to meet their various expenses in retirement when and as they occur. Some of these expenses, such as food, shelter, and clothing, require a regular flow of money. The need for shelter can be met either entirely by an income stream (for rent) or partly by an asset (home ownership) and partly by an income stream (for taxes, insurance, and expenses). The need for health care benefits, however, is unpredictable for many of the elderly. Some retirees have only minimal health care expenses. For some the expense is enormous and continues over many years. For others the expense is usually minimal, but may suddenly become overwhelming. *Average* health care costs are meaningless to individuals, who need to have their health care costs met when and to the extent they are incurred.

Retirement income adequacy cannot be thoroughly addressed without considering these separate needs for assets, for a regular flow of income for recurring expenses, and for resources to meet health care costs when and as they occur. We must ask whether the combination of economic resources is actually meeting the needs of retirees today, and whether their needs will be met in the future.

Health Care Needs

The typical American now retires at age 62, and some retire earlier, by choice or otherwise. For retirees under 65, Medicare is generally not available. Some of these retirees under 65 are covered by good programs provided by former employers, but most are not. Some of the retirees under 65 who are not covered under plans of former employers are covered under individual health insurance, but many cannot afford it and many cannot purchase it at any price because they are not insurable.

For the average retiree over 65, Medicare pays about half of health care costs. This statement is meaningless for any individual, who may have negligible health care costs not covered under Medicare or may have enormous costs. Thus all retirees need good supplemental protection to pay those significant costs not paid by Medicare. For retirees over 65, some are covered under retiree health programs of prior employers, although the proportion is smaller than for those under 65 because many employer programs only provide coverage until Medicare begins. Some retirees over 65 are covered under good individual Medicare supplement programs, but others have poor coverage or none at all.

The principal major health costs that are not covered by Medicare, often totaling thousands and sometimes hundreds of thousands of dollars for an individual, are coinsurance, prescription drugs, and care beyond the maximum number of days covered by Medicare.

Although Medicare leaves major gaps, it does play a major part in meeting the needs for health benefits. However, the outlook for Medicare Part A is quite uncertain because the Hospital Insurance Trust is currently projected to be exhausted in about 12 years. Either a significant increase in payroll taxes or other resources will be required or benefits must be substantially reduced.

The lack of adequate health insurance for the elderly is not essentially different from the lack for younger people, many of whom have no health insurance whatsoever. Every individual in America needs adequate health insurance regardless of age and regardless of whether employed. Almost every other industrialized country has recognized this need by providing a universal program of health insurance or health benefits regardless of employment status. National universal comprehensive health insurance is the obvious solution to the problem for Americans of all ages.

In the absence of universal comprehensive health insurance covering all Americans, Medicaid provides a vital back-up of benefits on the basis of a needs test. Here the relation to the adequacy of assets and retirement income is obvious, because the Medicaid recipient must first be reduced to poverty before receiving Medicaid.

Adequacy of Monthly Retirement Income

If the often unpredictable needs for health care benefits can be met by adequate health insurance, the remaining needs for ongoing expenses can be met by a regular flow of retirement income. Andrews looks at adequacy of retirement income in relation to three standards:

- preretirement income,
- income of younger adults,
- poverty levels.

Preretirement Income

Most people would like to continue their preretirement standard of living after retirement, and I concur that this is a reasonable goal. Andrews has assembled helpful information on the replacement ratios needed to accomplish this. She cites the studies by Bruce Palmer, which indicate that married couples earning $30,000 or more need to replace about 68 percent of their preretirement salary in order to maintain their preretirement standard of living. This needed replacement percentage is larger for those earning less than $30,000, increasing to 82 percent for those earning $15,000. Earlier studies by the President's Commission on Pension Policy indicate that the needed replacement ratios for single employees would be about 5 percent less than for married couples.

Based on studies by Susan Grad and by Alan Fox, Andrews reports estimated actual median replacement ratios for various segments of the retired population. These actual median replacement levels generally are well below the needed levels indicated previously. Medians of course do not indicate ranges. Some of those who receive both Social Security and an employer pension attain the replacement ratios needed to maintain their preretirement standard of living, while others fall significantly short. For those who do not receive an employer pension, almost all fall far short of being able to retain their preretirement standard of living.

Inflation

Replacement rates compare an individual's income just after retirement to his or her income just before retirement. For retirees whose only source of income is Social Security, income will be adjusted for inflation and thus their initial low standard of living at retirement will not fall further behind adequacy than it was on the retirement date.

Private employer pensions either receive no inflation adjustment at all or receive adjustments less than the cost of living. Most individuals with personal savings invest them primarily in fixed dollar investments, which they think are safe. This is actually very dangerous, because inflation is almost certain to substantially erode the purchasing power of such savings and the investment income it generates.

As a result of private employer pensions and investment income that fail to keep pace with inflation, the purchasing power of the retirement income declines after retirement for many retirees, gradually becoming less adequate.

Comparison to the Income of Younger Adults

Andrews, like others, compares the income of retirees with the income of active workers. She makes readers aware of the difficulty of making such comparisons. Taken as a whole, the aged population generally enjoys a standard of living comparable to the younger population.

Such comparisons serve no useful purpose. They ignore the fact that older workers earn substantially more than younger workers, because compensation increases with age in relation to performance, promotions, experience and longevity. Retirees might more appropriately be compared to workers between 50 and 60, who are more nearly comparable to their own status before retirement. Such comparisons would show that retirees have substantially less income than their friends a few years younger who have not yet retired. Both groups of course are much better off than workers in their twenties who started at the bottom of the ladder.

The process of comparing the income of retirees to that of *all* workers is not consonant with either equity or retirement-income needs.

Poverty Levels

Another view of retirement income adequacy is to consider the minimum needed by every American to provide some minimal standard of living. The most common measures are the "poverty level" and the "near-poverty level" (125 percent of the poverty level). For 1990 these levels were as shown in the table. There can be reasonable differences concerning exactly what dollar minimum should be considered the bottom limit below which no person should fall, and how such limits should be determined. In my view it is unacceptable for people to be

	Annual income	
Household composition	*Poverty level*	*Near-poverty level*
1 person 65 and older	$6,268	$7,835
2 persons 65 and older	$7,905	$9,881

forced to live below the near-poverty level shown, much less at or below the poverty line itself.

In 1989 11 percent of all Americans age 65 and older were living below the poverty line. Some ask whether such a poverty rate is too high. Unless one thinks that poverty among our fellow human beings is an acceptable condition, any poverty rate is too high. The real question is not whether the situation is unacceptable, but rather how widespread is this unacceptable situation. The goal must be to eliminate poverty to the greatest extent possible.

Future Retirement Income Adequacy

Andrews provides helpful information and insights regarding retirement income in the future. She focuses on forecasts under two micro-simulation models, DYNASIM and PRISM. Both models project very substantial improvement in retirement income levels in the future. But, as Andrews points out, forecasts are only as good as the underlying assumptions.

Both DYNASIM and PRISM project that the proportion of retirees receiving a pension under a plan of either a private or a governmental employer will rise from the current level of around 40 percent to roughly double that level. Andrews calls these projections "baffling." I call them unlikely. The proportion of employees covered under plans is unlikely to increase significantly. Defined benefit plans are being replaced by defined contribution plans. Defined contribution plans usually make payments in the form of a lump sum distribution, which may be consumed and not be available to provide a lifetime income. Even under defined benefit plans it is becoming more common to provide benefits in the form of a lump sum rather than a life annuity. Increasing mobility of workers makes it less likely that employees will continue employment long enough to receive a pension as a life annuity. All these factors bode ill for improvement in the number of persons receiving pensions.

Both DYNASIM and PRISM follow Social Security assumptions regarding future growth of real wages (in excess of inflation). PRISM followed the assumption of the 1991 Trustees Report that real wages will grow between 1.5 percent and 1.1 percent each year during the next several years, and grow at the ultimate rate of 1.1 percent each year thereafter. A rising tide raises all ships. These assumptions would result in real wage increases of 43 percent in the next thirty years and resulting increases in all of the sources of retirement income. The proportion of individuals below the poverty line would fall drastically among both active and retired workers, but would not entirely disappear.

The above results are contingent on the underlying assumptions. Those who endeavor to project the level of real wage growth do so with considerable humility, realizing how uncertain it is. This is not meant to imply that the 1.1 percent growth rate is unreasonable, but only to indicate that it might be very much higher or lower than this level, leading to very different results than those indicated by the models.

Even with overall gains, some retirees would still be left in poverty. While the models indicate increasing levels of absolute retirement income, Andrews points out that they do not indicate whether replacement ratios will improve, and she does not anticipate much change from current levels if there are no significant legislative changes. I concur.

Policies to Improve Retirement Income Adequacy

Andrews states that "the most effective retirement-income policy ought to be targeted toward the maintenance of preretirement living standards and toward the eradication of pockets of poverty among the aged." I concur.

Social Security is the only form of retirement income that almost all retirees receive. By itself Social Security clearly is not adequate to prevent poverty or to provide adequate replacement ratios. Under present law, replacement levels from Social Security are scheduled to gradually decrease until, for those born after 1959, they reach approximately 87 percent of the level for current retirees, unless those future retirees elect to retire at a higher age than current retirees. Employer pensions are an uncertain source because many workers are not covered, many change jobs without vesting, many receive their benefits in the form of lump sum distributions, and even those who receive life annuities have those annuities eroded by inflation. History shows that, for many of the retired, personal savings cannot be counted on as a significant source of income.

There are only three possible ways both to eradicate poverty among the elderly and to enable all Americans more nearly to maintain preretirement living standards. The first is to increase benefits under Social Security so that Social Security by itself provides an adequate minimum retirement income for all retirees and so that replacement ratios will be more adequate. This could include minimum benefit levels for individuals regardless whether the individual has any wage history at all, perhaps replacing both the spouse's benefit under Social

Security and needs-tested benefits under the SSI program. The second possible solution is to require every employer to provide a minimum pension for every employee, with these minimum pensions fully and immediately vested and payable only in the form of a life annuity with at least minimum postretirement cost-of-living adjustments. The third possible solution is a combination of the first two, with every employer required either to contribute to a second layer of Social Security or to maintain its own plan providing at least minimum pensions for all employees. There is no other approach that can assure that all retirees will have adequate retirement incomes in the future. Experience offers no hope that individual savings will fill the gap for most Americans.

Can we afford such benefit increases in the years ahead? With the projected growth in real wages of 43 percent over the next thirty years, allocating a small portion of this gain to retirement income needs could easily solve the problem without undue hardship.

The Larger Problem

Andrews's paper addresses retirement income adequacy only in the United States. The paper is not to be criticized for this, since all projects must as a practical matter limit their scope. However, we need to remember that the United States constitutes only 4.5 percent of the world's population, and that only a small portion of the world shares our relative affluence.

Is retirement income adequacy of any importance at all? Yes, but only because human beings are individually important. There is no rationale to think that the needs of Americans are important while the needs of others are not.

It is difficult to have any real understanding of the poverty of much of the rest of the world if one has not seen it on an individual basis. Most of us cannot even imagine life in Bangladesh, where the per capita income is approximately 1 percent of that in the United States. We see pictures of people actually starving to death in Somalia, but the reality is difficult to grasp. In such countries poverty is almost universal at all ages.

A fundamental part of the world problem is overpopulation and the escalation of that overpopulation. In much of the world the population already far exceeds the resources that would be needed to provide income adequacy under even the most modest definition. Yet the world's population is expected to approximately double during the next forty years. In Bangladesh and other countries where the problem is already acute, the growth rate is faster.

Those of us who care about our fellow humans must ask both what can be done as a matter of public policy and what we can do as individuals. The problem is so large that one could give up in despair. However, there are many steps that can be taken by individuals, by governments, and by international institutions that can greatly improve the situation in the years ahead. The scope of this discussion does not enable me to discuss the solutions herein.

Comments by Gary D. Hendricks

Overall this paper does an excellent job of pointing out issues that have been forgotten or ignored recently.

Measures of Retirement Income Adequacy

Andrews's discussion in this area is excellent. I don't recall having seen such a review for some number of years now, and, frankly, I was surprised that so much had been done of which I was not aware. My one criticism here is a minor one. I would like to have had the author share her opinion of all this work at the end of the section. The technical issues are daunting and the different measures yield substantially different results. I would have appreciated the author telling me what she, who had thought about this much more than I, concluded. What really matters here? As a person who works almost daily with policy makers, what should I care about and why?

In the end Andrews does give the reader some guidance. The last sentence of her paper reads, "Consequently, the most effective retirement income policy ought to be targeted toward the maintenance of preretirement living standards and toward the eradication of pockets of poverty among the aged." What this sentence suggests to me is that those who deal with public policy take a pragmatic view. For purposes of public policy debate, crude measures will do. Besides, with the current budget deficit, we can only afford to use public funds to remove the most serious gaps in income inadequacy among the aged, and these are the pockets of aged poor. For the nonpoor, maintenance of preretirement living standards crudely measured is a good political measure of how we as a society are doing in this area.

Although fairly basic measures will do for policy purposes, this fact does not mean that research is not needed and is not useful. To the contrary, to make life better for future generations of retirees we need to understand the forces that drive the distribution of income after retirement, and we need to monitor that distribution. Knowing the median income of the aged won't do. Averages mask many problems and tell us very little about how individuals are doing.

Current Gaps in Retirement Income Adequacy

I don't think anyone would question Andrews's conclusions here. The findings from analysis done over the past decade seem clear, and we owe the author a debt for having so carefully reviewed the extensive work in this area and isolated the major findings.

Despite the fine work, I found many parts of this discussion unsatisfying. The discussion highlights not only the major findings to date but also the need for further research and data collection. This is especially true for the factors underlying the gaps in retirement income adequacy. For example: How many of the aged poor or near-poor were in this status most of their lives? Did most of these people only enter near-poverty status when they were no longer able to work or were no longer able to get a job? Also, how does the adequacy of income change over the entire period of retirement?

The author discusses the inadequacy of the income of many aged widows and even suggests some ways that their income could be improved. However, she does not discuss the problem of increased longevity, the problem of exhausting assets, having a fixed income from a private pension and institutionalization. It appears that much more is known about who is poor during retirement than how they became poor. Here again, the need for further research is obvious.

Future Retirement Income Adequacy

As a former microsimulation modeler, I was most fascinated by this section of the paper. Here the author relies on work done with two simulation models: PRISM and DYNASIM. Andrews tells the reader enough about these models to make people who are knowledgeable about such models very nervous and to make the less knowledgeable total disbelievers. Unfortunately, the information she gives us about the models is not the right information. It's not so important that a model systematically overstates or understates an income component. It is much more important that the distribution is correct and that the covariance of the components of income for individuals is correct.

Moreover, the usefulness of the numbers from long-range projections using dynamic microsimulation models is not the magnitude of the numbers themselves but rather the trends in the numbers—the magnitude of changes over time. And even the trends produced by the models are by themselves of only limited use.

The most useful information from the models is the explanation of why the model produced the trends: mechanically what factors in the model led to the results. We learn from these models by explaining their results. This is how we discover important interactions that it would be difficult to uncover without the models. This is how we discover that factors that are statistically important in static research studies may have little to do with long-run results because they will be overwhelmed by other factors that can't be included in static research studies.

If you think about these models as I do, I think you would seriously question the conclusions Andrews suggests based on the projections she reviewed. Let me be more specific.

Although only 46 percent of the full-time workforce is covered by a private pension, 85 percent of workers in the models end up with one. This might well be true if job changes were strictly random. However, a job change in one time period may be a function of past job changes in ways that are not properly specified in the simulations. There may also be a high correlation between pension coverage on the old job and pension coverage on a new job. I have no evidence that this is true, although I think Alan Gustman has done research that suggests a correlation. In any case, it seems reasonable that many people tend to work for the same type of employer in job after job (larger employer to larger employer or small employer to small employer). Moreover, many job changes are probably between employers with somewhat similar benefit packages. Only a minority of job changes—less than 20 percent as I recall—are involuntary.

I think a closer look at the mechanics of the models that produced the results would point out the need for further research to support the operation of the models. The likelihood of pension coverage before and after a job change is only one such possible area. There are certainly others. However, it is hard to guess what they are without analyzing the mechanics of the models that produced the results on which Andrews is relying.

I was also distressed by the real wage growth assumptions used in both simulation models. It is difficult to justify real wage rate growth of 1.1 percent over the next twenty to thirty years when real wage rates, on average, have grown much more slowly over the past twenty years. What is going to make real wage rates suddenly start growing more rapidly? This overly optimistic real wage rate growth assumption is even more disconcerting because I don't know how it is being applied in the model. And I would even venture to guess that the studies Andrews reviewed probably don't contain the answer to my question.

DYNASIM, for example, simulates earned income through a string

of stochastic determinations that include whether the person partici-
pates in the labor force, the number of hours worked, and the wage
rate. If the real wage trend is applied at the wage rate level, then the
simulation may be grossly overstating the growth in real earnings.
Even with a zero real wage trend, the model should produce real
increases in annual wages. This is true because of increased labor force
participation and the number of workers, especially women, who are
working more hours each year than previously. It is critical at what
point in the simulation the trend factor is applied. I think my concerns
here only underscore my own belief that these models are best used to
increase our understanding of interactions, rather than as black boxes
that produce numbers to be accepted at face value. I wonder how
different the simulation results would look if (1) there were almost no
real wage rate growth, on average, over the next twenty years and
(2) the inequality of the income distribution of the nonaged population
continues to increase at the same rate as over the last decade.

There is little doubt that Andrews has focused on the right groups in
her review of the simulation results. However, I think the improvements she reports from the simulations may be illusionary. There is
nothing in the discussion of the simulations to convince me that, for
the next generation of retirees, many of those in the groups with the
greatest need will find their situation greatly improved.

Before leaving this section of the paper I would like to make one
other comment. Based on her review of the simulations, Andrews
concludes that restructuring of employer-sponsored pensions does not
appear to be the most efficient means of filling in the most important
gaps—relative poverty and maintenance of middle-class living standards. I am inclined to agree. However, I would hasten to point out
that the private pension system is being dramatically restructured
through the substitution of defined contribution plans for defined-
benefit plans. There is no reason in theory why defined contribution
plans cannot provide the same income replacement in retirement as
defined benefit plans. In fact, defined contribution plans have an
inherent advantage because of their portability. However, in practice
this is not what is happening.

The defined contribution plans that are being created are not generous enough to replace defined benefit plans. Moreover, the money
often does not remain in these plans until retirement. An employer
pension frequently means the difference between a very modest and a
modestly comfortable retirement income. Contrary to the simulation
results, even with stricter vesting standards withdrawal from defined
contribution plans could mean that fewer retirees will have meaningful
private pension benefits twenty to thirty years from now.

Policies to Improve Retirement Income Adequacy

Andrews's suggestions in this section are excellent. The changes she proposes are modest and would clearly help fill the most significant gaps. They are also changes that have not captured the attention of policy makers. Her suggestions deserve our careful consideration and the attention of those who regularly communicate with policy makers.

In closing, I would like to point out that Andrews's analysis seems to me to suggest one other way to help workers save enough to make a difference to their retirement income adequacy. According to Andrews's review, even a modest $100 to $150 a month in income from assets makes a large difference in determining whether one is near-poor during retirement. This suggests that even a small mandated employer contribution to a defined contribution plan could ease the financial stress of retirement for many who might otherwise become near-poor when they leave the labor force. Such a scheme would only help, of course, if the money set aside were preserved for retirement. As pointed out earlier, this is often not the case currently.

Comments by Bruce D. Schobel

Introduction

In her paper, Emily Andrews presents useful definitions of retirement income and measures of its adequacy. She also provides substantial information with respect to both the adequacy of retirement income today and how the situation may be expected to change in the future, based on two well-known computer models. Andrews envisions a future not too different from today.

In this discussion of Andrews's paper, I make some general observations, especially regarding the projections of the future situation, and some specific points regarding the likely contribution of Social Security to retirement income in the future. Finally, I make a few technical observations and note some possible errors.

Measures of *Adequacy*?

One general observation about measures of adequacy: My preference is to consider "adequacy" relative to *minimum* living standards. Of course other definitions have validity, too, but most combine other concepts with the concept of adequacy.

A common measure of retirement income adequacy—and one used repeatedly in Andrews's paper—is the replacement rate: retirement income relative to preretirement earnings, often adjusted in some way to reflect inflation. The philosophy underlying the use of these rates seems to be that, as a matter of fairness, retired people should be able to maintain their preretirement standard of living. Obviously, they need to receive some reasonable percentage of preretirement earnings in order to accomplish this goal.

These lifestyle-maintaining replacement rates, which vary by income level for a variety of well-known reasons, are not too difficult to compute, and many analysts have done this. Most, however, do not make sufficient distinction, in my view, between maintaining preretirement living standards and having a retirement income that is *adequate.* After all, expecting wealthy people to reduce their living standards after retirement may not be so unreasonable and may even be "fair," depending on one's definition.

For example, if that stereotypical American millionaire, Lee Iacocca, were to receive only 10 percent of his enormous and much publicized preretirement earnings after he retires from Chrysler this year, few would consider this level of retirement income to be "inadequate." He would probably have difficulty maintaining his preretirement lifestyle on that level of income and might have to make certain adjustments. Even at the 10-percent replacement rate, however, his retirement income would put him easily in the top 1 percent of American taxpayers.

Thus measures of adequacy based on poverty rates and the like may have greater meaning than those based on replacement rates. Still, these other measures provide important information, even if they do not relate all that well to my own concept of adequacy.

Validity of Projections

Andrews's vision of the future situation is based largely on results from the PRISM and DYNASIM computer models. Anyone with experience in this field knows that computer models can be only as good as the assumptions on which they are based (if they are even that good!). In this instance, the assumptions have to be regarded with considerable skepticism, simply because they extend so far into the future.

Analyses of *short-range* economic forecasts by even the most highly respected economists demonstrate the great uncertainty that exists. Economists (and everybody else, for that matter) have demonstrated little ability to forecast even a few years ahead, let alone decades. The problems of developing *long-range* forecasts are likely to be much greater, although we have not had enough experience yet to demonstrate this greater uncertainty.

The PRISM model attempts to make projections for 30 years into the future; DYNASIM looks ahead for 40 years. Of course, the Social Security Administration tops both of these, attempting the perhaps impossible task of projecting economic and demographic variables for the next 75 years!

Such very long-range projections can be put into perspective in the following way. Consider an economist (or actuary) sitting in his or her office in 1962 and trying to predict what the United States economy would be like 30 years hence, in 1992. How close to reality would the predictions have been? How about another expert in 1952 trying to look ahead 40 years? Then make the enormous leap to an economist in the year 1917, just before the United States entered World War I, trying to forecast 75 years down the road to the present time. Obviously, none of these people—no matter how brilliant—would have had a chance of coming even close to what actually occurred. Because today's economists are probably not much better at predicting the far-distant future than their predecessors were, we need to take all these projections with at least a few grains of salt. The use of computers really should not give us much more confidence in the results.

None of this discussion is intended to suggest that long-range projections should not be performed, just that they should not be taken too seriously. In addition, sensitivity analyses are essential, so that users of these projections can get a sense of how volatile the results are. Unfortunately, many analysts do not bother with this last step.

Social Security's Contribution to Future Retirement Income

The magnitudes of the most likely future sources of retirement income are quite difficult to project. We have no way of accurately estimating future investment income, for example, because we cannot project with any real confidence how much people will save during their working years or what future interest rates will be. One item that may be an exception to this general rule, however, is Social Security (by this term, I refer to the Old-Age, Survivors, and Disability Insurance, or OASDI, program).

We can probably start from the premise that the Social Security law will remain basically the same as it is today for several decades. (This is probably true with respect to OASDI, but certainly not with respect to Medicare, which has such enormous problems that it will certainly be changed drastically.) The present-law OASDI benefit formula produces absolutely stable and predictable replacement rates under any economic conditions. Very briefly, a worker with average earnings in every year (slightly less than $23,000 in 1992) who retires at his or her normal retirement age (NRA) will receive benefits at retirement that are about 41 percent of the earnings in the year before retirement. Similarly, an otherwise identical worker with maximum OASDI-covered earnings ($55,500 in 1992) will, in the long run, receive benefits at retirement that are about 27 percent of the last year's earnings.

These figures, and the continuum of replacement rates for earnings between average and maximum and at earnings levels below the average, were essentially fixed by the Social Security Amendments of 1977 (Public Law 95-216). Because Social Security's financial picture is pretty good for 30 to 40 years, according to the annual reports of its

Trustees, we can probably anticipate that the benefit provisions of the law—the most difficult provisions to change—will remain about the same as they are today for at least that long. Thus Social Security's contribution to future retirement income—the "floor of protection," as it is often called—can probably be predicted with greater confidence than that of any other source.

Still, Social Security has some surprises awaiting the unwary retiree. The stable replacement rates cited above are for workers retiring at NRA. The NRA was age 65 when Social Security began, and it remains there for workers born before 1938 (who will become eligible for Social Security early retirement benefits before the year 2000). For workers born in 1938 and later, however, the NRA rises, under provisions enacted into law as part of the Social Security Amendments of 1983 (Public Law 98-21). Eventually, for workers born after 1959, the NRA reaches 67. Thus, to get the same Social Security replacement rate that a worker gets today at age 65, retirees in 2027 and later will need to wait 2 years, until age 67.

The fact that the increase in NRA is a benefit reduction, which may be obvious enough, becomes much more obvious when considered in light of the large percentage of beneficiaries who claim early-retirement benefits before reaching their NRA. Currently, something like three-fourths of the non-disabled fully-insured population claim benefits at age 62. At exact age 62, the early-retirement reduction required under the law is 20 percent today; therefore, these early retirees receive 80 percent, or slightly more, of the benefit that they could receive if they waited until age 65 (ignoring the effects of additional earnings, which are relatively small in most cases). Their replacement rates are therefore lower. For example, the hypothetical average earner described above could receive 41 percent of his or her last year's earnings from Social Security at NRA; at age 62 today, the replacement rate would be only 33 percent.

In the future, early-retirement benefits will continue to be available at age 62, but because the number of years of early retirement will increase (from 3 to 5), the early-retirement reduction factor increases also. Starting in 2022, workers who retire at exact age 62 will receive just 70 percent of the benefit that would be payable at NRA, instead of 80 percent today. This represents a 12.5 percent relative reduction in benefit amount. The replacement rate for our hypothetical average earner who retires at NRA would be just 29 percent in 2022, instead of 33 percent today. Clearly, unless retirement behavior changes, Social Security will contribute less toward the adequacy of retirement income in the future than it does today.

The question of whether retirement behavior *will* change is worth investigating. Everyone knows that Americans have been retiring earlier and earlier for many decades, and nobody has been able to show that this trend will ever reverse. Of course, Americans have been living longer, and we might anticipate that some of this extra longevity will be reflected in longer working lives rather than going entirely to longer periods of leisure. On the other hand, we could speculate that greater affluence, which is projected to occur even under so-called "pessimistic" economic assumptions, will allow the trend toward earlier retirement to continue indefinitely or maybe just level off sometime. Perhaps most Americans do not like their jobs very much and will retire as soon as they can afford to do so. This issue raises questions that we simply cannot answer, and it serves to emphasize the uncertainty of all long-range projections.

Social Security has more surprises in store for future retirees. In one-earner families, which were the norm years ago and are predominant in today's retired population, the non-working spouse (usually, the wife) receives a benefit roughly equal to half of the retired-worker spouse's benefit, depending on their respective ages. In other words, if our hypothetical average earner who retires at NRA has a non-working spouse the same age, then their *combined* replacement rate is not 41 percent but 62 percent.

When today's predominantly two-earner couples retire, they will ordinarily not be eligible for any such spousal supplements, because each worker's own retired-worker benefit will offset any potential spouse's benefit, reducing it to zero in most cases. (The point at which reduction to zero occurs depends on many factors, but it almost always happens when one spouse has average indexed monthly earnings of one-third of the other spouse's average indexed monthly earnings.) Without supplemental spouse's benefits, the combined replacement rate for the retired couple, both with average earnings in every year, would be just 41 percent at NRA, a huge reduction from 62 percent today.

These reductions in future Social Security benefits resulting from changes in family work patterns will continue after one spouse dies. Under Social Security law, the surviving spouse receives a benefit essentially equal to the benefit that had been received by the higher-earning spouse. (If that spouse dies, the other spouse gets a widow(er)'s benefit equal to what the deceased spouse had been receiving; if the lower-earning spouse dies, the higher earner simply continues to get whatever benefit had been payable before the other spouse's death, and the deceased spouse's benefit ends.)

For the traditional one-earner retired couple that we see today, this means that the benefit reduction at the first spouse's death is about 33 percent (as found by Hurd; see page 14 of Andrews's paper). For our hypothetical average earner with a non-working spouse the same age, the replacement rate while both are alive is 62 percent; after the first spouse dies, the replacement rate drops to 41 percent.

When today's two-earner couples retire, they will have less survivor protection because of the absence of spousal supplements. When our hypothetical married average earners retire at NRA, each will receive a retired-worker benefit replacing about 41 percent of that person's last year's earnings. The overall replacement rate is therefore 41 percent. When one spouse dies, that person's benefit will end, reducing the overall replacement rate to 21 percent, as compared to 41 percent today. Again, this is a huge reduction.

Finally, the percentage of single-person families has been increasing. When these people retire, they obviously can receive no spousal supplements and consequently will have replacement rates that are lower than average.

All the preceding discussion shows that, while the Social Security law may not change very much in the next 30–40 years, already scheduled changes in the law and the way that it functions in the context of changing family situations and other circumstances will cause the level of benefits to fall substantially relative to previous earnings. Thus, everything else being equal, retirement income can be expected to be less adequate in the future than it is today.

The appropriate response to this prediction would be to increase savings of various kinds, but Americans seem to be doing exactly the opposite. The retirement years may be very bleak for large numbers of people. As a result, I am much less confident that "retirement income will improve in the future," as Andrews predicts. The reverse may be true.

Technical Observations

I have a number of technical observations and, in some cases, corrections of Andrews's paper. These are as follows:

1. On page 4, factors are presented for equating the living standards of two hypothetical families, using three possible scales. Using the "poverty-line" scale, I computed the equivalence factor to be 84 percent [2.01/(2 x 1.19)], rather than 65 percent. Also, I computed the equivalence factor using the van der Gaag and Smolensky measure to be 88 percent [1.56/(2 x 0.89)], rather than 87 percent. Considering that the factors on the three scales range from 84 percent to 96 percent, perhaps they are not so divergent and therefore uncertain as Andrews suggests.

In any event, I wondered whether these equivalence factors are intended to be pre-tax or after-tax. Because the higher-income younger family pays more taxes as a percentage of income, an equivalence factor less than 1 might be reasonable. (The younger family will be in a higher tax bracket, it does not get certain special advantages available to the elderly, and the two additional personal exemptions are not worth enough to offset these effects.)

2. On page 6 and in Table 2, the necessary replacement rates may not be comparable because of inflation. For example, Andrews notes that the replacement rates computed by Palmer in 1989 "are generally higher than those of earlier studies." While this is true, it may be at least partially due to inflation—the $20,000 earner examined by the President's Commission in 1980 was higher on the American income scale than a $20,000 earner was in 1989. The figures are numerically identical but not comparable.

3. On page 11, the two sets of actual replacement rates computed by Fox are not comparable, because they use different measures of income in their denominators. The first set, showing how much preretirement income is replaced by Social Security and employer-sponsored pensions, uses earnings in the four "middle" years of the last ten before retirement, adjusted for inflation. The second set, showing how much preretirement income is replaced by all sources, uses earnings in the last year before retirement only. Clearly, these two sets of figures cannot be compared to each other in a meaningful way, especially considering the unusual earnings patterns that often occur close to retirement.

4. The paper seems to use the Gini coefficient inconsistently. On page 7, it is defined as follows: "A Gini coefficient of 1 indicates complete income equality. The smaller the Gini coefficient, the less equal the distribution of income." Then, on page 12, reporting on the work of Radner, the paper says that income inequality rose between 1979 and 1984, because the Gini coefficient "rose" from 0.416 to 0.426. If the coefficient rose, then income inequality declined, based on the earlier definition. The change in the coefficient reported by Radner seems to be trivial in any case and hardly the basis for any real conclusions. Again, on page 23, we are told that "a less equal distribution of assets among the baby boom cohort will also increase the Gini coefficient." Shouldn't it decrease?

5. On page 15, the paper notes that "many women will be entitled to higher Social Security benefits on their own account and to pension payments from employer sponsored plans." As noted previously, women's entitlement to Social Security benefits on their own account actu-

ally means that replacement rates will decline! Of course, other measures of adequacy should improve, especially those based on poverty rates.

With respect to employer-sponsored pension plans, five-year vesting may have virtually no effect because most of the pensions earned in such brief periods, especially long before retirement, have so little value. On the other hand, the trend toward defined contribution plans works in the opposite direction and probably has a larger impact.

6. On page 22, the paper reports the predictions of Zedlewski et al. regarding the greatly declining percentages of elderly families with income below $10,000 in the case of married couples and $5,000 in the case of unmarried individuals. Because the reductions are so extreme, one must conclude that the earnings thresholds are not indexed for inflation. Without such indexing, the figures really have little meaning. They give no information with respect to poverty rates, for example (as noted by Andrews).

7. On page 24, the paper notes that the scheduled increase in the Social Security NRA penalizes "persons unable to work." As noted above, the increase has a negative impact on everybody, not just those unable to work. At least those unable to work have the possibility of receiving Social Security disability benefits, which are payable at any age without reduction, unlike early-retirement benefits.

Social Security's rules for evaluating disability take into account the applicant's age, so that older applicants can receive benefits with medical conditions that would not allow benefits to be paid to younger applicants. How such rules will be extended to ages 65 and 66 remains to be seen, but they can be expected to be at least as liberal as those used currently at ages 60–64.

8. On page 25, the paper notes that "there appears to be little political will to force employers into providing pensions that could be easily transferred." Maybe so, but employers are making these changes on their own, without being forced, for a variety of reasons. Defined benefit plans are disappearing, while defined contribution plans are generally replacing them. The latter type of plan provides benefits that are inherently portable and that retain their value over time. At the same time, as Andrews observes, the benefits from defined contribution plans are often used for other purposes long before retirement occurs.

Chapter 2
Innovations and Trends in Pension Plan Coverage, Type, and Design

Olivia S. Mitchell and Anna M. Rappaport

Introduction

Business and labor market developments over the last two decades, and the expectation of continued changes, offer new challenges to the form and structure of employer-sponsored pension plans. Work lives are becoming more varied and shorter, spanning multiple employers and careers, and reaching retirement at an earlier age than ever before. Business conditions have also undergone tremendous change during the last decade, as witnessed by the decline of traditional large manufacturers (e.g., steel, auto, electronics, and heavy equipment) and the transition to smaller firms in an information and service based economy, changes in business ownership and corporate restructuring, the escalation of international competition, changes in corporate and individual taxation, and a decline in unionization.

In this paper, we outline recent trends in employer pension plan structure in the United States, focusing on plan coverage, plan type, and plan design. We then identify the key factors that we believe will shape company-sponsored pension design in the future, drawing conclusions from reviewing recent research and practice. Finally, we offer a cautious prognosis about the future of pension plan coverage and design, focusing on the role of labor force aging, as well as anticipated developments in the business environment and anticipated changes in public policy.

I. Recent Trends in Pension Plan Coverage, Type, and Design

A. Pension Plans Have Many Functions

Pensions have many economic and other functions responding to employee needs and plan sponsor objectives. Perhaps the most important reason employees want pensions is to help them *save for retirement*, thus reducing old-age economic insecurity. A companion role of pensions is to *provide annuities*, since outliving one's savings is for many a major source of economic insecurity in the last third of life. Many pensions, particularly defined benefit plans, offer insurance against extended longevity by promising an annuity payment from retirement to death. Employer-sponsored pensions cost less than individually purchased retirement annuities, in part, because there is no adverse selection by the purchaser.

In addition, workers want pensions because dollars saved in a pension plan generate more retirement benefits by virtue of *economies of scale and risk pooling*. Larger investment pools can be shown to save substantially on administrative costs and investment expenses when they are compared to individually purchased annuities.

Another central reason that people seek to save for retirement using pensions rests in U.S. tax law. In the United States, employees are permitted to pay lower current taxes when a portion of employee compensation is deposited in a pension plan, rather than being paid in cash. The opportunity to *save on a pre-tax basis* has been shown to be a tax-effective form of compensation, particularly for people in higher marginal tax brackets. (For evidence on each of these points, see Gustman and Mitchell, 1992; and Gustman et al., 1992.)

Unions have also played an important role in shaping the pension environment, by bargaining for and influencing plan type, benefit levels, and plan design. Negotiated plans were preeminently defined benefit plans, typically with relatively generous benefit levels and multiple options for early retirement. Historically, these plans also set the standard for nonunion companies, but this pattern has diminished as the unionized fraction of the workforce declined over the last decade. (Unique features of union plans are discussed in Gustman et al., 1992.)

Employers institute pension plans for a variety of reasons, but their overall goal is generally thought to be to *design compensation patterns consistent with their human resource policy*. Human resource policies, in turn, are driven by company business strategy. Some organizations, particularly larger ones, tend to emphasize selection, retention, and motivation of the "right" employees as central to their business success. This perspective is seen in recent efforts to implement "total quality management" efforts in the United States, and implies long-term worker/company attachments as well as pension plan design that favors this practice.

Consistent with this notion is the view that pensions are frequently offered *to attract and keep valuable workers*. In part, this is achieved by pension plan features that *encourage effort and discourage worker mobility*. For example, vesting rules tend to discourage workers from changing jobs before gaining a legal right to a pension benefit, which is frequently attained after five years of service. Benefit accrual formulas, particularly in defined benefit plans, can *reduce turnover and increase effort* by offering, in effect, higher compensation to those employees who stay longer and whose pay rises with seniority.

Another aspect of pensions that employers find useful is that they are perceived as *attracting and retaining certain kinds of workers over others*. Thus some businesses find it essential to attract workers who will remain with the firm for a long period of time. This can be important when, for instance, the workforce has a great deal of firm-specific training and knowledge that is not easily duplicated. Because pensions are a form of deferred compensation, only those workers who intend to remain at the company will tend to be attracted to pension covered jobs. Thus the pension itself tends to be a recruitment and retention tool for workers with desired characteristics. In still other cases, pensions which reward workers based on company profitability *generate the incentives for covered employees to more closely align their work effort with company objectives*, as in the case of profit sharing and stock ownership plans. (See Gustman et al., 1992; and Ippolito, 1992.)

Employers have also found pension plans to be helpful in other contexts, particularly with regard to *regulating retirement flows*. When productivity begins to plateau, or when technological change renders skills obsolete, a company's pension offerings can provide the opportunity for career employees to leave the company with dignity and with adequate income security. In some cases, companies have also used pensions, particularly early retirement windows, to *minimize involuntary terminations* when faced with the need for corporate restructuring and downsizing. (More discussion on these points appears in Gustman et al., 1992; Luzadis and Mitchell, 1991; and Lazear, 1983.) The pension plan can, therefore, be designed to make retirement appealing by making retirement benefits more generous overall, and by making early retirement benefits generous as compared to pension payments for delayed retirement.

B. Differentiating Defined Benefit and Defined Contribution Plans

The two major types of pension plans in the United States are defined benefit (DB) plans, and defined contribution (DC) plans. In the former case, the employer generally specifies a formula for benefits defined as income and payable at retirement, whereas in the latter case, the employer typically states a formula for plan contributions (often as a fraction of pay) during an employee's working lifetime. DB plans are the predominant form of employer-provided pension plan in the

United States, covering about 63 percent of employees of medium and large employers and 20 percent of employees of small employers (those with under 100 employees), and 93 percent of government employees, as is shown in Tables 1–2.

DB plans are usually structured to achieve multiple outcomes (see Table 4):

- They meet employee needs for retirement income (often assumed to be the maintenance of preretirement living standards).
- They are associated with reducing worker turnover, encouraging career employment and employee loyalty, thereby protecting the employer's investment in human capital.
- They help career employees leave the labor force with dignity at a retirement age that fits the employer's human resource policy.
- They support other human resources needs, including workforce downsizing.
- They meet competitive practices and conform to the general practices in the community.

DC plans have some of the same features, but many different ones as well. In a DC plan the employer generally specifies contributions into the pension plan rather than formula defined benefits, and the funds thus accumulated are invested until the worker reaches retirement age. In a DB plan, the obligation is fixed by the benefit defined and the application of minimum funding rules, but in a DC plan, the contribution can be defined or discretionary. Table 4 compares features of these plans. DC plans currently cover 48 percent of employees of medium and large employers and 31 percent of employees of small employers, as well as 9 percent of employees of public employers. Some of these employees are also covered by DB plans. Because DC plans are subject to the same tax qualification rules as DB plans, many of the same retirement savings goals can be met with these plans. In addition, DC plans can meet other corporate goals including:

- Encouraging employees to save pre-tax for their own retirement, including perhaps savings to meet the need for medical care after retirement.
- Increasing worker motivation and giving workers a "stake" in the company, particularly when contributions depend on company profitability, or when pension assets are invested in company stock.
- Helping the company finance itself in an effective manner.
- Providing lump sum cashouts to workers who leave the firm before reaching retirement age.

TABLE 1   Employees Participating in Private Sector Retirement Plans, 1989 and 1990 (Percentages)

	From 1989 Survey of Medium and Large Firms				From 1990 Survey of Small Firms			
	All employees	Prof. and admin.	Tech. and clerical	Prod. and service	All employees	Prof. and admin.	Tech. and clerical	Prod. and service
All retirement plans	81	85	81	80	42	49	47	37
Defined benefit pension plans	63	64	63	63	20	20	23	18
Wholly employer financed	60	61	61	60	19	18	21	18
Partly employer financed	3	3	2	2	1	2	1	1
Defined contribution plans	48	59	52	40	31	40	36	24
1. Uses of funds								
Retirement	36	43	39	31	28	36	32	21
Wholly employer financed	14	15	14	12	16	19	17	15
Partly employer financed	22	28	24	18	11	17	16	6
Capital accumulation plans	14	18	14	11	4	5	4	2
Wholly employer financed	2	1	1	3	1	2	2	1
Partly employer financed	12	17	13	8	2	3	3	2
2. Types of plans								
Savings and thrift	30	41	35	21	10	16	15	5
Deferred profit sharing	15	13	13	16	15	17	17	13
Employee stock ownership	3	4	3	3	1	1	1	*
Money purchase	5	8	6	3	6	9	6	6

Sources: USDOL (1990), Table 1; (1991), Table 1.
*Less than 0.5%

TABLE 2   Employees Participating in Public Employer Retirement Plans Compared to Private Sector Participation (Percentage)

	Private sector medium and large firms	Private sector small firms	State and local governments—1987			
			All employees	Regular employees	Teachers	Police and firefighters
All retirement plans	81	42	98	97	99	98
Defined benefit pension plans	63	20	93	92	95	93
Wholly employer financed	60	19	20	22	17	17
Partly employer financed	3	1	73	70	78	76
Defined contribution plans	48	31	9	9	8	13
1. Uses of funds						
Retirement	36	28	9	9	8	12
Wholly employer financed	14	16	4	4	5	4
Partly employer financed	22	11	4	5	3	8
Capital accumulation	14	4				
Wholly employer financed	2	1				
Partly employer financed	12	2				
2. Types of plans						
Savings and thrift	30	10				
Deferred profit sharing	15	15				
Employee stock ownership	3	1				
Money purchase	5	6				

Sources: USDOL (1990), Table 1; (1991), Table 1; (1988), Table 1.

TABLE 3 Patterns in Defined Benefit and Defined Contribution Pension Plans (1975–1989)

	1975	1980	1985	1986	1987	1988	1989
Number of plans in operation (000s)							
Defined benefit	107	179	224	230	234	NA	NA
Defined contribution	233	410	581	617	638	NA	NA
Total	340	589	805	847	872	NA	NA
Annual rate of increase from prior year							
Defined benefit		10.8%	4.6%	2.7%	1.7%		
Defined contribution		12.0%	7.2%	6.2%	3.4%		
Total							
Percentage of total							
Defined benefit	31.5%	30.4%	27.8%	27.2%	26.8%	NA	NA
Defined contribution	68.5%	69.6%	72.2%	72.8%	73.2%	NA	NA
Total	100.0%	100.0%	100.0%	100.0%	100.0%	NA	NA
Number of private multi-employer plans (000s)							
Defined benefit	2.1	2.3	2.3	2.2	2.2	2.1	NA
Defined contribution	0.3	0.4	0.8	0.9	1.0	1.2	NA
Total	2.4	2.7	3.1	3.1	3.2	3.3	NA

Favorable determination letter applications issued by IRS (000s)
Note: 1987 includes three quarters only

	1975	1980	1985	1986	1987	1988	1989
Initial applications							
Defined benefit	NA	19	17	22	16	17	5
Defined contribution	NA	50	30	45	40	46	23
Total		69	47	67	56	63	28
Termination applications							
Defined benefit	NA	4	12	11	11	12	16
Defined contribution	NA	9	14	15	13	13	13
Total		13	26	26	24	25	29
Initial applications as a percentage of existing plans							
Defined benefit		10.6%	7.6%	9.6%	6.8%	NA	NA
Defined contribution		12.2%	5.2%	7.3%	6.3%	NA	NA
Total		11.7%	5.8%	7.9%	6.4%	NA	NA
Termination applications as a percentage of existing plans							
Defined benefit		2.2%	5.4%	4.8%	4.7%	NA	NA
Defined contribution		2.2%	2.4%	2.4%	2.0%	NA	NA
Total		2.2%	3.2%	3.1%	2.8%	NA	NA

Sources: EBRI (1990c), p. 79; EBRI (1991), p. 8 (multi-employer plan data only).

TABLE 4   Major Differences Between Defined Benefit and Defined
Contribution Pension Plans

Plan feature	Defined benefit	Defined contribution
Benefit accrual pattern	Higher in later years	Higher in earlier years
Cashouts for early leavers	Not usually	Lump sum
Retirement benefit payment	Annuity until death	Lump sum
Early retirement subsidy possible	Yes	Not usually
Postretirement benefit increases	Often	Not usually
Investment risk	Borne by employer	Borne by employee
Benefits fully funded	No	Yes
PBGC benefit guarantee	Yes	No
Employee makes asset allocation decision	No	Often

Employees also seem to understand and appreciate DC plans more than DB plans, which may explain their recent growth. This may be because plan sponsors offer periodic statements of account balances in DC plans, whereas this concept is not applicable in the DB case, where statements are usually less frequent and generally show accrued and projected retirement income rather than a lump sum account balance. (A few DB plans are designed for lump sum payouts, however.) In addition, DC account balances are often portable from one job to the next, whereas a DB annuity payment beginning at age 55 or later seems remote to young workers. Nevertheless, this apparent better understanding of DC plans is probably somewhat illusory because employees cannot readily translate DC plan balances into retirement income. In addition, DC portability does not ensure retirement security since the pension balances are often spent rather than saved (Rappaport and Schieber, 1993).

Evaluating the efficacy and usefulness of the two plan types requires one to recognize that over the long run a dollar invested in a DB plan often produces more investment income than in a DC plan. This is because DB plan sponsors typically use a balanced portfolio to maximize investment returns consistent with their risk profiles, but in DC plans where employees have investment choices they frequently invest in fixed income securities. Thus "401(k) plan participants described themselves as conservative investors who prefer to direct their own investments toward insurance and bank contracts . . . and said they were more inclined to choose low-risk/low-return investments" (EBRI,

TABLE 5   Rates of Return by Plan Type for Period Ending December 31, 1989 (Percentages)

	1 year	3 year	5 year
All pension plans	20.7	14.4	16.7
Single employer defined benefit	20.7	15.0	17.3
Single employer defined contribution	21.4	14.4	16.4
Multi-employer	18.4	11.8	14.7
Consumer price index	4.7	4.5	3.7

Source: EBRI (1990c), p. 6.

1992). The different investment mix can easily result in a lower average return by 1 to 3 percentage points for a typical DC plan as compared to a typical DB plan. Data on reported returns of DB and DC plans for the five-year period ending in 1989 confirm that DB plan investments outperformed those of DC plans (see Table 5). These trends will probably continue because the fraction of DC plans permitting individual direction in investment options has probably increased, while in DB plans more aggressively managed portfolios became more popular over time.

Of course DC plans are quite varied in form and differ among themselves with regard to whether and what investment choices are available. Some plans offer only investments in company stock, whereas others offer a choice between different investment portfolios. When a DC plan is wholly invested in company stock, as in the case of an employee stock ownership (ESOP) plan, there is substantially higher investment risk in the DC plan, and a higher expected average investment return. Nevertheless, stock ownership plans have grown over time, covering 11 million employees as of 1989 (see Table 6).

Another difference between DB and DC plans that has received increasing attention in recent years is the fact that DB plans typically provide monthly income, whereas DC plans typically pay lump sums. If early lump sum payments are spent rather than saved, this brings into question the tax-favored status of such plans. Those concerned about retirement security have proposed outlawing these lump sum cashouts, or favor higher penalties if cashouts are not transferred to another retirement savings plan; on the other hand, the availability of lump sum cashouts can make it easier for companies to downsize if tax law remains relatively favorable toward pension lump sums.

TABLE 6   Number of Plans and Participants in Employee Stock Ownership Plans

Year	Number of plans	Number of employees (000s)	Average number of employees per plan
1975	1,601	248	155
1980	5,009	4,048	808
1985	7,402	7,353	993
1986	8,046	7,860	977
1987	8,777	8,860	1009
1988	9,400	9,630	1024
1989	10,230	11,530	1127

Source: U.S. Department of Commerce, Bureau of the Census (1991), Table 890, "Employee Stock Ownership Plans—Number of Plans and Participants: 1975–1989," p. 540.

C. Typical Pension Plan Structures by Type of Employer

Pension plan features differ greatly across employer size and type of plan sponsor. In order to illustrate the rich variety of benefit practices currently in effect, it is useful to review and compare data on pension plans covering employees of large and small private sector firms, multi-employer groups, not-for-profit organizations, and public sector employee groups.

Medium- and Large-Sized Employer Plans

Data for pension plans offered by private establishments with 100 or more employees were last collected in a 1989 Employee Benefit Survey conducted by the U.S. Department of Labor (USDOL, 1989). This evidence (see Table 1) shows that nearly all medium and large employers sponsored pension plans: 81 percent of employees were covered by retirement plans, with 63 percent covered by DB plans and 48 percent by DC plans (some employees have both). Most DB plans also structured formulas to replace generous percentages of earnings: three-quarters based benefits primarily on earnings, especially earnings during the final years of employment with the plan sponsor so as to protect benefits against inflation (prior to retirement). Average replacement rates in the DB plans were about 1 percent for each year of service. Therefore, a typical worker with twenty years of service at retirement might expect a benefit worth 20 percent of his or her final average earnings, while the retiree with thirty years of service would anticipate a replacement rate closer to 30 percent (USDOL, 1989, Table 85).

Determining whether these benefits meet income adequacy standards must take into account Social Security and personal funds and the extent to which benefits are indexed after inflation. Medium and large employers have for many years offered a measure of inflation protection for retirement, inasmuch as 41 percent of their employees had retiree health coverage prior to age 65, and 36 percent had retiree health coverage after 65 in 1989. On the other hand, inflation protection after retirement is not complete and appears to have declined in the last decade, which suggests that inflation remains a challenge to pension retirement income adequacy (Allen, Clark, and McDermed, 1991; Gustman and Steinmeier, 1992a).

In the very largest companies, a typical pension program included a first tier non-contributory DB plan, with a second tier that was often a matched savings plan of the DC variety. In the past, most larger employers also tended to offer retiree health insurance along with the pension, but the future is uncertain as health care costs continue to rise. Some employers offered profit sharing for salaried workers and a DB plan for hourly employees. Relatively few employers adopted stock ownership plans as primary retirement vehicles, though many use them to supplement basic retirement programs. Medium-sized employers were more likely to use DC plans frequently with a cash (lump sum) retirement benefit. Here, too, retiree health benefit plans were less prevalent.

Small Employer Plans

Pension data for private establishments with fewer than 100 employees were last collected in a 1990 Employee Benefit Survey (USDOL, 1990). A review of coverage and benefit patterns indicates that small employers were much less likely than large employers to offer retirement benefits, and where plans were offered, they tended to be DC plans (see Table 1). Thus 42 percent of employees in small companies were covered by retirement plans: 20 percent had DB plans and 41 percent had DC plans (some employees had both). These employers were also less likely to offer retiree health insurance coverage: only 13 percent of these employees offered retiree health benefits. While data on benefit levels for small employers have not yet been published, they are probably lower than those reported above for medium and large employers. This conclusion is suggested by other studies which have found that small companies offer lower compensation levels in general (Brown and Medoff, 1989).

Multi-Employer Plans

Multi-employer pension plans incorporate workers from a number of different employers, and are commonly found in the unionized trucking, construction, and retail trade sectors. In the past they were used to provide private retirement benefits to workers employed in a trade who worked for different employers over relatively short periods. Most multi-employer plans permit workers to carry their coverage with them from one job to the next, so long as they remain in covered employment (usually in the same occupation or industry, as a member of the same union). For historical reasons, these pensions face different economic constraints and regulatory obligations from those affecting single employer plans (Luzadis and Mitchell, 1991; Mitchell and Andrews, 1981).

These plans have not grown much over time: there are only about three thousand plans currently in existence, and multi-employer plans constitute less than one-half of one percent of total private plans (see Table 3). They are likely to shrink in the future because of the continued fall in private sector union membership, and projected declines in industries that traditionally used multi-employer plans. In addition, many employers have grown concerned about the financial solvency of these DB pensions with continued increases in negotiated flat-dollar benefit levels; many plans are underfunded and employers joining the plans face potentially high withdrawal liabilities. While these issues are beyond the scope of the present paper which focuses primarily on single employer plans, policy makers concerned with retirement security must also consider multi-employer plan issues (USGAO, 1992).

Pension Plans in Not-For-Profit Firms

Not-for-profit organizations are a diverse group including membership associations, charities, universities, religious orders, and health care providers. Their diversity also implies pension plans with divergent structures and aims. Thus, for instance, universities often offer faculty a DC plan funded by individual annuity contracts under the teachers' portable nationwide plan. In contrast, the human resource concerns of health care providers and larger membership associations resemble those of for-profit employers, and their pension plans are more similar to those of their for-profit counterparts. Larger not-for-profit employers offer pension benefit plans that are similar in structure to those of private employers, except that their DC pensions are subject to substantially different regulations. Religious orders can set up plans under the Church Plan rules, which are considerably different from general qualified plan rules. Smaller not-for-profits rely heavily on tax sheltered annuities under special sections of the tax code. Relatively few not-for-profits offer retiree health benefits.

Pension Plans in the Public Sector

Human resource concerns of public sector employers frequently differ from those in the private sector, partly because of civil service requirements and partly because more workers are unionized in governmental entities. Also, pension regulation that covers private sector plans does not typically govern plans of federal, state, and local workers, so that benefit plans have some special characteristics not found in the private sector.

Data on public sector plans are drawn from a 1987 Benefits Survey on full-time state and local government employees in groups with 50 or more participants (USDOL, 1987). Table 2 shows that pension coverage was more common than among private sector workers, with 98 percent of state and local employees having a retirement plan, including 93 percent covered by a DB plan and 9 percent by a DC plan (some employees had both). Of course, many public sector workers were traditionally excluded from Social Security, so higher coverage rates are not directly comparable with private sector figures. Public sector plans also tend to offer generous retirement income: they facilitate earlier retirement, they tend to offer postretirement indexation of benefits, and 48 percent of all covered public sector workers have retiree health coverage (USDOL, 1987). Typical replacement rates for regular retirees (excluding Social Security benefits) amounted to about 35 percent of final pay for a worker with 20 years of service, and more than 50 percent for a retiree with 30 years of service (USDOL, 1987). Public sector plans are much more likely to require employee contributions than private sector plans.

Diverse problems and issues face governmental plans, including the fact that many plans are quite underfunded (Mitchell and Smith, 1992). Unfortunately, data for public plans are much more difficult to obtain than for the private sector because public plans are not required to conform to common reporting and disclosure requirements. While our focus in this paper is primarily on private sector pension concerns, additional work is needed to explore public sector pension issues. Specifically, it will be important to ascertain whether public sector employees' retirement needs differ greatly from those in the private sector; whether public employers' objectives, resources, and constraints differ greatly from those in the private sector; and whether pensions play a different economic role in the public and private sector.

D. Recent Trends in the Mix of Defined Benefit and Defined Contribution Plans

There has been much written about the apparent decline in private sector DB pension coverage in recent years, and a concomitant increase in DC plan coverage (Society of Actuaries, 1990). These trends are illustrated in Table 3, which shows the number of DB and DC plans over time, and the number of determination letter applications for new plans as well as for plan terminations. The figures confirm that there was an increase in DC plans relative to the number of DB plans: DB plans decreased from 32 percent of the total plan universe in 1975 to 27 percent in 1987.

The leading explanation for this trend is that the industrial composition of employment changed over the last fifteen to twenty years in ways that favored a shift to DC pensions. Sectors that traditionally favored DB plans (e.g., durable manufacturing, unionized companies) contracted, while the service and finance sectors grew—and the latter have traditionally had DC plans. There are mixed signals in the data, however. Only about half the overall movement toward DC plans has been linked to these national employment shifts, and the shift was concentrated among smaller businesses (with between 100 and 1,000 participants), but there was no similar trend among very large companies (with 1,000 employees or more). (See PBGC, 1990a; Clark and McDermed, 1990; Gustman and Steinmeier, 1992a.)

A companion explanation for the downward drift in DB coverage is that DB plans became increasingly expensive to administer over the last decade, especially compared to DC alternatives. Note, however, that for many larger plans this higher administrative cost has been more than offset by reduced contributions resulting from favorable investment returns. Numerous legislative and accounting changes during the 1980s increased the relative complexity of managing DB plans as compared to DC plans. Indeed, one study reported that DB pension plan administrative costs almost tripled for small plans (with 15 or fewer participants) between 1981 and 1991, while small employers' costs for DC 401(k) plans were far lower. (See Hay/Huggins, 1990; Clark and McDermed, 1990.)

Whether this administrative cost advantage of DC plans will persist in the future is open to question. Several recent regulations and litigation may challenge the current perception that DC plans are less costly to administer. For instance, recent troubles in the insurance and financial industries have highlighted responsibilities of plan sponsors to carefully select and then monitor investment managers. Another issue is that a host of increasingly complex and stringent nondiscrimination tests must be applied to plans permitting employee contributions and/ or employer matching funds, which make DC plans more costly than in the past. (This has been a primary area of focus in discussions about pension simplification.) Reforms are also being proposed to clarify the status of a worker's DC pension plan status in personal bankruptcy. This legislation will probably prevent an increase in the cost of administering such plans, as courts today are increasingly looking to DC pension plan assets in bankruptcy. Last, but not least, regulations from the U.S. Department of Labor are promoting more employee choice with regard to investments, increasing the complexity of plan management and communication to employees.

On the other hand, insurance companies, banks, and other financial intermediaries continue to offer packaged "pension products" for smaller employers that typically are DC plans. These products enable a small employer to use the package without requiring custom design or much management. A decade ago, "off the shelf" DB plan products were also sold, but are now a rarity because of the regulatory complexity of operating DB pension plans.

E. Innovations in Defined Benefit Pension Plan Design

During the last decade, two factors strongly influenced the structure and design of DB pension plans: regulation regarding specific plan features and plan termination. In both cases, Congress has enacted legislation, that, with the implementing regulations, will result in major changes from past practice. As of early 1993, many of these changes have not yet been fully implemented. For instance, major changes in pension law were contained in the Tax Reform Act of 1986 (TRA), most of which became effective in 1989. Interpretations of the TRA along with additional regulations were not, however, issued in final form until September 1991, when a 600-page package of "Final Regulations" was issued, effective for 1992 plan years. Subsequently, in 1992, the U.S. Treasury agreed to delay the effective date of many regulations until 1994 plan years; and for the tax-exempt sector and governmental plans the effective date is now for plan years beginning in 1996. In the interim, TRA remained in effect and employers were required to meet a standard of good faith compliance. Therefore much regulatory policy is still undergoing change and many plans are awaiting revisions. The uncertainty wrought by this continuous change is certainly depressing new plan formation and plan updating, and may be hastening plan termination.

Despite the state of flux in which pension regulation finds itself, a few common themes are likely to be persistent. Through much of the 1980s, Congress became progressively more interested in limiting access to tax-qualified pension savings, unless the plans could be shown to balance benefits to higher-paid employees with relatively generous benefits to lower-paid employees. For instance, TRA requirements restricted annual compensation for qualified plan purposes to $200,000. The maximum benefit limits permitted under Section 415 of the Internal Revenue Code were reduced three times during the 1980s. TRA also limited the extent to which employers can coordinate pension payments and workers' Social Security benefits. These new limits on so-called Social Security integration required major changes in some very large plans and significantly complicated plan administration for those seeking maximum integration. As a result of eliminating or reducing integration, pension benefits rose for lower paid, and/or were reduced for higher-paid employees. While equalization of benefits could increase retirement income security for the lower-paid employees, it did limit employers' ability to reward higher-paid employees with tax-qualified pension benefits, and in some cases it resulted in an overall decrease in benefit amounts.

Pension plan sponsors have sought innovative approaches to these restrictions. One has been to establish "non-qualified" pension plans for key executives. Here, highly compensated employees who cannot be fully covered in a company's qualified plans because of legal restrictions are offered a pension plan whose contributions are subject to tax (just as cash compensation would be) once there is constructive receipt. In other cases, a non-qualified plan may be offered to an executive hired in mid-career; here the plan grants, in effect, additional service. Unfortunately, no nationally representative data are available on the incidence and structure of these plans.

The increasing complexity of nondiscrimination regulations has also produced ever more complicated pension plan administration problems, and makes it challenging for employees to understand their plans. Many plans have multiple layers, with different formulas applying to different years of service. Plan sponsors have called for simplification of pension regulation; this is a popular political slogan, but has yet to be translated into legislation that Congress can agree on. Plan sponsors have criticized many of these simplification proposals as not having gone far enough.

A different solution for some employers has been to terminate their DB pensions. This phenomenon increased rapidly over the last decade: for instance, Table 3 indicates that the number of DB termination applications increased from 4,000 in 1975 to 16,000 in 1989. At the same time, applications for new plans plummeted. Nevertheless, the termination trend cannot be blamed on regulation alone, because many of these coincided with leveraged buyouts (LBOs). In one study, for instance, 20 percent of the DB plans that had been sponsored by bought-out companies were terminated after the LBO (USGAO, 1991). Most plans terminated after LBOs were replaced, and most active participants were provided replacement DB plans, suggesting that at least some of these terminations were primarily financial transactions to remove surplus from the plans (Ippolito, 1989).

In assessing the potential for future terminations of DB plans, it must be kept in mind that legislation has made plan termination increasingly difficult and expensive over time. In addition, taxation of pension plan reversions has increased, so that using pension surpluses to help finance takeovers will probably decline in importance in the future (Ippolito, 1989). Finally, many small and medium employers had already terminated their DB plans during the 1980s so this is largely a closed issue. To the extent that terminations are seen, they will be more likely to coincide with company bankruptcy, or changes in direction for overall benefit management purposes, rather than playing a key role in company buyouts as seen during the 1980s.

In addition to plan termination and regulation, several other important developments emerged over the last decade in the DB arena. An interesting one for human resource analysts has been employers' increasing awareness of pensions as a human resources policy tool, where DB pension offerings have been structured to help corporations downsize their labor force. Sometimes the traditional DB formula has included liberal early retirement offerings, at other times early retirement window arrangements were offered providing for additional retirement benefits for people retiring within a specified time. Early window plans have become widespread among larger firms, as indicated by a recent report by Charles D. Spencer and Associates (1990) on early retirement incentives. This study showed that 15 percent of 273 large employers queried had offered early retirement incentive programs in 1989 and 24 percent had offered windows in 1986. Few, if any, employers offered incentives annually, but many offered multiple incentives. Early retirement window plans are attractive because they concentrate retirements during a shorter time period than otherwise would be likely to occur (Luzadis and Mitchell, 1991; Lumsdaine, Stock, and Wise, 1990a).

Along with early-out plans has come growing awareness that the retirement benefit package also includes medical benefits, and plan sponsors are increasingly facing the need to link medical and pension programs in designing coherent retirement offerings. On the other hand, retiree health insurance costs are rising in tandem with active worker health insurance costs, forcing careful management of total compensation, including tradeoffs between health and pension offerings. Thus far, only anecdotal instances of this tradeoff can be cited, but it is possible that retiree health insurance cost pressures may force more employers to revisit the entire cost, structure, and contents of their retirement package offerings in the next few years.

Another development in the DB arena is a trend toward new pension "designs," including cash balance or account based pension plans. While these are fundamentally DB plans that specify benefits as an account, they permit employers flexibility in converting to a different type of benefit formula without undergoing plan termination. In such a plan, benefits are defined according to a contribution formula, yet minimum benefit payouts (in the form of life annuities) can be offered as in a traditional DB plan. The plan sponsor has the option of later changing benefits and/or offering early retirement windows. Administratively, these plans require actuarial valuations and are covered by Pension Benefit Guaranty Corporation (PBGC) insurance (which may be seen as an advantage or disadvantage depending on one's viewpoint). Thus far, relatively few employers offer them: 2 percent of the 1989 DB participants in medium and large employers had account-based plans, and 1 percent of the 1990 DB participants in small plans (USDOL, 1989, 1990). On the other hand, the plans' legal status has recently been clarified: regulations issued at the end of 1991 clearly sanctioned these plans and provided a well-defined set of rules for passing nondiscrimination tests. It is anticipated that these plans are likely to be very popular in years to come. There has also been an increase in employers offering both DB and DC plans, and this trend too will probably grow more prevalent among employers with DB plans.

F. Recent Developments in Defined Contribution Pension Plan Design

The most significant DC plan development in the last decade was the growth of 401(k) plans. At the same time, regulatory changes challenged administrators of DC plans in some of the same ways detailed above. One key change was brought about by TRA rules that tightened nondiscrimination tests. Many plans had trouble meeting these tests and were forced to modify plans or reduce contributions for highly compensated employees. Some employers responded by liberalizing their 401(k) plans and increasing the amount they "match," or contribute when an employee deposits money into the plan. Others have turned to non-qualified plans, to make up amounts which cannot be contributed into a tax-qualified account due to the TRA limits.

As in the case of companies offering DB pension plans, employers providing DC plans have become increasingly aware of the need to coordinate pension and retiree medical insurance offerings. There is growing interest in the use of DC plans as a vehicle to finance retiree health benefits. Some benefits analysts and attorneys suggest that profit sharing plans can be used to pre-fund retiree health insurance plans on a pre-tax basis. Some employers have sought to provide funds for retiree health coverage with other benefit structures, including stock ownership plans which permit retirees to elect to apply funds to cover retiree health insurance. So far, few companies have adopted these programs, pending clarification of these new arrangements' tax status.

Perhaps the most interesting development in the DC arena over the last decade is the increased effort on the federal government's part to permit employees to make choices about their pension funds and to limit employees' access to these funds prior to retirement. Response to restrictions on early withdrawals is seen in plans' increased use of loan and hardship withdrawal provisions, giving workers limited access to funds for non-retirement purposes. Many DC plans also offer lump sum cashouts if workers leave their employers. This is sometimes a cause of concern for those hoping to force workers to save more for retirement, because available evidence suggests that workers spend rather than save the lump sum cash amounts (Piacentini, 1990).

In addition, there is growing concern about the implications of the way employees make investment choices when they are permitted to do so with their retirement funds. There is evidence that employees offered an investment choice tend to be extremely risk averse, often putting 80 percent or more of their dollars in a fixed income investment (Table 7). As a consequence, their investment returns often suffer. Low return assets have also proved to be riskier than expected in recent years, as "guaranteed" investments held by insurance companies and banks have turned out to be worth less than expected. Failures at Executive Life and Mutual Benefit Life have changed expectations drastically, placing new concerns about fiduciary burdens on plan sponsors' shoulders, and creating new financial worries for covered employees. The choice of investment options is probably more

TABLE 7 Defined Contribution Plan Asset Mix, by Size of Plan (Percentages)

	Total plans		By size of plan assets in 1990			
	1989	1990	>$500M	$201–500M	$50–200M	<$50M
Company stock	26.0	24.2	26.5	18.1	12.4	31.0
Other common stock	16.4	19.1	19.1	17.7	20.6	19.5
Bonds	6.9	9.0	9.2	8.2	8.1	9.5
Guaranteed investment contracts	41.2	38.2	36.6	43.6	46.6	28.0
Cash and short term securities	6.7	7.1	6.5	9.0	9.5	8.3
Other	2.8	2.4	2.1	3.4	2.8	3.7
Total	100.0	100.0	100.0	100.0	100.0	100.0

Source: Greenwich Associates (1991), p. 62.

complex than was generally perceived in the past, a troublesome development for small and medium sized employers who previously turned their plan management over to an insurance company for investment management and administrative service.

II. The Coming Challenges to Company-Sponsored Pensions

It appears unlikely that the nation will return to an era like that of the 1970s and early 1980s, when pension coverage was growing and DB plans were the most commonly offered plan in both the private and public sectors (Kotlikoff and Smith, 1983). There are, however, several factors that suggest further growth of pensions, particularly in the DC area, though many other influences will imply slower growth than over the last twenty years. As we look to the next decade, several factors will pose challenges to company-sponsored pensions. These include demographic trends, the business environment and human resource policy, and public policy and federal regulation.

A. Factors Influencing Employees' Desire For Pensions

A variety of demographic and economic factors in the years to come will influence workers' desires for pensions, not all of them uniformly positively or negatively. One serious challenge to the future of pensions arises from the stagnation in *earnings* experienced over the last decade or two. Indeed, the average American worker's pay has declined in real terms in seven out of ten years during the 1980s (U.S. President, 1990). While part of this stagnation in earnings may turn around as the economy moves toward recovery, it remains the case that U.S. workers' earnings are not likely to rise quickly in the face of increasing global competition.

Shrinking take-home pay leaves less for retirement savings, and implies that economic recovery is a necessary ingredient for future pension growth. Related to this question is that of what will become of older workers' earnings as the baby boom ages? On the one hand, the increased supply of older people could depress their earnings, thus reducing the capacity to save for retirement. On the other hand, a declining number of younger workers may induce increased demand for older employees. Though future wage patterns are uncertain, forecasts suggest that older workers' earnings will probably rise slightly as the baby boom ages (Levine and Mitchell, 1988). If true, this should somewhat offset the overall downward pressure on pensions due to stagnant real earnings.

Another response to depressed earnings is *increased work effort*, which, in fact, seems to be happening already. After three decades of declining labor supply among men 55 years old and over, there is now some suggestion that labor force participation rates have stabilized and even begun to increase in the latter half of the 1980s (Quinn, Burkhauser, and Myers, 1990). If this turnaround in retirement persists, older workers may need less pension savings inasmuch as a shorter period will be spent out of the labor force.

The *aging of the workforce* is likely to increase the demand for retirement savings in general, and for pensions in particular. As baby boomers age, they will become increasingly *aware* of retirement savings needs, and the tax-preferred status of pensions will continue to make them more appealing than non-pension alternatives. The *long-term trend toward earlier retirement* among males has also implied that retirement saving must be accomplished in a shorter time (Fields and Mitchell, 1984), though women have continued to enter the workforce in greater numbers even among the older age groups. Many of today's workers also had their *children later in life*, leaving a relatively short time to save for retirement after children complete their education. *Two-earner families* have increased greatly in numbers in the last three decades, and it may be easier for them to devote income to retirement pensions once the child-rearing demands are over. Among such couples, high family *marginal income and payroll tax* rates will also increase pension plans' appeal. Last, but not least, higher than anticipated housing values have meant benefits for today's retirees that future retirees will probably not approach. If baby boomers cannot count on *housing* appreciation for much of retirement wealth, they will need to look to pensions more than the previous generation.

Factors working in the opposite direction should also be considered, however. If pension contributions and pension investment earnings lose all or part of their *tax-protected* status, this will surely reduce the tax-preferred role of pensions versus other forms of saving (Woodbury and Huang, 1991). In addition, employment paths are changing in such a way as to make pension coverage less valuable. Many Americans, particularly women, *move between jobs* and *out of the labor force* during much or all of their working lives. This implies that they tend not to vest even when pension coverage is available, or when they do vest, they do not reap the rewards of a pension based on final average earnings.

Corporate downsizing has also cut short career jobs for many long term employees, meaning that they will not receive retirement benefits based on a full career with one company. Also, many overfunded DB plans terminated during the 1980s, a phenomenon that provided annuities, or perhaps a lump sum, to covered workers based on a partial rather than a complete career. Even if an employee earns a vested benefit with several employers, the sum of the vested benefits is usually less valuable than the benefit earned for one continuous period of employment.

The prevalence of pensions may be tapering off because of declines in private sector *unionization*: in 1983 the fraction of employed wage and salary workers represented by unions was 23 percent, which dropped to 19 percent in 1989. Unions played a major role in demanding pension plans, particularly DB plans through the 1970s, but this has not been true for the last decade and will probably not be true in the future. Additionally, more businesses are relying on *contingent workers* who are unlikely to have benefits of any type, but particularly pensions (Belous, 1990). Growth in the use of contingent workers will reduce both DB and DC plan coverage.

Finally, workers are becoming increasingly concerned about *health care insurance* both prior to and during retirement. Increasing health care cost inflation leaves fewer dollars in the compensation pool for pay increases and other benefits including pensions. In some cases, employees directly confront these tradeoffs, as in flexible or "cafeteria" benefit plans that require workers to allocate benefit credits between health and other benefit options. In other cases, the pressure from health care costs is at retirement. Increasingly, it seems that workers' decisions about when to retire are being conditioned not only by their pensions but also by the health care insurance offerings they will have during retirement. Whether this tradeoff becomes more acute will depend on efforts to control national health care costs, but this topic is beyond the scope of our paper.

B. Factors Influencing Employers' Willingness to Offer Pensions

In the past, employers offered pensions when they were *profitable* enough to pay relatively high benefits along with wages. In addition, pension growth, particularly of the DB plan variety, was fostered by employers' desire to achieve *long-term employee attachment* to the company (Gustman et al., 1992).

What changed during the 1980s? In the private sector, especially in durable manufacturing, global and local competition drove down wages as well as profits, and leveraged buyouts threatened business as usual. Increasing global competition, new technology, and the long recession also induced widespread corporate downsizing and brought shifts in the industrial composition of the U.S. economy. *Firm size* also played a role: in the past, larger employers were typically those most likely to offer pensions, but many of these were also the businesses most vulnerable to shrinkage in the last decade. For these reasons, overall pension coverage leveled off and even declined slightly during the 1980s (Allen, Clark, and McDermed, 1991; Gustman and Steinmeier, 1992a; PBGC, 1990a).

These changes brought labor costs into the limelight in the 1980s, a trend that will continue to characterize the 1990s. Particular attention is being devoted by employers to an evaluation of the benefits, and the costs, of offering health care benefits for active employees and retirees, as well as pensions. Many conclude that retirement benefit plans look increasingly expensive, particularly as health care inflation exerts increased pressure on labor costs. There is also no indication that *health care inflation* rates will slow down, forcing some companies in crisis to control other benefit costs and possibly to terminate pension plans or freeze benefit accruals. Massive plan termination is unlikely in the future because pension regulation has made termination less attractive, both where plans are overfunded, and where plans are underfunded but plan sponsors have assets adequate to cover liabilities. However, there remains the danger of underfunded pension plan termination when businesses are in severe financial trouble.

Lest our description of these trends be misinterpreted, we must state that many employers will continue to want and need pensions (and retiree health benefits) in their compensation packages. DB plans remain a very important tool in human resource management for employers who wish to promote long-term career employment. They are necessary tools for *reducing turnover* among middle-aged workers, and for *facilitating subsequent retirement*. In the business restructuring of the last few years, early retirement windows have also been an important vehicle to help implement workforce reductions. Particularly in larger businesses, DB plans have been quite successful in *encouraging early retirement* on a temporary (or an ongoing) basis through subsidized early retirement provisions, and through early retirement windows (Fields and Mitchell, 1984). Though recent legislation and regulations have restricted the choices once available for early retirement windows, DB plans remain an important tool in human resources management. Many plan sponsors favor the DB plan because their goal is to pay benefits to those who stay until retirement. DC plans, though they offer less opportunity to influence mobility, will probably also grow in importance, particularly if Congress were to undertake a meaningful pension simplification effort. Investments of DC plan assets are likely to change. Falling interest rates, as well as the solvency problems and negative publicity about insurance companies, may encourage covered workers to shift into stocks and move out of the lower return "guaranteed" assets offered by financial intermediaries.

In many ways, the pension environment during the 1980s became *more segmented* and *less stable* than in the past. As the business environment grows *more competitive*, large employers that remain economically viable will probably retain their commitment to career employment, offering DB plans as well as retiree health coverage to both hourly and salaried employees. (Many of these companies often also provide a supplementary DC plan, more often for salaried employees.) These larger businesses have historically espoused a *corporate culture* emphasizing responsibility for employee security. Larger employers will probably continue to foster pension plans, and particularly DB plans, as part of their drive toward "quality management" and the resulting human resource policies. In some cases, *nonqualified supplemental plans* are likely to grow in importance as regulations restrict what can be done overall. *Securing* these nonqualified benefit promises should also grow in importance.

In contrast, small businesses have found it increasingly difficult to provide high wages and generous benefits, particularly in light of increasingly complex legal and accounting rules resulting in rising pension administrative costs (Hay/Huggins, 1990). Unless pension law is significantly simplified so that administrative costs are radically reduced, small companies will not adopt DB plans. Similarly, companies facing frequent *ownership changes* are less likely to be stable and may not have human resources policies favoring career employment. Smaller companies are less likely to demand and reward career employment, so that pensions are less likely to be offered, and when they are offered they will be more likely to be DC plans. As we look to the future, the great unknown is how strong large businesses will be, and how strong the traditionally unionized manufacturing component will be relative to the total American economy.

Corporate bankruptcies, buyouts, and downsizing have also cut short career jobs for many long-term employees, who often lose the opportunity to receive retirement benefits based on a full career at one firm. When businesses are bought and sold, they sometimes develop stable human resource policies that include pensions, but in many cases employment arrangements become less stable. On balance, benefit coverage is sure to fall as a result of bankruptcy. For private sector pensions, this loss will primarily be in the form of future accruals, because plan assets tend to cover most accrued benefits and government-provided pension insurance under the PBGC serves as an additional safety net. (Whether the PBGC's current financial problems will necessitate an additional infusion of funds to remain viable is beyond the scope of our paper, but see Ippolito, 1989.) Growth in short-term employment as well as in the number of contingent workers (see discussion in the previous section) will probably reduce coverage under both DB and DC plans.

In the public sector, there is more risk of benefit loss when state and local government budget needs cannot be met by tax revenues. There is no pension termination insurance in the public sector akin to that offered by the PBGC for private sector pension plans, and plans appear rather less well funded than in the private sector (Mitchell and Smith, 1992). As a consequence, public workers' pension accruals could be threatened, along with future benefit accruals, cost-of-living provisions, and retiree health coverage. More oversight and reporting in the public pension arena would vastly benefit both covered pensioners and taxpayers, and would increase economic security of those in the public pension plan business.

C. Pensions and the Public Policy Environment

New pension legislation was enacted several times during the last decade, so that requirements seemed to change constantly. This vast body of law and regulation radically altered the pension environment, and some of the effects of this movement are still unfolding. Major changes in pension law were incorporated in TRA with key provisions effective on January 1, 1989. As indicated above, there remain questions and uncertainties about major portions of the regulations under this legislation, and effective dates were delayed again in February 1992. While the authorities are revisiting the regulations, TRA remains in effect, and employers are required to meet a standard of good faith compliance. Therefore, many legal pension questions remain open at present, and a large number of plans await revisions.

It is highly likely that *pension law and regulation* will continue to evolve in the next several years. What will happen to tax rates in the future is not known, but as of early 1993 there remain two conflicting forces confronting both Congress and the Administration. On the one hand, there is a great desire to lower taxes; on the other, there is a great need to raise revenue. Three primary types of income on which taxes are not currently paid include pensions, other employee benefits, and interest on home mortgage loans. There is great temptation to tax these items because doing so would raise revenue without increasing tax rates.

Tax preferences for pensions have been challenged several times over the last decade, as Congress imposed penalties on early distributions and termination reversions, increased taxes on lump sum cash distributions from pension plans, and reduced the limits on tax-preferred contributions to, and benefits payable from, both DB and DC plans. There have also been proposals to tax part of pension investment earnings. Marginal changes in the tax status of pensions may not dramatically change overall coverage rates, but if Congress were to repeal entirely the pension tax preference, this would probably curtail growth and cause more plan sponsors to freeze or terminate their plans (Zeisler and Rappaport, 1992). Available evidence suggests that increasing taxes on pension contributions and/or investment earnings will reduce pensions' appeal, though the exact size of the pension response to tax changes has yet to be precisely measured (Gustman et al., 1992). In any event, a narrow Congressional policy focus on taxes forgone will certainly deter the development of sound pension regulation and thoughtful consideration of pension issues within a larger retirement income security policy.

Other forms of government regulation have also played an important role in shaping the pension environment. New pension legislation appeared almost annually over the last decade, and delays in releasing *interpretative regulations* have made the pension environment extremely difficult for plan sponsors (for a summary of recent pension regulation see EBRI, 1990a). Over at least the last six years, large employers seeking to comply with the rules, and small companies contemplating new plans, have been faced with a chaotic regulatory environment that makes it costly and complex to offer tax-qualified plans. Some employers cannot absorb or offset these costs readily (through lowering wages or other benefits), particularly in smaller operations.

Policy makers have been somewhat sympathetic to these developments and have begun to design so-called "pension simplification proposals," particularly for smaller employers. For example, the federal government recently proposed relaxing nondiscrimination rules for small employers who offered a DC plan with specific design features. While some hailed this as a movement in the right direction, others expressed concern that it tended to disfavor DB plans and might possibly reduce coverage for lower paid workers. Additional concerns expressed included worries that the proposals themselves did not go far enough in the simplification direction. Unfortunately, conflicts have developed in the last decade between the ostensible goals and the results of pension legislation, producing a great deal of skepticism about the possible outcomes of further legislation. Taxation and regulation remain key areas of uncertainty; here is where policy makers can help determine whether employer-sponsored pensions grow, or wither.

These regulatory burdens on employer-sponsored benefits are exacerbated by powerful pressures on other components of the retirement income system. Private savings rates are the lowest they have been in years, and many believe that Americans are not saving enough to ensure retirement-age well-being (Bernheim, 1991). Government retirement programs such as Social Security and Medicare will certainly become more financially troubled as the baby boom group matures (Aaron, 1982). In response, these government programs have been reformed in ways which may place employer-sponsored pensions under increasing stress. For instance, Social Security benefits were cut and the normal retirement age raised in 1983; these reforms may have to be extended if demand for benefits continues to be high. Payroll taxes for Medicare and Social Security have also been increased almost annually in the last decade. In addition, many foresee passage of some type of national health insurance plan. If all employers are required to offer a minimum health care coverage, this will exert severe cost pressures on employers not currently offering these benefits (Mitchell, 1991). Because most of these are smaller employers who can ill afford to pay increased labor costs, the health care mandate might further reduce pension coverage offered by smaller employers.

Each of these policy concerns highlights the fact that employer-provided pensions are only one leg of the "three-legged retirement income stool," and that public policy in the retirement income area broadly speaking will influence both employers' willingness to offer pensions, and workers' demand for pensions, in years to come.

III. Implications for Pension Coverage, Plan Type, and Plan Design

Retirement income security for the baby boom generation remains a goal but not a certainty in the United States. Two legs of the traditional three-legged stool are weak, and in this essay we show that grave problems have also undermined the third leg, employer-sponsored pensions.

Major structural changes in employer-sponsored pension plan design and coverage occurred over the last decade, largely in response to a changing business structure, different employee demands, the financial problems of plan sponsors, and a dynamic public policy environment. Overall, these changes did not increase American workers' retirement income security, and it is critically important that policymakers seek ways to create a more positive retirement future. These same forces affect both pensions and retiree medical benefits.

A. Pension Plan Coverage and Plan Type

Several forces at work today point to further declines in pensions and, particularly, DB coverage for the average employee, though it is possible that DC coverage will stabilize or even increase slightly. The most important factors *depressing* pension plan coverage overall, and DB coverage in particular, include:

- Lower real pay levels and lower marginal tax rates.
- More competitive labor and product markets, causing buyouts and downsizing.
- Reduced profits, pay, worker-firm attachments, unionization, and firm size.
- Increased administrative costs and complexity from pension regulation on top of which rising health care costs are superimposed.
- Extensive and complex pension regulation, including nondiscrimination requirements, premiums charged for pension insurance, and fees, reducing employers' ability to offer pension plans.

On the other hand, we have also identified several factors which will somewhat offset the prevailing trend to lower coverage by tax-qualified employer-sponsored pension plans. The factors *supporting* pension growth include:

- The aging of the workforce, which will probably heighten awareness of retirement income needs.
- Increasing desire for early retirement, which raises the need for pension income.
- The continuing appeal of pensions as tax-preferred savings vehicles, combined with higher family income taxes among dual-earner couples.
- Employers' need to provide retirement benefits which reduce turnover for younger employees while increasing retirement rates among older workers.
- Increasing concerns about the long-term level of Social Security and Medicare benefits.

If Congress wishes to enhance the chances that employer-sponsored pensions survive this time of transition, policy makers can take several steps. It is imperative to recognize that company pensions can continue to play an important role in workers' retirement income security only if there is a *more supportive policy climate* regarding retirement income policy as a whole. Linked with this is the recognition that the labor market and the economy of the next twenty years will differ from that which we have become accustomed to. Jobs are located in new regions and industrial sectors, competition is now global, and cost pressures are everywhere. This implies that labor market policies will change.

Retirement age policy at the national level will probably also have to change, because early retirement trends experienced up until recently cannot persist, given the slow growth in economic productivity. American workers will probably need to be encouraged to save more for their own retirement, which suggests that pensions should benefit from government encouragement in the decades to come.

It is also essential for policy makers to recognize that *both DB and DC plans have an important role to play*, so that regulation should not overtly advantage one form of pension versus another. American employers and employees are quite diverse and require different solutions for different problems. Linked to this is our view that pension nondiscrimination requirements are too complex at present. Employers seeking to make employees secure in retirement are probably overly regulated so as to prohibit a small minority of employers from benefiting a limited group of employees. A more rational, stable, and coherent retirement income policy is needed, and pension legislation should fit into this policy rather than being formulated in terms of deficit reduction needs.

Finally, though a full consideration of the public sector is beyond the scope of this paper, Congress and taxpayers should confront the fact that *public sector pension plans are not especially healthy* and should be considered in a systematic overview of pension legislation and reform.

B. Expected Changes in Pension Plan Design

A variety of important changes in pension plan design may be anticipated, extrapolating from trends over the last ten years. Both employers and employees have devoted increasing emphasis to *pension choice and individual responsibility* in benefit plans, as is evident from the rapid growth of supplemental savings plans, mainly 401(k) plans and tax-sheltered annuities. *Use of matched savings plans* and other DC plans giving workers investment choices are also likely to increase.

Nevertheless, from a policy perspective Americans have very poor overall records as savers, and it seems dangerous to rely too heavily on individual savings as a source of retirement benefits. The distribution of risk among employer, employee, and the public sector is an important issue in retirement savings plans and policy. If DC plans permit more employee savings and expanded employee investment choice, employers will certainly find it necessary to take a more active role in educating employees about savings and investment choice. DB plans do not permit covered workers to exercise choice over investment options, though participants potentially face a different type of risk— that of plan underfunding. Pension insurance is beyond the scope of this paper, and is the subject of other analysts contributing to this conference. Nevertheless, it must be kept in mind that allocation of risk remains a central concern in future discussions of retirement security.

A related point pertains to the form in which benefits are paid. DB plans have traditionally offered benefits in the form of annuities (except for small benefit amounts, generally less than $3,500, which are often paid out as a lump sum). In contrast, the conventional DC plan traditionally paid out a *cash lump sum*, although it was common to offer an annuity option. Lump sums were favorably taxed in the past and still are today, but to a lesser extent than previously. There is also pressure on some DB plan sponsors to offer lump sums. This area is a controversial one at present, and Congress may place limitations on the availability of lump sums, and/or require that they be rolled over into other pension funds.

In addition to these changes, we see other plan design innovations developing out of recent experience. Plan sponsors will probably seek *innovative plan designs*, as long as regulations do not make it too difficult to implement them. For instance, the cash balance plans mentioned earlier are likely to grow because they offer many of the advantages of DB plans, while also offering some features and advantages common to DC plans.

Compliance with layers of regulations over the years has led to ever more complex plans, and many such plans now have multiple layers of benefit formulas with different rules applying to service accrued at different points in time. We expect that this increased complexity will cause employers to place increasing weight on *simpler plan design* in the future. The changing business environment will increase emphasis on *plans that link company profitability and benefits provided*. The number of plans *integrated with Social Security* will probably continue to grow if trends shown in Table 8 continue. However, TRA has materially changed the rules and attractiveness of integration so that we may also see a reversal of this trend. TRA rules have also forced a decrease in the degree of integration within integrated plans.

There are opposing views about whether pension plan benefits will become more or less generous over time. On the one hand, *benefit levels may have to be reduced somewhat and early retirement ages raised* if employers are to be able to offer retiree health insurance to better manage phased retirement and early retirement window plans, and to design plans

TABLE 8   Integration of Defined Benefit Plans with Social Security (1980–89)*

Type of formula	Percent of full-time participants								
	1980	1981	1982	1983	1984	1985	1986	1988	1989
Without integrated formula	55	57	55	45	44	39	38	38	37
With integrated formula	45	43	45	55	56	61	62	62	63
Benefit offset by SS payment†	30	33	35	35	36	40	43	39	41
Excess formula‡	16	10	10	20	20	27	24	26	24

Source: Mitchell (1992a), Table 9.11. Data cover plans in medium and large firms only. An Employee Benefits Survey (EBS) for this group was not conducted in 1987. The EBS sampling frame changed in 1988 to include smaller firms and more industries than before, so data for 1988 and 1989 are not precisely comparable with previous years' tabulations.

* Data exclude supplemental pension plans. Sums may not equal totals because of rounding.
† Pension benefit calculated is reduced by a portion of primary Social Security payments.
‡ Pension formula applies lower benefit rate to earnings subject to Social Security taxes or below a specified dollar threshold.

which better match retirees' income needs. On the other hand, a review of DB plan design trends over the 1980s suggests that *subsidization of early retirement trends remains the norm, and indeed has become more prevalent over time* (Table 9). As the workforce continues to age, some workers and employers will rely on pensions to enhance the appeal of retirement.

There remain important unanswered questions about how *nondiscrimination requirements* will affect benefits offered to different groups of employees. Many of these nondiscrimination issues are not yet fully resolved, yet there is reason to expect that companies will begin to *consolidate plans across hourly and salaried workers*. Because of continued declines in collective bargaining coverage, we predict *continued decline of multi-employer plans*. On the other hand, there will be continued *growth in nonqualified supplemental plans*. There may be some overall reduction in benefit levels as management finds it can benefit less from qualified plans than in the past.

C. Policy Issues

Without going into extensive detail, it is important to review a few of the most important policy proposals that have been the subject of intense debate in recent years, to see how their passage might change the pension environment in years to come.

Great strides have been made in improving workers' chances of vesting, first under ERISA, and then subsequently by reducing vesting requirements to 5 years of service. This has probably improved pension participation, since many Americans change jobs repeatedly during their worklives. Despite this, some analysts contend that increased *pension portability* should remain an important policy goal so that workers who change jobs or spend part of their careers out of the workplace, will benefit from increased retirement income. On the other hand, many recognize that limiting access to retirement funds is necessary by requiring rollover into another retirement vehicle, so that workers are not tempted to spend lump sum amounts that should be saved for retirement. Thus DC plans are seen as meeting portability needs, primarily because they can pay benefits in the form of lump sums when a worker changes employers. However, when benefits are spent rather than saved, they cease to be available as retirement benefits. Requiring more liberal pension portability would undermine some of the good reasons employers offer pensions—to reduce turnover and to regulate retirement flows—and would probably not encourage pension growth overall. If Congress limits the availability of lump sums with requirements that they be rolled over, this could benefit many,

TABLE 9   Minimum Requirements for Early Retirement in Defined Benefit Pension Plans (1980–1989)*

	Percent of full time participants								
	1980	1981	1982	1983	1984	1985	1986	1988	1989
Plans permitting early retirement*	98	98	97	97	97	97	98	98	97
Service requirements alone									
30 years required	10	5	5	6	5	4	5	7	6
Age requirements alone	9	10	9	10	10	9	10	10	6
Age 55	8	9	9	10	9	9	10	10	6
Age and service requirements									
Age 55 and 5 years	3	4	4	3	4	3	3	4	9
Age 55 and 10 years	NA	36	35	35	39	43	41	44	43
Age 55 and 15 years	NA	11	10	9	7	8	7	10	8
Age 60 and 10 years	NA	4	4	5	5	4	4	5	4
Age 62 and 10 years	NA	—	—	—	—	—	—	—	2
Age plus service sum	5	9	10	9	10	10	9	4	1
Sum equals 80 or less	NA	NA	NA	6	6	5	5	2	—
Sum equals 85 or more	3	6	5	5	5	4	4	1	—
Plans not permitting early retirement	2	2	3	3	3	3	2	2	3

Source: Mitchell (1992a), Table 9.3. Data cover plans in medium and large firms only. A comparable Employee Benefits Survey (EBS) was not conducted in 1987. The EBS sampling frame changed in 1988 to include smaller firms and more industries than before, so data for 1988 and 1989 are not precisely comparable with previous years' tabulations.

*Early retirement as the point when a worker can retire and immediately receive accrued benefits based on service and earnings; benefits are reduced for years prior to the normal age. Data exclude supplemental pension plans. Sums may not equal totals because of rounding. NA means data not available; — means less than 0.5 percent.

though some are concerned that too much labor force immobility might be detrimental.

Another policy concern alluded to above is the continuing issue of *who bears risks related to retirement,* and how they should be divided among active workers, retirees, employers, and the government. For example, many retirees currently bear virtually all the risk of non-Medicare retiree health care costs, while the federal government bears much DB plan termination risk (Bodie, 1992). Restructuring the retiree health care benefits, or the DB pension promise and its insurance system, would dramatically alter employers' and employees' willingness to keep plans or to start new plans. DC plans offer yet a different pattern of risk-sharing, depending on their specific structures; for example, in a common money-purchase plan the worker bears diversified capital market risk, while in a profit-sharing or stock-ownership plan the risks are much more concentrated (Blasi and Kruse, 1991). The worker bears the full inflation risk with all DC plans, although in some plans this can be partially offset by the type of investments chosen. Understanding how these risks differ across benefit plans, and how they relate to company profitability as well as the overall economic environment, deserves much more attention in years to come.

Stepping back and viewing pensions from a broader perspective, there remains the ultimate public policy question of *whose responsibility should retirement saving be, and what role should pensions play in achieving the savings targets?* Over the years, many have urged increased private saving, but the efforts have not worked: personal savings as a percentage of personal income dropped between 1970 and 1990. This trend is even more alarming when considered in combination with pressures on long-term government and business spending for retirement. The savings debate will have to be paired with a national debate over the socially optimal retirement age, as the workforce continues to grow older and more diverse, and as pressures grow stronger on the Social Security and medical care systems. *We believe that public policy should preserve a central role for pensions in the decades ahead, and both DB and DC pension plans should be available in service to a diverse business and labor community.* On the other hand it must be recognized that pensions have many important functions beyond their retirement savings role. Increasingly burdensome restrictions and the frequency of change in those restrictions on pensions are threatening the multi-dimensional benefits that pensions offer to employees, the sponsoring employers and the economy as a whole.

Without implicating them, the authors acknowledge helpful suggestions from Alan Gustman, Chip Kerby, Jerry Levy, and Ray Schmitt, and research support from Cornell University's Industrial and Labor Relations School as well as William M. Mercer, Incorporated and the Pension Research Council.

Bibliography

Aaron, Henry. 1982. *Economic Effects of Social Security.* Washington, DC: Brookings Institution.

Allen, Steven G., Robert L. Clark, and Ann A. McDermed. 1991. "Pension Bonding and Lifetime Jobs." National Bureau of Economic Research Working Paper 3688. April.

Andrews, Emily. 1985. *The Changing Profile of Pensions in America.* Washington, DC: EBRI.

———. 1989. *Pension Policy and Small Employers: At What Price Coverage?* Washington, DC: EBRI.

"Are Defined Benefit Plans Dead?" 1991. *Mercer Bulletin* 194 (August; William M. Mercer, Inc.).

Beller, Daniel J. and Helen H. Lawrence. 1992. "Trends in Private Pension Coverage." In *Trends in Pensions: 1992*, ed. John Turner and Daniel J. Beller. Washington, DC: U.S. Government Printing Office.

Belous, R. S. 1990. "Flexible Employments: The Employer's Point of View." In *Bridges to Retirement,* ed. Peter Doeringer. Ithaca, NY: ILR Press.

Bernheim, B. Douglas. 1991. *The Vanishing Nest Egg.* New York: Priority Press Publications for the Twentieth Century Fund.

"Big Employers Retain Defined Benefit Plans." 1991. *Business Insurance* (November 18).

Biggs, John H. 1993. "Implications of Demographic Changes for the Design of Retirement Programs." In *Demography and Retirement: The Twenty-First Century,* ed. Anna M. Rappaport and Sylvester J. Schieber. Westport, CT: Pension Research Council and Praeger Publishers.

Blasi, Joseph and Douglas Kruse. 1991. *The New Owners.* New York: Harper Business.

Bodie, Zvi. 1990. "Pensions as Retirement Income Insurance." *Journal of Economic Literature* 28, 1 (March): 28–49.

———. 1992. "Federal Pension Insurance: Is it the S&L Crisis of the 1990's?" Paper presented at the Industrial Relations Research Association meetings, New Orleans, January.

Brown, Charles and James Medoff. 1989. "The Employer Size-Wage Effect." *Journal of Political Economy,* 97, 5 (October): 1027–59.

Clark, Robert L. and Ann A. McDermed. 1990. *The Choice of Pension Plans in a Changing Regulatory Environment.* Washington, DC: American Enterprise Institute.

Ehrenberg, Ronald G. and George Jakubson. 1988. *Advance Notice Provisions in Plant Closing Legislation.* Kalamazoo, MI: Upjohn.

Employee Benefit Research Institute (EBRI). 1990a. *Databook on Employee Benefits.* Washington, DC: EBRI.

———. 1990b. *Quarterly Pension Investment Report* 5.

———. 1990c. "Types of Pension Plans and Their Assets." *EBRI Issue Briefs* (April).

————. 1991. "Questions and Answers on Employee Benefit Issues." *EBRI Issue Briefs* (October).

————. 1992. "New Evidence That Employees Choose Conservative Investments for Their Retirement Funds." *EBRI Notes* (February).

Fields, Gary and Olivia S. Mitchell. 1984. *Retirement, Pensions and Social Security.* Cambridge, MA: MIT Press.

Grant, Paul B. 1991. "The Open Window—Special Early Retirement Plans in Transition." *Employee Benefits Journal* (March).

Greenwich Associates. 1991. "Going Global, Good Going." *Greenwich Associates Reports.* Greenwich, CT.

Gustman, Alan and Olivia S. Mitchell. 1992. "Pensions and Labor Market Activity: Behavior and Data Requirements." In *Pensions and the Economy: Sources, Uses, and Limitations of Data,* ed. Zvi Bodie and Alicia H. Munnell. Pension Research Council. Philadelphia: University of Pennsylvania Press: 39–87.

Gustman, Alan, Olivia S. Mitchell, and Thomas Steinmeier. 1992. "The Role of Pensions in the Labor Market." Cornell University Department of Labor Economics Working Paper.

Gustman, Alan and Thomas Steinmeier. 1992a. "Pension Cost of Living Adjustments." In *As the Workforce Ages: Benefits, Costs and Policy Challenges,* ed. Olivia S. Mitchell. Ithaca, NY: ILR Press.

————. 1992b. "The Stampede Toward Defined Contribution Plans: Fact or Fiction?" *Industrial Relations* 31, 2 (Spring): 361–69.

Hay/Huggins Company, Inc. 1990. *Pension Plan Expense Study for the Pension Benefit Guaranty Corporation.* September.

Ippolito, Richard A. 1986. *Pensions, Economics and Public Policy.* Pension Research Council. Homewood, IL: Dow Jones-Irwin.

————. 1989. *The Economics of Pension Insurance.* Pension Research Council. Homewood, IL: Dow Jones-Irwin.

————. 1990. *An Economic Appraisal of Pension Tax Policy.* Pension Research Council. Homewood, IL: Dow Jones-Irwin.

————. 1992. "Selecting Out High Discounters: A Theory of Defined Contribution Pensions." PBGC Working Paper.

Kotlikoff, Laurence J. and Daniel Smith. 1983. *Pensions in the American Economy.* Chicago: University of Chicago Press, 1983.

Lazear, Edward P. 1983. "Pensions as Severance Pay." In *Financial Aspects of the United States Pension System,* ed. Zvi Bodie and John Shoven. National Bureau of Economic Research. Chicago: University of Chicago Press.

Levine, Philip and Olivia S. Mitchell. 1988. "The Baby Boom's Legacy: Relative Wages in the Twenty-First Century." *American Economic Review* 78, (May).

Lumsdaine, Robin, James Stock and David Wise. 1990a. "Efficient Windows and Labor Force Reduction." *Journal of Public Economics,* 43 (November).

————. 1990b. "Three Models of Retirement: Computational Complexity Versus Predictive Validity." National Bureau of Economic Research Working Paper 3558, December.

Luzadis, Rebecca A. and Olivia S. Mitchell. 1991. "Explaining Pension Dynamics." *Journal of Human Resources* 26, 4 (Fall).

Mitchell, Olivia S. 1982. "Fringe Benefits and Labor Mobility." *Journal of Human Resources* 17, 2 (Spring): 286–98.

————. 1988. "Worker Knowledge of Pension Provisions." *Journal of Labor Economics* 6, 1 (January): 212–39.

————. 1991. "The Effects of Mandatory Benefit Packages." In *Research in Labor Economics*, ed. L. Bassi, D. Crawford, and R. Ehrenberg. Greenwich, CT: JAI Press, 297–320.

————. 1992a. "Trends in Retirement Provisions." In *Trends in Pensions: 1992.* ed. J. Turner and D. Beller. Washington, DC: U.S. Government Printing Office.

————, ed. 1992b. *As the Workforce Ages.* Ithaca, NY: ILR Press.

Mitchell, Olivia S. and Emily Andrews. 1981. "Scale Economies in Private Multi-Employer Pension Systems." *Industrial and Labor Relations Review* 34, 4 (July): 522–30.

Mitchell, Olivia S. and Robert S. Smith. 1992. "Public Sector Pensions: Benefits, Funding and Unionization." In *Industrial Relations Research Association Papers and Proceedings.* Madison: University of Wisconsin Press.

Munnell, Alicia H. 1989. "It's Time To Tax Employee Benefits." *New England Economic Review* (July/August).

Pension Benefit Guaranty Corporation (PBGC). 1990a. *Pension Plan Choice.* Washington, DC: U.S. Government Printing Office.

————. 1990b. *Pension Plan Cost Study.* Washington, DC: U.S. Government Printing Office.

————. 1991. "Creating a Sound Insurance Program." *1990 Annual Report.* Washington, DC: U.S. Government Printing Office.

Piacentini, Joseph. 1990. "An Analysis of Pension Participation at Current and Prior Jobs, Receipt and Use of Preretirement Lump-Sum Distributions, and Tenure at Current Job." Employee Benefit Research Institute Report to the U.S. Department of Labor. Washington, DC: EBRI, May.

Quinn, Joseph F., Richard V. Burkhauser, and Daniel A. Myers. 1990. *Passing the Torch: The Influence of Economic Incentives on Work and Retirement.* Kalamazoo, MI: W. E. Upjohn Institute. New York: Basic Books.

Rappaport, Anna. 1991. "Defined Contribution Plans: Do They Offer a Solution to Retiree Medical Liability Problems?" *Postemployment Benefits* 8, 1 (Winter 1991).

Rappaport, Anna. 1987. "New Ideas in Employee Benefits Planning." *Journal of Pension Planning and Compliance.* 12, 1 (Spring).

————. 1988. "Human Resources Implications of a Changing Labor Force." *Benefits Quarterly* IV, 2 (second quarter).

————. 1989. "The Future of Employee Benefit-Related Public Policy." *Employee Benefits Journal* 14, 3 (September).

————. 1992a. "Retirement Benefit Structure in the 1990s—Defined Benefit vs. Defined Contribution Plan Structure." International Association of Consulting Actuaries.

————. 1992b. "The Role of the Actuary in Defining Public Policy Implications of an Aging Society." International Congress of Actuaries.

Rappaport, Anna and Sylvester Schieber. 1993. "Overview." In *Demography and Retirement: The Twenty-First Century,* ed. Anna M. Rappaport and Sylvester Schieber. Westport, CT: Pension Research Council and Praeger Publishing.

Rosenbloom, Jerry S. and G. Victor Hallman. 1991. *Employee Benefit Planning.* Third Edition. Englewood Cliffs, NJ: Prentice-Hall.

Spencer, Charles D. and Associates. 1990. *Spencer's Research Report on Employee Benefits.* June 22.

Society of Actuaries. 1990. "Plan Design for the Next Decade." *Record.* 16, 4B (October): 2779.

Turner, John A. and Daniel J. Beller, eds. 1990. *Trends in Pensions, 1989.* Washington, DC: U.S. Government Printing Office.

U.S. Congress, Congressional Budget Office. 1987. *Tax Policy for Pensions and Other Retirement Savings.* Washington, DC: U.S. Government Printing Office, April.

U.S. Department of Commerce, Bureau of the Census. 1991. *Statistical Abstract of the United States, 1991.* Washington, DC: U.S. Government Printing Office.

U.S. Department of Labor, Bureau of Labor Statistics (USDOL). 1987. *Employee Benefits in State and Local Governments.* Washington, DC: U.S. Government Printing Office.

———. 1989. *Employee Benefits in Medium and Large Firms.* Washington, DC: U.S. Government Printing Office.

———. 1990. *Employee Benefits in Small Firms.* Washington, DC: U.S. Government Printing Office.

U.S. General Accounting Office (USGAO). 1991. *Pension Plans: Terminations, Asset Reversions and Replacements Following Leveraged Buyouts.* Washington, DC: U.S. Government Printing Office, GAO/HRD 91-21.

———. 1992. *States Need Labor's Help in Regulating Multiple Employer Welfare Arrangements.* Washington, DC: U.S. Government Printing Office, GAO/HRD 92-40, March.

U.S. President. 1990. *Economic Report of the President 1990.* Washington, DC: U.S. Government Printing Office.

Woodbury, Stephen A. and Wei-Jang Huang. 1991. *The Tax Treatment of Fringe Benefits.* Kalamazoo, MI: Upjohn Institute.

Zeisler, Paul and Anna Rappaport. 1992. "Public Policy and Pension Plan Taxation: The Implication for Plan Design and for Participants." *Journal of Pension Planning and Compliance* (Spring).

Comments by Alan L. Gustman

Olivia Mitchell and Anna Rappaport have produced a very useful paper, one that has a number of interesting things to say about trends in pensions and pension policies. They have been very careful to limit their inquiry, in most cases providing qualitative rather than quantitative answers to the questions they address.

Mitchell and Rappaport have good reason for limiting much of their discussion to qualitative effects and to the direction of the impact of specific causal factors, rather than to a quantitative analysis of these outcomes. Economists do not know enough about the importance of the various forces shaping workers' demands for pensions, and firms' willingness to supply them, to determine the size of the effect of each of the motivations for pensions on the pension-related outcomes observed in the labor market. Accordingly, we are not in a position to make fully reliable and comprehensive quantitative predictions about pension trends or policies. Those forecasts of pension outcomes, and quantitative evaluations of specific regulations or policies that we do make, must be strongly hedged.

What Are the Limitations of Economists' Knowledge About the Role of Pensions in the Labor Market?

To indicate the weaknesses in our knowledge, let me borrow from a paper Olivia Mitchell, Thomas Steinmeier and I have written on the role of pensions in the labor market, a paper to which Mitchell and Rappaport refer (Gustman et al., 1992).

A survey of empirical studies suggests that economists have a better idea of the forces shaping workers' demand for pensions than they do of the forces shaping firms' willingness to supply them. But in neither case do we have any reliable estimates of the importance of each of the separate effects operating on workers' and firms' sides of the markets.

Workers want pensions to take advantage of tax benefits to retirement savings. Moreover, there is the insurance motivation for pensions, especially because pensions provide a highly valuable annuity that is otherwise subject to market failure. A useful framework for analyzing these effects is created by applying consumption theory. For example, pension choice may be modeled in the context of a standard life cycle model. In the choice of the optimal path for savings, the pension is not exogenously given, but is an instrument and is determined as part of the savings decision along with nonpension savings. An appropriately specified model would tell us about the forces shaping the demand for pensions, and would provide enough information to gauge the likely effects of changes in public policy on the workers' demands. But while the empirical models we have available generate results with appropriate signs, so that special tax treatment of pensions increases demand for pensions, and higher incomes are associated with higher demand, the models are relatively crude. For example, the best of the econometric models available (Woodbury and Huang, 1991) implicitly assumes that all retirement savings must take place through the pension, and treats the tax advantage of a pension as if pensions were tax free rather than a mechanism to defer taxation. That model also ignores the role of pension insurance, and pays no attention to social security. Studies of worker choices of pensions are subject to such serious specification error that we must have significant doubts about the parameters that are estimated.

On the firm side of the market, it is argued that, in addition to wanting pensions because their workers do, it is in the firms' interest to provide pensions for their workers due to cost advantages from tax benefits and economies of scale. Moreover, firms may adopt and design pensions with the intent of influencing retirement, regulating turnover, and encouraging enhanced work effort. Almost all the empirical analyses concerned with motivation on the firm side of the market involve indirect tests of available theories. The major tests involve determining whether retirement outcomes vary with incentives created by the pension, with greater incidence of early retirement being observed where the incentives for early retirement are greater. Analogous tests also attempt to relate pension incentives to worker mobility, in my view, less successfully. Empirical evidence from these indirect tests supports some of the theories, while others are left unproved or in doubt. But, most important, there are no direct attempts to estimate econometrically the relationships among pension policy, compensation, labor inputs, and output produced. That is, there are no econometric analyses that estimate models of the firm and its production function, while taking into account the effects of retirement flows, worker quits, or induced work effort on the firm's output or costs, building in an explicit role for pensions.

Our most fundamental problem is that we do not know enough about what the firm side model looks like. Moreover, there still are a number of key questions to answer about the details of behavioral relations on the worker side of the market. We simply do not have the behavioral parameters necessary to make reliable forecasts of the quantities of pension related outcomes.

As a result, there are questions that we are in no position to answer:

- How big are the effects of the regulations that Mitchell and Rappaport discuss on past trends in pension coverage and plan type which they document? What exactly are the effects of tax benefits on pensions and their structure? We know the direction of these effects, that is, we know the qualitative answers, but we do not know their quantitative importance.
- What would be the effects of relaxing these regulations on future trends? We know the direction, but we do not know, and cannot, given current information, determine any magnitudes.
- We have direct estimates of the effects of pension regulation on the costs of administering the pension plan. But we do not know the extent to which the constraints on compensation structure created by pension regulations affect worker productivity—inhibiting human resource policies which are designed to regulate retirement, turnover, and productivity. We can guess the direction, but cannot determine whether the costs are in millions or in billions.

Certainly, having no estimates of structural econometric models of the determination of pensions limits our understanding of the importance of forces shaping pension outcomes, explaining plan type, plan features, and plan values, and related employment outcomes, compensation and productivity. Nevertheless, as some portions of Mitchell and Rappaport suggest, it is possible to attach magnitudes to some effects of interest. To provide an example of what we can and cannot do given the current state of knowledge, it is useful to take the case of the trends in plan type, which Mitchell and Rappaport discuss. This is a subject that can be analyzed quantitatively with less knowledge about the underlying process generating choice of plan type. The analyst can avoid some of the need for modeling by asking questions about forces generating *changes*, paying less attention to how the *levels* are determined. Nevertheless, as we will see, as long as the full model is not available and estimated, there remain important gaps in what we can learn.

In a paper dated this March, entitled "The Proliferation of Defined Contribution Plans" (1992), Richard Ippolito illustrates what we can and cannot accomplish under what are the most favorable of circumstances. In that paper Ippolito finds, consistent with earlier results based on cruder data by Tom Steinmeier and myself (Gustman and Steinmeier, 1992), that over the last decade about half the trend away from primary defined benefit plans is due to the changing mix of firm size, industry, and unionization. Thus half the trend to primary defined contribution plans is purely mechanical. He labels the rest of the trend as due to preferences, which really means that the rest of the trend is unexplained. He then attempts to reduce the range of our ignorance. First, he presents data from a Hay/Huggins report to the PBGC suggesting that new pension regulations significantly raised costs for DB plans at small firms but had a much smaller impact at large firms. Based on the size of the cost increases, Ippolito concludes that regulation probably is not the reason for the trend observed at large employers. But in the absence of a model it is difficult to determine the extent to which cost changes induced by regulatory changes would translate into a change in plan type. Ippolito also does a nice analysis of the trend in 401(k) plans, relating the adoption of 401(k) plans to firm size, industry, and unionization and attempting to determine the extent to which 401(k) plans substituted for primary DB or DC plans. He concludes that 401(k) plans were more than twice as likely to substitute for DB as for DC plans. There are models of how 401(k)s might affect demand for labor and labor productivity, but these, which are mainly due to Ippolito, are theoretical and still very rough and untested. Ippolito then mentions other causes of declining demand for DB plans, including changes in the structure of taxes, anti-discrimination rules, and funding limits; but again there is no model to evaluate how exactly these factors influence pension choice, plan type, or plan value.

The research on trends in plan type proceeds as if it is possible to analyze the trends without quantitative estimates of the importance of each of the forces on the worker and firm sides of the market shaping the determination of plan type at a moment in time. If we are lucky, or if the researcher has very good instincts, as I believe Ippolito does, then the factors we are not measuring will truly not have changed, or had only weak impact, and we can measure what underlies the *trend* without measuring how the *level* of the outcome is determined. If we are not lucky, we will have left out some important influences on the trend. The only buffer against serious specification error is a solid model of the process determining plan type at a moment in time.

What Can be Done to Extend the Range of Questions We Can Answer?

Olivia Mitchell and I have written two reviews, one for the PRC (Gustman and Mitchell, 1992) and another which I referred to earlier, which address this question. The first highlights needs for data that would foster progress; the second points to advances in empirical analysis that would fill major gaps in our behavioral models, gaps which must be filled to provide a basis for more useful policy analysis and to enable us to improve prediction of trends. Both tasks are doable.

To date, economic analysis has told us a limited amount about the role of pensions in the labor market. But our knowledge is slowly expanding. As behavioral analysis progresses, we will be able to say more about pension policies; analyses will be more useful to policy makers and to practitioners.

Let me end these comments with a plea to an influential audience. We all wish that behavioral analysis were progressing more quickly. One way to increase progress in this area is to attract more labor market analysts with the appropriate analytical skills to do research on pensions. Many qualified labor economists are working in other areas, which they find as important and interesting as pension research. In many cases, their choices are correct. Scarce research time is being allocated among a number of important topics. If it is allocated in an efficient manner, the returns to marginal research hours are similar in each activity.

If we want to attract more and better researchers to pension analysis, we need to raise the returns to pension research, or reduce the costs. There are important barriers to entry into pension research which make it an unusually costly type of research. These barriers can be reduced in a number of ways. One way to do so is to encourage firms to make more detailed information available, even if it is on a confidential basis, to improve understanding of firms' demand for pensions. Second, there is a need for a central depository for pension data. Third, pension software is highly specialized and difficult to develop. A center that collected and perhaps refined pension related software would perform an extremely useful function. These activities would lower barriers to entry into pension research, and encourage more researchers who have appropriate econometric tools to undertake basic research on this important topic. Such activities will speed the day when we move beyond the barriers that have constrained the analysis of Mitchell and Rappaport, enabling us to say more about the quantitative effects of pension policies and about pension trends, and thus to contribute more fundamentally to the policy process.

References

Gustman, Alan L. and Olivia S. Mitchell. 1992. "Pensions and the Labor Market: Behavior and Data Requirements." In *Pensions and the Economy: Sources, Uses, and Limitations of Data,* ed. Zvi Bodie and Alicia H. Munnell. Pension Research Council. Philadelphia: PRC and University of Pennsylvania Press,

Gustman, Alan L., Olivia S. Mitchell, and Thomas L. Steinmeier. 1992. "The Role of Pensions in the Labor Market." Cornell University Department of Economics Working Paper.

Gustman, Alan L. and Thomas L. Steinmeier. 1992. "The Stampede Toward Defined Contribution Pension Plans: Fact Or Fiction?" 1992. *Industrial Relations* 31, 2 (Spring): 361–69.

Ippolito, Richard A. 1992. "The Proliferation of Defined Contribution Plans." Pension Benefit Guaranty Corporation, xeroxed.

Woodbury, Stephen A. and Wei-Jang Huang. 1991. *The Tax Treatment of Fringe Benefits.* Kalamazoo, MI: Upjohn Institute.

Comments by Marc M. Twinney, Jr.

Introduction

This is an excellent paper, both in its breadth of view and in its detail in describing normal practice and future trends. My discussion will be limited to those few issues on which I can sharpen the emphasis or understanding, at the risk of repeating a few of the paper's views.

My comments will be in three parts: first, why large firms sponsored defined benefit plans in the past and why they are likely to continue to do so in the future; second, three provisions in large company plans that are not well known but are important in supporting the rationale given for sponsoring or designing the plans; third, a few comments on the policy issues and the form and direction of pension regulation in the United States.

The Past and Future of the Defined Benefit Form

The primary reason larger, international manufacturing firms provide private pensions is to remove the older, less efficient employee from the workforce in a socially responsible way. Firms do not provide pensions to recruit and hire employees. Firms do not provide pensions to tie employees to the workforce and avoid recruiting or training costs. The fact that this occurs is incidental to the primary goal. These secondary effects result from controlling the costs of providing retirement income and are acceptable to the firm and to employees.

Viewing the firm's purpose in sponsoring a pension in this way helps to explain why the firm is willing to vest the accrued benefit after some reasonable period of time in the workforce, but is not as willing to increase prior service benefits for future inflation after work has ceased. Today when "lean" production is necessary as a way to compete in global markets, most workforces must be "size constrained." We see this as company after company, even some of those in industries employing the latest technology, announce workforce reductions and restructuring. Few of these employers would resist voluntary termination by their trained employees when they are downsizing. If termination occurs after vesting and prior to retirement eligibility so much the better. But the voluntary quits decline abruptly in periods when economic activity slows and firms must regroup.

Large firms prefer the defined benefit form for the retirement objective not only because of cost but also because of its effectiveness. Defined benefit plans allocate more of the contributions to those who must retire than to those who depart before retirement. This is true for the defined benefit relative to both cash balance and defined contribution forms. The sponsor's assumption of the investment risk has driven costs down compared with the defined contribution form. The defined benefit plan can be focused at a selected retirement age or maximized at a specific period of service, thus encouraging orderly retirement not dependent on high market values or subjective factors. Any one of these advantages of the defined benefit forms could be compelling; collectively they are overwhelming.

As to the future, there may be further shrinkage in manufacturing jobs as the international competition intensifies. In this future "long" hour jobs will prevail in manufacturing, to make the teamwork and quality goals work and to support any opportunity of improved wages and benefits. Thus the forces that created the effectiveness of the defined benefit form in the large setting will be reinforced.

Three Specific Plan Provisions

Three provisions in large firm plans are of design interest.

One pension provision is how certain industrial plans treat involuntary termination of employment that occurs before eligibility for retirement. For employees who reach age 45 with at least ten years of service, involuntary termination prior to retirement eligibility is considered not to break service. Thus the employee is eligible at age 55 for a regular early retirement benefit, not the more reduced deferred vested benefit. The regular early benefit is worth about 80 percent more than the deferred vested benefit at that age. The employee also is eligible for postretirement life and health insurance. This policy applies to hourly and salaried people covered by these provisions.

A second design point relates to the history of lump sum provisions at my company. Since the inception of the plan in 1950 we have never allowed the basic life pension to be paid as a lump sum (except in cases of very small benefits). This applies to negotiated and unilateral plans. The policy makers did not want to face the situation of a retiree or spouse whose retirement income was gone because of wasting a lump sum distribution. This resolve prevailed despite the added costs of postretirement increases for the life income distribution. It also applies outside the United States, where Ford tries as a policy to maximize monthly life incomes and to minimize lump sum commutation.

The third design relates to the design of the U.S. retirement income formulas. In 1952 or so a major appliance manufacturer adopted a very simple formula—2 percent per year of service, 30 years maximum—of final five year average compensation. No employee contributions, no integration with Social Security, and almost no need to continue accruals after age 65 (when that regulation was promulgated). In forty years, vesting has been liberalized and some of the early retirement and survivor provisions revised, but the basic formula remains essentially unchanged.

This formula was criticized at its adoption as too generous and too expensive, especially for the lower paid, too dynamic, too front loaded, and so forth. In practice, it has worked out very well. Management took its cost into account in their long term planning. The pension fund returns have been better than expected at its inception and to date. This plan has been one of the firm's greatest successes in personnel policy. It has stood the test of time—and it will cause little problem under tax reform.

After much effort, change, revision, and improvement, it is interesting to note that my company plan is now providing a benefit formula of about 1.9 percent of five-year final average salary. We also have an executive formula for early retirement that provides a maximum of 60 percent of final salary. This 2 percent rate appears to be the neighborhood of convergence because of adequacy and the availability of surveys of the competitive benefit levels. This rate is likely to continue to be desirable in the future for similar reasons.

It is doubtful that the appliance company will seek out an innovative design. I suggest that more plan formulas may emulate its longstanding design, perhaps with the exception of integration with Social Security, when the fundamentals are thought through carefully.

Pension Policy

The policy issues have been largely neglected by the nation since ERISA was passed. The nation tried to face the idea of mandating a minimum private plan benefit in 1980 and failed. One of the consequences of that failure I believe is the web of law and regulation requiring voluntary plans to accrue benefits for lower-paid employees and coverage and participation requirements. These regulations are literally incomprehensible except for the full-time practitioner.

The U.S. situation now is worse than for the employers and employees in the United Kingdom. First, because of the required second level of Social Security or private benefits contracted out, all U.K. employees are accruing some benefit. Second, because everyone is covered by some future accrual the regulation of the private plans is made less complex. The U.K. environment is not necessarily less harsh for the employer—plans must pass solvency tests and provide indexing with inflation in future service accruals and the smallest employer must contribute.

Many of the U.K. plans are contributory because of contracting out. Fewer of these plans look like the DC form than in the U.S., but most of the U.K. plans permit a 25 percent lump sum distribution. There is diversity in formulas and simplicity in detail that is quite healthy. It would be interesting to compare the savings rates in the United States versus the United Kingdom since 1980, by which time the contracted-out plans were well established in the latter.

It seems doubtful now that the United States could solve this pension policy issue by requiring a miminum private benefit when that requirement is probably key to any solution on the health care coverage issues. As a result, we have successive layers of regulation requiring plan changes, each one by itself apparently worthwhile but in the aggregate objectionable. "Simplification" is not the answer as it is proposed to date. It simply puts another layer of complexity in force for another time period.

I would think minimal pensions and health care plans would be a valid long-term policy goal. If we cannot reach an acceptable level voluntarily, we may have to follow the European example. The question is, how do we continue our progress?

Chapter 3
Roundtable Discussion: Defined Benefit/Defined Contribution Trends

Ray Schmitt

The current trend away from defined benefit plans and toward defined contribution arrangements has been alluded to earlier by some of the discussants and is a much debated issue. There are differences in opinion as to what is causing this movement. Moreover, it is unclear what effect these trends will have on future retirement income security. Leading our panel will be Angela Chang. Angela is going to set the analytical framework for the discussion. She is a Ph.D. candidate in economics at MIT, and her dissertation topic is "The Moral Hazard Problems with PBGC Insurance." Joining her is Professor Robert Clark, who is currently the Interim Head of the Division of Economics and Business at North Carolina State University. Dr. Clark has written numerous articles and books on retirement and pension policies, including *The Choice of Pension Plans in a Changing Regulatory Environment*, which has served as a good backdrop and focus for today's round-table discussion. Joining us also will be Edwin Hustead, Senior Vice President and Actuary at Hay/Huggins. Ed is in charge of government actuarial and benefit consulting. He is a noted and respected employee benefits expert who is frequently called upon to testify before Congressional committees. Ed has authored numerous studies for the executive and legislative branches, including a study for the Pension Benefit Guaranty Corporation, "Pension Planning Tips in Complying with Regulatory Changes."

Angela Chang

(The text of Chang's discussion is substantially identical to her paper, pp. 111–14 of this volume, and is omitted here.)

Robert L. Clark

It is very nice to have the eyes of a young scholar looking at some of these old issues concerning employer pensions. Angela has done a very nice job of examining a series of studies and determining how and why they differ. I started examining trends in the choice of pension plans a few years ago. My initial study examined data provided by the Department of Labor and culminated in the book with the American Enterprise Institute to which Angela has referred. That study examined the choice of a pension plan. When firms and workers evaluate the type of pension plan to establish, they consider the various differences in those plans and assess which type of plan is most practical and applicable for them.

As Angela stated, firms can provide a dollar's worth of benefit or cost from either kind of plan. Thus the choice of plan type is not an issue of how much money to allocate to the company pension. Instead, selection of a plan type is an issue of the nature of retirement security that the plan sponsor seeks to provide its workers. What are the objectives that a firm is trying to achieve? And what are the objectives that a worker is trying to achieve? Defined benefit and defined contribution plans differ substantially in who bears various types of risks. Individuals and firms can assess the importance of financial market risk, labor turnover risk, and inflation risk. People look at what types of risk they must bear, and make the decision on what type of plan is best for them.

It certainly would be presumptuous for us to decide that one type of plan is necessarily better for all types of workers in all situations. In fact, differences in firm and worker preferences are why we see distribution of these types of plans across the various companies in the United States. Some firms and workers examine the two types of plans and conclude that it's in their best interest to have a defined benefit plan. They then proceed to establish and maintain such a plan. Other firms choose defined contribution plans. The issue I have been examining is why, over time, the distribution of plans has changed. Is it because of government regulation? Is it because of shifts in the economy? Are there other determinants of this trend? Concern over the shift away from defined benefit plans and toward greater use of defined contribution plans is how my earlier study began. The objective was to measure the changes in the use of various types of pension plans and to determine why the distribution of pension plans is changing.

Since my study, several other researchers have examined this trend. The specific question has become blurred with the publication of these studies. If you read the papers that Angela reviewed, you will notice that there is debate over whether the sample observations should be weighted. I have had long conversations with each of the other authors. Each begins by agreeing that the question of interest is the choice of a pension plan. All parties agree that one needs to specify a plan choice function. I conclude that to analyze this choice process one must examine the decisions by plan sponsors, that is, decisions to offer a pension plan and what type of plan to establish. Several others involved in this debate agree that we want to examine the decisions of plan sponsors but argue that the observations need to be weighted. That is simply wrong.

The issue concerning weighting is, do you want to look at the distribution of plans, which I have done, or do you want to look at the distribution of workers covered. Weighting shifts the unit of analysis from plans to participants. These are two separate issues. Angela's paper clearly outlines the differences in these two separate questions. My real disagreement with the other studies cited by Angela is that they examine the second question concerning the distribution of participants while asserting that they are answering the first question concerning the distribution of plans. This is the basic difference in the papers. I would encourage you to read the papers carefully and consider the difference in the two questions.

Today I want to discuss the distribution of plan choices and how they change over time. Angela has indicated that in our earlier work we estimated that about 20 percent of the decline in the proportion of plans that are defined benefit plans is attributable to compositional changes in the economy, such as changes in the proportion of plans in various industries and of various plan size. About 80 percent is due to the change in the estimated coefficients in our model. The changes represent shifts in the plan choice structure or a change in firm preferences. One does not know why these changes in plan choice have occurred. We can, however, speculate on why this trend is occurring. We examined potential determinants of these trends in the book and were able to rule out certain possible influences. The evidence suggests that regulatory changes have been one of the primary factors driving the trend towards greater use of defined contribution plans.

Part of the disagreement across the studies under review may be due to the jargon problems Angela described. In the book we use "regulation" to refer to all government policy, including changes in the opportunity for new types of defined contribution plans, tax policy, and regulation that affects administrative costs. We use "regulation" broadly defined, not narrowly defined. In her talk, Angela mentioned regulation ("regs," as she called it), and then she had tax policy and other aspects of government policy. We put all of these items under one heading.

I would like to focus the remainder of my remarks on some new research examining these trends. After Ray asked me to make this presentation, I agreed to update and extend our previous analysis. Our paper includes an update of our earlier analysis to include data from 1988. In addition, we present a more detailed assessment of the trends by firm size. The unit of analysis is firms with at least one primary defined benefit plan. Thus we are biasing this result to show more defined benefit plans. If a company had both defined benefit and defined contribution plans, obviously it has at least one defined benefit plan and would be included in the defined benefit category.

Table 1 in the paper (p. 118) shows a change in the size distribution of firms with pension plans. A larger percentage of pensions in 1988 were in small firms. This is part of a structural change in the economy. Table 1 also shows the change in the percent of the firms in each size category that have a defined benefit plan. Notice that even the largest plans, with 10,000 or more participants, show a 10.4 percentage point decline in the proportion of firms with defined benefit plans between 1977 and 1988. An examination of these numbers indicates that a larger proportion of the decline is among small plans, but it's incorrect to assert that there is no change in the distribution of pension plans among large firms.

If you have read our book, you may recall the results shown in Table 3 (p. 119). This is an estimation of the plan choice process equation using a logit equation. The dependent variable is (zero/one) "Does the company have at least one primary defined benefit plan?" You can see that the results for 1977 and 1985 are the same as those that we presented in our book, while the 1988 results are extensions of our earlier analysis. The results contain several interesting observations. For instance, the smallest plans are much less likely to have a defined benefit plan than the larger plans. Notice also that there is a time trend away from defined benefit plans. More recently established plans are less likely to be defined benefit plans. This is shown in the relative size of the coefficients on the effective date variables in all three equations.

The issue has been raised that relatively few changes were occurring among large firms. To examine this assertion, we estimated the plan choice equation by firm size category. Table 5 (p. 122) shows independent estimates for each of the five firm size categories in 1977. Not included in the table are the estimated coefficients for 110 three-digit SIC coding industries that are included in the equations. Thus the analysis holds constant the weighting of companies across these 110 categories. A similar exercise using the 1988 data is shown in Table 6 (p. 123). Notice that in both years, for all size categories, there is a trend away from the use of defined benefit plans shown by the estimated coefficients on the effective start date of the pension plan. Even among the largest plans there is a substantial difference in the probability of a firm having a defined benefit plan the more recently established the plan. Among the large firms starting new plans, they are much more likely to be defined contribution plans than defined benefit plans.

Next we determined the difference between the probability of a company having at least one defined benefit plan in 1988 and the probability of a company having at least one defined benefit plan in 1977. These results are shown in Table 4 (p. 121) of the paper. The difference between the probabilities of having a defined benefit plan in 1988 and in 1977 indicates the total change in the probability of having defined benefit plans between the two years. Earlier Angela mentioned that the change using plans of all size categories together was 15 percent between 1977 and 1985 across all plans. Table 4 shows the magnitude of decline between 1977 and 1985. Declines in the likelihood of a firm having a defined benefit plan were 15.0 percent between 1977 and 1985 and 11.2 percent between 1985 and 1988. The change in probability can be decomposed into how much is due to holding constant the coefficients in the 1977 equation while changing the values of the explanatory variables. Simply stated, this allows the structure of the economy to change while holding constant the firms' preferences. The actual change in the structure of the economy between 1977 and 1985 accounted for 3.2 percent of the total change in the likelihood of a firm having a defined benefit plan. Between 1985 and 1988, the decline due to structural changes was only 1.7 percent. Thus approximately 20 percent of the total decline in the probability of a firm offering a defined benefit plan is due to structural changes.

To indicate that this is not due just to changes among small plans, we estimate the plan choice equation separately by firm size categories and complete the decomposition calculation again for each of the five groups. These results are shown in Tables 5, 6, and 7 (pp. 122–24). For each of the five size categories, Table 5 shows the estimates of the 1977 predicted probability equation, Table 6 shows the same results for 1988, and Table 7 reports the results of the decomposition of the decline in defined benefit coverage between 1977 and 1988. For each size category, the 1988 predicted probability of a firm having a defined benefit plan is lower than the probability found in 1977. The bottom part of Table 7 separates the total percentage point decline due to the structural change in the economy from the proportion due to the change in the plan choice. You can see that in each of these size categories the proportion due to the change in the structure of the economy is less than the 20 percent that we reported overall. Looking within the size categories does not support the conclusion that there is no decline in the use of defined benefit plans among the larger plans.

Remember, these results relate to the distribution of pension plans and not to the distribution of pension participants. Comparing the results with what you might find in the other papers reviewed by Angela, the differences are clear. For example, consider the case of Ford Motor Company mentioned earlier by Marc. Ford Motor Company has had a substantial reduction in employment resulting in a large reduction in the number of people covered by its pension. Our research methodology, which examines the distribution of plans, indicates that there has been no change at Ford. They still have the same plan; they still are offering that plan; the company is still in existence. The methodology of the other authors would examine this change and conclude that coverage by defined benefit pension plans has declined. Both observations are correct. The key difference is the issue being examined. Are you trying to determine changes in the distribution of plans or changes in participant coverage?

Within the analysis that we have discussed today, there are major changes in the determinants affecting the choice of pension plans among firms of all sizes, including large firms. This is primarily due to new companies, companies trying to decide whether or not to offer pension plans. These firms are now much more likely to offer defined contribution plans rather than defined benefit plans. While there are some terminations of defined benefit plans and new starts of defined contribution plans among mature companies, most of the trend away from the use of defined benefit plans appears to be due to new companies that are growing larger and establishing defined contribution plans.

Thank you for the opportunity to discuss trends in the use of pension plans. Once again, I thank Angela, who has done an outstanding job of crystallizing and clarifying some points that were being debated among pension analysts. Her paper and this symposium will help advance research examining trends in the choice of pension plans.

Edwin C. Hustead

I will take the dubious responsibility for having said to Ray, "Was this a memorial service for the defined benefit plan or not?" I do not know if that is why I was placed in the dubious role of being the last person before lunch. I do have one chart (Figure 1) that shows exactly what everybody else has said, but I guess they will let me show it. It's kind of

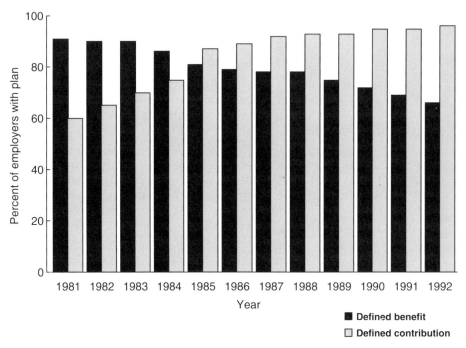

Figure 1. Prevalence of plans by type. Source: Hay/Huggins Company, Inc., *Hay/Huggins Benefit Report*, September 1992.

nice when everyone is saying the same thing. This is the trend from the Hay/Huggins Benefits Report (1991) over the last ten years. It shows the defined benefit plan declining from around 90 percent down to 69 percent, whereas defined contribution plans in medium to large employers have grown to 95 percent. Of course, most employers have both kinds, so the total is more than 100 percent. Let me mainly suggest that all of these variables—behavioral patterns, workers' demands, tax policy, replacement rates, production versus income—come down to one thing and that is the interaction between the benefits specialist and the employer when the employer decides to put in a pension plan. All of these occur with this type of organization, but this is what has happened. About ten or fifteen years ago we began to hear that almost all new plans were defined contribution plans. We said, "Don't worry. These are all small employers; they come and go; the large employers are going to keep their plans." What we did not recognize then and lost sight of is that small employers become medium employers and medium employers become big employers. I think that underlies most of the trends that are on these charts that we have just shown.

So, consider the cycle and what happens when an employer decides to put in a retirement plan. Now let me refer to three decades: the 1960s, the 1970s, and 1980s. You have a small employer. He has made it through the Darwinian scuffle of the first five years. He is one of the hundred or so that survive; he is now doing well. He has fifty or seventy-five employees and is paying good salaries. He is giving leave and has taken care of insurance and says, "Now I've got to think about retirement plans. Let's call in one of those, what are they called, actuaries. . . . Let's see what I can do. How can I be competitive and help my employees save money?" In the 1960s we said, "Well, put it in a retirement plan." Now to us, that was like the man who when he was 65 years old found out he had been speaking prose all his life. We now know that these are called defined benefit plans. But back then all we knew was a retirement plan was a retirement plan. There was only one plan. If you wanted to put in a savings plan, okay, but a defined benefit plan was the answer, and we helped them choose one and put in that plan.

The 1970s came along. ERISA, of course, was very significant; and we began to be aware of defined benefit, defined contribution; and there were choices; and there were pros and cons on both sides. During that period, if you had gone with the benefits consultant or the actuary to that critical meeting, you would have gotten a fairly balanced perspective on what should have been put in place.

Since the 1980s, however, employers have been hearing something like this, "Well, there are two types of plans, there's a defined benefit plan and there's a defined contribution plan. Let me explain a little bit of what they are and what your choices are. First of all, on the defined benefit side; it's going to cost you $10,000 just to put that plan in place, it's going to cost you $5,000 to $10,000 a year just to keep it going." Despite what Anna said, it is going to cost you twice as much to fund that plan. It is true that if you are going to pay equal dollars, you are going to get equal percentage benefit, but as a practical matter, the typical plan you would install is going to cost six to eight percent of payroll for a defined benefit plan and two to three percent for a defined contribution plan. "As far as your employees are concerned, they are going to be much more excited and interested in the defined contribution plan than the defined benefit plan. You're going to get much more return for that expenditure than you put in. So, I would be glad to tell you about defined benefit plans, if you really want me to, but you don't want one, unless you have unusual circumstances, so let's install a defined contribution plan. Let's talk 401(k), profit sharing, and all the other avenues that are there and pick what's best for you." That is what has happened, and I emphasize what we will hear, I think, over the next couple days several times: that much of change is driven by the expense and much of that, most of that, is driven by the laws and the regulations put on defined benefit plans. As long as we have that, the small employers who become the medium-sized and large employers are going to adopt defined contribution plans. Ten years from now perhaps you will see only governments and only the large, very long-term organizations having defined benefit plans; and the defined contribution plans will be the name of the game. Thank you.

References

Hay/Huggins Company, Inc. 1992. *Hay/Huggins Benefits Report.* September.

The Trend Away from Defined Benefit Pension Plans
Angela Chang

1. Introduction

Between 1975 and 1988, of all workers covered by primary pension plans, the proportion with defined benefit plans declined from 87 percent to 66 percent. This trend away from defined benefit plans has occurred among firms of all sizes and across all major industries.

I have reviewed three studies by the following economists about the declining prevalence of primary single-employer defined benefit plans: Clark and McDermed (1990), Gustman and Steinmeier (1992), and Ippolito (1992). These studies focus on two explanations for the trend away from defined benefit plans: a shift in preferences of firms and a shift in employment. The first emphasizes the effects of pension regulations. Regulations of defined benefit plans have become complex and have raised the costs of sponsoring defined benefit versus defined contribution plans. A Hay/Huggins study (1990) reports that the per-worker administrative cost for a 15-worker defined benefit plan increased from $162 in 1981 to $455 in 1991, an increase of 181 percent. During the same period, the per-worker administrative cost for a 15-worker defined contribution plan increased by only 99 percent and were half as large as those for defined benefit plans. The cost disadvantage of defined benefit plans exists for larger plans as well.

The second explanation, a shift in employment, stresses the importance of changes in the U.S. labor market. For example, employment has grown in service-oriented industries where defined contribution plans are more commonly offered, and has declined in manufacturing industries where defined benefit plans traditionally have been favored. Also, the fraction of workers covered by unions has fallen; unions have typically favored defined benefit plans.

2. Review of Studies

The three studies (see Table 1) use data from the IRS Form 5500 Annual Pension Plan Reports. They use different measures of the trend away from defined benefit plans and of the shift in employment. They also use different statistical techniques.

Clark and McDermed focus on the decline in the percentage of firms that offer primary single-employer defined benefit plans as the measure of the trend away from defined benefit plans. They estimate a decline of 15 percentage points between 1977 and 1985. They estimate that 21 percent of this decline is due to a shift in the distribution of firms away from sectors that have traditionally favored defined benefit plans. They assume the remaining 79 percent is due to a shift in firms' preferences.

Unlike Clark and McDermed, Gustman and Steinmeier focus on the decline in the percentage of employees covered by defined benefit plans as the measure of the trend away from defined benefit plans. They estimate a decline of 10.3 percentage points between 1977 and 1985. They estimate that 40 percent of the decline is due to a shift in firms' preferences. They assume the remaining 60 percent is due to a shift in the distribution of workers across sectors.

Like Gustman and Steinmeier, Ippolito focuses on the decline in the percentage of employees covered by primary defined benefit plans as the measure of the trend away from defined benefit plans and the shift in the distribution of workers across sectors as the measure of the shift in employment.

Ippolito uses more recent and more complete data than those used in the other two studies. He examines a later period, 1979 to 1987, and uses information on the union status of pension plans. He estimates a decline of 11.7 percentage points during the period. He estimates that 45 percent of the decline is attributable to a shift in firms' preferences and assumes that the remaining 55 percent is due to a shift in the distribution of workers across sectors.

3. Conclusion

The conclusion we can draw from these studies is that how we choose to measure the trend away from defined benefit plans is quite important. If we define the trend in terms of the decline in the number of firms offering defined benefit plans, then the study by Clark and McDermed suggests that the trend is due primarily to a shift in firms' preferences. If we define the trend in terms of the decline in the

TABLE 1   Summary of Findings: Decomposition of the Trend Away from
            Defined Benefit Plans Among Primary Single-Employer Plans

| | *Percent of trend away from defined benefit plans due to a shift in:* | | |
| | | Employment | |
Author(s)[a]	Firms' preferences	Distribution of workers	Distribution of firms
Clark and McDermed	79	[b]	21
Gustman and Steinmeier	40	60	[b]
Ippolito	45	55	[b]

[a]These figures are not exactly comparable because of differences in samples, explanatory variables, and procedures. Three major differences deserve mentioning. First, the focus of the studies is different. Clark and McDermed (1990) focus on the number of firms that offer defined benefit plans. Gustman and Steinmeier (1992) and Ippolito (1992) focus on the number of employees covered by defined benefits plans. Second, Clark and McDermed do not weight their data. Gustman and Steinmeier and Ippolito weight their data by plan size. Third, Clark and McDermed examine a change in the distribution of firms across sectors. Both Gustman and Steinmeier and Ippolito examine a change in the distribution of workers across sectors.
[b]Not estimated.

number of workers covered by defined benefit plans, then the studies by Gustman and Steinmeier and by Ippolito suggest that a shift in firms' preferences explains less than half of the decline.

A caveat applies to the results from these studies. Each of the three studies directly estimates the portion of the trend away from defined benefit plans due to only one of two factors: a shift in firms' preferences or a shift in employment. Each assumes the remaining portion of the trend is due to the other factor, which is not directly estimated. This procedure may overestimate the portion of the trend due to the factor that is not directly estimated.

Although a shift in firms' preferences does seem to be a significant factor, none of the studies examines the specific reasons for this diminished popularity of defined benefit plans with employers such as whether regulations have raised the costs and have reduced the advantages of defined benefit plans or whether changes in the U.S. labor and product markets have made employers more reluctant to bear the investment risk associated with defined benefit pensions. Moreover, the studies provide little insight into the effects of the trend away from defined benefit plans on the welfare of workers, in terms of pension coverage or future retirement income.

References

Chang, Angela. 1991. *Explanations for the Trend Away from Defined Benefit Pension Plans.* U.S. Library of Congress Congressional Research Service, CRS Report for Congress No. 91-647 EPW. Washington, DC: U.S. Government Printing Office.

Clark, Robert L. and Ann A. McDermed. 1990. *The Choice of Pension Plans in a Changing Regulatory Environment.* Washington, DC: American Enterprise Institute.

Gustman, Alan L. and Thomas L. Steinmeier. 1992. "The Stampede Toward Defined Contribution Pension Plans: Fact or Fiction?" *Industrial Relations 3,* 1 (Spring): 361–69.

Hay/Huggins Company, Inc. 1990. *Pension Plan Study for the Pension Benefit Guaranty Corporation.* September.

Ippolito, Richard A. 1992. "The Proliferation of Defined Contribution Plans." Unpublished manuscript. March.

Firm Choice of Type of Pension Plan: Trends and Determinants
Robert L. Clark, Ann A. McDermed, and Michelle White Trawick

Introduction

In our recent book (Clark and McDermed, 1990), we outlined the factors that influence firms' decisions to offer pension plans and examined the determinants of whether a firm chooses to offer a defined benefit or defined contribution pension plan. A central theme of the analysis was that defined benefit plans offer firms greater opportunity for modifying worker retirement patterns, quit rates, and effort. In addition, the two plan types have different levels of various types of risk for the worker and firm. These risks include those associated with mobility or turnover, rate of return to pension investments, and inflation before and after retirement.

Given the different nature of the two types of plans, it is not surprising that some firms select defined-benefit plans while other firms believe defined contribution plans are the better type of retirement plan. Historically, most small, non-union, non-manufacturing firms have selected defined contribution plans as their primary retirement plan while larger, unionized firms have opted for defined benefit plans. Defined benefit plans were the preferred choice until the late 1970s for firms with 100 or more employees across all major industrial and size categories.

Beginning in the 1970s, the distribution of pension plans began to change rapidly. Using data from the Internal Revenue Service Form 5500 (Annual Return/Report of Employer Benefit Plan), we (Clark and McDermed, 1990) examined the choice of pension plan type in 1977, 1980, and 1985. The analysis was restricted to firms that offered some type of pension and had at least 100 employees. We reported changes in the distribution of primary pension plans and the distribution of participants in primary plans. For both measures, the proportion in defined benefit plans declined in every one-digit SIC group and for all size categories that we examined. When comparing changes within more detailed SIC industries (two- and three-digit industries), we found that the proportion of firms with defined benefit plans declined in over 95 percent of these industrial groups.

To explain why these changes were occurring, a model of plan choice was estimated. Because the objective was to determine why the proportion of firms with defined benefit plans was changing, the analysis focused on the choice of plan type by firms. The estimated decision function was whether a firm with a pension plan offered at least one primary defined benefit plan.

The results indicated that for firms of the same size and in the same three-digit industrial group, those who established their plans more recently were much more likely to have only defined contribution plans. Comparing the 1985 results to those for 1977, we estimated that only about 20 percent of the 15 percentage point decline in the proportion of firms with primary defined benefit plans was caused by structural changes in the economy. The other 80 percent of the decline was due to changes in the plan choice process. We speculated that this shift in plan preferences was caused by changes in public policies that increased the price of offering defined benefit plans and made defined contribution plans more accessible.

This work has been reviewed by researchers and policy makers for its implications for pension regulation and other public policies. The findings have been criticized on several grounds. These criticisms include that the analysis did not properly weight the data, that the results stop in 1985 and should be extended using more recent data, and that we did not isolate changes among larger plans. This paper addresses each of these criticisms. The results of this new study strongly reinforce the conclusions of our earlier work.

Should Plan Choice Equations Be Weighted?

The primary objectives of our study were to examine the choice of pension plans by firms, to determine changes in the distribution of pension plans by type in the United States, and to estimate the reasons for these changes. Papers by Ippolito (1992), Gustman and Steinmeier (1992), and Kruse (1991) have also attempted to examine the trend toward greater use of defined contribution plans.

These studies weighted the observations of primary plans by the number of participants in the plan. After weighting, they conclude that the proportion of the trend attributable to structural changes in the economy is approximately 50 percent instead of the 20 percent reported in our book.

Although there are other differences in statistical methodology across these studies, the main source of variation in the estimated proportion of the trend toward defined contribution plans attributable to changes in the plan choice process is the result of weighting the plan observations by the number of participants in the plan. Are participant-weighted estimates appropriate if one is trying to understand changes in distribution of pension plans? The answer is clearly no. Weighting the data by number of participants in the plan transforms the analysis from a study of the distribution of plans to a study examining the distribution of participants.

Consider the following hypothetical example. Suppose that total employment in 1980 in manufacturing was ten million and all these workers were covered by 100 primary defined benefit plans, while employment in the retail trade was five million with all these workers participating in 200 primary defined contribution plans. Assume that changes in the economy altered employment patterns between 1980 and 1985 such that in 1985 only eight million people are employed in manufacturing, no firms have gone out of business, and no pension plans have been terminated. There still remain 100 primary defined benefit plans in this sector, but now they cover only eight million workers. In contrast, employment increases in retail trade from five to seven million, there are no new firms, and no new pension plans are established. In this industry, there remain 200 defined contribution plans that now cover seven million workers.

In this example, there has been no change in the distribution of pension plans but there has been a major change in the distribution of participants by plan type. Chang (1991) provides a clear discussion of how weighting transforms the nature of the research study. Our point is not that the distribution of participants by plan type is uninteresting or unimportant. It is, however, a different question than the one that we have been studying. It is clear that, if one wants to examine changes in the distribution of pension plans, weighting by the number of participants in each plan is inappropriate.

Updating the Analysis Through 1988

The trend toward greater use of defined contribution plans continued between 1985 and 1988. As Table 1 shows, the proportion of firms with pension plans that had at least one defined benefit plan declined in each of six firm-size categories. Among firms with fewer than 2,500 employees, declines ranged from 7.7 percentage points for firms with

TABLE 1   Distribution of Firms with Pension Plans and Proportion of Firms with at Least One Defined Benefit Plan by Firm Size*

Firm size (number of employees)	Distribution of firms with pension plans			Proportion of firms with at least one defined benefit plan		
	1977	1985	1988	1977	1985	1988
100–249	27.2	30.9	32.0	60.0	45.4	37.7
250–499	24.3	24.6	24.3	63.8	47.8	35.5
500–999	17.9	16.2	15.6	71.6	56.2	45.6
1,000–2,499	14.5	12.5	12.6	78.5	67.4	58.2
2,500–9,999	9.8	8.8	8.6	82.6	74.4	68.4
10,000+	6.3	7.0	6.9	90.0	85.4	79.6

Source: Data tape containing the IRS Form 5500 reports for all firms with 100 or more participants was provided by the U.S. Department of Labor.
*Sample is limited to primary pension plans as determined by the Department of Labor.

100 to 249 employees to 12.3 percentage points for firms with 250 to 499 employees. Somewhat smaller declines occurred among larger firms, with the decline in the two largest categories being about 6 percentage points. It is important to note that the trend toward greater use of defined contribution plans was large and significant even among the largest firms.

Table 2 reports similar changes in the distribution of participants by firm size. Among firms with less than 1,000 employees, the decline in participants in primary defined benefit plans is of similar size to the decline in the proportion of primary plans that are defined benefit. Among larger firms, however, the absolute decline in the proportion of defined benefit participants is somewhat less than the decline in the proportion of firms with defined benefit plans reported in Table 1. Surprisingly, for firms with 10,000 or more employees there is a slight increase between 1985 and 1988 in the proportion of participants that are in defined benefit plans.

The first two columns of Table 3 repeat the results reported in our book for 1977 and 1985, while the third column presents new estimates for 1988. The dependent variable in this analysis is "Does the firm have at least one primary defined benefit plan?" The equations are estimated using a probit model and include 109 dichotomous industrial variables as well as the variables for firm size and effective date of the oldest plan offered by the firm. The table entries are the estimated change in the probability of a firm offering a defined benefit plan when the indicated variable has a value of one instead of zero when the other variables in the model are held constant at their sample means. The comparisons are made relative to a plan established between 1964 and

TABLE 2   Distribution of Pension Participants and Proportion of
Participants in Defined Benefit Plans by Firm Size*

Firm size (number of employees)	Distribution of pension participants by firm size†			Proportion of participants in defined benefit plans‡		
	1977	1985	1988	1977	1985	1988
100–249	3.2	4.2	4.5	63.4	46.9	36.7
250–499	4.9	5.6	5.8	68.9	51.1	39.5
500–999	6.5	6.8	6.9	76.9	60.7	51.1
1,000–2,499	10.7	11.0	11.7	83.3	71.1	65.0
2,500–9,999	19.9	18.4	19.3	88.6	77.4	74.6
10,000+	54.8	53.9	51.9	90.1	85.2	87.0
Total	100.0	100.0	100.0			
Total participants (millions)	16.3	26.3	27.0			

Source: See Table 1.
*Sample is limited to primary pension plans as determined by the Department of Labor.
†Entries in each column indicate the proportion of pension participants enrolled in plans sponsored by firms of various sizes. For example, the first entry for 1977 indicates that 3.2 percent of all pension participants were in plans sponsored by firms with 100–249 employees. Column entries total 100.0 percent.
‡Entries indicate the proportion of pension participants enrolled in defined-benefit plans. For example, the first entry for 1977 indicates that 63.4 percent of pension participants in plans sponsored by firms with 100–249 employees were in defined benefit plans and, therefore, 36.6 percent were in defined contribution plans.

TABLE 3   Estimated Defined Benefit Coverage: 5500 Forms*

Variables	1977	1985	1988
Number of employees			
100–499	−0.187†	−0.251†	−0.266†
500–999	−0.118†	−0.180†	−0.184†
Effective date			
Before 1942	0.203†	0.262†	0.326†
1942–1953	0.092†	0.169†	0.216†
1954–1963	0.010	0.049†	0.068†
1974–1979	−0.116†	−0.159†	−0.154†
1980–1985		−0.302†	−0.282†
1986–1988			−0.353†
Constant	0.249†	0.239†	0.213†
Proportion defined benefit	0.697	0.561	0.465
Predicted probability	0.728	0.580	0.462
Log likelihood function	−6,901	−12,722	−14,237
Number of firms	13,016	22,880	26,336

Source: See Table 1.
*The dependent variable in these equations is *Does the firm have at least one primary defined benefit plan?* The variable has a value of 1 if yes and a value of 0 if no. All equations also contain 109 dichotomous variables indicating the three-digit SIC of the plan sponsor.
†Estimated coefficient is significantly different from zero at the 0.01 confidence level.

1973 in a firm with 1,000 or more employees. The 1988 results are similar to those for 1977 and 1985. The estimated effects for the effective date variables indicate that the trend for firms with more recently established plans not to offer defined benefit plans accelerated between 1986 and 1988.

To examine the cause of the trend away from defined benefit plans shown in Table 3, we re-estimate the model without the effective date variables. The estimated probit coefficients and sample means are used to predict the probability of having at least one defined benefit plan. This process predicts the probability that the average firm in a given year would have at least one defined benefit plan. Table 4 reports these results for two time periods: 1977 to 1985 and 1985 to 1988. The first row shows the predicted probability of the average 1977 firm having defined benefit plans in 1977. This is computed using the estimated plan choice model for 1977 and the sample mean values for 1977. This describes the distribution of pension plans that actually existed in 1977.

The second row shows the probability predicted by the 1977 estimates and the 1985 sample means. This is an indication of how the probability of a firm having a defined benefit plan would have changed for the average firm if the plan choice process had remained at its 1977 level but the structure of the economy shifted as it actually did between 1977 and 1985. The third row shows the probability of the average firm in 1985 having at least one defined benefit plan predicted from the 1985 estimates of plan choice and the 1985 means.

The difference between the first and third rows shows the total change in the predicted probability between 1977 and 1985. The difference in the first and second row is the estimated change due to structural shifts in the economy while the difference between the second and third row is the estimated impact of shifts in preferences by employers. The bottom half of the table indicates that only 21 percent of the 15 percentage point decline is estimated to have been attributable to structural change in the economy.

The results of the 1985 to 1988 period show that the change in the predicted probability of a firm having at least one defined benefit plan declined from 57.4 percent in 1985 to 46.2 in 1988. Holding constant the plan choice process but allowing for structural changes in the economy, the probability would have declined from 57.4 to 55.7 percent. Thus, during this more recent period, the proportion of the decline due to structural changes in the economy is estimated to account for only 15.2 percent of the decline in the use of defined benefit plans.

This update of the analysis of trends in the use of defined benefit plans indicates that the movement away from the use of defined bene-

TABLE 4 Decomposition of Total Decline in Probability of a Firm Having at Least One Defined Benefit Plan

Predicted probability of having at least one defined benefit plan, 1977–88

1977	0.724
1985 (no change in coefficients)	0.692
1985	0.574
1988 (no change in coefficients)	0.557
1988	0.462

Decline in probability of having at least one defined benefit plan

	1977–1985	1985–1988
Total decline in probability in percentage points	15.0	11.2
Decline due to structural change	3.2	1.7
(Percent of change)	(21.3)	(15.2)
Decline due to change in plan choice	11.8	9.5
(Percent of change)	(78.7)	(84.8)

fit plans continued during the last half of the 1980s and that the driving force for this change continued to be the shift in firm preferences away from the relative use of defined benefit plans. In fact, the annual rate of decline in use of defined benefit plans actually increased and the proportion of the decline attributable to structural changes declined.

Assessment of Trends by Firm Size

The final criticism of our earlier study was that we had not given sufficient attention to the differences in plan choices between small and large firms. The estimates for 1977 and 1985 reported in our book included control variables for three firm sizes (100–499, 500–999, and 1,000 and over). The estimates clearly indicated that smaller firms were less likely to have defined benefit plans and that the difference between small and large firms grew over time. Table 3 shows that firms with 100 to 499 employees were 18.7 percent less likely to have a defined benefit plan in 1977 than firms with 1,000 or more employees while in 1985 this difference had increased to 25.1 percent. Our updated findings show that this gap continued to widen to 26.6 percent in 1988.

The methodology used in the earlier study calculated changes in the distribution of pension plans taking into account differences in firm size. However, the statistical procedure did require the other plan choice parameters (the estimated probit coefficients) to be the same across the various firm sizes. Given the different costs and incentives

TABLE 5   Estimated Defined Benefit Coverage: 5500 Forms by Size Categories, 1977*

	Number of employees				
	100–249	250–499	500–999	1,000–2,499	2,500+
Effective date					
Before 1942	0.286†	0.210‡	0.041	0.162†	0.107†
1942–1953	0.118†	0.123†	0.070‡	0.061‡	0.045†
1954–1963	0.048‡	−0.010	−0.008	0.000	0.005
1974–1979	−0.127†	−0.118†	−0.111†	−0.102†	−0.085†
Constant	0.100	0.193†	−0.019	−0.234‡	0.012
Proportion defined benefit	0.601	0.639	0.714	0.785	0.851
Predicted probability	0.614	0.654	0.741	0.828	0.902
Log likelihood function	−2,110	−1,862	−1,226	−824	−724
Number of firms	3,531	3,173	2,334	1,892	2,086

Source: See Table 1.
*All four equations also contain 70 dichotomous variables indicating the three-digit SIC of the sponsor.
†Estimated coefficients are significantly different from zero at the 0.01 confidence level.
‡Estimated coefficients are significantly different from zero at the 0.05 confidence level.

facing small and large firms, it is reasonable to expect that the plan choice process itself would be different in small firms compared to large firms.

To explore the differences in plan choice, we divided plan sponsors into five size categories: 100–249, 250–499, 500–999, 1,000–2,499, and 2,500 or more employees. Separate estimates of the plan choice equations by firm size are shown in Table 5 for 1977 and Table 6 for 1988. Each equation also includes 70 dichotomous variables indicating the three-digit SIC of the plan sponsor.

The results show a clear time trend away from the use of defined benefit plans in all firm-size categories. In the 1988 estimates, firms with 100 to 249 employees whose oldest pension plan had been established prior to 1942 were 32.6 percent more likely to have a defined benefit plan than firms with plans established between 1964 and 1973. In contrast, firms with plans established in the 1980s were over 25 percent less likely to have defined benefit plans.

The sharp trend away from having defined benefit plans is observed in every size category even among firms with 2,500 or more employees. Statistical analysis confirms that the plan choice process was significantly different in 1988 compared to 1977 in every size category. This analysis indicates that firms of similar size and industry were behaving

TABLE 6 Estimated Defined Benefit Coverage: 5500 Forms by Size Categories, 1988*

	Number of employees				
	100–249	250–499	500–999	1,000–2,499	2,500+
Effective date					
Before 1942	0.326†	0.466†	0.085	0.202‡	0.200†
1942–1953	0.192†	0.233†	0.222†	0.154†	0.161†
1954–1963	0.088†	0.079†	0.039	0.037	0.029
1974–1979	−0.142†	−0.139†	−0.137†	−0.157†	−0.111†
1980–1985	−0.257†	−0.242†	−0.301†	−0.297†	−0.233†
1986–1989	−0.315†	−0.293†	−0.330†	−0.397†	−0.323†
Constant	−0.120	−0.134‡	−0.259‡	−0.067	0.013
Proportion defined benefit	0.377	0.355	0.456	0.582	0.734
Predicted probability	0.354	0.332	0.447	0.609	0.791
Log likelihood function	−4,705	−3,502	−2,276	1,699	−1,848
Number of firms	8,424	6,401	4,118	3,326	4,067

Source: See Table 1.
*All four equations also contain 70 dichotomous variables indicating the three-digit SIC of the sponsor.
†Estimated coefficients are significantly different from zero at the 0.01 confidence level.
‡Estimated coefficients are significantly different from zero at the 0.05 confidence level.

differently in 1988 relative to 1977 when selecting the type of pension plan to offer.

Table 7 reports changes in the predicted probability of the average firm having at least one defined benefit plan between 1977 and 1988 for each of the firm-size categories. For plan sponsors with fewer than 2,500 employees, the decline in the likelihood of having at least one defined benefit plan ranged between 22 and 31 percentage points. Among firms with over 2,500 employees, the decline was approximately 13 percentage points. The second row of the table shows the decline in the probability of the average firm having a defined benefit plan that is predicted to have occurred if the plan choice process had remained constant but the economy had evolved as it actually did between 1977 and 1988. The bottom half of the table illustrates the decomposition of the changes into the portion due to structural changes in the economy and that due to shifts in the plan choice process. In each of the size categories, the proportion of the change attributable to structural changes in the economy is less than 18 percent. The estimated impact of structural changes in the economy is lowest for large firms.

TABLE 7   Decomposition of Total Decline in Probability of Having at Least
One Defined Benefit Plan

	Number of employees				
	100–249	250–499	500–999	1,000–2,499	2,500+
Predicted probability of having at least one defined benefit plan					
1977	0.611	0.651	0.739	0.821	0.889
1988 (no change in coefficients)	0.568	0.602	0.702	0.787	0.878
1988	0.367	0.343	0.449	0.598	0.757
Decline in probability of having at least one defined benefit plan					
Total decline of probability in percentage points	24.4	30.8	29.0	22.3	13.2
Decline due to structural change	4.3	4.9	3.7	3.4	1.1
(Percent of change)	(17.6)	(15.9)	(12.8)	(15.2)	(8.3)
Decline due to change in plan choice	20.1	25.9	25.3	18.9	12.1
(Percent of change)	(82.4)	(84.1)	(87.2)	(84.8)	(91.7)

Source: See Table 1.

Summary of Findings

In our earlier work, we examined the decision process of firms selecting a type of pension plan and applied this model of plan choice to data
from IRS Form 5500 files for 1977 and 1985. These estimates are for
all firms with at least 100 employees that offer a pension plan. We
documented a substantial trend toward greater use of defined contribution plans and estimated that only a small proportion of the trend
could be explained by structural changes in the economy.

Our findings have been reviewed by researchers and policy analysts
because of their important implications for pension policy. The results
have been criticized on three grounds: the lack of participant weighting, the need for more recent data, and the necessity for greater
attention to the diversity in the choice process among small and large
firms. This chapter considers each of these items. First, it is clear that
when studying the distribution of pension plans observations should
not be weighted by the number of plan participants and that our model
is the appropriate method for examining changes in the distribution of
pension plans across firms.

Second, updating the results provides further support that the trend away from the use of defined benefit plans is continuing and that structural changes in the economy account for only a small part of the total shift away from defined benefit plans. Third, examining the distribution of plans separately by firm size shows that the trend toward fewer defined benefit plans is present in all firm-size categories but is larger among plans with less than 2,500 employees. However, in all cases, structural changes in the economy are estimated to account for less than 18 percent of the total decline in the relative use of defined benefit plans.

References

Chang, Angela. 1991. *Explanations for the Trend Away from Defined Benefit Pension Plans.* U.S. Library of Congress Congressional Research Service, CRS Report for Congress 91-647 EPW. Washington, DC.

Clark, Robert and Ann McDermed. 1990. *The Choice of Pension Plans in a Changing Regulatory Environment.* Washington, DC: American Enterprise Institute.

Gustman, Alan and Thomas L. Steinmeier. 1992. "The Stampede Toward Defined Contribution Pension Plans: Fact or Fiction?" *Industrial Relations 3,* 1 (Spring): 361–69.

Ippolito, Richard. 1992. "The Proliferation of Defined Contribution Plans." Unpublished manuscript, March.

Kruse, Douglas. 1991. "Pension Substitution in the 1980's: Why the Shift Toward Defined Contribution Pension Plans?" Unpublished manuscript, Rutgers University.

Chapter 4
Death and Taxes: Can We Fund For Retirement Between Them?

Gordon P. Goodfellow and Sylvester J. Schieber

Introduction

From its very beginning, the U.S. government has made a significant commitment to the retirement income security of its older citizens. Initially, this commitment was only to its own employees. It subsequently expanded its commitment to retirement income security by encouraging other employers to offer retirement programs for their own employees' retirement security. The government broadened this commitment once again by directly providing a broad level of retirement benefits with the establishment of Social Security. Over the years, each of these areas of governmental commitment to retirement income security has been amended to account for changing times, needs, etc.

Any commitment implies associated costs, and governmental commitments imply the associated need to pay for them. Today, the governmental commitments to retirement income security are coming under increasing scrutiny and criticism because of the relative burden they place on the current level of government finance and because they pose an even larger burden in the future. This paper seeks to investigate the tradeoffs between the government's commitment to the income security of its older citizenry and the equitable financing of that commitment.

In the next section of this paper we review the evolution of government commitment to retirement income security in the United States and the concerns being voiced about the funding and equity of each of the elements of our retirement system. To be sure, the government plays a major role in each of the elements of our retirement system as they exist today. We believe that it is important to understand the breadth and duration of the government's commitment to retirement income security at each level of the system. This commitment is often overlooked in discussions about the workings or costs of particular elements of the retirement system.

In the third section we focus on Social Security and the funding and equity concerns that relate to the provision of retirement cash income to the eligible aged and disabled under the program. While cash benefits are currently secure under the program, the program is not adequately funded under current law to meet the demands that will be placed on it as the baby boom passes into retirement after the turn of the century. The longer we wait to address the projected underfunding in Social Security, the more disruptive it will be to the retirement planning of those affected. As we address the funding issue, however, it will heighten existing concerns about the value of benefits provided under Social Security in comparison to the taxes workers pay into it. We address this issue, and indeed show that for some workers Social Security, by itself, is not providing a positive return on tax contributions. We argue that returns realized through Social Security should be evaluated in the larger context of federal support for all elements of the retirement system.

In the fourth section we evaluate the federal government's commitment to employer-sponsored retirement programs. Our analysis and conclusions suggest that the estimated costs of the tax preferences accorded these plans has been systematically exaggerated. We also look at the relationship age and work force attachment have with access to pension protection and the utilization of pension-related tax preferences. Here we show that more than 60 percent of the total population between the ages of 45 and 59 are now receiving a pension, participating in one, or married to someone who is. If the people who are not already receiving a pension or who have had no attachment to the work force for more than one year are excluded from the base, the percentage of the population accruing benefits or already receiving a pension jumps to more than 70 percent of this age group.

In the fifth section we look at the combined tax effects of pensions and Social Security on workers at various income levels. Looking at each element of the retirement system without consideration of the others is a bit like the three blind men describing an elephant when one had hold of the trunk, the second had hold of an ear, and the third had hold of a leg. The aggregate structure or equity of the benefits or tax elements supporting our retirement income security system can only be understood by looking at all the component elements. Our analysis suggests that the combined system is somewhat progressive, with lower-paid workers benefiting more than higher-paid workers. The combined pension and Social Security systems results suggest that middle- and higher-paid workers can expect no subsidization of their lifetime retirement savings even though they may participate in generous pension programs.

In the final section of the paper we draw a number of conclusions regarding retirement program policies. Specifically, we argue that the relative strengths of various aspects of the retirement system should be capitalized upon in further modifications to its elements, so the long-term commitment to retirement income security may be met in an efficient manner. We note that the underfunding of Social Security should be addressed with future benefit reductions for higher-paid workers who will reach retirement after the turn of the century. Because employer-sponsored pension plans will never be effective vehicles for providing retirement income security to the lowest-paid workers, whose careers are characterized by short periods of employment with many different employers and frequent periods of unemployment between them, we argue that the retirement income security of such workers should be enhanced through Social Security. Middle- and upper-income workers should be encouraged to support these types of policy changes by the continued support of their employer-sponsored pensions encouraged by the existing incentives in the federal tax system.

I. Background

A. Providing Retirement Income Security

The first national pension law, which dates back to 1776, provided half pay for life or during disability for soldiers disabled during the Revolutionary War. Military provisions based on service date back to 1780. Gradually, service pensions came to be provided separately for veterans of each war. In 1861 the first major nondisability program provided for voluntary retirement of military officers after forty years of duty. In 1885 nondisability retirement was extended to marine and army enlistees, providing voluntary retirement after thirty years of service.[1] In 1920 the federal Civil Service Retirement System was begun. While the federal government's initial commitment was only to the retirement income security of its own employees, when it established the Civil Service Retirement System (CSRS) for its own civilian employees, it began to encourage other employers to establish their own retirement security programs.

The 1921 Revenue Act eliminated current taxation of income for employer-sponsored stock bonus and profit-sharing plans established for "some or all" of their workers. By administrative ruling, pension trusts also were accorded preferential tax treatment, and the 1926 Revenue Act permitted reasonable deductions in excess of currently accruing liabilities, allowing the funding of past service credits.[2] In 1935, the Social Security Act became law, initially extending coverage to roughly 60 percent of all workers engaged in commerce and industry. Gradually, coverage has been extended to cover almost all workers today.

Until 1938, retirement trusts set up by employers were revocable. This allowed plan sponsors to set up such trusts during profitable periods and to revoke them during unprofitable ones. The 1938 Revenue Act modified the revocability provisions and required that retirement trusts be for the exclusive benefit of employees covered under the plans until all plan obligations were met. The pension regulatory environment that was evolving during this period allowed plan sponsors to be selective in the extension of pension benefits among their workers.

In 1940 Social Security began to pay its first annuities. In that year there was also a sharp increase in corporate income tax rates, increasing the value of the tax incentive for employers to set up tax-qualified retirement programs. The 1942 Revenue Act and amendments to it in the 1954 Internal Revenue Code modified the tax qualification standards and changed the tax code to preclude plan sponsors from discriminating in favor of their owners and officers.[3]

In 1974 the Employee Retirement Income Security Act (ERISA) was adopted to assure the widespread and equitable delivery of retirement benefits through employer-sponsored plans. ERISA introduced participation requirements, vesting standards, and a host of other requirements to assure that benefits were provided equitably to large segments of an employer's work force when a plan existed. It also established funding requirements and the Pension Benefit Guaranty Corporation (PBGC) to insure the delivery of certain accrued benefits under a qualified plan in cases where the sponsor cannot meet those obligations.

Each of these diverse commitments to retirement income security has been modified over time. Many of the changes that have been implemented have expanded coverage, offered new kinds of protection, or raised the levels of benefits provided under the programs. Generally these changes have been considered improvements to the programs. In the current environment of large and growing federal deficits, however, various policy analysts are beginning to question the affordability of these commitments to income security, especially for the upper-middle- and high-income segments of society.

B. Paying for Our Promises

Table 1 shows the level of benefits provided in fiscal 1971 and fiscal 1991 by federal employee retirement and disability programs, Social Security, and Medicare. It also shows the total level of federal government outlays in the two years and the compound annual rates of growth in each of the measures over the 20-year period. Over the last 20 years, each of these programs has grown more rapidly than the total level of government expenditures. In combination they grew from comprising just less than one-quarter (23.4 percent) of total outlays in 1971 to slightly more than one-third (34.5 percent) in 1991. Current projections suggest these programs will continue to overtake the other elements of our government's fiscal operations.

In addition to concerns about the size of direct government outlays for retirement income security, some policy analysts are also concerned about the level and distribution of the tax preferences that encourage employers to establish and maintain retirement programs for their workers. The particular concern about pension-related tax preferences flows from an ongoing discussion about "tax expenditures" that began in the 1950s.[4] In 1974 the Congressional Budget Act formalized the tax expenditure concept as a required element of the official budget document that the President submits to Congress each year.

The measurement of tax expenditures in the Annual Budgets submitted since the passage of the Congressional Budget Act have highlighted the federal revenue implications of the various preferences woven throughout the Internal Revenue Code. Tax expenditures are defined in the act as "revenue losses attributable to provisions of the federal tax laws which allow a special exclusion, exemption, or deduction from gross income or which provide a special credit, a preferential rate of tax, or a deferral of tax liability."[5] For fiscal 1993 the U.S. Treasury Department estimates that the federal government will incur a $51.2 billion loss in tax revenues because of the preferences in the tax code favoring employer-sponsored retirement plans. It estimates that the special treatment accorded individual retirement accounts (IRAs) will result in an added $5.5 billion loss of revenues, and that Keogh plans will account for another $2.9 billion loss in revenues.

The loss in federal tax revenues has been particularly highlighted in recent years because the U.S. government's deficit has been higher over the last 10 years than over any comparable time in history. It is now approaching $400 billion for this fiscal year alone. As the deficit has mounted there has been a growing clamor to cut back on some of the direct and preferential commitments included in our fiscal system, including those providing retirement income security. For example,

TABLE 1   Selected Federal Outlays and Growth in Outlays Between Fiscal
1971 and Fiscal 1991 ($ millions)

Program	1971	1991	Annual growth rate (percent)
Federal employee retirement programs	$6,575	$56,106	11.3
Social Security	35,872	296,015	11.1
Medicare	6,622	104,489	14.8
Total outlays	210,072	1,323,001	9.6

Source: Executive Office of the President of the United States, *Budget of the United States Government, Fiscal Year 1993* (Washington, DC: U.S. Government Printing Office, 1992), Supplement Table 3.2, pp. Part Five 49–57.

Senator Warren Rudman (R-N.H.), long a critic of the federal deficit levels we have been experiencing, announced that he would not seek reelection in 1992 because he was "disgusted with Congress's inability to deal with a problem that is the surest agent of American decline."[6] The problem referred to here is the deficit. To do something about it "means curbing entitlements (Social Security, Medicare, etc.) and/or raising taxes."[7]

In some analysts' minds, the concern about the federal deficit also applies to reconsideration of the tax preferences afforded employer-sponsored retirement plans. For example, in the *New England Economic Review*, Alicia Munnell argued: "In an era of large budget deficits and a future that includes the rising costs of an aging society, it is difficult to understand why such a large source of potential revenue is allowed to go untapped."[8] While the short-term budget considerations should be considered in justifying any government endeavor, there are a number of other considerations that have been raised about our public commitment to retirement income security programs.

C. Keeping Our Promises

The concerns about the current fiscal imbalances, and the role retirement income security commitments play in operating federal budgets, do not begin to reveal the magnitude of our future obligations under these programs. Table 2 shows the unfunded future promises shown in the fiscal 1993 Budget submitted to Congress for a variety of income security programs operated by the government. The magnitude of the promises made, for which revenues have not been committed, raise questions about the long-term viability of these programs.

Haeworth Robertson, a former Social Security chief actuary, has

TABLE 2   Actuarial Deficiencies of Federal Retirement Annuity and Health
Programs ($ billions)

	Amount of deficiency
Annuity programs	
Social Security	$1,111
Civil service retirement system	660
Military retirement system	533
Federal employees retirement system	6
Railroad Retirement Board	33
Other retirement system	21
Health programs	
Medicare—hospital insurance	402
Federal employees health benefits	115
Military health facilities and CHAMPUS	295

Source: Executive Office of the President of the United States, *Budget of the United States Government, Fiscal Year 1993* (Washington, DC: U.S. Government Printing Office, 1992), Table 13-5, p. Part One 280.

recently published a book suggesting that the combined payroll tax required to fund the system could increase from roughly 15 percent today to 25 to 43 percent (including Medicare; including just OASDI, the respective numbers would be 12 percent and 17 to 26 percent) during the working lifetimes of today's youth.[9] The former Chairman of the President's Council of Economic Advisors, Michael Boskin, published his own observations on the subject a number of years ago in a book entitled *Too Many Promises: The Uncertain Future of Social Security.* He begins by saying: "Public retirement policies in the United States are in deep trouble, and we are heading toward a crisis of unprecedented proportions."[10] More recently, a former commissioner of Social Security, Dorcas Hardy, has written a book with her father, C. Colburn Hardy, entitled *Social Insecurity: The Crisis in America's Social Security System and How to Plan for Your Own Financial Survival.* Echoing Boskin, the opening paragraph in the Introduction to the book observes: "In the next century, just a few years away, the United States will face a potentially devastating crisis: the retirement checks that should be sent to benefit millions of Americans will *not* be there."[11] While the Hardys' overall analysis may be more sensationalist than sound, Dorcas Hardy's former position will give the statement credence to the casual observer.

Less than 10 years ago, the 1983 Social Security Amendments were hailed for restoring the long-term solvency of the cash benefits programs. At that time the stream of projected revenues was expected to cover benefit obligations for the next 75 years, although the cash benefits programs (OASDI) under Social Security were projected to exhaust their cash balance in 2063. Since 1983, there have been a number of changes in assumptions about OASDI operations, and the 1991 projections suggest the cash balances in the trust funds will be depleted by 2041. The Bush administration's proposed Budget for 1993 indicates that experience and revised assumptions about the program since 1983 "have advanced by 22 years the time when the trust fund balance would be exhausted."[12] While the long-term viability of cash benefits provided by Social Security may be called into some question, the concerns regarding Medicare suggest those promises are even less tenable.[13]

If we are concerned about the burden of unfunded promises in Social Security and Medicare that touch the lives of virtually all workers in the nation, it is only logical that we should be at least equally concerned about unfunded taxpayer obligations of similar magnitude that apply to less than 3 percent of the population. The President's fiscal 1993 Budget points out that the actuarial deficiencies reflected in Table 2 are not fully comparable across the range of programs reflected there.[14] Even considering the differences in the method of measuring unfunded promises, the existence of $1.7 trillion in statutory obligations that are not reflected as government debt is sobering.

In 1974 ERISA established funding standards for tax-qualified pension and profit sharing plans. In 1978 only 25 percent of large defined benefit pension plans had sufficient assets to cover benefits already accrued under their existing provisions. A similar portion had assets that were less than half their accrued obligations, and 52 percent had assets that would cover less than 75 percent of their accrued benefits. By 1991 only 13 percent of plans held assets that were less than 75 percent of their accrued benefit obligations and two-thirds had assets that would at least cover accrued benefits.[15] Despite the improvement in funding of pension obligations by private pension sponsors, the federal government has been increasingly concerned about the exposure to underfunded plans by the PBGC. President Bush's 1993 Budget points out that: "Between 1989 and 1991, . . . the present value of benefits it must pay in excess of the value of assets—grew 127 percent to $2.5 billion. . . . The agency's exposure to 'reasonable possible' losses has grown approximately $10 billion since 1989."[16]

The Bush administration's concern about the PBGC's "vulnerability" led it to propose faster amortization of pension underfunding, freezing of guaranteed benefits with respect to plan amendments for structurally underfunded plans, and improvement of the PBGC's status in bankruptcy claims. While the PBGC exposure must seem to make its ongoing support vulnerable, it is a small piece in the looming debate over our retirement income security system.

D. Reassessing Our Commitments

Increasingly, the issues of maintaining existing commitments to our retirement income security system focus on questions of equity. The concerns about fairness come from across the range of the political spectrum and target virtually every element of the U.S. retirement income security system.

With regard to Social Security, the concerns about equity cut across several issues. The primary concern, though, is the dual goals of providing social insurance protections through the program, while also attempting to meet minimal welfare needs. Peter Ferrara contends that because of the competing insurance and welfare goals in Social Security:

> Some beneficiaries will therefore receive more than they have paid for in past taxes, while others will receive less than they have paid for. The result is to make social security an unfair insurance program because beneficiaries cannot count on getting full value for their tax dollars. . . .
> Just as the pursuit of welfare objective through social security makes it a bad insurance program, the pursuit of insurance objectives through social security makes it a bad welfare program. Because of the program's insurance objective, social security is financed by a payroll tax on wage income. . . .
> But the payroll tax is an inappropriate way to finance a welfare program because the payroll tax is regressive.[17]

The concerns about federal pension programs tend to focus on the overall generosity of the benefits provided in comparison to retirement benefits provided by other employers in combination with Social Security. Former Representative Barber Conable has said that "Unless some reasonable limit is imposed on the federal pension systems, its excesses will not only exacerbate our deficit problem, but will also bring about a popular reaction punitive to the interests of retired public employees."[18] Another former Representative, Hastings Keith, estimates that 62 percent of his current combined federal pensions and Social Security benefits are composed of cost-of-living increases that he has received on them. Keith is in the unusual position of receiving three federal pensions plus Social Security, currently totaling $106,920 per year. He argues that it is unfair that the full amount of federal pensions should be indexed for changes in the cost of living. He supports the full indexation of amounts that would cover basic living costs, which he estimates to be roughly the equivalent of the maximum level of Social Security benefits. He argues that it is unfair that the common taxpayer, who does not have guarantees that his or her earnings or pension income will keep pace with inflation, should be burdened with the obligation of fully insuring high-income annuitants against inflation.[19]

In terms of employer pensions, the concerns being voiced relate to the inequity inherent in a tax system that provides preferences for pensions that are not universally used. For example, Alicia Munnell argues that "the failure to tax nonwage compensation creates serious inequities between those workers who receive all their earnings in taxable cash wages and those who receive a substantial portion in nontaxable fringe benefits."[20]

As the issues relating to our ability to sustain the commitments we have made to provide retirement income security become clearer, the concerns over equity will be heightened. Because of the long time horizons required in providing for individual retirement income security, it is imperative that any changes in national retirement policy be anticipated as far in advance as possible. Then such changes in policy can be implemented on a phased basis that provides the maximum opportunity for people to adjust their own expectations and behavior accordingly. Before striking off piecemeal to fix this or that component of our retirement systems, we should give some careful thought to how we might coordinate policy adjustments to most affordably and efficiently achieve our long-term goals. In order to do this, we must first understand how the current components of our retirement system operate separately, and then together in the delivery of retirement income security.

II. Social Security

A. Benefit Design and the Tilt Toward Adequacy

In its statement of basic principles on the design of Social Security, the Committee on Economic Security that did the design work on the original Social Security legislation stated that the benefits should bear a "definite relationship to the previous earnings of the beneficiary." As a counterweight to this principle, the committee also felt that benefits would be sufficient to "prove a considerable item of income to the recipient."[21] The committee also believed that benefits should be graduated so low-wage earners and people entering the system late in life should receive proportionately higher benefits. The proposed weighting of benefits toward lower-wage workers was intended to make the program redistributional. But the committee also recommended that white-collar workers earning over $250 per month be excluded from the program, somewhat dampening the redistributive aspects of the proposal. The legislation actually passed in 1935 included all workers in covered employment, covering only the first $3,000 of earnings. This made the legislation more redistributive than the committee's proposal.

The 1939 Social Security Amendments altered the redistributional characteristics of the program by moving from a formula that based benefits on lifetime, cumulative, covered earnings to one based on average monthly covered earnings. The 1939 Amendments moved the program from being heavily weighted toward equity, with benefits based on cumulative covered earnings, more toward adequacy considerations by providing greater protection against hardship. Because of the way the program was started, virtually all beneficiaries with normal life expectancy at retirement could expect to get back more from the program than the value of the taxes they and their employers contributed to it. With benefit enhancements over the years, this situation persisted up until the early 1980s. The maturing of the program in recent years has raised questions about the competing adequacy and equity goals.

The Committee on Economic Security proposed the financing of Social Security through a tax on a percentage of employees' earnings, taxes on a percentage of employers' payrolls, and "subsidies from the Federal Government financed through taxes not borne by workers."[22] The reason the committee advocated the employee tax was that it would assure that benefits would be provided as a "matter of right without a test of means." In support of the employer tax the committee argued, "Just as industry, generally, has become accustomed to meeting charges for the depreciation and replacement of its material equipment, many employers have developed programs for the payment of retirement allowances for their superannuated workers."[23]

At the payroll tax rates on employees and employers proposed by the committee, revenues were expected to be adequate to support benefit payments and establish a reserve fund until about 1965 when a general fund subsidy would be required to maintain the benefits and reserves built up in the earlier years of the program.[24] The committee observed that old-age benefits would become an increasing part of the public cost of the system that maintained adequate benefits. Covered employees should not bear the entire burden of providing insurance benefits that reduced the need for public assistance benefits for the elderly that were paid from general revenues.[25] In other words, the essence of the proposal by the committee was that the inherent subsidization of benefits for lower-wage workers to provide them with adequate income security was to be funded through the more progressive income tax.

When President Roosevelt discovered that after 1965 a large deficit would develop in the proposed program because benefits would exceed payroll tax collections, he insisted that the proposal be changed. The program that was enacted contained no provision for partial general revenue financing, a situation that continued until the 1983 Amendments, which imposed an income tax on a portion of the benefits and directed the taxes collected on benefits to the Social Security trust funds. Currently, the taxation of Social Security benefits contributes about 0.56 percent of taxable payroll to the 75-year average balance in the OASDI trust funds.

The history of the early years of the program has been described by a number of knowledgeable observers[26] and it is not necessary to repeat their analyses here. Several elements of the early experience of the system are relevant for our discussion. Financing the system in the early years was relatively painless. The benefit expansions in the 1939 amendments were financed without a tax increase by eliminating refunds of contributions for individuals dying prior to retirement and other benefit adjustments. During the 1950s, benefits and coverage were further expanded. The real value of benefits during the 1960s was relatively stagnant. But in the early 1970s benefits were increased by 15, 10, and 20 percent under three ad hoc increases. Over the three years benefit levels increased by 52 percent while the consumer price index (CPI) was increasing 14 percent. After 1972 individuals receiving benefits received automatic cost-of-living increases based on growth in the CPI.

B. Maturing Program Encounters Funding Problems

During the 1970s, it became increasingly clear that the automatic benefit increase provisions of the 1972 amendments would likely have a detrimental effect on the long-term financial soundness of the system under the benefit computation formula then in effect. The 1977 amendments were designed to correct the flaws in the benefit formula and to create stable replacement rates for successive cohorts of beneficiaries. While benefits to new retirees were reduced by about 5 percent and the runaway growth in replacement rates ended, economic conditions conspired to create a short-term funding crisis in the early 1980s.

The 1983 Social Security Amendments went a long way toward restoring confidence in the near-term viability of the system and extended the period over which beneficiaries could expect to receive a timely payment of promised benefits. Prior to the adoption of those Amendments, in 1982 the OASI trust fund was expected to be exhausted by 1984.[27] After the Amendments were passed, the 1984

TABLE 3   Long-run Balances in the Old Age and Survivors Insurance Trust
Fund as a Percentage of Taxable Payroll

Year	1st 25-year period	2nd 25-year period	3rd 25-year period	75-year period
1983[a]	1.63	.33	−1.99	−.01
1984[b]	1.84	.06	−1.99	−.03
1985[c]	1.87	−.62	−2.28	−.35
1986[d]	1.99	−.61	−2.24	−.29
1987[e]	2.01	−.90	−2.40	−.43
1988[f]	1.98	−1.20	−3.07	−.45
1989[g]	2.05	−1.56	−3.31	−.53
1990[h]	1.80	−1.82	−3.30	−.69
1991[i]	1.52	−1.99	−3.38	−.82
1992[j]	1.32	−2.23	−3.54	−1.01

Source: *Annual Report of the Board of Trustees of the Federal Old-Age and Survivors Insurance and Disability Insurance Trust Funds* (Washington, DC: U.S. Government Printing Office, various years). Values are based on the intermediate assumptions in each report (1983–1990, II-B; 1991–1992, II).
[a] 1983 Report, Table 31.
[b] 1984 Report, Table 32.
[c] 1985 Report, Table 32.
[d] 1986 Report, Table 28.
[e] 1987 Report, Table 26.
[f] 1988 Report, Table 27. Balances are based on the present value of income and costs. Earlier reports based the fund balances on a simple average method. The three 25-year period balances do not include the initial balance in the fund. The 75-year average balance includes as income the value of the initial fund.
[g] 1989 Report, Table 27. See note f.
[h] 1990 Report, Table 27. See note f.
[i] 1991 Report, Table 27. The 75-year average balance includes as income the value of the initial trust fund and as a cost the value of maintaining a target trust fund equal to one year's costs.
[j] 1992 Report, Table II.F.14. See note i.

Trustees Report projected that the OASI trust fund would not be exhausted in the 75-year projection period.[28]

Although the 1983 Amendments solved the short-term funding crisis and initially put off the day when financing would be inadequate to pay full benefits, the Amendments did not permanently guarantee the long term viability of the old age portion of the Social Security cash benefits program. Table 3 shows the actuarial balance of the OASI program over the 75-year valuation period as a percent of taxable payroll from each of the Trustees Reports from 1983 to 1992. The balances in these reports are not strictly comparable due to a change in the method of calculating the balances that was initiated in the 1988 report. Nevertheless, the message from the reports is clear: the estimated day when the system will be unable to meet its benefit obligations under its current structure is coming closer and closer. If Social Security is underfunded, new adjustments to its revenue sources, benefit promises, or both will have to be implemented some time in the future. That means the relative balances that have currently been struck in the program will be modified. The required modifications will undoubtedly heighten concerns about the program's equity goals.

C. The Value of Benefits in Comparison to Payroll Taxes

Because Social Security benefits are proportionately larger for lower income than for higher-income employees, the question naturally arises whether employees with different earnings histories can expect to receive benefits commensurate with the taxes collected. The relative gains and losses of persons with different earnings levels were not particularly important when everyone in the system was a winner. First, until the early 1980s (or 1990s if you do not consider the taxation of Social Security benefits) nearly all beneficiaries at retirement could expect to receive back from the system more than the value of their and their employers' contributions toward retirement benefits, as Table 4 shows. However, the OASI program was underfunded in both the short and long terms in the early 1980s, which led to the 1983 Amendments. The 1983 Amendments included a variety of changes that modified its relative worth to participants.

Anthony Pellechio and Gordon Goodfellow calculated the present value of Social Security benefits and taxes for employees age 25, 40, and 55 in 1983.[29] They calculated the present value of Social Security benefits that would be received after 1983. No past benefits (benefits before 1983) were included in the benefits side of the analysis. Taxes paid before 1983 were carried forward with interest only. Their results are summarized in Table 5. The results for single men indicate that younger men receive benefits that are worth less than their tax payments even at low salary levels. This finding may be due to the fact that benefits were reduced to account for the taxation of benefits under the 1983 Social Security Amendments and that the age at which full benefits are paid is 67 for an employee aged 22 in 1983.

For this paper, the authors developed a simplified calculation of the net present value of Social Security benefits to illustrate the relative value of the retirement portion of Social Security benefits for single persons with different lifetime earnings histories. Only retirement benefits at age 65 for a single person are used in the calculation of the

TABLE 4   Comparison of Combined Employer-Employee OASI Taxes Accumulated with Interest and Present Value of Retirement Benefits for Persons at Age 65 in Various Years

Year of attaining age 65	OASI taxes accumulated with interest to age 65	Ratio of the present value of future OASI benefits at age 65		
		Single man	Single woman	One-earner couple
For average wage earner				
1960	$1,972	7.10	8.88	13.18
1970	6,991	3.34	4.30	6.31
1980	24,206	2.75	3.53	5.17
1990	79,565	1.55	1.99	2.90
2000	174,860	1.24	1.58	2.31
2010	338,063	1.12	1.42	2.08
2020	593,144	1.11	1.41	2.06
For maximum wage earner				
1960	$2,753	5.66	7.07	10.50
1970	9,000	2.93	3.76	5.53
1980	33,865	2.49	3.20	4.69
1990	126,856	1.29	1.65	2.41
2000	318,422	0.97	1.24	1.82
2010	688,030	0.84	1.07	1.56
2020	1,347,509	0.76	0.97	1.41

Source: Robert J. Myers and Bruce D. Schobel, "A Money's-Worth Analysis of Social Security Retirement Benefits," *Transactions*, Society of Actuaries 35 (1983): 542–43.

accumulated value of benefits and the OASI portion of FICA taxes is used in the calculation of the present value of taxes.[30] The results of the calculations are shown in Table 6.

Social Security retirement benefits are calculated assuming that individuals' earnings grow at 6 percent per year while national average earnings grow at 5 percent per year. The reason for assuming that wages of workers considered here would grow more rapidly than those in the national economy is that these workers in the subsequent parts of the paper are also assumed to be covered by an employer sponsored pension. Because workers covered by pensions tend, on average, to have higher earnings levels than those not covered, higher earnings growth rates were assumed for this analysis. In the calculations the Social Security benefit is reduced because of the taxes that apply to such benefits.

To calculate the reduction due to taxes, retirement benefits are calculated for each hypothetical employee based on the qualified pension and savings plan provisions of 308 companies in the Wyatt Com-

TABLE 5   Ratio of Present Value of Social Security Benefits to Taxes for Single Men Aged 25, 40, and 55 in 1983 for Selected Wage Levels

	Age in 1983		
Wages in 1983*	25	40	55
$10,000	.76	.81	1.11
$20,000	.61	.66	.92
$30,000	.47	.56	.81
$37,500	.43	.53	.78

Source: Calculated by the authors from Tables 6, 7, and 8, Anthony Pellechio and Gordon Goodfellow, "Individual Gains and Losses from Social Security Before and After the 1983 Amendments," *Cato Journal* 3, 2 (fall 1983).
*Denotes a hypothetical employee whose earnings are always at the Social Security Wage Base.

TABLE 6   Ratio of the Present Value of Social Security Retirement Benefits and OASI Taxes for a Single Person at Selected Ages and Earnings in 1991*

	Age in 1991				
Earnings in 1991	30	35	40	45	50
$ 10,000	.95	1.06	1.19	1.29	1.43
$ 20,000	.74	.80	.88	.97	1.10
$ 30,000	.62	.68	.74	.82	.97
$ 50,000	.45	.49	.54	.60	.70
$100,000	.43	.48	.53	.58	.66

Source: Calculated by the authors.
*Earnings are assumed to increase (decrease) at 6 percent per year after (before) 1983. The value of Social Security benefits at retirement is based on the value of an annuity that increases at 4 percent per year. The annuity interest rate is 6 percent and the 1984 Unisex Pension mortality is assumed.

pany's COMPARE™ data base. Additional income ranging from 0 percent to 15 percent of final earnings was assigned to retirees. Taxes on Social Security benefits were calculated following current law. The hypothetical employees were assumed to be single and to have three sources of retirement income: pension benefits, Social Security, and additional income from personal savings (the latter was zero for low wage workers). Thus the ratio of Social Security benefits to taxes in Table 6 represents the average after-tax present value of such benefits when other sources of income in retirement are included in the present value of taxes for the hypothetical employee.

The results of "money's-worth" analyses indicate that younger and higher earning employees will not receive benefit payments commensurate with the taxes they pay. Although the data presented here show only single persons, these data may be indicative of the situation faced by the majority of future retirees. As time passes, more and more women will become entitled to social security benefits that are greater than the spouses' benefits provided by Social Security. In the same way, widows' benefits may become a relatively small residual paid on top of widows' own retirement benefits. Thus very few retired families will have the advantage in the current system for the married, one-earner family.

D. Current Policy Issues

Presently there are two elements of public policy that are again bringing Social Security benefits under increased scrutiny. First, the current budget deficits have raised interest in curtailing entitlement benefits for middle- and upper-income persons. For example, a 1990 article in *Business Week* argues that government entitlements—read Social Security, government pensions, Medicare, etc.—can be cut without harming those who rely on government programs for most or all of their incomes.[31] Second, the increasing awareness that Social Security is underfunded in the long term will mount pressures to address the funding and benefits issues that are behind the growing projected deficits. Addressing either of these policy concerns will undoubtedly diminish Social Security's value for most workers from a money's-worth perspective. Efforts to reduce retirement benefits for middle- and upper-income persons are sure to stimulate more analyses of who gets what under our current system. Our current system, however, is not just Social Security with its inherent tax burdens and implied benefits.

III. Employer-Sponsored Retirement Programs

Until recently, Social Security has been run largely on a pay-as-you-go basis. This has generally meant that expansions in benefits have been linked fairly directly to increases in payroll tax rates. In the case of Social Security, the conflict between the desire to expand benefits and the need to raise taxes to support them has been clear. In the case of employer-sponsored retirement programs, the relationship between benefits provided and the role of tax policy has not been nearly as well understood. Even though the relationship is not as direct, the conflict between retirement policy and tax policy as they apply to qualified plans has been far more contentious than in the case of public pensions or Social Security. The contentiousness in this case has been the result of fundamental disagreements between pension advocates and critics over two issues. The first is the measurement of "tax expenditures" in the federal budget as they apply to pension and savings programs. The second is whether the distribution of the benefits provided by the tax incentives is equitable.

A. Measuring Pension-Related Tax Expenditures

Theoretical Issues

In theory, a true measure of a person's "income" during any given period is his or her level of consumption plus the increase or decrease in wealth during the period. If this theoretical concept of income were applied to tax-qualified income deferral plans, the tax expenditure during any period would be the foregone taxes on the increase in the real present value of benefits rights during the period.

Under the existing tax code, the preferential treatment of qualified retirement programs makes part of the tax system operate more as a consumption tax system than as a pure income tax system. Contributions to the plans are deductible from income for tax purposes at the point the contribution is made, and the contributions and interest returns on the contributions are not taxable until benefits are actually paid out. Critics of the current tax code preferences favoring employer-sponsored pensions argue that we should move more toward a comprehensive income tax. In order to do so, they advocate the immediate taxation of contributions made to retirement trusts and ongoing taxation of investment returns to the trusts. These critics do not always fully explain the implications of their proposals.

For example, Alicia Munnell has explored the relative implications of moving from the current tax treatment of pensions towards a more comprehensive income tax treatment.[32] She begins by positing a simple case where there are no taxes applied against income. In this case, a consumer can enjoy a level of consumption C equal to his or her entire income Y in the time period P in which it is earned.

(1) $$C_P = Y_P \, .$$

Alternatively, the consumer can invest his or her income and earn interest at a rate i, and enjoy future income as follows:

(2) $$C_F = Y_P \, (1 + i) \, .$$

The consumer can trade off current versus future consumption at the rate

(3) $$\frac{C_P}{C_F} = \frac{Y_P}{Y_P(1+i)} = \frac{1}{(1+i)}.$$

If a comprehensive income tax is introduced into this world, current consumption is redefined as

(4) $$C_P = (1-t)\,Y_P\,,$$

where t is the income tax rate. Future consumption in this regime is

(5) $$C_F = (1-t)\,Y_P\,[1 + i(1-t)]$$

and

(6) $$\frac{C_P}{C_F} = \frac{1}{1 + i(1-t)}.$$

The application of the "comprehensive" tax to qualified retirement plans, as Munnell defines it, will equalize the tax treatment of pension savings with the tax treatment of a regular savings account.

Advocates of the move to a comprehensive income tax, and the current measurements of tax expenditures, overlook the fact that some portion of the returns on assets over time do not reflect real economic return for deferring consumption, but rather make up for the decreased purchasing power of money resulting from price inflation. So the interest rate i that Munnell describes is composed of two elements:

(7) $$i = \frac{dP}{P} + r\,,$$

where P is the price level in the current period, and dP is the change in prices from the current period to the future period, and r is the real rate of return on assets in excess of inflation. In other words

(8) $$\frac{C_F}{C_P} = \frac{1}{[1 + (dP/P)(1-t) + r(1-t)]}.$$

In order for deferred consumption to at least be of equal value to present consumption, the rate of return on deferred consumption has to at least equal the rate of inflation. Since the return defined by the factor dP/P is merely maintaining the purchasing power of income across periods, taxing that factor subjects income to an added tax if it is not consumed immediately. It is this conception of a "comprehensive tax" where the return on assets that cover inflation is taxable that is the theoretical basis for measuring tax preferences for retirement and savings plans. Under this model, income deferred for retirement purposes outside a tax qualified plan is subjected to a higher tax than if it is used for immediate consumption purposes if there is any inflation at all in the economy.

As an example, consider an extreme case where the total return on assets equals the inflation rate. Consider an individual who has $1,000 in earnings that can either be consumed today or saved for future retirement consumption purposes. Assume this individual is subject to a marginal tax rate of 25 percent, so that the $1,000 in earnings will yield $750 in disposable income. It is actually only the $750 that the individual can use for current consumption or invest for future purposes. For the sake of the initial example, assume that inflation is steady at 5 percent per year and that the individual can invest in a risk-free bond that pays a nominal rate of return of 5 percent per annum, a zero yield in real terms.

Using an interest rate that merely equals the rate of inflation in the economy is meant to show the effects of the tax system on inflationary gains on savings. It is not meant to suggest that savers cannot realize positive real rates of return. The effects reflected in this example where the interest rate equals the inflation rate are equally applicable to situations where the interest rate exceeds the rate of inflation in the economy, as will be shown later.

Table 7 shows that deferring consumption under this type of regime results in a gradual deterioration of the purchasing power of money saved relative to that of the income originally earned. If the earnings are put toward consumption in the year earned, the taxpayer can consume 75 percent of the value of earnings. If consumption is deferred just one year, the purchasing power of the account is only 74.1 percent of the value of the initial earnings. This loss in purchasing power results because the inflationary return on the asset is taxed. No added income accrues to the account holder under the assumptions, just added tax because of the decision to defer consumption. If the savings are held in this environment for ten years, the effective tax on the original earnings rises to 33.5 percent. After twenty years it is 41.0 percent, and after thirty years it is up to 47.6 percent. Further analysis of this phenomenon shows that the effective tax rate on earnings not immediately consumed varies in relation to a number of factors as shown in Table 8. The results in the table show that the effective tax

TABLE 7   Relative Value of Money in a Normal Savings Account Paying a
Rate of Return Equivalent to a 5 Percent Inflation Rate and
Subject to 25 Percent Tax Rates

Year	Nominal value of constant purchasing power	Nominal value of savings	Gross interest	Net interest	Purchasing power of savings as percentage of original earnings	Effective tax rate on original earnings
0	1,000.00	750.00	37.5	28.1	75.0	25.0
1	1,050.00	778.13	38.9	29.2	74.1	25.9
2	1,102.50	807.30	40.4	30.3	73.2	26.8
3	1,157.63	837.58	41.9	31.4	72.4	27.6
4	1,215.51	868.99	43.4	32.6	71.5	28.5
5	1,276.28	901.57	45.1	33.8	70.6	29.4
6	1,340.10	935.38	46.8	35.1	69.8	30.2
7	1,407.10	970.46	48.5	36.4	69.0	31.0
8	1,477.46	1,006.85	50.3	37.8	68.1	31.9
9	1,551.33	1,044.61	52.2	39.2	67.3	32.7
10	1,628.89	1,083.78	54.2	40.6	66.5	33.5
20	2,653.30	1,566.11	78.3	58.7	59.0	41.0
30	4,321.94	2,263.10	113.2	84.9	52.4	47.6

Source: Calculated by the authors.

TABLE 8   Effective Tax Rates on Current Versus Future Consumption
When Consumption is Deferred Through a Regular Savings
Account at 5 and 10 Percent Interest and Inflation Rates

Consumption time frame	Effective tax rate at statutory rate of:	
	25 percent	33 percent
At 5 percent interest and inflation rates		
Immediate	25.0	33.0
After 10 years	33.5	42.8
After 20 years	41.0	51.2
After 30 years	47.6	58.3
At 10 percent interest and inflation rates		
Immediate	25.0	33.0
After 10 years	40.4	50.6
After 20 years	52.6	63.6
After 30 years	62.4	73.1

Source: Calculated by the authors.

TABLE 9   Relative Value of Money and Returns in a Normal Savings Account Paying 10 Percent Rate of Return with 5 Percent Inflation Rate and Subject to 25 Percent Tax Rates

Year	Nominal value of constant purchasing power	Nominal value of savings	Gross interest	Net interest	Inflation return on savings balance	Real return in excess of inflation
1	750.00	750.00	75.00	56.25	37.50	18.75
2	787.50	806.25	80.63	60.47	40.31	20.16
3	826.88	866.72	86.67	65.00	43.34	21.67
4	868.22	931.72	93.17	69.88	46.59	23.29
5	911.63	1,001.60	100.16	75.12	50.08	25.04
6	957.21	1,076.72	107.67	80.75	53.84	26.92
7	1,005.07	1,157.48	115.75	86.81	57.87	28.94
8	1,055.33	1,244.29	124.43	93.32	62.21	31.11
9	1,108.09	1,337.61	133.76	100.32	66.88	33.44
10	1,163.50	1,437.93	143.79	107.84	71.90	35.95
20	1,895.21	2,963.62	296.36	222.27	148.18	74.09
30	3,087.10	6,108.11	610.81	458.11	305.41	152.70

Source: Calculated by the authors.

rate varies with the underlying statutory tax rate, the duration of time that consumption is deferred, and the economy's underlying inflation rate.

In the analysis thus far, it has been assumed that the inflation rate and the rate of return on deferred consumption are identical. Table 9 shows a situation where a savings account is assumed to have a 10 percent nominal rate of return during a period with 5 percent inflation. The statutory tax rate is assumed to be 25 percent for the calculation. In this case, the after-tax return on the savings can be broken into its component elements to show the effective yield on savings after the effects of inflation on the purchasing power of money are taken into account. Under these assumptions, 50 percent goes to keep up with the eroding purchasing power of money, and 25 percent of the gross interest goes to pay taxes. The effective yield on the deferred consumption in this case implies a 50 percent tax on the real return, double the statutory tax rate.

Some critics of pension policy acknowledge that it would be desirable to eliminate the inflation component of return on capital under our tax system on theoretical grounds, but that the actual tax expenditure calculation related to pensions should still consider them since indexing is not part of our tax system. They argue that it does not make sense to single out pensions for special treatment relative to the measurement of tax expenditures. But there is considerable confusion about what should be considered a tax expenditure for purposes of developing budgetary estimates because the Congressional Budget Act of 1974, which requires that a list of such expenditures be included in the budget, failed to specify the baseline provisions of the tax law against which they could be estimated. The Budget document submitted to Congress is unequivocal in its observation that decisions on whether specific provisions of the tax law are preferential exceptions to the baseline provisions "is a matter of judgement."[33] The Fiscal 1993 budgetary document specifically addresses the issue that is being raised in this section. It states: "A comprehensive income tax would adjust the cost basis of capital assets and debt for changes in the price level during the time the assets or debt are held. Thus, under a comprehensive income tax baseline the failure to take account of inflation in measuring . . . interest income would be regarded as a negative tax expenditure (a tax penalty)."[34]

Given that inflationary returns on pension assets are not real income, that the budget indicates the inclusion of certain items is judgmental, and that it specifically indicates that the failure to take account of inflation in considering interest income issues is wrong, it is hard to understand why the inflationary return on pension assets is included in the calculation of pension-related tax expenditures. *It hardly seems reasonable to use the current methodology as the model against which to evaluate the "tax expenditures" related to pensions, given the longstanding history of governmental commitment to the income security of retired workers. If government policy makers believe it is desirable for workers to save for their own retirement, why would it impose a "tax penalty" on them for doing so?*

Practical Measurement Issues

In the actual measurement of the tax expenditures related to pensions, the Treasury staff estimates the taxes that would be paid on contributions to the trusts if such contributions were paid as regular income. They add to that amount an estimate of the taxes that would be paid on the earnings accruing to the trusts if they were treated as regular income and subtract from that sum their estimate of the taxes paid on benefits currently being paid through the plans. For several reasons this method of estimating the tax expenditure relating to deferred income programs exaggerates the size of the stated tax expenditure relative to the concepts on which it is built.

Tax-deferred savings accounts are more efficient for retirement accumulation than regular savings accounts. Tax-deferred savings accounts would generally be more efficient for retirement accumulation than regular savings accounts in which only real returns were taxed. But the taxes that are not collected on a contribution to a pension trust in the period the contribution is made are ultimately collected when the benefits are paid. By looking at the forgone taxes on contributions being made to trust funds today, and subtracting from that the taxes on benefits paid today, the Treasury methodology exaggerates the long term loss of tax revenues. This is the case for at least four reasons.

First, today's retirees worked during periods when pensions were much less prevalent, and the current prevalence of pensions has little effect on their retirement income levels. A retiree who is 85 years old today worked in an economy where the pension participation rate among private sector wage and salary workers averaged less than 30 percent throughout his or her career. Most retirees today over age 85 are women. These women had extremely low labor force participation rates relative to women today. Most women in this age group are getting only a small survivor pension, if any. Retirees currently between ages 75 and 84 worked in an economy where the average pension participation rate was between 30 and 35 percent throughout their career. Overwhelmingly, most retirees in this age group retired prior to ERISA's passage, and virtually all did so prior to the passage of the Retirement Equity Act. The retiree who is 65 today spent a career with average pension participation rates around 40 percent. Only 40 percent of today's retirees over age 65 are receiving a pension. Today's private sector wage and salary workers, on the other hand, work in an environment where more than half can expect to receive a pension, generally one much larger than that being paid today to current retirees. By offsetting current contributions based on today's high level of worker participation in pensions by relatively low amounts of taxable benefits based on low pension participation rates of former workers, the U.S. Treasury underestimates the taxes that will ultimately be recouped when pensions being currently earned will be paid as benefits and taxed.

Second, Social Security benefits have been accorded preferential treatment for years. Half the annual Social Security benefit and nontaxable interest is included in the computation of adjusted gross income (AGI) for determining whether Social Security benefits are to be taxed. For individuals with a modified AGI over $25,000, and for joint returns with the modified AGI over $32,000, some portion of the Social Security benefit is taxable. In the future, the benefit of the preferential treatment of Social Security is going to diminish because the $25,000 and $32,000 thresholds are frozen, and a declining number of households will benefit from the tax preference. The current tax preferences for Social Security lower the marginal tax rates some pension recipients face, and thus, the estimated tax collections on current pension benefits do not reflect the ongoing operation of the tax system. The current treatment of Social Security exaggerates the effects of pensions on federal revenue collections. If the tax preferences for employer-sponsored retirement programs are reduced now because of this exaggeration, it will only be future pensioners who will be penalized, even though they will not get current Social Security preferences.

Third, today pensions cover many workers, including the baby boom workers, and relatively few retirees. Because pension plans are funded on a benefit accrual basis during covered workers' lifetimes, one should expect the relative growth in pension trusts to be even more rapid than in Social Security, which is only partially prefunded. The Treasury methodology calculates tax expenditures when contributions are abnormally high and benefit payouts are abnormally low because of the age composition of society. By calculating the tax expenditures the way it does, completely ignoring the demographic effects of the baby boomers, the Treasury significantly underestimates the taxes that will ultimately be recouped when pensions being currently earned will be paid as benefits and taxed.

Fourth, employees covered by the pension programs sponsored by governmental and tax-exempt employers are included in calculations. While it can be argued that employees or such organizations accruing future income rights should be treated exactly the same as private sector employees, there is an incongruity between the inclusion of these plans in the "tax expenditure" estimates but their exclusion when specific "revenue enhancement" measures are considered. The incongruity occurs because there are no deduction issues raised when the nontaxable employers contribute to their pensions. The contributions would not be taxable anyway. In fact, if we look at the largest of these programs—those sponsored by the federal government—the funding of employee retirement is largely a mirror game anyway. For its civil service and military pensions, the government funds benefits by issuing government securities. In other words, the federal government can increase the general level of tax expenditures by issuing additional IOUs to its pension plans.

A specific instance of this incongruity between including nontaxable entities' pension plans in the tax expenditure calculations but not considering them a source of revenue during legislative considerations is the Tax Reform Act of 1986 (TRA86). Tax reform accorded governmental and other nonprofit employer-sponsored plans special provisions that increase the tax expenditure estimates under the methodology used for measuring them. TRA86 reduced the maximum benefits that private plans could fund, for anyone retiring prior to Social Security's normal retirement age. Public employees, including members of Congress, and those working for tax-exempt employers were exempted from these benefit reductions because imposing them on these nontaxable entities would not raise any additional revenues.[35] So the tax laws are being written to grant special treatment for government and nonprofit employees because the exemptions do not have revenue effects, but then the tax expenditure calculations are increased as though the exemptions do have revenue effects.

Adding to these four problems with the treatment of contributions to and benefits paid out of pension trusts, the double taxation inherent in the normal tax treatment of interest accruals leads us to conclude that the estimated tax expenditures relating to pension plans are significantly exaggerated. We acknowledge that there is a beneficial effect provided by the tax incentives and that it is significant. But it is not the $51 billion per year that it is estimated to be, even taking into account loss of payroll taxes as Munnell suggests.[36]

Arithmetic Problems with the Estimates

In the case of employer-sponsored pension and savings plans, the tax expenditure estimates developed by the Treasury Department treat a given year's contributions to pension trusts as taxable wages and treat the return on assets in the trust funds as taxable income accruing to participants in the plans. The tax rate used in estimating the lost tax revenues on contributions to the funds and the fund income is 23.5 percent, a weighted average marginal tax rate for covered workers. The estimated tax revenues collected from benefits paid by employer-sponsored plans is calculated using a 20.0 percent weighted average marginal tax rate for beneficiaries.

We have applied this method of calculating pension-related tax expenditures for 1990 in an effort to roughly replicate the estimated $46.8 billion in forgone federal revenues for fiscal year 1990 as presented in the fiscal 1992 Budget. We calculated the net tax expenditure in two ways: (1) using the traditional method of treating inflationary returns to pension trusts as taxable; and (2) using the more reasonable method of treating only real returns to pension trusts as taxable for purposes of developing the tax expenditure estimates. Our results are presented in Table 10.

The tax expenditure estimates that we derive using published government statistics do not come close to the estimated numbers included in the federal budget submitted to Congress for 1990. Our estimates of

TABLE 10   Pension Balances and Flows for 1989–1990 ($ billions)

	Private plans	State & local plans	Federal plans	Total plans
1989 balance	1,749.1	734.9	298.6	2,782.6
1990 employer contributions	52.5	32.7	58.4	143.6
1990 employee taxable contributions	N/A	14.0	4.4	18.4
1990 interest earned	105.8	1.0	21.2	128.0
1990 benefits paid	141.2	39.2	53.6	234.0
1990 balance	1,766.3	743.4	328.9	2,838.6
Nominal return rate	6.0	0.1	6.7	4.6
Inflation rate	5.4	5.4	5.4	5.4
Total interest plus pre-tax contributions	158.3	33.7	79.6	271.6
Real interest earned	10.9	−38.9	4.2	−23.7
Real interest plus pre-tax contributions	63.4	−6.2	62.6	119.8
Taxes on benefits	28.2	7.8	10.7	46.8
Forgone taxes—nominal basis	37.2	7.9	18.7	63.8
Tax expenditure—nominal basis	9.0	0.1	8.0	17.0
Forgone taxes—real basis	14.9	−1.5	14.7	28.2
Tax expenditure—real basis	−13.3	−9.3	4.0	−18.6

Sources: 1989 and 1990 balances held by private plans and state and local plans are based on Federal Reserve Flow of Funds data taken from EBRI *Quarterly Pension Investment Report* 6, 3 (third quarter, Dec. 1991): 43. The federal plan data were accumulated from the annual reports submitted in compliance with PL 95-595 for the Federal Reserve Bank, the Public Health Service, the Army-Air Force Exchange Service, the Coast Guard, the Military Retirement System, and the Civil Service Retirement/Federal Employee Retirement Systems.

Private sector employer contributions to private pension and profit sharing plans and the benefits paid by these plans are taken from U.S. Department of Commerce, Bureau of Economic Analysis *Survey of Current Business* 72, 1 (January 1992): Table 6.11C, p. 69. Contributions to state and local employee retirement programs were taken from Table 3.6, p. 44 and the benefits paid by these plans were taken from Table 3.12, p. 48. Contributions and benefits from federal retirement programs were aggregated from the respective PL 95-595 reports.

"Interest earned" was derived from beginning and ending balances and contributions made to the plans and benefits paid by them. "Inflation rate" is the change in the consumer price index (CPI) for all urban consumers from 1989 to 1990, derived from Table B-56 in *Economic Report of the President* (Washington, DC: U.S. Government Printing Office, 1992), p. 361.

Estimated forgone taxes were calculated at a rate of 23.5 percent and taxes collected were calculated at a rate of 20.0 percent, consistent with rates reportedly used by the U.S. Treasury in estimating tax expenditures.

the total tax expenditure using the conventional measure is only $17.0 billion for 1990, of which 47 percent is attributable to federal retirement plans alone. Our estimate using the more correct measure, which does not include inflationary returns on pension assets, estimates that employer-sponsored plans were net tax contributors to the federal tax system by approximately $19 billion. The only elements of the pension system that were a drain on the public fisc from the perspective of this more reasonable tax expenditure concept during 1990 were the federal plans.

The reason our estimate of the 1990 pension tax expenditure is so far from the Treasury estimate is because the latter uses an estimated rate of return relatively constant over time to estimate the interest return and capital gains on pension assets. Estimates developed by the conventional measure of tax expenditures for pensions for 1988 and 1989 yield estimates that are somewhat higher than published tax expenditure estimates—$64 billion and $87 billion respectively. The estimate for 1987 using this methodology would be $44 billion. Over the four years for which there are data since the passage of tax reform, the estimated average tax expenditure would be $53 billion dollars using the conventional measure, relatively close to the estimates developed by the Treasury Department. If we were to use the modified calculation procedure that only considered the tax preference accorded to real returns on pension assets, the average tax expenditure estimate for the first four years after tax reform would be $27 billion, half of which would be attributable to public employer plans. In other words, half the estimated tax expenditures related to pensions can be attributed to returns on assets related to inflation, and half of that has nothing to do with plans sponsored by taxable entities.

Alicia Munnell has suggested an alternative method for estimating the value of the tax losses attributable to preferences in the federal tax code favoring employer-sponsored pension and savings programs. She estimates the value of the deferral to be the difference between the present discounted value of the revenue from the current taxation of pensions as they accrue over the employee's working life and the present discounted value of the taxes collected when the benefits are received after retirement.[37] To estimate the value of the tax expenditure in a given year she uses the employer contributions to their plans as the basis. Then, using a range of assumptions about return on the assets, average age of workers participating in plans, etc., she estimates the tax expenditure would currently range between $40 and $69 billion per year assuming an average age of 35 for covered workers and a return on trust funds of 7 percent—within proximity of the Treasury Department's published estimates. Her results show that using an average age of 45 for covered workers yields an estimate that is about one-third lower than using an average age of 35. Since pension accruals and their commensurate contributions naturally tend to occur later in life, and are driven to do so by provisions in the Omnibus Budget Reconciliation Act of 1987, using an average age of 45 or higher is probably most reasonable in using this methodology. The average age used in the calculation notwithstanding, this methodology is subject to the same taxation on inflation bias discussed above. Under Munnell's proposed methodology, if 3 to 4 percent of the 7 percent return she assumes can be attributed to inflation—for example, the real return is in the 3 to 4 percent range—then at least half the tax expenditure she estimates is attributable to the taxation of inflationary returns on the assets held by the pension trusts.

B. The Distribution of Benefits Provided Under Pension Plans

While the size of the tax expenditure number related to pensions may be important, it has, for the most part, distracted policy analysts and policy makers from focusing on a more comprehensive evaluation of our retirement income security system. Pensions have come under much criticism because they cover less than half the total work force, and because the lack of coverage tends to be somewhat concentrated above the lowest wage strata in the economy. These criticisms generally ignore two extremely important points: (1) pensions are earned across a long period of a career, and cross-sectional looks at coverage do not give a good life cycle perspective, especially as they relate to family units; and (2) for some individuals a pension can never be an effective retirement savings vehicle, no matter how much we wish it would be.

The estimates that pensions cover slightly less than half the U.S. work force are derived from the Current Population Survey (CPS) done by the Bureau of the Census for the Department of Labor. The survey is representative of the U.S. population and its various elements. It is done monthly and is the basis for government estimates of the U.S. work force, unemployment, etc. Each March, a special supplement is added to the survey that gathers information on employment and income during the whole prior year. The March survey also ascertains whether people covered in the survey were participants in employer- or union-sponsored pension or savings plans. In addition to the annual survey in March, the CPS has occasionally looked at pension coverage and participation in somewhat more detailed surveys. These more detailed surveys generally focus on current participation in a pension or savings program in the immediate time period during which the survey is conducted. Typically these latter special looks at pensions get the most attention and they are used to determine what share of the work force is participating in pension plans. Based on these special looks at pensions in 1979 and again in 1988, most people agree that pension participation fell during the 1980s.

The information on participation in employer-sponsored plans gathered each March is more interesting in some regards than the

TABLE 11   Pension Plan Participation Rates During 1990 by Age and Sex of Workers

Age	Men	Women	Total
15–19	3.4	3.0	3.2
20–24	18.7	16.6	17.7
25–29	37.5	34.6	36.2
30–34	45.7	41.0	43.6
35–39	51.5	45.6	48.8
40–44	56.1	45.8	51.2
45–49	57.0	47.8	52.7
50–54	56.4	46.9	52.0
55–59	55.3	42.9	49.8
60–64	46.3	41.5	44.2
65+	24.6	21.7	23.3
Total	42.4	36.2	39.5

Source: Authors' tabulations of the March 1991 Current Population Survey.

more detailed information gathered periodically, because it presents a more continuous picture of evolving changes in coverage. Because it focuses on the whole prior year, it yields somewhat different estimates of pension participation from those of moment-in-time surveys. For example, Table 11 shows the pension participation rates for various age and sex groupings during 1990 based on the March 1991 CPS.

The pension participation rates for all workers calculated in the March 1991 CPS fall about 7 percentage points less than similar tabulations on the last pension survey done as part of the CPS in May 1988. The reason the rates are lower when calculated on this basis is that there are substantial numbers of workers, in any given year, who have only a brief or partial attachment to the work force. The summary of work patterns shown in Table 12 indicates that only 68 percent of the men and 51 percent of the women who held jobs some time during 1990 worked full time for the full year for only one employer or at least one full-year, full-time employer where the individual worked more than one job at a time. Full-time, part-year employment captures people engaged in seasonal employment, or those who experienced a period of unemployment from a full-time job during the year. Between ages ranging from the late 20s to the late 50s, there is a relatively stable percentage of both men and women working on a steady full-time basis.

Part-time attachment to the workforce, on either a steady or a temporary basis, was particularly prevalent among younger workers. It was also twice as prevalent, on average, among women as men, but generally three or four times as prevalent for women compared to men

TABLE 12   Percentage of Workers by Age-Sex Cohort and Work Force Attachment during 1990

| Age | Percentage of cohort working | | | | Percentage of total work force |
	Full-time, full-year	Full-time, part-year	Part-time, full-year	Part-time, part-year	
Men					
15–19	10.6	22.4	16.3	50.7	3.6
20–24	45.9	30.1	10.3	13.6	5.8
25–29	71.2	20.6	3.6	4.6	7.3
30–34	76.9	17.5	2.2	3.3	7.7
35–39	80.1	14.9	1.9	3.0	7.1
40–44	81.1	14.1	2.2	2.5	6.3
45–49	82.7	13.7	1.7	2.0	4.8
50–54	80.8	13.8	2.2	3.1	3.7
55–59	77.5	15.8	2.6	4.1	3.2
60–64	64.3	19.8	6.0	9.9	2.4
65+	34.6	15.7	23.3	26.5	2.1
Total	67.9	18.2	5.1	8.7	53.9
Women					
15–19	6.6	16.2	19.9	57.4	3.3
20–24	37.7	27.1	13.6	21.6	5.4
25–29	57.3	22.1	8.3	12.3	6.2
30–34	56.6	19.4	10.4	13.6	6.4
35–39	57.4	17.1	11.8	13.7	6.1
40–44	61.2	15.6	11.0	12.2	5.6
45–49	64.4	13.9	11.6	10.0	4.2
50–54	62.7	14.4	11.8	11.1	3.2
55–59	56.7	14.0	15.5	13.8	2.5
60–64	47.8	15.8	16.7	19.7	1.8
65+	23.9	14.3	27.7	34.2	1.6
Total	51.3	18.2	12.8	17.8	46.1

Source: Authors' tabulations of the March 1991 Current Population Survey.

between the ages of 25 and 64. In separate tabulations of the March 1991 CPS not shown, 71 percent of the individuals indicated they had worked part time throughout the whole year and 68 percent who indicated they had worked part time for part of the year also indicated that they worked part time because they wanted only part-time work. Those working part time on a continuous basis reported working a median of roughly 22 hours per week. Those working only part of the year had median reported hours that are roughly equal to working 20 to 25 percent of a full-time job on an annualized basis. For the younger individuals, part-time income is desirable because it helps meet needs during periods when they are making a significant time commitment to

TABLE 13   Pension Plan Participating Rates During 1990 by Age and Sex of Workers and Work Force Attachment

	Percentage of workers participating in pension plans				
Age	Full-time, full-year	Full-time, part-year	Part-time, full-year	Part-time, part-year	Total
Men					
15–19	16.3	4.3	3.1	0.4	3.4
20–24	29.2	11.3	13.4	3.7	18.7
25–29	45.5	20.1	19.4	5.1	37.5
30–34	52.9	25.3	15.9	6.7	45.7
35–39	58.2	27.9	15.6	15.9	51.5
40–44	62.5	34.5	14.9	5.1	56.1
45–49	62.9	32.8	15.1	10.9	57.0
50–54	62.0	38.4	32.1	9.7	56.4
55–59	60.9	42.0	33.0	13.7	55.3
60–64	54.4	42.6	15.3	19.8	46.3
65+	39.3	33.5	14.6	8.8	24.6
Total	54.1	24.6	13.6	5.3	42.4
Women					
15–19	18.2	3.1	3.5	1.0	3.0
20–24	29.2	13.4	8.8	3.6	16.6
25–29	46.6	23.3	22.7	7.0	34.6
30–34	54.8	30.1	25.7	10.4	41.0
35–39	61.2	29.9	28.3	14.7	45.6
40–44	58.4	36.0	25.7	12.9	45.8
45–49	59.6	37.0	23.3	15.6	47.8
50–54	58.8	39.1	22.4	16.1	46.9
55–59	56.3	39.5	23.6	13.1	42.9
60–64	59.1	39.1	23.1	16.0	41.5
65+	42.8	34.5	10.2	10.7	21.7
Total	53.4	26.8	19.3	8.5	36.2

Source: Authors' tabulations of the March 1991 Current Population Survey.

education. Many of them work only during vacations and holidays from school. For many married women, steady part-time employment helps augment family earnings.

   Variations in workers' attachment to the workforce are extremely important in explaining variations in pension or savings plan participation as shown in Table 13. Full-time, full-year workers were more than twice as likely to be participating in a pension plan as the full-timers working only part of a year. Part-timers were even less likely to be pension participants, with less than 10 percent of part-time, part-year workers being included under plans. In Table 13, controlling for attachment to the work force, the differential in pension participation noted between women and men in Table 11 largely disappears within the various groups. Women under age 40 generally have higher pension participation rates within each group of workers than their male counterparts. Women over age 40 and working full time may have slightly lower rates, but only by a couple of percentage points on average. The relatively high labor force participation rates of women, compared to earlier generations, and their participation in pension plans would seem to suggest that future generations of retiring women should receive significantly more pension income than current older women retirees.

One other aspect of Table 13 worth noting is the relationship between age and pension participation. For full-time, full-year workers especially, there is a clear pattern of increasing participation rates until workers reach their mid 30s, and then a leveling out until retirements start occurring when workers reach their mid to late 50s. Throughout most of the "middle age" portion of the career, pension participation rates are 10 to 15 percentage points higher than they are on average for typical full-time workers.

In assessing pensions, we sometimes overlook the time horizon over which pensions are accrued and the lifetime exposure that workers will have to qualify for one. The lowest levels of pension participation tend to occur in the youngest age cohorts. But the people in these age cohorts have to pass through middle age to get to retirement. As they age, they tend to move from tenuous attachments in their employment relationships to more stable ones. As they do so, many accrue benefits from the pension system. The experience of the baby boom generation with pensions over the last decade is a good example of how the system works over the life cycle.

The baby boom generation were born between 1946 and 1964. In 1980 they ranged in age from 16 to 34. Table 14 shows the pension participation rates of full-time, full-year workers from the baby boom in 1980, 1985, and 1990. Reading across a single line on the table allows comparison of a single cohort's progression through the pension system over a 10-year period. For example, of men aged 15 to 19 in 1980, 19.1 percent were participating in a pension, increasing to 31.9 percent in 1985 and 45.5 percent in 1990. While looking at the 1981 data might suggest that only 19 percent of 15- to 19-year-old men will receive a "tax benefit" from the pension system, a much larger group actually will. Even though male baby boomers' pension participation increased by 70 percent during the decade, and corresponding female participation increased by 76 percent, with the rapid influx of new baby boom workers during the decade overall participation rates increased only 3 and 4 percentage points respectively. One disturbing element in the table is

TABLE 14   Changing Pension Plan Participation Rates of Specific Cohorts of Full-Time, Full-Year Workers by Age in 1981 and Sex

| Age in 1981 | Pension participation rate (percent) | | | Age in 1991 |
	1980	1985	1990	
Men				
15–19	19.1	31.9	45.5	25–29
20–24	42.1	47.7	52.9	30–34
25–29	56.5	55.7	58.2	35–39
30–34	60.7	64.0	62.5	40–44
Total	53.4	52.0	56.5	
Total workers (millions)	17,275	24,714	29,436	
Women				
15–19	23.3	34.1	46.6	25–29
20–24	41.3	50.2	54.8	30–34
25–29	56.9	59.2	61.2	35–39
30–34	62.3	59.8	58.4	40–44
Total	52.4	51.7	56.5	
Total workers (millions)	10,693	15,776	18,844	

Source: Authors' tabulations of the May 1981, May 1986, and May 1991 Current Population Survey.

that as you look diagonally across the table to compare individuals of equivalent age in 1980 and 1990, you see the participation rates, especially for young men, have fallen significantly.[38]

The intensity of a worker's attachment to a job bears a direct relationship to annual earnings. Part-time workers tend to cluster at the lower end of the distribution of earnings and full-time workers tend to cluster at the upper end. As a practical matter, low levels of earnings tend to leave one with little discretionary income. Because hunger and other pressing current needs tend to drive up the discount rate on future consumption relative to meeting current needs, low-wage workers are less likely to save than high-wage workers. Thus workers with relatively low earnings levels would not be so likely as higher wage earners to look for employment that provided pensions. Table 15 shows the distribution of all workers, both male and female, by the four classifications of attachment to the work force used earlier, and also shows their labor force participation rate. The familiar pattern of higher participation in pensions at higher income levels is apparent. Critics of the tax preferences accorded pensions often point to distributions of this sort to claim that those policies are inequitable.

TABLE 15   Earnings and Pension Plan Participation Rates During 1991 by Age and Sex of Workers and Work Force Attachment

Annual earnings	Full-time, full-year	Full-time, part-year	Part-time, full-year	Part-time, part-year	Total
Number of workers (millions)	80.9	24.5	11.6	17.3	134.3
Percentage of workers in income class					
None	0.1	0.1	0.6	0.3	0.2
Under $5,000	2.1	28.8	30.4	73.8	18.7
5,000– 9,999	6.3	23.0	37.5	16.1	13.3
10,000–19,999	29.1	26.2	21.4	6.9	25.1
20,000–29,999	26.0	11.9	5.7	1.7	18.5
30,000–39,999	16.7	5.4	2.1	0.6	11.3
40,000–49,999	8.6	2.6	0.9	0.3	5.8
50,000–69,999	6.8	1.3	0.6	0.2	4.4
70,000+	4.3	0.7	0.7	0.2	2.8
Total	100.0	100.0	100.0	100.0	100.0
Percentage of workers by work force attachment					
None	34.8	11.3	30.0	23.9	100.0
Under $5,000	6.9	28.1	14.1	50.9	100.0
5,000– 9,999	28.5	31.5	24.4	15.6	100.0
10,000–19,999	70.0	19.1	7.4	3.5	100.0
20,000–29,999	84.5	11.7	2.7	1.2	100.0
30,000–39,999	89.0	8.7	1.6	0.7	100.0
40,000–49,999	89.7	8.3	1.4	0.6	100.0
50,000–69,999	93.0	5.4	1.1	0.5	100.0
70,000+	92.4	4.5	2.2	0.9	100.0
Total	60.2	18.2	8.6	12.9	100.0
Pension participation rates (percents)					
None	2.3	14.3	0.0	0.0	2.4
Under $5,000	9.9	6.6	4.2	3.5	4.9
5,000– 9,999	15.8	16.5	15.7	13.5	15.6
10,000–19,999	39.0	31.2	28.3	24.6	36.2
20,000–29,999	59.3	49.9	42.5	29.8	57.4
30,000–39,999	69.7	59.9	41.2	24.5	68.1
40,000–49,999	75.2	62.1	43.1	52.0	73.6
50,000–69,999	72.4	46.9	42.6	13.3	70.3
70,000+	65.5	41.8	48.1	28.6	63.7
Total	53.8	25.6	17.5	7.3	39.5

Source: Authors' tabulations of the March 1991 Current Population Survey.

In a number of regards, distributions like those shown in the bottom panel of Table 15 are misleading. First, they are person weighted, and a part-time, part-year worker who works an annualized average of eight hours a week is counted as equivalent to a full-time, full-year worker. Second, including very young cohorts of workers, many of whom have only casual attachment to the workforce, tends to inflate the perception of workers not getting benefits from the plans. Finally, many of the part-time workers who are not accruing a pension in their own right are married to someone who is. Given the structure of our income tax program, which taxes married couples primarily on the basis of their combined incomes, the tax benefits that accrue to one spouse because of pension coverage generally accrue to the other as well. This has become especially the case since the passage of the Retirement Equity Act in 1984, which expanded spouse and survivor protections originally included in ERISA.

A better way of evaluating the potential delivery of benefits is to focus specifically on a group of workers well established in their careers, who should be beginning to focus on their retirement needs. In order to do this we have focused specifically on the age group ranging from age 45 to 59. The pension status of single and married individuals in this age range are shown in Table 16. The table reflects all the people in the population who fell within the age range stipulated, not just the people who were working. In 1990 there were approximately 36.4 million people in this age range. Slightly more than one-fourth of them, 27.1 percent, were single.

Among the single individuals, 3.9 percent were receiving a benefit, and another 35.7 percent were participating in a retirement pension or saving plan sponsored by their employer. Another 22.3 percent of these single individuals had not received any earned income during the year in 1990. In other words, among single individuals who had worked in the prior year, or who had previously retired with a benefit, 51 percent were receiving some form of benefit from the tax preferences favoring pensions.

Among the married individuals, 69.4 percent were receiving some benefit from the pension system. Among them, 5.6 percent already appeared to have fully retired on some form of pension, reporting that they, their spouse, or both were receiving a pension, and had no earned income in 1990. For another 6.9 percent, one or both spouses were already receiving a pension, and one or both of them were still employed and actively participating in a retirement plan. For 38.0 percent, neither member of the couple was yet receiving a pension but one or the other spouse was participating in a pension; and in 18.5 percent, both members were participating in a pension plan. Among those not

TABLE 16   Marital and Pension Status of Individuals Aged 45 to 59 in 1990

	Single (percent)	Married (percent)
Neither participating nor receiving	60.4	31.5
Respondent only receiving	2.8	1.9
Spouse only receiving		3.7
Both receiving		0.4
Respondent only participating	35.7	19.5
Respondent participating and receiving	1.1	1.0
Respondent participating and spouse receiving		1.0
Respondent participating and both receiving		1.4
Spouse only participating		18.5
Spouse participating and respondent receiving		0.8
Spouse participating and spouse receiving		1.4
Spouse participating and both receiving		0.0
Both participating and neither receiving		18.5
Both participating and respondent receiving		0.6
Both participating and spouse receiving		0.7
Both participating and both receiving		0.0
Total percentage with some benefit	39.6	69.4
Total persons (millions)	9.86	26.5
Total number getting some benefit (millions)	3.90	18.39

Source: Authors' tabulations of the March 1991 Current Population Survey.

covered or not receiving a pension benefit of any sort, 2.4 million individuals reported no earnings in the prior year. If the people who had not worked in the prior year and were not already receiving a pension are removed from the basis for calculating the share of the population benefiting from a pension program, 75.3 percent of the remaining married individuals were receiving some benefit.

Looking at everyone within the age bracket being considered shows that 22.3 million out of 36.4 million people, or 61.3 percent, were participating in an employer-sponsored pension or saving program in some fashion. For a base population narrowed to those already retired and receiving a pension plus those still working, 22.3 million out of 31.8 million, or 70.1 percent were included in such a retirement program. These levels of exposure to employer-sponsored retirement benefits far surpass those that simply look at current participation rates across the whole population that are generally cited by critics of the current tax treatment of pension programs.

While the exposure to pensions may be considerably greater than critical characterizations would have us believe, the fact that some segment of society may be getting to retirement without any enhancement of Social Security benefits also bears scrutiny. Table 17 shows the

TABLE 17   Annual Earnings of Individuals Aged 45 to 59 in 1990 Not
Getting Any Sort of Benefit from Pension System

	Single (percent)	Married (percent)
Earnings ($)		
None	36.9	28.5
Less than $10,000	22.6	21.6
$10,000–19,999	21.1	19.2
20,000–29,999	9.8	12.5
30,000–39,999	5.0	6.9
40,000–49,999	1.8	4.0
50,000–69,999	1.7	3.7
70,000 or more	1.1	3.6
Total	100.0	100.0
Income ($)		
Less than $10,000	50.3	44.8
$10,000–19,999	26.2	21.3
20,000–29,999	11.3	13.4
30,000–39,999	5.5	7.5
40,000–49,999	2.7	4.4
50,000–69,999	2.0	4.4
70,000 or more	1.2	4.2
Total	100.0	100.0
Total persons (millions)	5.96	8.34

Source: Authors' tabulations of the March 1991 Current Population Survey.

1990 earnings and income of those individuals in the 45 to 59 age group completely detached from the pension system. The table indicates that the lack of pension protection as workers approach retirement is heavily concentrated in the lower wage and income strata. As the earlier discussion indicated, it is at the lower wage levels that Social Security provides the greatest return, at the expense of the earnings classes of people that get the greatest benefit from pensions. This general observation raises the question of how these two major elements of the retirement system distribute their respective benefits and tax preferences as they work in concert.

IV. Combined Tax Effects of Pensions and Social Security

In the previous section, the documentation that pension participation is relatively low among lower-wage earners is consistent with prior research findings. While there has been considerable research evaluating the coverage of pensions, there has been little work focusing on the distribution of the tax incentives accorded pensions, and how they interact with Social Security. One exception is an estimate of the distribution of retirement-related tax preferences based on the relative generosity of a sample of pension plans for workers at different earnings levels, participation in plans at the various earnings levels, and average tax rates for various income classes. That analysis concluded that the biggest group of gainers from U.S. pension policies were workers in families with annual incomes falling in the $30,000 to $50,000 range, encompassing roughly 40 percent of all workers' families.[39] There are two factors that contribute to this concentration of benefits from the tax preferences. First, pension participation reaches its highest levels within this income range. Second, higher tax rates accentuate the benefits of participation over the value of participation at lower income levels where tax rates are much lower.

Workers falling into the $30,000 to $50,000 income corridor are butting up against the upper end of Social Security protection, while heavily subsidizing lower-wage workers' Social Security benefits. To consider the pension related income-tax benefits accruing to workers in the middle to upper income ranges without considering their subsidization of the retirement benefits of lower-wage workers through Social Security only shows a partial picture of the total federal tax effects on workers' retirement accruals. Looking at the combined effects of Social Security and pensions provides a perspective on how the overall federal tax structure treats individuals accruing retirement income rights.

In order to assess the interaction of pensions and Social Security, we calculated the present value of Social Security benefits and taxes and the tax advantage of qualified pension and savings plans. Benefits and taxes are calculated for 25 hypothetical employees. These persons are assumed to be 30, 35, 40, 45, or 50 in 1991 and to have earnings in 1991 equal to $10,000, $20,000, $30,000, $50,000, or $100,000.

A. Social Security Benefits and Taxes

For purposes of Social Security, the hypothetical employee is assumed to enter covered employment at age 22 and to work continuously until retirement. Earnings are assumed to have increased at 6 percent per year before 1991, and to continue to increase at 6 percent beyond that point until retirement. All employees retire at age 65. Qualified plan benefits are based on the hypothetical employees' last jobs. Tenure in the last jobs is 35, 30, 25, 20, and 15 years beginning in 1991.

Social Security benefits are calculated for age 65 retirement under current law, projected into the future. We assume that workers covered by pensions might realize more growth in their earnings levels over their careers than workers who do not earn pension protection. In our projections of benefits, we assume that national average wages increase by 5 percent per year after 1990. The inflation rate is assumed to be 4 percent per year.

Unlike previous estimates of money's worth, we calculated an after-tax Social Security benefit. We assume that taxable retirement income consists of benefits from the qualified plans, other income, and 50 percent of the Social Security benefit. Other income is calculated by assuming that the hypothetical employees have additional income in retirement equal to a percentage of final earnings that varies with earnings. Persons with $10,000 of starting earnings are assumed to have no other income. The assumed percentage of final earnings is 5 percent at $20,000, 7.5 at $30,000, 10 percent at $50,000 and 15 percent at $100,000.

Total income at retirement is compared to the $25,000 threshold amount for a single person and the excess up to 50 percent of the Social Security benefit is taxed. The income tax rate is 15 percent for hypothetical employees whose starting wages in 1991 are $10,000, $20,000, and $30,000; it is 28 percent for employees whose starting wage is $50,000; and it is 31 percent for employees whose starting wage is $100,000. Income tax rates do not vary over the working and retired life of the employee.

Once after-tax Social Security benefits are calculated, the lump sum equivalents are calculated using the 1984 unisex pension mortality rates with a 6 percent interest rate and a 4 percent cost-of-living increase. Payroll taxes earmarked for OASI benefits are calculated using the current law rates applicable to employees and employers. Interest on taxes is accumulated to retirement assuming a 6 percent interest rate and no taxation of interest earnings. No preretirement mortality is assumed.

B. Qualified Plan Benefits and Taxes

The Wyatt Company has detailed information on pension and savings plan benefits that allow computation of plan benefits for about 675 companies. Of these companies, 308 have a 401(k) arrangement for employee tax-deferred savings and provide a defined benefit plan for employees. For each such company, the retirement annuity under the defined benefit plan is calculated under the terms of the plan as the terms apply to new hires. The defined benefit annuity is converted to a lump sum equivalent. The lump sum account balances for the 401(k) arrangements of the companies are calculated using current employee contribution rates and current employer matching rates.

Employee contribution rates to the defined contribution plan for non-highly and highly compensated employees are assumed to be equal to the current actual deferral percentage (ADP) rates reported by companies for such employees. If the company did not report its ADP rates, the average of all companies that did report rates is used. The income level at which employees are considered to be highly compensated is $60,535 in 1991. For computational simplicity, once a hypothetical employee is placed in the non-highly compensated group, he or she does not switch to the highly compensated group even if future earnings exceed the indexed threshold. This calculation procedure affects hypothetical employees whose starting wage is $50,000 in 1991 and whose tenure in the last job is more than 11 years. Thus, the hypothetical employees whose starting wages are $50,000 remain in the non-highly compensated group though wage growth at 6 percent per year will result in earnings larger than the crossover income level in a future year. Contributions accumulate until retirement with 6 percent interest.

The tax advantage of qualified plans is calculated in three steps. First the lump sum equivalent of retirement benefits under the qualified savings and pension plans is calculated for each hypothetical employee for each defined contribution and defined benefit plan of the companies in the Wyatt COMPARE® data base. Based on the lump sum, a level contribution rate as a percentage of earnings is calculated such that annual contributions at the calculated contribution rate accumulated at 6 percent interest equal the actual lump sum calculated for each employee and plan. In effect, each plan is treated as if it were a money purchase plan that is not coordinated with Social Security. Finally, based on the contribution rates calculated above, the lump sums that would accrue by retirement under two taxation schemes are calculated. The difference between the after-tax actual lump sum equivalent benefit and the lump sums calculated under the two alternative taxation schemes represents the tax benefits for qualified plans.

Qualified plan benefits accumulate without current taxation. To estimate the tax benefits of qualified plans, we first estimate the annual contribution amounts made to the plans and then estimate the taxes that would be made on contributions and the yield on account balances under the two schemes. In the first scheme, all contributions and earnings are taxed as they accrue. The difference between the after-tax lump sums of the qualified plans and the lump sum that would accrue if contributions and earnings were fully taxed each year is the estimated tax benefit of the current treatment of qualified plans. Under the estimated alternative tax benefit contributions to the plan and only that portion of the annual yield on the account balance in excess of the inflation rate are considered to be the tax preference.

Table 18 shows the distribution of the estimated tax benefits that might be accrued under three different tenure scenarios for individuals with five different levels of beginning salary in 1991. In this table the definition of the tax benefit is based on the nominal returns to the accumulating account, which includes the return on inflation. At each higher 1991 salary, other things being equal, the plans generate higher levels of tax benefits. Similarly, for each increase in the period of service under the plan, the accrual of tax benefits increases. While there is some variation in the tax benefits in each tenure-salary class, there is considerable clustering in each case.

Table 19 shows the distribution of the estimated tax benefits based on the real returns to the accumulating account. We believe the underlying methodology behind these calculations to be a more reasonable basis for estimating the tax benefits for retirement oriented savings. The results generally yield tax benefits that are only about one-third the level of those estimated using the underlying methodology usually applied by the critics of pension programs. Still the same general pattern of tax-related benefits results from the calculations when they are done in this fashion. Workers with higher-paid jobs derive greater benefits from the pension system than lower-paid workers. Workers who have longer tenures under their pension plans derive greater benefits than those with shorter periods of service.

Juxtaposing the tax benefits that accrue to various individuals because of their participation in an employer-sponsored retirement plan with Social Security gains and losses gives a completed picture of the net effects of the combined tax effects of the payroll and income tax systems. The results in Table 20 show such a juxtaposition. The essence of our findings is that above middle earnings levels, expected losses overwhelm the benefits provided through the tax incentives accorded employer-sponsored retirement programs. This is true regardless of which measure of tax preferences is used in estimating the pension accrual gains and the combined gains and losses from Social Security. The pension accrual gains shown in the table are the average of those estimated for all of the plans for which we could estimate benefits. Even the tax benefits provided by the most generous plans could not overcome the Social Security losses at the higher income levels.

The overall system appears to be somewhat progressive up to the Social Security maximum taxable income level, where the stabilization of Social Security losses is gradually offset by increased benefits provided through the pension system. There is a limit, though, to the

TABLE 18   Estimated Accrued Nominal Tax Benefits Received at Age 65 from Job Begun at Various Ages

Accrued tax benefits at age 65 taxing all returns	Percentage of plans for 1991 wage level				
	$10,000	$20,000	$30,000	$50,000	$100,000
Age 50					
Less than $1,000	5.8				
$1,000– 4,999	94.2	98.1	60.1		
5,000– 7,499		1.9	37.7	1.9	
7,500– 9,999			1.9	9.4	
10,000–19,999			0.3	86.4	3.2
20,000–29,999				2.3	36.7
30,000–39,999					52.6
40,000–49,999					6.8
50,000–79,999					0.3
80,000 or more					0.3
Age 40					
Less than $1,000					
$1,000– 4,999	59.1	1.3			
5,000– 7,499	38.6	12.0	1.3		
7,500– 9,999	2.3	40.6	4.5		
10,000– 19,999		46.1	84.1	1.6	
20,000– 29,999			10.2	9.4	
30,000– 39,999				39.9	
40,000– 49,999				33.8	1.0
50,000– 79,999				15.3	14.0
80,000– 99,999					37.7
100,000–129,999					43.5
130,000 or more					2.9
Age 30					
Less than $1,000					
$1,000– 4,999	1.9				
5,000– 7,499	7.5	0.3			
7,500– 9,999	29.2	1.0			
10,000– 19,999	60.4	33.4	3.2		
20,000– 29,999	1.0	57.1	25.0		
30,000– 39,999		7.1	47.4	1.3	
40,000– 49,999		1.0	20.8	1.9	
50,000– 79,999			3.6	26.0	
80,000– 99,999				44.1	1.3
100,000–199,999				26.3	29.9
200,000–299,999				0.3	62.0
300,000 or more					6.8

Source: Calculated by the authors.

TABLE 19   Estimated Accrued Real Tax Benefits Received at Age 65 from Jobs Begun at Various Ages

Accrued tax benefits at age 65 taxing real returns ($)	Percentage of plans for 1991 wage level				
	$10,000	$20,000	$30,000	$50,000	$100,000
Age 50					
Less than $1,000	99.4	45.8	2.9		
$1,000– 4,999	0.6	54.2	97.1	70.8	
5,000– 7,499				27.6	4.5
7,500– 9,999				1.6	23.1
10,000–19,999					71.8
20,000–29,999					0.3
30,000–39,999					0.3
40,000–49,999					
50,000–79,999					
80,000 or more					
Age 40					
Less than $1,000	3.6				
$1,000– 4,999	96.4	94.8	43.5		
5,000– 7,499		5.2	49.7	1.6	
7,500– 9,999			6.2	4.5	
10,000–19,999			0.6	87.3	1.9
20,000–29,999				6.5	16.9
30,000–39,999					50.7
40,000–49,999					27.4
50,000–79,999					2.2
80,000 or more					0.9
Age 30					
Less than $1,000					
$1,000– 4,999	87.0	6.5	1.0		
5,000– 7,499	12.0	37.3	4.5		
7,500– 9,999	1.0	41.9	12.7		
10,000–19,999		14.3	80.5	4.5	
20,000–29,999		1.3	26.3		
30,000–39,999				51.0	1.3
40,000–49,999				16.6	3.2
50,000–79,999				1.6	40.3
80,000–99,999					42.8
100,000 or more					12.4

Source: Calculated by the authors.

extent that high-salaried workers can derive added benefits through the tax preferences afforded pensions because of the section 415 limits that cap them. In our calculations, the youngest individual that we considered (the 30-year-old) at the 1991 wage level of $100,000 per year would have his or her benefits capped by the section 415 limits in

TABLE 20   Gains and Losses from Social Security, Average Pension Accrual
Gains, and Net Gains and Losses Combined

1991 wages	Years in last job	Social Security gains/ (losses)	Pension accrual gains		Net gains/(losses)	
			All yield taxed	Real yield taxed	All yield taxed	Real yield taxed
$10,000	15	$23,109	$1,550	$530	24,659	23,639
	20	17,685	2,929	1,010	20,614	18,695
	25	13,239	4,891	1,703	18,130	14,942
	30	5,148	7,557	2,655	12,705	7,803
	35	(4,879)	22,415	7,945	17,536	3,066
$20,000	15	11,355	3,130	1,070	14,485	12,425
	20	(3,433)	5,988	2,066	2,555	(1,367)
	25	(17,556)	10,044	3,497	(7,512)	(14,059)
	30	(30,975)	15,494	5,433	(15,481)	(25,542)
	35	(46,741)	22,408	7,942	(24,333)	(38,799)
$30,000	15	(5,384)	4,818	1,647	(566)	(3,737)
	20	(32,762)	9,221	3,181	(23,541)	(29,581)
	25	(53,838)	15,513	5,401	(38,325)	(48,437)
	30	(74,932)	23,943	8,411	(50,989)	(66,521)
	35	(101,720)	34,724	12,308	(66,996)	(89,412)
$50,000	15	(69,565)	13,038	4,553	(56,527)	(65,012)
	20	(111,677)	24,622	8,744	(87,055)	(102,933)
	25	(149,688)	40,894	14,763	(108,794)	(134,925)
	30	(189,055)	62,314	22,862	(126,741)	(166,193)
	35	(227,110)	89,292	33,483	(137,818)	(193,627)
$100,000	15	(82,715)	31,912	11,273	(50,803)	(71,442)
	20	(121,551)	60,506	22,135	(61,045)	(99,416)
	25	(160,433)	100,601	37,962	(59,832)	(122,471)
	30	(202,067)	154,264	60,749	(47,803)	(141,318)
	35	(240,971)	224,662	95,127	(16,309)	(145,844)

Source: Calculated by the authors.

slightly over half of the plans for which we estimated benefits. In any
event, the combined pension and Social Security systems yield results
that suggest younger workers in the middle up through the highest
income ranges can expect no subsidization of their lifetime retirement
savings even though they may participate in relatively generous pension programs.

V. Policy Issues and Considerations

Critics of current tax incentives encouraging employers to establish
pension or retirement savings plans for their workers often cite a

number of reasons why these incentives are bad policy. The major reasons include concerns about vertical and horizontal equity among taxpayers, and the loss of federal revenues badly needed within the context of the budget deficits that have persisted since the early 1980s. Throughout the 1980s, the legislative measures affecting pensions were propagated on the combined needs to provide greater equity and to reduce the federal budget deficit. Both were partly, if not largely, a ruse.

Critics of Social Security policy worry about the conflicting adequacy and equity goals underlying the program, and a broader group of policy analysts are increasingly concerned about the long-term funding status of the program. Critics of federal pension policy affecting its own workers are concerned about the excessive levels of benefits provided through federal pensions and the massive unfunded burden they pose for future generations of taxpayers.

A. Pensions and the Presumption of Inequity

For the sake of discussion, we assume that we live in a hypothetical economy comprised of 10 workers, and that their earnings represent all the income in the economy. Let us further assume that their earnings are distributed in accordance with the distribution shown in column 1 of Table 21. Let us finally assume that the benevolent despots that govern this society of workers have decided on a "perfect tax structure" such that they legislate a comprehensive income tax that taxes "all" earnings at rates shown in column 2 of Table 21. Having implemented this tax structure results in the collection of taxes from each of the workers as reflected in column 3 of the table.

For the sake of further discussion, let us now assume that the benevolent despots in charge of this society decide they want to encourage retirement savings, and so they decide to depart from a comprehensive income tax by establishing certain tax preferences for retirement savings. Let us assume that the rate of take-up of these preferences is represented by the rates shown in column 4 of Table 21, such that after partaking of the preference our workers end up with net taxable income as represented in column 5 of the table.

Finally, for the sake of discussion, let us assume that our benevolent despots have a firm policy that the government of their great land has to realize as much revenue under the revised tax structure as it did under the comprehensive income tax, and that the distribution of tax collections should also be the same. As a result of their decision, they implement a "modified tax rate" structure applied against net taxable salary as reflected in column 6 of Table 21. In this case, the modified

TABLE 21   Hypothetical Tax Rates and Tax Collections under "Perfect" and Alternative Tax Structures

Gross salary	Perfect tax rate	Perfect tax distribution	Tax preference	Net taxable salary	Modified tax rate	Perfect tax distribution
$10,000	0.01	$100	0.03	$9,700	0.010	$100
20,000	0.03	600	0.03	19,400	0.031	600
30,000	0.05	1,500	0.03	29,100	0.052	1,500
40,000	0.07	2,800	0.04	38,400	0.073	2,800
50,000	0.09	4,500	0.04	48,000	0.094	4,500
60,000	0.11	6,600	0.05	57,000	0.116	6,600
70,000	0.13	9,100	0.06	65,800	0.138	9,100
80,000	0.15	12,000	0.06	75,200	0.160	12,000
90,000	0.17	15,300	0.07	83,700	0.183	15,300
100,000	0.19	19,000	0.07	93,000	0.204	19,000
Total taxes		71,500				71,500

Source: Calculated by the authors.

tax structure collects exactly the same amount of taxes from each individual as the comprehensive tax structure did. Yet the higher paid workers appear to have received a greater advantage from the tax incentives than lower paid workers. In fact, they have received no advantage at all.

The example suggests that the mere existence of tax incentives, or their utilization at different rates across the income strata, does not necessarily result in any redistribution of the tax burden intended by the despots who set taxes. Looking at the existence of the preferences and their varying utilization after the fact may suggest that higher paid workers are being unduly favored under the modified tax system, but only because the intended tax structure is not considered as the basis for evaluation. There is nothing in the U.S. Constitution or any of its government's laws that explicitly specifies an intended tax structure for this land. Since the passage of the Congressional Budget Act in 1974, budget analysts at the Treasury Department and the Joint Committee on Taxation have estimated the "tax expenditures" related to various preferences in the U.S. Tax Code against their respective definitions of a *tax baseline*. Any tax expenditures is a preferential exception to the *baseline provisions* of the tax structure. But, as the *Budget of the United States Government* points out: "The 1974 Act does not, however, specify the baseline provisions of the tax law. Deciding whether provisions are preferential exceptions, therefore, is a matter of judgement."[40]

In the example cited above, the vertical equity intended in the comprehensive tax structure is maintained by manipulation of tax rates to meet the vertical equity goals. Under the U.S. tax structure, higher-paid workers take greater advantage of the incentives encouraging pension participation than their lower-paid counterparts. This fact is generally the basis for criticism of pension incentives on vertical equity grounds. The vertical equity criticisms ignore the a priori intentions of federal policy makers relative to the distribution of the tax burden across the income spectrum. It is also a myopic perspective that ignores the participation of most pension participants in Social Security and the interactions of the incentives and burdens across the federal taxing authority.

Another concern about pension policy relates to the horizontal equity issues raised because individuals equally well off participate at different rates in the incentives offered pensions. The problem of less than universal participation in federal programs is universal because even under the best of circumstances not everyone eligible takes advantage of the benefits offered by most federal programs. For example, only about 65 percent of the individuals eligible for cash assistance take it from the Supplemental Security Income (SSI) program run by the Social Security Administration.[41] Likewise, only 66 percent of the individuals eligible for food stamps actually receive them.[42] Among all farm operations, only 36 percent benefit from the distribution of direct government payments to farm operators.[43] Among undergraduates who are dependents of parents with family incomes below $10,000, 34 percent receive no direct federal aid, although 21 percent of those in families with incomes between $40,000 and $50,000 receive such aid, and 9 percent with incomes between $70,000 and $80,000 do.[44] As long as we are dependent on individuals choosing to take advantage of the opportunities presented to them, we will have incomplete success in attaining universal utilization in any program, be it an incentive or direct benefit. While less than universal participation in every public endeavor at providing benefits to members of society raises questions about horizontal equity, we will unlikely scrap them all simply because some of those eligible to benefit from them fail to participate.

Evidence supporting our contention that pure equity concerns were not the motivation for 1980s pension reforms relates to lawmakers' protection of their own self interests relative to restrictions they have imposed on other citizens. In the passage of ERISA, Congress had established maximum funding standards, limiting the amount of benefits that could be funded for highly compensated workers. While Congress considered exempting governmental workers from these limits, it struck the exemption from the final legislation.[45] In passing the Tax Reform Act of 1986, Congress lowered the maximum level of benefits private plans could fund for early retirees, but exempted themselves and other governmental and nonprofit workers from the new lower limits. In a similar vein, Congress exempted the federal government from having to meet the actual deferral percentage (ADP) tests in its own 401(k) type savings plan that it requires of all private employers. If lawmakers were truly interested in equity this is an odd way of delivering it.

B. Gaining Control of Our Federal Fiscal Incontinence

The federal budget deficit is often cited as a reason to eliminate the tax preferences accorded employer-sponsored retirement programs. Through the 1970s and the beginning of the 1980s, the tax incentives accorded pensions were more generous in several ways than they are today. In real terms, the maximum level of benefits that could be funded then was higher than it is now. In addition, defined benefit plans could be funded on the basis of projected benefit obligations back then, whereas funding limits are now based on accrued benefit obligations. Yet the deficits we are experiencing today are much larger than they were back when the tax code treated pensions more generously. The deficits we are suffering now did not grow out of the tax preferences encouraging employers to establish retirement oriented savings and pension programs for their workers. They grew out of the fact that we reduced the government's revenue stream during the 1980s by cutting tax rates without commensurate reductions in government expenditures.

Because our government leaders manufactured the government deficits we now endure, they have used them repeatedly as an excuse to reduce the scope of pension incentives, especially for private sector workers. During the 1980s, the Tax Equity and Fiscal Responsibility Act of 1982, the Deficit Reduction Act of 1984, the Tax Reform Act of 1986, and the Omnibus Budget Reconciliation Act of 1987 significantly reduced the incentives for employers to provide pensions. A host of other lesser bills also affected the sponsorship of plans. The burden of repeated legislation was only outdone by the onerous rules propagated by the regulators implementing new laws.

Since 1982, lawmakers have been looking for an easy way out of the structural imbalance that we have in our fiscal policy. The early theory was that low tax rates would stimulate such rapid growth that higher incomes would more than offset lower tax rates. They didn't. The intermediate theory was that base broadening coupled with further rate reductions would stimulate growth sufficiently to offset the deficit. It didn't. Most recently, there is hope that a "peace dividend" realizable now that we are at the end of the Cold War might help us resolve this problem. It is unlikely that it will. The laws of simple arithmetic preclude a painless way out of our federal budgetary deficits.

It appears that we have only three choices to deal with the problem: (1) we can raise taxes through either raising existing rates or creating new taxes; (2) we can cut expenditures, but must include entitlements in the equation if we wish to have a significant effect on aggregate expenditures; or (3) we can use some combination of the first two. As we seek a solution, we should seek one that helps us begin to close in on our short-term dilemma, while at the same time positioning us to deal with our long-term contingencies as well.

C. Providing Retirement Income Security Across the Income Spectrum

Given the long-term planning horizons required for retirement preparations, now is the best time to begin addressing the revisions in our national retirement policy that are necessary to deal with the demands baby boomers will pose as they begin to move into retirement. As we look at the policy options that are facing us, we should seek to take maximum advantage of each segment of the retirement system. Public policy initiatives should acknowledge that the most effective way to deliver retirement income security to lower wage workers is through a mechanism like Social Security. They should also acknowledge that pensions provide the greatest protection to workers with higher incomes.

In Table 17, where we were looking at individuals between the ages of 45 and 59, we saw a marked decline in the number of people between the $30,000 and $40,000 earnings levels without any attachment to a pension program. We also saw from Table 19 that it is above the $30,000 earnings level that workers begin to realize some substantial benefit from the tax incentives accorded employer-sponsored programs, especially if they have careers of any substantial duration in their job leading up to retirement. As we look out into the future and face the prospect that in 20 to 30 years we will have no choice but to deal with the Social Security funding issue, why not begin to take advantage of the characteristics of pension coverage now? If pensions are providing widespread protection to workers in the top 20 to 40 percent of covered earnings, why not begin to reduce their Social Security benefits on a prospective basis, with the clear message that they will need to fill the gap created by the prospective benefit reductions? To the extent that reductions in Social Security benefits at the upper end of the earnings scale net savings, these can be used to further subsidize the benefits at the lower end and to reduce the underfunding in the program.

Social Security benefits can be manipulated to accomplish the result proposed here in more than one fashion. One way to accomplish the goal would be to adjust the current replacement of average indexed monthly earnings (AIME) that is used in the calculation of the primary insurance amount (PIA) used to determine benefit levels. For example, the PIA for a person first eligible for benefits in 1992 equals to 90 percent of the first $387 of AIME, plus 32 percent of the next $1,946 of AIME, plus 15 percent of any AIME in excess of $2,333. These dollar thresholds where the replacement of AIME changes are often referred to as the "bend points" in the formula. If we raised the bend point where the rate goes from 90 to 32 percent and lowered the bend point where the rate goes from 32 to 15 percent, our suggestion could be accomplished. An alternative way to accomplish essentially the same outcome would be to move to a formula without bend points that provides a declining replacement of AIME as that measure increases (e.g., 140 percent of AIME equal to $400, declining at x percent with each $100 increase in AIME). In either case, maximum benefits paid through Social Security would be lower than they are now. It is possible even to conceive of a case where Social Security benefits decline with increases in AIME at the upper end of covered earnings levels.

Implementing a proposal of this sort would undoubtedly bring added criticism in the money's-worth context. They can be somewhat diffused by arguing that, in return for their support of Social Security's redistributive aspects, higher-wage earners are given tax incentives to save for their retirement through employer-sponsored pension and savings programs. On the qualified plan front, there is a need to review the discrimination requirements that are imposed on both defined contribution and defined benefit plans if Social Security benefit levels are reduced at the upper end of the current formula.

For example, in the application of the ADP tests for 401(k) plans, workers just above the earnings limits that classify them as highly compensated often are limited by the percentage tests to contributions significantly below the maximum dollar contribution they might otherwise make. Someone earning $80,000 per year might want to contribute 10 percent of pay to the plan, but would not be able to because the ADP rate among non-highly compensated workers would disqualify it. The worker earning $200,000, on the other hand, might be well within the percentage test. These tests particularly limit the contributions of workers nearing retirement who have discretionary income to invest during their latter working years, even though they may not have been able to take full advantage of tax preferences for retirement savings earlier in their career. The tests for permitted disparity in benefit accruals between highly compensated and non-highly compensated employees under integrated defined benefit plans give a similar result. When the test is applied it is the workers whose earnings are just above the Social Security covered compensation level that cause the most problem in passing the tests.

One criticism of shifting retirement income dependence from Social Security more toward private provision for higher-paid workers is that very few pension programs provide full indexation of retirement benefits. If the government is concerned about providing some level of real income protection it could do so in a couple of ways. First, it could allow higher paid workers at retirement to buy back some additional Social Security benefits that could be fully indexed. Alternatively, it could provide indexed securities to serve as the funding basis behind an indexed annuity. In any event, the federal government should not be obliged to fully insure all annuitants against inflation regardless of their relative economic well being. If there is one thing the last decade or two has taught us, it is that many members of society do not have automatic inflation protection. If farmers, homeowners, workers, and others do not enjoy inflation insurance, it is hard to understand how high income pensioners, including federal retirees, can be guaranteed full immunity from inflation at the expense of those who are not so immunized. Certainly, the frailties of age warrant some special consideration against the cost of rising prices as it affects some standard of basic living needs. Beyond that, classification as a pensioner does little to distinguish those of us receiving them from those of us who are not.

The authors thank Lex Miller and David Webb of The Wyatt Company for their assistance with the statistical and computational development of this paper. We also thank Dick Joss and Linda Moncrief of The Wyatt Company for their help in checking our results. The authors' comments and opinions expressed in this paper are solely their own and do not necessarily represent the opinions of The Wyatt Company or any of its other associates.

Notes

1. U.S. Department of Defense, Office of the Actuary. *Valuation of the Military Retirement System: September 30, 1990* (Washington, DC: U.S. Department of Defense, 1991), pp. B-2–B-5.

2. Dan M. McGill, *Fundamentals of Private Pensions*, 4th ed. (Homewood, IL: Richard D. Irwin, Inc., 1979), pp. 23–28.

3. Ibid.

4. For a complete discussion of the evolution of this concept and its applica-

tion to retirement plan issues, see Sylvester J. Schieber, *Benefits Bargain: Why We Should Not Tax Employee Benefits* (Washington, DC: Association of Private Pension and Welfare Plans, 1990).

5. U.S. Office of Management and Budget, *Special Analyses, Budget of the United States Government for Fiscal Year 1990* (Washington, DC: OMB, 1989), p. G-1.

6. Charles Krauthammer, "Looking for a Real Scandal? The U.S. Government, not the House Bank, is Insolvent," *Washington Post* (March 27, 1992): A21.

7. Ibid.

8. Alicia H. Munnell, "It's Time to Tax Employee Benefits," *New England Economic Review* (July/August 1989): 49.

9. A. Haeworth Robertson, *Social Security: What Every Taxpayer Should Know* (Charlotte, NC: Retirement Policy Institute, 1992).

10. Michael J. Boskin, *Too Many Promises: The Uncertain Future of Social Security* (Homewood, IL: Dow Jones-Irwin, 1986), p. 2.

11. Dorcas R. Hardy and C. Colburn Hardy, *Social Insecurity: The Crisis in America's Social Security System and How to Plan For Your Own Financial Survival* (New York: Villard Books, 1991), p. vii.

12. Executive Office of the President of the United States, *Budget of the United States Government, Fiscal Year 1993* (Washington, DC: U.S. Government Printing Office 1992), Table 13-5, p. Part One-281.

13. See Sylvester J. Schieber, "Can Our Social Insurance Systems Survive the Demographic Shifts of the Twenty-First Century?" in *Demography and Retirement: The Twenty-First Century*, ed. Anna M. Rappaport and Sylvester J. Schieber (Westport, CT: Pension Research Council and Praeger Publishers, 1993).

14. The Budget indicates that the underlying economic assumptions are not consistent in developing the estimates. Also, the Social Security and Medicare estimates are developed on an "open system" basis that considers future entrants into the programs as well as current participants. The federal annuity estimates, on the other hand, are calculated on a "closed system" basis that does not consider new entrants into the systems. The estimates of unfunded health benefits for federal plan participants are calculated on the basis of service accrued to date.

15. The Wyatt Company, *1983 Survey of Actuarial Assumptions and Funding* and *1991 Survey of Actuarial Assumptions and Funding* (Washington, DC: The Wyatt Company, 1983, 1991).

16. *Budget . . . Fiscal Year 1993* (note 12), Table 13-5, p. Part One-276.

17. Peter J. Ferrara, *Social Security: The Inherent Contradiction* (Washington, DC: Cato Institute, 1980), pp. 10–11.

18. Barber Conable, "A Formula with a Future," *U.S. News and World Report* (September 30, 1985): 80.

19. Hastings Keith, "Fairness Is One Thing; Pigs at a Trough Another," *Los Angeles Times* (January 29, 1992): Part B, p. 7.

20. Munnell (note 8).

21. Committee on Economic Security, *Social Security in America* (Washington, DC: U.S. Government Printing Office, 1938), p. 203.

22. Ibid.

23. Ibid., p. 205.

24. Ibid.

25. Ibid.

26. For example, see Robert J. Myers, *Social Security*, 4th ed. (Philadelphia: Pension Research Council and University of Pennsylvania Press, 1993) and Martha Derthick, *Policymaking for Social Security* (Washington, DC: Brookings Institution, 1979).

27. *1982 Annual Report of the Board of Trustees of the Federal Old-Age and Survivors Insurance and Disability Insurance Trust Funds* (Washington, DC: U.S. Government Printing Office, 1982), Table 32, p. 71.

28. *1984 Annual Report of the Board of Trustees of the Federal Old-Age and Survivors Insurance and Disability Insurance Trust Funds* (Washington, DC: U.S. Government Printing Office, 1984), Table 33, p. 76.

29. Anthony Pellechio and Gordon Goodfellow, "Individual Gains and Losses from Social Security Before and After the 1983 Amendments," *Cato Journal* 3, 2 (fall 1983).

30. No mortality was assumed before retirement age; therefore the OASI portion of FICA taxes overstates the taxes paid for retirement benefits. Pre-retirement survivor benefits amount to about 4 percent of the long range cost of the system and, thus, our overstatement of the taxes is not large.

31. "We Must Cut the Deficit Now; Here's How to Do It," *Business Week* (August 6, 1990): 60–61.

32. Alicia H. Munnell, "Current Taxation of Qualified Pension Plans: Has the Time Come?" prepared for American Law Institute-American Bar Association, Pension Policy Invitational Conference (Washington, DC, October 1991).

33. *Budget . . . Fiscal Year 1993* (note 12), p. Part Two-23.

34. Ibid.

35. Similarly, the federal government as an employer is exempted from having to meet the actual deferral percentage (ADP) tests for its own 401(k) type savings plan that it requires all private employers to meet.

36. Munnell (note 32).

37. Ibid.

38. This finding corresponds with that of David E. Bloom and Richard B. Freeman, "The Fall in Private Pension Coverage in the U.S.," NBER Working Paper 3973, (Cambridge, MA, 1992) where they find that pension coverage fell most heavily on younger and less educated men.

39. Schieber (note 4), pp. 35–38.

40. *Budget . . . Fiscal Year 1993* (note 12), p. Part Two-23.

41. John F. Sheils et al., "Elderly Persons Eligible for and Participating in the Supplemental Security Income Program," report prepared for the U.S. Department of Health and Human Services by Lewin-ICF (January 1990).

42. Pat Doyle and Harold Beebout, "Food Stamp Program Participation Rate," report prepared for the U.S. Department of Agriculture, Food and Nutrition Service by Mathematica Policy Research (November 1988).

43. James Duncan Shaffer and Gerald W. Whittaker, "Average Farm Incomes: They're Highest Among Farmers Receiving the Largest Direct Government Payments," *Choices* (second quarter 1990): 31.

44. National Center for Education Statistics, *National Postsecondary Student Aid Study: Estimates of Student Financial Aid, 1989–1990* (Washington, DC: U.S. Department of Education, October 1991), p. 7.

45. Senator Lloyd Bentsen's comments in *Legislative History of the Employee Retirement Income Security Act of 1974*, prepared by the Subcommittee on Labor of the Committee on Labor and Public Welfare, U.S. Senate (Washington, DC: U.S. Government Printing Office, April 1976), p. 1735.

Comments by David C. Lindeman

Syl Schieber and Gordon Goodfellow have written a paper that is long overdue in its attempt to analyze social security and tax preferenced pensions together. Though I think that aspects of their analysis are flawed, the paper makes the useful point that the United States in fact does have a "retirement income policy" and that the policy should be examined as a whole. This policy is not novel. Most other developed countries have the same policy—that is, an organized public program that runs through the governmental fisc and a conscious decision by the public authority to allow complementary or supplementary private arrangements, usually employer-based, to accumulate according to the rules of what can be described as either a consumption tax or a lifetime income tax. As with other public goods, the relative importance of the nominally private, but publicly suffused, tier is greater in the United States than in, at least, the countries of continental Europe.

Their analysis attempts to quantify what we know already. Tax-preferenced pensions and similar arrangements—qualified plans in tax code talk—are a middle-class and upper-income institution and, accordingly, that is to whom the tax advantages accrue. To the extent that a commensurately higher income tax burden is borne by non-participants, in particular those in the lower portions of the income distribution, that extra income tax burden is compensated—arguably, more than compensated—by the redistributional configuration of Social Security measured on a lifetime accounting basis.

The problems with doing this kind of analysis are many. Somehow, everything must be reduced to a common measure. In addition, there has to be a stable reference point—a normative position—against which to measure advantages and disadvantages. Because such norms are hard to agree on, because the tax system is such a compromise of theory, practical constraints, and incentives, this kind of analysis is illusive. Take two examples from the paper presented here. In one case, I think the authors overstate the redistribution effects of Social

Security. In the other, I think they overstate the tax advantages of qualified plans.

My understanding of their money's-worth analysis of Social Security is that they are comparing after-tax benefits to gross payroll taxes. I think that is incorrect. Under the 1983 Amendments, Social Security increasingly will be taxed according to consumption tax principles—in effect, the same principles that apply to qualified plans. The piece of Social Security derived from after-tax employee contributions always has been so taxed. We do not require Social Security recipients to compare their benefits to their basis—that is, employee contributions paid from after-tax income—and then tax them on the difference. Instead, in accord with the "pre-payment" or "opportunities" variant of consumption taxation, because half the Social Security contributions were once included in the tax base, therefore half the benefits are non-taxable.

On the other hand, until the 1983 Amendments, the other half of the benefits—the portion derived from never-taxed "employer" contributions—were never included in the income tax base. This is a tax preference by either standard, consumption tax or conventional income tax. The 1983 Amendments provide for taxation of this excluded half above a statutory threshold. Because the threshold is not indexed, the exclusion will wither away. If this second half of benefits, the increasingly taxable half, is compared to the full amount of before-tax employer contributions, then the rate of return within Social Security is being understated. Under consumption tax rules, the tax paid on benefits is merely a deferred tax on the contributions not previously included in the income tax base. This is the amount that the government has chosen to co-invest with the saver. Accordingly, the after-tax benefits should be compared to prior contributions with the government's initial co-investment subtracted out. In addition, I think we have the familiar stacking problem. It appears that the top marginal rate is being applied to the taxable half of social security. This too may be exaggerating the effects of taxing benefits.

My other major example relates to their analysis of tax benefits of qualified plans. If only for reasons of administrative practicality, the Haig-Simmons measure of income—yearly employment income and annual changes in wealth—has never been implemented in the United States or, as far as I know, any other country. Approximately 80 percent of wealth is taxed on some sort of exceptional basis, whether as "normal" deferral (as in taxation capital gains or the inside buildup in insurance or annuity contracts purchased from after-tax income) or as "consumption tax" deferral (as in qualified plans or the $125,000 exemption for home sales).

Consequently, in measuring the preference given qualified plans, I would recommend using as a benchmark a tax rate on capital that reflects the realities of taxation rather than the much ignored ideal. Normal income taxation, therefore, would incorporate the effect of capital gains deferral, at least to the extent it now exists. Arguably, the norm should be further adjusted to reflect a more extensive shifting toward such investments in a world in which qualified plans were abolished. Compared to such a benchmark, the incremental advantage of qualified plans in the authors' analysis would be diminished.

The analysis presented here is also influenced by the tax rate structure. By definition, those in higher brackets benefit more than those in lower brackets. I would have also liked to see a supplementary analysis that assumed a uniform tax rate on capital income, thus separating out the pure tax rate effects from the structural effects of benefit formulas in the plans that were examined.

I think that these examples indicate a more basic problem—establishing a stable reference point against which the measure departs from a norm. When the exceptions in the tax code swallow the theoretical rules, then those rules become increasingly vulnerable as a normative measure. As one commentator has put it, it's almost impossible to define what is the "essential structure" of most tax systems in the developed world—virtually all such tax systems are hybrids that contain a mix of income tax and consumption tax rules. As I noted earlier, practical considerations have established realization, rather than annual accrual, as the primary means by which we tax capital income. Similarly, considerations of administrative practicality, at least at the level of the individual income tax, have helped shape the current cash-flow rules that we apply to qualified plans. Consequently, we have a tax system that taxes capital income in three different ways—annual accrual, "normal" deferral, and "consumption tax" deferral.

Even these conventional tax base distinctions break down, however, if a long enough accounting period is adopted. As Aaron and Galper (1985) have argued, if bequests and gifts are generally included in the tax base—if, in effect, death is constructively treated as the final act of consumption—then the differences between a consumption tax and an income tax evaporate. Further, as they suggest, there is no logical reason why the astronomical regularity of a calendar year has to be enshrined in the tax law, especially if holding to that fetish distorts choices between current and future consumption and reduces national savings.

The irony for me in reading this paper is that I have always wanted to see an analysis done along the lines attempted by Syl and Gordon. I even will admit to having encouraged this effort from time to time.

Now having seen it, however, I've come to the conclusion that a less consistent and more qualitative analysis would be more helpful. Rather than a money's worth analysis of Social Security, I think it would be more helpful to compare results under Social Security's existing redistributional formulas to a hypothetical system in which everyone received the same replacement rate in Social Security with full actuarial adjustments for survivors. This comparison could easily incorporate taxes paid on the benefits in both worlds. Among other things, this type of analysis would not depend on the antecedent level of payroll taxes, thus removing the inter-generational transfer effects that are probably contributing to the rather surprising results of so many losers relative to winners. Inevitably, however, it would demonstrate that the system is generally progressive with respect to lifetime earnings.

I would then compare those different Social Security outcomes to an analysis of pension participation and outcomes along the lines presented on pp. 154–63. One of the problems with Section IV of the paper is that it overlays the analysis of the tax advantages of qualified plans on top of the money's-worth analysis of Social Security and thus presumes more participation in lower parts of the income distribution than actually occurs—indeed, than can be supported by the paper's own analysis of CPS surveys. If, instead, the outcomes were weighted according to the probabilities of participation, then the measured advantages would be skewed upward more than what is presented here.

In fact, the most useful and illuminating part of the paper is the part contained in the section I just referred to. What emerges confirms what we know from other sources. Pensions are middle class and middle aged. They are part of a compensation package tied to good jobs for people with stable work histories in firms and occupations that have been relatively successful in coping with the structural changes in the economy.

Is that enough? Apparently not, for we have had two basic responses to that question over the last decade. One has been to limit the preferences through indirect means like tighter section 415 limits, the OBRA 87 full funding limit, and the section 4980A excise tax imposed on distributions from qualified plans that exceed certain levels. The other has been tighter and more rigorous coverage and non-discrimination rules.

Why have we had these responses? In no small part, it is because, being unwilling to explicitly raise taxes on current consumption, policy makers are driven by fiscal policy imperatives to accelerate receipts over the short term. Another reason is an equal reluctance to tamper very much with the structure of social welfare spending on the aged.

Consequently, we try to achieve our social ends through more tax code regulation.

I want to raise what I see as two major problems with this trend. The first relates back to my earlier point about the mutable nature of our tax code. When I consider all the unfinished business left after the 1986 Tax Reform Act—inflation and the taxation of capital income, integration of corporate and individual income taxation, arbitrage opportunities from the mismatch of deductions and the inclusion of capital income—I conclude that the society eventually will move to some version of a cash-flow tax as the only means to resolve most of these problems in a manner that is administratively simple and economically efficient. The degree to which such a cash-flow tax would be a consumption tax or an income tax would depend on how bequests and gifts are treated and whether capital equipment at the business level is expensed or depreciated. Regardless of those choices, if the essential structure of the tax code becomes more like the current exception for qualified plans, then the theoretical basis for today's tax code regulation of qualified plans no longer exists.

But, even if we continue to have the current muddle of a tax structure, eventually we are going to have to ask what we are getting for the regulation relative to the costs. If our concerns about qualified plans were solely ones of tax equity as usually defined, we could deal with them at the individual level. We could expand IRAs for those not currently participating in an employer plan; with appropriate offsets, we could even expand IRAs for participants whose employer-provided contributions or benefit accruals are suboptimal. The Canadian experience suggests that such individually based arrangements can work. On the other hand, if we want to go after the doctors, lawyers, and other members of the undeserving rich from getting too much, we could tinker with the section 4980A excise tax to lower the threshold or include other components of AGI, including Social Security, in the calculation. Similarly, we could submit any unused distributions from qualified plans to income taxation at death, although this suggestion is not without its tracing problems.

But, instead, we regulate the tax benefit at the firm level because, I conclude, we must be trying to affect behavior—that is, we are trying to force individuals to save more for their retirement than they might otherwise and, in so doing, possibly redistribute the costs of such saving from the highly compensated to the rank and file. Given compensating wages, widespread borrowing against residences, and the steady drift toward lump sum distributions, I suggest that the theoretical case for achieving such ends, particularly if a lifetime perspective is taken, is very weak. If anything, the net result of our current policies may only encourage wasteful tax arbitrage. In any event, before we continue down this road, we might want to pause and see if there is any empirical evidence one way or the other.

In contrast, the experience of the last decade suggests the costs are not trivial. A great deal of the decline in pension coverage, especially defined benefit plan coverage, relates to major structural changes in the economy. In the small plan area, I suspect that changes in the overall tax environment—lower tax rates, combined with the suspicion that rates are likely to increase—may be affecting behavior. But, there is a substantial residual that plausibly can be correlated with the costs of regulation. Some of these costs were particularly high in the 1980s because of repeated changes in law and major regulations. Other costs represent a higher cost for ongoing compliance. In effect, an implicit tax is being imposed on what is notionally a tax-free savings vehicle. Expressed as a fraction of plan assets or even as a tax on annual investment earnings, these costs—at least $2 billion in a conventional year, more than $5 billion in an exceptional year—appear small in the aggregate. Compared to an annual tax expenditure of approximately $40 billion for the exemption of investment income from current taxation, the ratio is more significant. In effect, these are monies that are going neither to participants nor the fisc, but rather to overhead.

In short, I believe that we are pushing on a string by trying to shape retirement outcomes in what is, after all, a voluntary pension system. Though I have no wish to visit unemployment on our growing private bureaucracy of benefit lawyers and actuaries, I have to ask the question of whether we know what value is added by their efforts. There are alternatives: for example, expanded individual savings on a cash-flow basis coupled with more selective taxation at time of distribution. And, as Syl and Gordon remind us, there is Social Security (and, I would add, its functional equivalent, a mandatory pension tier) through which society can achieve its retirement income objectives. Further, in Social Security at least, any redistribution of costs relative to benefits can be achieved with a great deal less ambiguity and deadweight losses.

Whatever the means, however voluntary or mandatory, it is worth reminding ourselves that we are only playing an accounting game with ourselves and the next generation if these retirement claims are not translating themselves into increased levels of aggregate savings, investment, productivity, and, therefore, national product in the future when the claims become due. To use Pierre Pestieau's phrase, if "negative pensions"—that is, public debt owing to current consumption—rise in tandem with the putative funding of either our private or public pensions, we will have accomplished very little, however equitable the arrangements.

The views expressed here are the author's and do not reflect the views of the Pension Benefit Guaranty Corporation. Please do not cite this paper without the author's permission.

References

Aaron, Henry J. 1991. Summary of Remarks at a Conference on Private Pensions and Public Policy sponsored by the OECD. Paris, July 1–3.
Aaron, Henry J., Barry P. Bosworth, and Gary Burtless. 1989. *Can America Afford to Grow Old? Paying for Social Security*. Washington, DC: Brookings Institution.
Aaron, Henry J. and Harvey Galper. 1985. *Assessing Tax Reform*. Washington, DC: Brookings Institution.
Andrews, Emily S. 1990. "Private Pensions and Retirement Income: The U.S. Experience." Paper prepared for the OECD, November.
Dilnot, Andrew. 1991. "Taxation and Private Pensions: Costs and Consequences." Presented at a Conference on Private Pensions and Public Policy sponsored by the OECD. Paris, July 1–3.
Hay/Huggins Company, Inc. 1990. *Pension Plan Cost Study for the PBGC*. Final Report submitted to the PBGC, September.
Ippolito, Richard A. 1991. "The Productive Inefficiency of New Pension Tax Policy." *National Tax Journal* XLIV, 3 (September): 405–17.
Lindeman, David C. 1990. "Changes in Pension Fund Taxation: How Would Federal Regulation and Programs Be Affected?" Presented at a Conference on Assessing the Implications of Proposals for Pension Fund Taxation, Employee Benefit Research Institute—Education and Research Fund Policy Forum, May 3.
Lindeman, David C. and Larry Ozanne. *Tax Policy for Pensions and Other Retirement Savings*. Washington, DC: Congressional Budget Office, April 1987.
Lindeman, David C. and Kathleen P. Utgoff. "Pension Taxes and the U.S. Budget." In *Pensions and the Economy: Sources, Uses, and Limitations of Data*, ed. Zvi Bodie and Alicia H. Munnell. Pension Research Council. Philadelphia: PRC and University of Pennsylvania Press, 1992.
Pestieau, Pierre. 1991. "The Distribution of Private Pension Benefits: How Fair Is It?" Presented at a Conference on Private Pensions and Public Policy sponsored by the OECD, Paris, July 1–3.
Steuerle, C. Eugene. 1992. *The Tax Decade: How Taxes Came to Dominate the Public Agenda*. Washington, DC: Urban Institute Press.
Utgoff, Kathleen P. 1991. "Towards a More Rational Pension Tax Policy: Equal Treatment For Small Business." *National Tax Journal* XLIV, 3 (September): 383–91.

Comments by Alicia H. Munnell

The argument for taxing pensions on a current basis rests on two propositions. First, in the absence of wealth transfer taxes, an income tax is more equitable than a consumption tax and is in fact the standard against which the Treasury, with the apparent concurrence of Congress, measures deviations. A comprehensive income tax would include in its base the change in the present value of pension benefits. Second, taxing pensions on a deferred basis can be justified only if such favorable treatment achieves desired social goals. In the case of pensions, the argument would have to be that pension plans provide rank and file employees with retirement benefits that they would not have accumulated on their own, or, failing that test, that they increase the saving of those who are covered so that national saving and capital accumulation are greater than they would have been otherwise.

The evidence does not support either of these justifications. Pension benefits are a trivial source of income for retirees in the bottom two-fifths of the income distribution; that is, they do not appear to be providing benefits to those who would not save on their own. And the assets of pension plans do not represent a net increment to national capital accumulation, but rather a shift in the composition of saving and capital accumulation; that is, they do not appear to increase national saving. Given that the revenue loss associated with qualified plans does not appear to be achieving major social goals, the taxation of benefit accruals should be shifted to a current basis.

Against this bulwark, Goodfellow and Schieber fire the following salvo. First, they argue that an income tax should include in its base only the real increment to wealth; taxing the full increase in pension wealth, which includes an inflation component, would be unfair. Second, they contend that the tax expenditure figures are exaggerated. Third, they claim that pension coverage is more widespread than current surveys suggest, once attention is focused on the "relevant" group. Fourth, they argue that high-income people lose so much under the Social Security system that they deserve favorable treatment under the pension system. Finally, they make the point that the distribution of tax revenues depends not only on the base but also on the rate structure, and that the system could compensate for any item omitted from the base by adjusting rates. While all these contentions contain a kernel of truth (the kernel is larger in some instances than in others), not one makes a dent in the case for taxing pensions.

I. Taxation of Inflationary Gains

Public finance theory does indeed state that the income tax base should include all *real* economic income. Any returns to capital that are simply compensating for inflation should not be in the tax base; that is, nominal capital gains and the inflation component of interest should not be taxed. Likewise, deductions should not be allowed for the inflation component of interest expense.

When the Office of Tax Policy of the Treasury Department in 1984 issued its report on *Tax Reform for Fairness, Simplicity, and Economic Growth* (Treasury I), it devoted considerable attention to the inequities and inefficiencies that result from including both inflationary and real returns in the tax base. As part of its comprehensive and theoretically pure reform proposals, the Treasury suggested explicit inflation adjustments for depreciation allowances, for cost of goods sold from inventory, for capital gains, and for interest income and expense.

Interest indexing did not make it as far as the much watered-down report *The President's Tax Proposals to the Congress for Fairness, Growth, and Simplicity* (Treasury II, 1985), which appeared six months later. The reasons given for dropping this critical provision were that it greatly increased the complexity of taxpayer compliance, caused a loss in revenue, and provided a windfall for financial institutions (McLure, 1986). (The proposal also did not extend to interest on mortgages on the taxpayer's principal residence—a flaw that would have created serious misallocations.) Some indexation of capital gains was recommended in Treasury II, but was never enacted.

The point is that, while eliminating the inflation component of the return to capital is clearly desirable on theoretical grounds, inflation indexing is not currently part of our tax law nor likely to be in the foreseeable future. Thus it makes little sense to apply such an adjustment in the area of pensions when it is not applicable to any other part of the economy. Including the increase in pension wealth in the tax base simply would bring this increment in economic well-being in line with that accorded other components of income.

II. The Size of the Tax Expenditure

The authors cite four reasons why the current estimate of tax expenditures overstates the revenue loss from pensions. Three relate to the fact that in the future more retirees will be paying taxes on more pension benefits. The fourth is a faulty argument regarding nonprofit employers; whether or not the Treasury loses money through employer deductions of pension contributions is irrelevant to the current tax expenditure calculation. The current cash-flow calculation focuses on the individual and estimates the difference it would make if pension accruals were taxed as wages at the time the accrual was earned rather than in retirement.

A generous interpretation of the major thrust of the authors' concern with the revenue estimates is that the cash-flow calculation may not be the best way to measure revenue loss in those instances where tax concessions take the form of deferral as opposed to deductions or exclusions. Indeed, the cash-flow approach may not be the best, but the reason has little to do with systematic overestimates of the revenue forgone.

The limitation of cash-flow accounting for the value of deferral in the case of pension plans can be seen clearly by considering a situation in which (1) annual contributions to private plans and pension fund earnings exactly equal benefit payments during the year, and (2) workers face the same marginal tax rate in retirement as they do during their working years. Under these assumptions the revenue loss would equal zero, according to the Treasury calculations of tax expenditures. Yet individuals covered by private plans would continue to enjoy the advantage of deferring taxes on employer contributions and investment income until after retirement.

A better estimate of the annual revenue loss resulting from the current deferral would be the difference between (1) the present discounted value of the revenue from current taxation of pensions as they accrue over the employee's working life, and (2) the present discounted value of the taxes collected when benefits are received by the employee after retirement. Such a calculation suggests that the current treatment of pensions reduces tax revenues between $40 billion and $69 billion in present value terms (Munnell and Yohn, 1992).

Thus the revenue loss associated with the favorable treatment of pension contributions and earnings under the personal income tax is substantial regardless how it is measured.

III. The Coverage Issue

The goal of federal tax policy since 1942 has been to encourage, through favorable tax provisions, the use of tax-qualified pension and profit-sharing plans to ensure greater retirement security for all employees, not just highly paid executives. In other words, the strategy is to secure retirement benefits for the rank and file by providing tax incentives that will induce higher paid employees to support the establishment of plans providing broad coverage.

Despite the near universal need for supplementary pension income, data on pension coverage from the March 1989 Current Population Survey showed that only 39 percent of full-time private wage and salary workers were covered by either a defined benefit or a defined contribution plan (Woods, 1989). Another 7 percent were covered by employer-sponsored pre-tax plans such as 401(k)s or 403(b)s. These kinds of plans are not necessarily employer-financed, however, nor do they necessarily provide retirement income since they frequently allow lump sum payments. Nevertheless, the sum of those covered by pretax plans and traditional plans equals only 46 percent of private full-time workers.

Pension coverage and pension benefit payments also tend to be concentrated among higher-paid employees. The incidence of pension coverage increases markedly as earnings levels rise. For example, in 1988 only 30 percent of nonagricultural wage and salary workers earning under \$20,000 were covered by a plan, compared with 73 percent of those with earnings over \$50,000 (EBRI, 1989).

Goodfellow and Schieber suggest that one need not be concerned about the extent and distribution of pension coverage. They argue that the percentage of people touched by pensions at some point in their lifetimes is much larger than that revealed by a snapshot and that pensions would never be an effective retirement saving vehicle for low-income people anyway.

To support their first point, the authors look at pension exposure for people aged 45 to 59. They find that 39.6 percent of single people are either participating or receiving benefits and 69.4 percent of married people are either participating or receiving benefits or married to someone who is participating or receiving benefits. If the "married to" component were dropped, their numbers show that only 45 percent of people in this prime age group were ever touched by pension plans. All indications are that this percentage will decline in the future.

Their argument that pensions would never be helpful to low-income people in any event undermines one of the major justifications for government subsidy of this vehicle. In short, the tax incentives do not appear to be meeting the goal of providing supplementary retirement income to those who would not save on their own, and are unlikely to do so in the future.

IV. Combined Tax Effects of Social Security and Pensions

The authors calculate that young workers in the middle- and high-income ranges are going to contribute over their lifetimes much more in Social Security taxes than they can hope to receive in benefits. They then compare this "loss" under the Social Security system with the estimated gain from the favorable tax treatment of pensions, and conclude that this group on balance receives no subsidization of their lifetime retirement savings. This analysis and the implied policy implication are flawed on two counts.

The first problem, which is evident in both their Table 6 and their current discussion, is the calculation of benefits relative to contributions under the Social Security program. For a given cohort, the return on combined employee and employer contributions, under a pay-as-you-go system, is equal roughly to the rate of real wage growth plus the rate of growth in the labor force. If average real wages are growing at a rate of 1 percent, the cohort as a whole should receive at least a 1 percent real return on its combined contributions. Table 6, however, suggests that almost everyone loses under Social Security. My sense is that the difficulty arises from the fact that the authors have assumed that individual real earnings grow by 2 percent while the aggregate grows by 1 percent. This inconsistency does not produce sensible results; it greatly exaggerates the expected net losses under Social Security (Table 19).

The more important point, however, is that even if these numbers were calculated correctly they would not provide any support for exempting pension accruals from current taxation under the personal income tax base. Social Security is a redistributive system and, with the reduction in the aggregate return to younger cohorts, most young, highly-paid workers will undoubtedly contribute more than they receive in benefits. That fact, however, does not provide any theoretical or practical justification for deviating from a comprehensive measure of income when defining the personal income tax base.

V. The Issue of Compensating Rates

It is true that Congress could offset any particular omission from the tax base with a compensating adjustment in rates. Such an approach, however, would be a very peculiar way of developing a tax structure. The more standard sequence is to establish the base and then apply the desired set of marginal tax rates. Moreover, the sharp decline in marginal personal income tax rates over the last 20 years is not what one would expect if Congress were trying to compensate for this exclusion from the tax base, which benefits primarily higher income tax payers.

VI. Conclusion

Goodfellow's and Schieber's main conclusion is that we should take advantage of the high-income bias in the current pension structure by reducing benefits under Social Security for highly-paid workers and letting them rely more on private pensions. This is a bad proposal; it will both harm high-paid employees and, in the long run, have an adverse effect on low and moderate-paid workers under Social Security.

Social Security has two unique advantages over even the best pension plans; it allows mobile workers to take the full value of accrued benefits with them as they move from job to job, and it provides a fully indexed annuity after retirement. Stripping high-income employees of part or all of this protection is likely to hurt many workers.

A large part of the success of Social Security can be attributed to the fact that it is a universal program. All workers contribute and receive benefits as an earned right. The fully indexed benefit is valued by the highly paid as well as by those earning much less. The program already faces a challenge as the return to successive cohorts of young workers necessarily declines as the program matures. In order to provide progressive benefits, higher-paid workers will inevitably receive less than they contribute. Worsening this tradeoff will only undermine support for the program, which in the long run will hurt low-paid workers.

The solution is not to alter the basic structure of Social Security, but rather to include pension accruals in the personal income tax base as suggested by the theory of comprehensive income taxation. In my view, that proposal has escaped completely unscathed from the Goodfellow-Schieber salvo, and remains the most desirable alternative.

The views expressed are solely those of the author and do not necessarily reflect the official position of the Federal Reserve Bank of Boston or the Federal Reserve System.

References

Employee Benefit Research Institute. 1989. "Pension Coverage and Benefit Entitlement: New Findings from 1988." *EBRI Issue Brief* 94 (September).

McLure, Charles E., Jr. 1986. "Rationale Underlying the Treasury Proposals." In *Economic Consequences of Tax Simplification*. Conference Series No. 29. Boston: Federal Reserve Bank of Boston.

Munnell, Alicia H. and Frederick O. Yohn. 1992. "What Is the Impact of Pensions on Saving?" in *Pensions and the Economy: Sources, Uses, and Limitations of Data*, ed. Zvi Bodie and Alicia H. Munnell. Pension Research Council. Philadelphia: PRC and University of Pennsylvania Press.

U.S. Department of the Treasury, Office of the Secretary. 1984. *Tax Reform for Fairness, Simplicity, and Economic Growth: The Treasury Department Report to the President*, vol. 1, Overview (November). Washington, DC: U.S. Department of the Treasury.

———. 1985. *The President's Tax Proposals to the Congress for Fairness, Growth, and Simplicity*. 1985. Washington, DC: U.S. Government Printing Office.

Woods, John R. 1989. "Pension Coverage Among Private Wage and Salary Workers: Preliminary Findings from 1988 Survey of Employee Benefits." *Social Security Bulletin* (October): 2–19.

Chapter 5
Pension Benefit Guarantees in the United States: A Functional Analysis

Zvi Bodie and Robert C. Merton

I. Introduction

In this paper we use *functional analysis* to examine the pension benefit guarantee system in the United States. The functional perspective on financial policy making begins with the set of *functions* required, and then looks for the optimal *institutional structure* to perform those functions.[1] Our analysis begins with a brief description of the functions served by the pension system and of the institutional structure currently in place to perform those functions in the United States. We explore the roles of the government and the private sector in providing retirement-income security and the complex interaction between them. The paper then focuses on the federal system for insuring private-sector defined-benefit pension promises against default risk. Finally, we consider how pension benefits might be adjusted for changes in both the cost of living and the standard of living.

The functions of a pension system are perhaps best described in the context of a household's life-cycle consumption/savings plan.[2] Institutions of many forms serve to facilitate life-cycle savings. The specific life-cycle purpose of the pension system (including the government-run Social Security system) is to provide households with income in the event that earnings stop due to death, disability, or retirement.[3]

An often-used metaphor for describing the retirement-income system in the United States is the three-legged stool. The first leg is Social Security and government welfare programs for the aged, the second is employer- or labor union-provided pensions, and the third is direct individual saving. The relative importance of these three sources of retirement income varies significantly, both across households within the United States and among different countries.[4] The Social Security part of the system provides a "floor" that is mandatory and nonassignable. The government actively encourages employers and households themselves to provide the other two legs of the retirement-income stool. Through tax incentives, it encourages employers to provide pension plans that—like Social Security—are mandatory and nonassignable. It also offers tax incentives to self-employed individuals and households who are not otherwise covered to provide a retirement fund for themselves, and imposes penalties on early withdrawal of money from the fund. Finally, in the United States, the government insures private-sector defined-benefit pension plans against default risk.

Some of the frequently cited economic justifications for having the government directly provide a layer of retirement benefits for everyone include:[5]

Informational Efficiencies

It is costly to acquire the knowledge necessary to prepare and carry out long-run plans for income provision. Strictly, each person's optimal lifetime financial plan depends on preferences known only to that person. But people may have enough in common in this regard that a standard retirement savings plan can prove to be suitably close to optimal for many. By providing a basic plan that saves enough to supply a level of retirement income that is at least the minimum that everyone would want, the government can help all people save more efficiently than they could on their own.

Adverse-Selection Problems

There is the risk that people will outlive their retirement savings. One way to insure against the risk of exhausting one's savings during retirement is by saving in the form of life annuity contracts. But because the private market for life annuities is voluntary it has the problem of adverse selection: there is a tendency for people with a higher than average life expectancy to have a high demand for this kind of insurance. In the competitive equilibrium, the average individual will find the equilibrium price unattractive and will tend to self-insure against longevity risk by providing an extra reserve of retirement savings.[6] Mandatory Social Security is one way of overcoming the adverse-selection problem. By making participation in the plan mandatory and offering life annuities as the only payout option, the deadweight cost of adverse selection is greatly reduced.

Free-Rider Problems

In virtually every country that has a national pension system, participation at some minimum level is mandatory. Some observers of government see such provisions for intervention as pure paternalism. But an alternative purpose for a government-mandated universal retirement-income system is to address the *free-rider* problem. That is, the citizenry may collectively feel an obligation to offer a "safety net" for everyone living in their midst. Thus, de facto there will be a safety net, even though no formal provision is made for one. But if this collective commitment were well understood by all, the existence of the de facto safety net would cause individuals to modify their saving behavior. For some, at least, there would be a tendency not to make full provision for their own retirement. Similarly, some may also take more risk in investing their retirement savings than they would in the absence of a safety net. Mandating participation by everyone forces people to pay for what they ultimately will receive from the system. Thus according to this view, the purpose of the mandatory system is to protect society against free riders. While this reasoning supports a mandatory *minimum* level of universal participation, it says nothing about what that level should be.

If those three reasons are the principal ones justifying the existence of the Social Security system, then what determines the level of benefits so provided? Differences in tastes and endowments among individuals argue for limiting the level of benefits provided by Social Security to an amount that is likely to be a minimum common to all; the other two parts of the retirement income system would provide the rest. Furthermore, direct government provision of retirement income has other potential drawbacks. In a strictly unfunded *pay-as-you-go* government-operated pension system, benefits are theoretically paid entirely from the stream of revenue generated by the payroll tax levied on currently active workers. If such were the case, benefits would fluctuate up and down with changes in collections. In most such systems, however, there is a benefit formula, and benefits accrued under that formula are viewed as a form of government debt. Without funding, however, a rising ratio of retired to active workers and/or large government deficits can lead to a concern that the level of future benefits will be reduced.

As a case in point, consider the 1983 reform of the United States Social Security system. A changing demographic structure for workers led many to become concerned that there could be dramatically reduced benefits in the future in a pure pay-as-you-go system. Hence, a key provision of that reform was to require substantial prefunding of future benefits.[7] To do this, the Social Security payroll-tax rate was raised and the excess of current revenues over current benefit payments is invested in government bonds held in a trust fund. While this procedure apparently funds the plan, some are less sure about the purpose for such funding. In a private plan, funding is used to insure against default by the plan sponsor. Here the promise to pay benefits has the same level of full faith and credit of the government as the bonds used to fund the plan. Yet there seems to be a belief that this change may help to ensure that, when they reach retirement, workers will indeed receive benefits approximating those promised under the current benefit formula (i.e., the one in effect in 1992).

Even with the 1983 prefunding provisions, there is some question about whether current Social Security benefit levels will be maintained in the United States. Such questions highlight the political risk endemic to the government-provided leg of the three-legged retirement income stool and offer an explanation and additional role for the other two legs. The political risk associated with Social Security arises from a basic paradox of power: the government is too powerful to bind itself credibly to any set of existing rules. The current Social Security benefit formula or the method of financing those benefits can be changed. The U.S. Congress has changed both in the past, and it can do so again in the future. Even if those currently running the government are committed to paying promised Social Security benefits, they cannot fully bind future governments to do so.

This brings out an important difference between government and private-sector obligations. A private-sector plan sponsor cannot unilaterally repudiate its legal liability to make promised payments. It can default because of inability to pay, but it cannot repudiate its legal obligations without penalty.[8] On the other hand, the government—because it has the power to legislate changes in the law—can sometimes find ways to repudiate such obligations without penalty. Indeed, an integrated system in which private plan sponsors supplement government-provided pension benefits to achieve a promised "replacement ratio" of preretirement earnings can be seen as a type of private-sector insurance against the political risks of the government-run system.[9]

One can therefore view a mixed public-private system of retirement income provision as a way of reducing the risks of each separate component by diversifying across providers. Public-sector pension plans can change the law and reduce benefits already promised. Private-sector pension plan sponsors are committed by law (and perhaps reputation) to pay promised benefits, but they may default. As an additional linkage reinforcing the first two legs of the retirement-income stool, there may be government insurance of private pension benefits.

Whether or not the government offers guarantees of private pension benefits, it may, as a matter of public policy, be on the hook for such guarantees anyway. Were there to be a system-wide failure of defined-benefit plans or private annuities, it is likely that the federal government would step in as the ultimate insurer. Indeed, when in 1990 First Executive Life, a large insurance company that had provided the annuities for several terminated private pension plans, was found to be insolvent and annuity payments were either not made or cut back, there were immediate calls in Congress to have the federal government guarantee those annuity payments.[10] If the government is de facto guarantor of at least some providers of pension benefits, it should manage those de facto obligations in the same way as its explicit guarantee activities.

II. Private Pension Plans

The second leg of the United States retirement-income system is pension plans sponsored by employers and labor unions. Pension plans are defined by the terms specifying the "who," "when," and "how much," for both the plan benefits and the plan contributions used to pay for those benefits. The *pension fund* of the plan is the cumulation of assets created from contributions and the investment earnings on those contributions, less any payments of benefits from the fund. In the United States, contributions to the fund by either employer or employee are tax deductible, and investment income of the fund is not taxed. Distributions from the fund, whether to the employer or to the employee, are taxed as ordinary income.[11] There are two "pure" types of pension plans: *defined contribution* and *defined benefit*.

In a defined-contribution plan, a formula specifies contributions but not benefit payments. Contribution rates usually are specified as a predetermined fraction of salary (e.g., the employer contributes 15 percent of the employee's annual wages to the plan), although that fraction need not be constant over the course of an employee's career. The pension fund consists of a set of individual investment accounts, one for each employee. Pension benefits are not specified, other than that at retirement the employee applies the total accumulated value of contributions and earnings on those contributions to purchase an annuity. The employee often has some choice over both the level of contributions and the way the account is invested. In principle, contributions could be invested in any security, although in practice most plans limit investment choices to bond, stock, and money-market funds. The employee bears all the investment risk; the retirement account is, by definition, fully funded by the contributions and the employer has no legal obligation beyond making its periodic contributions. For defined-contribution plans, investment policy is essentially the same as for a tax-qualified individual retirement account. Indeed, the main providers of investment products for these plans are the same institutions, such as mutual funds and insurance companies, that serve the general investment needs of individuals. Therefore, in a defined-contribution plan, much of the task of setting and achieving the income-replacement goal falls on the employee.

In a defined-benefit plan, a formula specifies benefits, but not the manner, including contributions, in which those benefits are funded. The benefit formula typically takes into account years of service for the employer and level of wages or salary (e.g., the employer pays the employee for life, beginning at age 65, a yearly amount equal to 1 percent of his or her final annual wage for each year of service). The employer (called the "plan sponsor") or an insurance company hired by the sponsor guarantees the benefits and thus absorbs the investment risk. The obligation of the plan sponsor to pay the promised benefits is like a long-term debt liability of the employer.

As measured both by number of plan participants and by the value of total pension liabilities, the defined-benefit form dominates in most countries around the world.[12] This is so in the United States, although the trend since the mid-1970s is for sponsors to choose the defined-contribution form when starting new plans.[13] But the two plan types are not mutually exclusive. Many sponsors adopt defined-benefit plans as their primary plan, in which participation is mandatory, and supplement them with voluntary defined-contribution plans. Moreover, some plan designs are "hybrids" combining features of both plan types. For example, a "cash-balance" plan is a defined-benefit plan in which each employee has an individual account that accumulates interest. Each year, employees are told how much they have accumulated in their account, and if they leave the firm, they can take that amount with them. If they stay until retirement age, however, they receive an annuity determined by the plan's benefit formula.[14] A variation on this design is a "floor" plan, which is a defined-contribution plan with a guaranteed minimum retirement annuity determined by a defined-benefit formula.[15] These plan designs usually take into account the benefits provided by the Social Security system.

With defined-benefit plans, there is an important distinction between the pension *plan* and the pension *fund*. The plan is the contractual arrangement setting out the rights and obligations of all parties;

the fund is a separate pool of assets set aside to provide collateral for the promised benefits.[16] In defined-contribution plans, by definition, the value of the benefits equals that of the assets, so the plan is always exactly fully funded. But in defined-benefit plans there is a continuum of possibilities. There may be no separate fund, in which case the plan is said to be unfunded. When there is a separate fund with assets worth less than the present value of the promised benefits, the plan is underfunded. And if the plan's assets have a market value that exceeds the present value of the plan's liabilities, it is said to be overfunded.

Why and how does funding matter? The assets in a pension fund provide collateral for the benefits promised to the pension plan beneficiaries. A useful analogy is that of an equipment trust. In an equipment trust, such as one set up by an airline to finance the purchase of airplanes, the trust assets serve as specific collateral for the associated debt obligation. The borrowing firm's legal liability, however, is not limited to the value of the collateral. By the same token, if the value of the assets serving as collateral exceeds the amount required to settle the debt obligation, any excess reverts to the borrowing firm's shareholders. So, for instance, if the market value of the equipment were to double, this would greatly increase the security of the promised payments, but it would not increase their size. The residual increase in value accrues to the shareholders of the borrowing firm.

The relation among the shareholders of the firm sponsoring a pension plan, the pension fund, and the plan beneficiaries is similar to the relation among the shareholders of the borrowing firm in an equipment trust, the equipment serving as collateral, and the equipment-trust lenders. In both cases, the assets serving as collateral are "encumbered" (i.e., the firm is not free to use them for any other purpose as long as that liability remains outstanding), and the liability of the firm is not limited to the specific collateral. Any residual or "excess" of assets over promised payments belongs to the shareholders of the sponsoring firm. Thus the larger the funding, the more secure the promised benefits. However, whether the plan is underfunded, fully-funded, or overfunded, the size of the *promised* benefits does not change.

III. The Nature of Defined-Benefit Pension Obligations[17]

As previously described, in a defined-benefit plan the pension benefit is determined by a formula that takes into account the employee's history of service and wages or salary. The plan sponsor provides this benefit regardless of the investment performance of the pension fund assets. The annuity promised to the employee is therefore the employer's liability. What is the nature of this liability?

Private-sector defined-benefit pension plans in the United States offer an *explicit* benefit determined by the plan's benefit formula. However, many plan sponsors have from time to time provided voluntary increases in benefits to their retired employees, depending on the financial condition of the sponsor and the increase in the living costs of retirees.[18] Some observers have interpreted such increases as evidence of *implicit* cost-of-living indexation.[19] These voluntary ad hoc benefit increases, however, are very different from a formal COLA (cost-of-living adjustment). It is unambiguous that under current laws in the United States the plan sponsor is under no legal obligation to pay more than the amount promised explicitly under the plan's benefit formula.

There is a widespread belief that in final-pay formula plans pension benefits are protected against inflation at least up to the date of retirement. But this is a misperception. Unlike Social Security benefits, whose starting value is indexed to a general index of wages, pension benefits even in final-pay private-sector plans are "indexed" only to the extent that (1) the employee continues to work for the same employer, (2) the employee's own wage or salary keeps pace with the general index, and (3) the employer continues to maintain the same plan. Very few private corporations in the United States offer pension benefits that are automatically indexed for inflation. This lack of inflation indexation gives rise to the portability problem. Workers who change jobs wind up with lower pension benefits at retirement than otherwise identical workers who stay with the same employer, even if the employers have defined-benefit plans with the same final-pay benefit formula.

Both the rulemaking body of the accounting profession (the Financial Accounting Standards Board [FASB]) and Congress have adopted the present value of the nominal benefits as the appropriate measure of a sponsor's pension liability. FASB Statement 87 specifies that the measure of corporate pension liabilities to be used on the corporate balance sheet in external reports is the accumulated benefit obligation (ABO)—that is, the present value of pension benefits owed to employees under the plan's benefit formula, absent any salary projections and discounted at a nominal rate of interest. Similarly, in its Omnibus Budget Reconciliation Act (OBRA) of 1987, Congress defines the current liability as the measure of a corporation's pension liability and sets limits on the amount of tax-qualified contributions that a corporation can make as a proportion of the current liability. OBRA's definition of the current liability is essentially the same as FASB Statement 87's definition of the ABO.

Statement 87, however, recognizes an additional measure of a defined-benefit plan's liability: the projected benefit obligation (PBO).

The PBO is a measure of the sponsor's pension liability that includes projected increases in salary up to the expected age of retirement. Statement 87 requires corporations to use the PBO in computing pension expense reported in their income statements. This is perhaps useful for financial analysts, to the extent that knowing the excess of the PBO over the ABO helps them to derive an appropriate estimate of expected future labor costs to use in valuing the firm as a going concern. The PBO is not, however, an appropriate measure of the benefits that the employer has explicitly guaranteed. The difference between the PBO and the ABO should not be treated as a liability of the firm, since those additional pension costs will only be realized if the employees continue to work in the future. If those future contingent labor costs are to be treated as a liability of the firm, then why not book the *entire* future wage bill as a liability? If this is done, then shouldn't one add as an asset the present value of future revenues generated by these labor activities? It is indeed difficult to see either the accounting or the economic logic for using the PBO as a measure of pension liabilities.

We can perhaps further clarify the issues involved by considering a numerical example. Suppose the plan pays a benefit equal to 1 percent of final salary per year of service. To keep the mathematics simple, we make additional assumptions that do not affect the basic qualitative conclusions. Plan participants enter the plan at age 25, retire at age 65, and live until age 85. There is immediate vesting, no early retirement option, and no employee turnover.[20] These assumptions allow us to ignore the actuarial adjustments necessary to account for mortality risk and turnover.

We further assume that the typical employee's salary increases at the rate of inflation. This implies no change in real wages over an employee's career and allows us to avoid the complications arising from the spread between nominal wage growth and inflation. Finally, we assume that the interest rate appropriate for discounting nominal annuities is 9 percent per year (the riskless real rate of 3 percent per year plus an expected rate of inflation of 5 percent per year plus a risk premium of 1 percent per year).

Under a final-pay formula of this sort, there is a "wage-indexation effect" that is central to understanding the difference between the ABO and the PBO. Consider an employee who has just turned 26 years old and who has received a salary of $30,000 for the just-completed work year. He has therefore accrued a deferred pension annuity of $300 per year for twenty years starting thirty-nine years from now when he retires. The present value of this deferred annuity is $95. This is the ABO. With inflation at 5 percent, if he works for another year he will receive a salary of $31,500. The pension annuity that he then is entitled to is 2 percent of $31,500, or $630 per year starting thirty-eight years from that date. This is $330 more per year in pension benefits than the $300 pension annuity he was entitled to after working only one year. We can decompose this $330 increase in pension benefits into two parts: (1) $315, which is 1 percent of the second year salary of $31,500; and (2) $15, which is the increase in the pension benefit arising from the increase in the salary base for computing the pension benefit. We call this second part the "wage-indexation increment." Had he not worked the additional year, he would have been entitled to only $300 per year at retirement. Thus he has earned the $15 indexation increment to his pension benefit through continued employment.[21]

By contrast, if the pension benefit were automatically indexed for inflation up to the age of retirement, then whatever happens in the future, the employee's projected pension benefit after one year of service is $300 x 1.05^{40} or $2,112 per year. The present value of this deferred annuity is $669. This is the PBO. The PBO would be the correct number to use for the firm's liability if benefits were tied to some index of wages up to the age of retirement, independent of whether the employee stays with the employer. Because private plans in the United States do not offer such automatic indexation, however, it is a mistake to use the PBO as the measure of what the sponsor is contractually obliged to pay to employees.[22]

IV. The Role of Pension Guarantees[23]

As has been noted, a major putative advantage of a defined-benefit pension plan over a defined-contribution plan is that it protects the employee against investment risk. The economic efficiency of this protection against investment risk is enhanced by the provision of guarantees against default risk. To understand the efficiency gains from guarantees of pension annuities, it is critical to distinguish between employees and investors (stockholders and bondholders) in firms that provide pension annuities. The distinction is that, unlike the firm's investors, the employees holding the sponsor's pension liabilities strictly prefer to have the payoffs on their contracts as insensitive as possible to the default risk of the firm itself. The function served by a pension annuity is for the beneficiaries to receive a specified benefit upon retirement. That function is less efficiently performed if the contract instead calls for the benefit to be paid in the joint event that the employee retires *and* the firm is still solvent.[24]

Even if the sponsoring firm offers an actuarily fair increase in the employee's cash wages to reflect the risk of insolvency, it is still likely that an employee would prefer a pension annuity with the least default risk. Employees typically have a large nondiversified stake in the firm already.[25] They may have invested in firm-specific human capital, which loses value if the firm does poorly. Thus few employees would consciously agree to accept default risk on their pension benefits in order to increase their expected cash wages. This is true even when the employee has all of the relevant information necessary to assess the default risk of the firm. In most cases the employees do not have the relevant information, and this fact makes the welfare loss even greater.

For example, consider the profile of a "typical" defined-benefit plan beneficiary. The vast majority of those covered by PBGC guarantees are blue-collar and white-collar workers for whom pension benefits constitute a large portion of total retirement savings. Such employees are unlikely to have asset portfolios of sufficient size or the investment expertise necessary to hedge the nondiversifiable risks of their defined-benefit pension asset. Only the most highly compensated managerial employees of the firm might have the financial wealth and knowledge required to diversify away the risks of their defined-benefit pension claims. But to hedge this risk they would effectively have to take a short position in the sponsoring firm's equity. Typically, managers and employees are prohibited from shortselling the firm's securities by the provisions of their incentive compensation package.

In contrast, an investor in the stocks or bonds issued by the sponsoring firm voluntarily and explicitly takes a financial interest in the fortunes of the firm itself. The function of these securities is to allow investors to participate in the risk and return prospects of the firm. Investors can diversify away much of the default risk associated with any one specific firm as part of their total portfolios. Employees with a substantial part of their wealth in firm-specific defined-benefit pension annuities usually cannot achieve such optimal diversification. They are like investors who are constrained to hold a large fraction of their wealth in the form of long-term bonds issued by a single firm, which is also their employer.[26] Thus both their tangible and human capital are significantly exposed to the fortunes of a single firm.

A firm sponsoring a defined-benefit pension plan can provide assurances against default risk to plan beneficiaries in three different ways:

1. By funding the plan or assuring that plan beneficiaries have a priority claim to the firm's non-pension assets. Thus even employees of a firm with an unfunded pension plan can be protected against default risk of their pension benefits if there are adequate non-pension assets and the other stakeholder claims against the

sponsoring firm's assets are clearly subordinated in the event of bankruptcy.

2. By purchasing guarantees of its pension liabilities from a private-sector third party. In the United States, private guarantees of a sponsor's pension liabilities are generally not available as such. However, some sponsors contract with insurance companies to provide pension annuities, thus effectively making the insurance company the guarantor of those benefits. If the solvency of the insurance company is in question, however, then the goal of guaranteeing employee pension benefits is not completely achieved.

3. Through government guarantees of its pension liabilities.

V. The Pension Benefit Guaranty Corporation[27]

The U.S. government provides insurance against default risk on private-sector defined-benefit pension promises through the Pension Benefit Guaranty Corporation (PBGC), a federal agency within the Department of Labor.[28] The PBGC was created under Title IV of the Employee Retirement Income Security Act of 1974 to guarantee only *basic* retirement benefits. There is therefore a ceiling on guaranteed benefits.[29] All private-sector defined-benefit plan sponsors must participate.[30] The PBGC has two different pension guarantee programs: one for single-employer plans and another for multi-employer plans. We restrict our attention to the single-employer program.

Although not a profit-oriented insurance company, the PBGC is intended to be self-financing and to operate on sound actuarial principles. It is expected to cover its operating expenses and annuity payments to beneficiaries from the annual premiums set by the Congress and paid by sponsors of defined-benefit plans, the investment earnings on its asset portfolio, and recoveries from terminated underfunded plans. In its annual report, the PBGC presents both an annual *flow* measure of its financial situation called the "profit" (or "loss"), and a *stock* measure called the "deficit."[31] In 1991 the loss for the single-employer program was approximately $600 million and the end-of-year deficit was $2.5 billion.[32]

When the PBGC was created in 1974, a uniform premium was initially set at $1 per yer per plan participant, regardless of the funding status of the plan or the financial condition of the plan sponsor. Subsequently, Congress legislated a series of premium increases, and in 1987 it made the premium depend on a plan's funding status. In 1992 the annual premium was raised to $19 per participant plus $9 per $1,000 of unfunded vested benefits (up to a maximum of $72 per participant).[33] To date, the PBGC has been able to cover all its cash outlays from its premium and investment income and from asset recoveries of terminated plans. It has not required funding from federal tax revenues.

Firms sponsoring single-employer defined-benefit plans have the option under the law to contract with a qualifying insurance company to assume all or part of their pension obligations.[34] The sponsor then pays premiums to the insurance company, and the insurance company becomes the private-sector guarantor of the pension benefits. Almost all 50 states in the United States, however, have state-sponsored insurance company guaranty funds. Hence, these state funds are the final or "last-resort" guarantor of the annuities provided by insurance companies. Under current law the federal government does not assume any responsibility for guaranteeing these benefits. Thus the system of guarantees of private-sector pension benefits in the United States is a mixed government-private system.

A. The PBGC's Deficit

The PBGC's $2.5 billion year-end deficit for 1991 is based on accrual accounting concepts, and it represents the difference between the PBGC's reported liabilities and its assets. The PBGC's measure of its liabilities is the present value of only those benefits payable to beneficiaries of plans that have been terminated with insufficient assets. It ignores the existing vested guaranteed benefits that will have to be paid by the PBGC to participants in plans that default in the future. That is, it implicitly assumes that there will be no further defaults in the future. If the insurance program of the PBGC were frozen at its year-end 1991 level (i.e., no new benefits guaranteed and no new premiums collected), the $2.5 billion reported by the PBGC would not be enough (in present-value terms) to fully cover the expected future shortfall. Neglecting the liability for future failures is similar to a casualty insurance company not taking account of the payments it will have to make to future accident and malpractice victims on policies currently paid for and in force.

Although not part of the reported deficit, the PBGC's 1991 *Annual Report* presents some measures of its exposure to future failures of underfunded plans. Thus it cites $31 billion as the total unfunded liabilities of all firms with underfunded plans. As the report points out, that number should not be used as a measure of the PBGC's liability. The $31 billion figure is the present value of the total unsecured pension debt guaranteed by the PBGC, but not the value of the guarantee itself. As already shown in sections II and III, the obligation of a firm to pay future pension benefits is a form of corporate debt, and PBGC insurance is thus a government guarantee of that debt.

A firm's pension debt is secured by the assets in the pension fund, but from the PBGC's perspective the unfunded part of the pension obligation is essentially unsecured corporate debt. For a firm in financial distress, the PBGC guarantee of the firm's unfunded pension obligation is the economic equivalent of a guarantee of "junk bonds." The economic value of that guarantee is the difference between the market value of the bonds with and without default risk. Thus if a particular corporate bond has a market price of $600 without the guarantee and would be worth $1,000 if free of default risk, then the value of the guarantee is $400. By simply comparing actual market prices of junk bonds with their present values computed using U.S. Treasury bond rates (cf. Merton, 1990, Table 7), it is straightforward to show that government guarantees can have substantial market value and that this market value can change significantly over time. Loan-guarantee values in excess of 50 percent of the bond price are common, and wide swings in prices caused by changes in the level of market interest rates and the economic prospects of the debtor corporation are frequent. Since unfunded pension liabilities are not traded, we cannot observe a market price for them as we can for junk bonds. Nevertheless, because PBGC insurance is essentially a guarantee of long-term corporate debt, we would expect its value to behave in a pattern similar to that of implied market prices for guarantees derived from traded bond prices.

It is beyond the scope of this paper to provide numerical estimates of the PBGC's true economic deficit. Considerable work first needs to be done to improve the quality of the raw data on corporate pension liabilities available to the PBGC.[35] The PBGC currently uses pension data as reported by the sponsoring firms themselves. Those data are unreliable because management has considerable discretion in determining the actuarial assumptions used in computing them. For example, Smalhout (1991) points out that Chrysler Corporation reported an unfunded pension liability of $3.6 billion in 1991, while the estimate by the PBGC for that same unfunded pension liability was $7.7 billion.[36]

B. Similarities Between the PBGC and FSLIC[37]

If the only goal of the PBGC were to operate a system of default-risk insurance according to sound economic principles, then as will be shown in the next section, there are a number of alternative ways to manage the guarantee function efficiently through some combination of monitoring, asset restrictions, and risk-based premiums. Every guarantor, regardless whether it is a private-sector or governmental entity, must employ some feasible combination of these three methods if it is to maintain economic viability without creating unintended and undesirable side effects.[38] Among the possible side effects in the case of the PBGC is the prospect that overcharging the sponsors of well-funded plans in order to subsidize the underfunded plans of financially distressed firms might cause financially healthy sponsors to terminate their defined-benefit plans. The United States could then be left only with bankrupt defined-benefit plans with the benefits financed directly by taxpayers.[39]

There are some significant similarities between the U.S. government system for guaranteeing pension benefits and the failed system for insuring savings and loan associations (S&Ls). The Federal Savings and Loan Insurance Corporation (FSLIC) was the government agency that insured the S&Ls until it was replaced in 1989. In FSLIC's case, poorly structured public policies and regulatory "forbearance" eventually led to misallocation of economic resources and an unintended and undesirable redistribution of wealth.[40] In the case of the PBGC, there is a growing body of evidence that current public policy is leading us in a similar direction.

Among the similarities are the following:

- The existence of multiple and conflicting goals for the guarantee program.
- Failure on the part of many in the legislative and executive branches of government to fully recognize or disclose the true costs, benefits and incentives of the guarantee program.
- A tendency to attribute losses of the guarantee fund to idiopathic causes such as individual abuses or incompetence rather than to structural ones such as predictable responses to the incentives built into the system.
- Failure to act promptly to limit such losses because of fragmentation and conflict of interest within the government regulatory apparatus.

Like FSLIC, the PBGC has several objectives, which can at times be in conflict with one another. The expressed purpose of establishing the PBGC was to insure a base level of promised defined-benefit pensions against default risk of the plan sponsor. However, some observers believe that an important latent function of the PBGC is to help revitalize some key depressed industries through assumption of part of the burden of providing pension benefits to their workers.[41] If firms can transfer their pension obligations to the PBGC, then the government effectively pays a portion of the workers' total compensation because these obligations are linked to workers' pay. The size of this government subsidy can be large.[42] Similarly, PBGC insurance provides a less transparent way for the government to guarantee the debt of financially troubled firms than the direct guarantee of the bonds issued by these firms.[43]

Beyond subsidizing depressed industries or financially troubled firms, the PBGC at times acts as if it has an additional charge to preserve defined-benefit pension plans in the face of the apparent trend to replace them with defined-contribution plans. ERISA assigns to the PBGC the goal of encouraging the growth of *private* pension plans, but it is silent on the issue of whether the institutional structure of such plans should be defined benefit or defined contribution. There are several indications, however, that the PBGC is reluctant to see the termination of defined-benefit plans even if they are to be replaced by defined-contribution plans.[44]

Thus the PBGC appears to have at least two and possibly three different objectives: (1) to provide default-risk insurance of basic pension benefits to participants in private defined-benefit pension plans on a sound economic basis, i.e., without taxpayer subsidies and without cross-subsidies among plans; (2) to provide subsidies to financially troubled firms and/or to workers in distressed industries; and perhaps (3) to encourage the continuation of the defined-benefit form of pension plan. Fulfilling these often-conflicting objectives involves tradeoffs.

Fragmentation of regulatory authority and conflicts of interest among government departments that oversee the private pension system are also a potentially serious problem for the PBGC's efficient operation. ERISA dictates that three governmental bodies should regulate private defined-benefit pension plans: (1) the Department of Labor, Pensions and Welfare Benefits Administration, which oversees the maintenance of fiduciary standards; (2) the Internal Revenue Service (IRS), which sets funding standards; and (3) the PBGC, which collects premiums and pays benefits but has few enforcement powers.

There are inherent conflicts between the objectives of the IRS and the PBGC. The IRS understandably would prefer minimal funding to prevent the loss of tax revenue to the U.S. Treasury; the PBGC would like to see maximum funding to prevent large insurance claims. The IRS has the right to grant contribution waivers to firms in financial distress. In the past, the granting of such waivers has resulted in reduced funding of defined-benefit plans with a consequent weakening of the collateral position of the PBGC as a secured creditor. In December 1987, as part of the Omnibus Budget Reconciliation Act (OBRA), major revisions were made to ERISA. The new law imposes stricter minimum funding standards on underfunded plans, but ironically it undoes much of the effect of these standards by enacting tough new *maximum* funding rules. The new maximum funding rules prevent over half of all pension sponsors from contributing anything to their plans for several years. Inevitably, some of those plans will become underfunded in years to come.[45]

A third important conflict within government is the one between the PBGC and the courts. In addition to its claim to the pension-fund assets, the PBGC also has a priority claim on part of a sponsoring firm's other assets if the pension plan is underfunded. This claim would seem to imply that even if a plan is underfunded the PBGC is protected against losses, because it can be reimbursed out of the sponsoring firm's other assets. However, recently the courts have ruled that the claims of the PBGC on the assets of a bankrupt firm with an under- funded pension plan are to be treated pari passu with those of other creditors (under Chapter 11 of the federal bankruptcy code.) Thus, unless the bankruptcy laws are changed, the PBGC has less protection than was intended in the pension laws.

As in the case of the S&L crisis, multiple objectives and conflicts among regulators of pension plans can lead to unintended and un- desirable consequences. For example, consider the case of one of LTV's pension plans, which had virtually all of its assets depleted several years before the firm went bankrupt in 1986. The plan was a large unfunded defined-benefit pension plan for salaried employees that LTV inher- ited when it acquired Republic Steel in 1984. Four years before, the plan was underfunded but it had about $300 million of assets. A year later senior officers of Republic Steel, some of whom were themselves approaching retirement age, changed the terms of the cash-out option in 1981 so as to make it particularly attractive to take a lump sum in lieu of an annuity. During the subsequent years preceding the merger, retiring employees (of Republic Steel) exercised their cash-out option en masse. When LTV went bankrupt in 1986, the PBGC thus found itself obligated to pay guaranteed benefits on an essentially unfunded plan ($230 million in liabilities and $7,700 in assets). Despite the ob- vious effect of the cash-out provision, both the PBGC and the Depart- ment of Labor concluded that there was no violation of the law. Thus, while lawmakers clearly did not intend for the PBGC to guarantee the full value of benefits of highly compensated employees, that is what in effect happened.

VI. Alternatives for Reforming the PBGC

The PBGC has recently proposed a package of legislative changes designed to eliminate its deficit, or at least to prevent it from growing.[46]

The main thrust of these proposals is to increase the funding of under-funded plans, to freeze future benefit increases in underfunded plans, and to enhance the priority of the PBGC's claims on a sponsor's non-pension assets in the event of bankruptcy. These changes however do not exhaust the range of economically feasible remedies available.[47] We have presented elsewhere a general framework for analyzing the man-agement of guarantee programs.[48] In the next two sections, we use that framework to analyze prospects for more efficient management of the PBGC.

There are three basic methods available to any guarantor—whether private or government—to manage its guarantee of pension benefits against failure of the sponsoring firm:

- Monitor the value of the pension assets with the right to seize them if they fall below a certain minimum funding ratio. If the premium charged for the guarantee is held fixed, the funding ratio required for viability increases with increases in the variance of the value of the collateral assets and with increases in the time between audits.
- Restrict the asset choice of the pension fund to ensure an upper boundary on the riskiness of the assets serving as collateral for the promised pension benefits.
- Set a premium schedule for the guarantee commensurate with the risk exposure. *Ceteris paribus*, the premium rate required for viability increases with increases in the variance of the value of the collateral assets and the time between audits.

No one of the three methods can be effective if used alone. They do however substitute for each other in varying degrees. Hence, there is room for tradeoffs among them. We now consider, in some detail, each method as it relates to guaranteeing defined-benefit pension plans.

A. Monitoring

Monitoring is widely used throughout the financial system as a method of managing both explicit and implicit guarantees that are part of loans or other financial contracts.[49] Under a monitoring system, the guaran-tor has the covenant right to conduct surveillance and seize assets of the borrower. Losses to the guarantor can be controlled by making sure that the assets accepted as collateral always have a value at least equal to the value of the promised payment.

As shown in Section V.A, the firm's defined-benefit pension obliga-tions are clearly a form of debt. Hence, the guarantor of those obligations holds a position analogous to an investor in the firm's bonds. Under the PBGC system, the specifically pledged collateral for a firm's pension debt is the assets in the pension fund itself.[50] When a corporation issues a bond, it obliges itself to make specific cash payments at specific dates in the future. The guarantor typically monitors the activities of the borrowing corporation, and moves as quickly as possible to seize the assets collateralizing the bonds in the event that the borrower misses a promised payment.

An example of an effective monitoring system for protecting the guarantor against default risk is the system used by the Federal Home Loan Banks in the United States for loans that they make to federally chartered thrift institutions. The twelve regional Federal Home Loan Banks require that their loans be collateralized by the borrowing thrift institution's highest quality assets. These are usually securities backed by mortgages guaranteed by the Federal government. The lending bank takes possession of the securities while they are serving as collateral. Even with the widespread failures of thrift institutions during the past decade, no Federal Home Loan Bank has lost money on any of these collateralized loans during the past sixty years.[51]

The key elements of this system of monitoring are: (1) the guarantor has possession of the collateral; (2) the value of the collateral is marked to market frequently at readily ascertainable market prices; and (3) the guarantor has the right automatically to liquidate the collateral to pay off the guaranteed liability if the ongoing capital requirement is violated. Each of these elements is essential for the system to function properly.

Could a system that relies primarily on monitoring be effective for the guarantor of defined-benefit pensions? For the moment we ignore how the system actually works and consider instead how it might be made to work. In order for a monitoring scheme to be effective, several conditions must be met.

By comparison with effective collateralized borrowing arrangements, if a monitoring system is the principal method used by a pension-plan guarantor, then insured plans should be *over*funded. That is, the market value of plan assets should exceed the present value of guaranteed benefits by some minimum amount—call it a funding "cushion." The guarantor must have the right to audit the plan's assets and liabilities at prescribed, frequent time intervals and, if the value of assets is insufficient to meet the cushion, the guarantor can terminate the plan and seize the collateral assets. Depending on the type of assets held, it can be very costly for the guarantor of a defined-benefit pension plan to audit the value of the plan's assets frequently. An increase in the required pension funding cushion can serve as a tradeoff alternative to greater frequency of surveillance.

A system of monitoring to control the risks faced by guarantors will work effectively only if there are mutually acceptable rules and valuation procedures to determine when the plan's assets can be seized and liquidated by the guarantor. If the collateral assets are traded in well-functioning organized markets such as national stock exchanges and government-securities markets, then reliable market values are readily observable, and marking to market is a relatively straightforward process. However, for assets that trade either infrequently or in significantly smaller lot sizes than the holdings of the fund, estimates of market prices are subject to significant errors, and reaching agreement on the proper mark-to-market procedure is more difficult. For example, if a pension sponsor were to collateralize its pension liability with corporate assets such as land, plant, and equipment, it would be difficult to estimate accurately the current market value of the fund.

In the context of a surveillance and seizure system, these estimation errors impose risks on both the guarantor and the insured pension plan. If the errors overstate values, the guarantor will not seize as quickly as it should, and the proceeds realized from seizure will be less than expected. If the errors understate values, the pension fund will be seized and liquidated when the plan is actually solvent. Thus, a "conservative" valuation method from the perspective of one party to the system will be an "aggressive" valuation method from the perspective of the other party. Hence, the valuation method should be unbiased. Protections for the parties from measurement errors in the prices can be provided by other rules of the monitoring system—such as the minimum size of the pension fund's surplus before seizure is permitted.

The relevant market price to use in valuing the assets for this purpose is the price at which they can be sold—the *bid* price. Any asset is therefore eligible to be held as collateral as long as it has a bona fide bid price for the quantity to be sold. If assets are marked to market at the bid price, illiquidity of assets serving as collateral is not a problem for the guarantor. Thus, in principle, a plan sponsor could pledge specific corporate assets as collateral—property, plant, equipment, etc. However, illiquid assets (which by definition have a large bid-ask spread) are probably not suitable because the *plan sponsor* is vulnerable to having the asset seized and liquidated when the bid price falls, even if the average of the bid and ask prices falls by a relatively small amount.[52] The spread cost from this "bid-ask bounce" is a deadweight loss to the collectivity of the sponsor and the guarantor. Thus, if it is large and the chances of a violation are not negligible, this form of handling guarantee risk is inefficient for illiquid assets. Therefore, when the underlying assets are illiquid, a pension guarantee system that relies heavily on monitoring is almost surely not efficient.

Just as it is important to mark the *assets* to market, so guaranteed *liabilities* must also be marked to market. Otherwise, the estimated exposure of the guarantor that equals the difference between the present value of guaranteed benefits and asset value is distorted, and the monitoring process can become dysfunctional. This happened with defined-benefit pension funds in the late 1970s and early 1980s. Under accounting rules in effect at the time, pension funds were required to mark their assets to market and to follow actuarial practice regarding the valuation of their accrued pension benefits. The interest rates that corporate sponsors used in computing their pension liabilities varied widely and differed significantly from the interest rates prevailing in the market.[53] FASB Statements 87 and 88 have largely corrected this particular problem.[54]

As part of its current legislative package, the PBGC is asking Congress to increase the priority of its claims in bankruptcy proceedings. The hope is that this increase in seniority for PBGC claims will induce the sponsoring firm's shareholders and subordinated creditors to pressure managements to reduce the firm's unfunded pension liabilities.[55] However, even if the PBGC succeeds in raising the legal priority of its claims, it will still have to carefully monitor the firms it insures. In the event of financial distress, the interests of subordinated creditors can diverge from those of the PBGC. Debt instruments, such as corporate bonds, often offer creditors ways of withdrawing cash out of a troubled institution before the guarantor can—high-coupon payments, call provisions, sinking funds, and put-option provisions are examples. The LTV case discussed in section V.B provides a more subtle example.[56]

In sum, if the PBGC chooses to rely more on monitoring to manage its guarantee activities, it must invest in a much better accounting system and be prepared to terminate plans and promptly seize the collateral assets of sponsors that violate funding standards.[57] The General Accounting Office, which audits the PBGC, has consistently criticized PBGC accounting practices. Indeed, the GAO has declared that it is unable to audit the PBGC because of the poor state of its records.[58] The accounting system currently employed by the PBGC therefore appears inadequate for the task of careful monitoring of the pension liabilities it guarantees and the pension assets backing them. But a better accounting system is only a necessary condition for monitoring to work as an effective control device. There must also be the ability and the willingness to terminate plans and seize the collateral assets of sponsors that violate funding standards.

B. Asset Restrictions and Risk-Based Premiums

The PBGC has to date all but ignored the impact of an insured pension fund's asset mix on the PBGC's exposure. Yet, as we show in the next sub-section, when there is a mismatch between the pension assets and liabilities, the economic value of the guarantee provided by the PBGC, even for well-funded pension plans, can be quite significant.[59] To continue a fixed premium policy independent of asset mix and remain viable, the PBGC must control the variability of the difference between the value of a plan's assets and the value of its promised payments. The pension benefits that are currently guaranteed in the United States are level-payment annuities fixed in dollar amount. Thus the plan sponsor could hedge all of the guaranteed annuities by investing in default-free fixed-income securities with the same cash flow pattern as the annu-ities—a procedure known as "immunization."[60] If, for example, the plan sponsor has an obligation to pay $100 per year for the next 5 years, it can provide this stream of benefit payments by buying a set of five sequentially maturing zero-coupon bonds, each with a face value of $100. This asset-allocation policy eliminates the risk to the guaran-tor stemming from uncertainty about future interest rates and from uncertainty about the solvency of the issuers of the fixed-income se-curities. The only remaining risk to the plan sponsor and therefore to the guarantor is mortality risk. If funding requirements are set to provide an adequate cushion for the mortality risk, the guarantor can charge low premiums and still be a viable entity.

While simple in concept, the immunization of pension liabilities is less simple to implement in practice. For instance, one might believe that plan sponsors can hedge the interest rate risk of their benefit liabilities by investing in long-term fixed rate mortgages or bonds. However, at least in the United States, virtually all mortgages and bonds have prepayment or call provisions that allow the issuer to retire them early. Plan sponsors that attempt to immunize must therefore deal with this prepayment risk.[61]

Starting in the 1980s, the development of trading in derivative secu-rities—futures, forward contracts, options, and swaps—greatly en-hanced the ability of pension funds to reduce their exposure to risk. Thus, by entering an interest rate swap contract, a pension fund can effectively convert a floating-rate asset into a fixed-rate one. Similarly, by entering an equity-for-fixed-rate-debt returns swap, a pension fund can in effect convert its stock portfolio into a fixed-income portfolio that matches its benefit liabilities. Alternatively, the pension-plan sponsor can change its liability exposure from fixed to floating rates by entering swap contracts matched to the payment pattern on its annuity liabilities. However, just as pension funds can quickly reduce both the variability of their net worth and the exposure of the guarantor by entering into swaps or taking hedging positions in futures contracts, so they can quickly reverse the process and become unhedged. Indeed, a pension fund can even increase rather than decrease its unhedged risk exposure by taking positions in derivative securities that accentuate the imbalance between its asset/liability positions. Thus the very efficiency of the derivative-securities markets in permitting rapid and low cost hedging of positions can also put greater demands on the guarantor to keep track of the pension fund's exposure to shortfall risk. If the guarantor is to monitor asset restrictions effectively, it must be able to observe and analyze the risk implications of the total positions held by the pension fund in derivative securities on a timely basis.

An alternative way for the guarantor to maintain solvency and create compatible incentives for plan sponsors is to charge risk-related premiums. The PBGC already has a premium structure that takes into account a plan's level of underfunding, but the premium schedule is unrelated to the mismatch between pension assets and liabilities. The fair market premium for a fully-funded plan that is fully immunized is zero. However, if the pension sponsor invests the pension assets in common stocks or other types of equity securities instead of fixed-income securities that immunize the guaranteed benefits, then the exposure of the guarantor to a potential shortfall increases.[62] The risk-related premium must therefore also be related to the future variability of the difference between the value of the pension assets (excluding the value of the guarantee) and the present value of guaranteed benefits. For risk-based premiums to work, the variability of net worth need not be reduced to zero, but it does have to be known (or at least bounded) and not subject to significant unilateral change by the insured pension plan after the premium has been set. If the insured pension-plan sponsor can unilaterally change the composition of its pension asset portfolio ex post, then the guarantor faces a problem of moral hazard.[63]

C. A Hypothetical Example

In general, there are tradeoffs among the methods of insuring the economic viability of the pension guarantor. To clarify these tradeoffs, consider the following hypothetical example, which uses a simplifying modification of the system actually used by the PBGC. The stream of guaranteed benefits stretches over many years and is free of default risk to the employees. Each plan sponsor contracts with the PBGC to pay a risk-based premium once a year. The premium is set to reflect both the fund's net worth—market value of pension assets less the present value of the guaranteed benefits—and its variability over the coming year. The variability of the fund's net worth is determined by the fraction of the guaranteed benefits immunized. With none immunized, the assumed annual variance rate of the logarithmic change in the pension fund's net worth is .04.[64] If, on the other hand, the guaranteed pension benefits are fully immunized, then the net-worth variability is zero. At the end of the year, either the fund must pay another premium for the period to follow that reflects its new funding status and net-worth variability, or the plan is terminated and the assets are seized by the PBGC. If the plan is terminated, then the PBGC makes up the shortfall to plan participants.

This hypothetical system differs from the current system in five important respects: in the hypothetical system, (1) premiums are charged on the basis of the present value of the guaranteed benefits rather than on a per capita basis; (2) the premiums charged by the PBGC reflect the volatility of the pension fund net worth; (3) included in the measure of pension-fund assets are any of the sponsoring firm's other corporate assets that are pledged as collateral;[65] (4) there is no maximum charge for the premium; and (5) the plan is terminated if the sponsor fails to make a premium payment. Under these assumptions, we can use well-known techniques to compute the competitive market premium for any combination of parameter values.[66] If the PBGC charges less than this premium, its guarantee operation will have a negative net present value.[67]

Table 1 and Figure 1 are designed to show how the risk-based premium varies with the fraction of benefits immunized and the funding ratio.[68] Figure 1 shows the tradeoffs between the premium charged and the fraction of benefits immunized for various funding ratios. Consider the case of full funding, for example, where the funding ratio is 100 percent. If the fraction of benefits immunized is zero, the premium is 8 percent of guaranteed benefits.[69] The premium falls as the fraction immunized rises. If half are immunized, the premium is 4 percent of guaranteed benefits. As the fraction of benefits guaranteed rises to 100 percent, the premium falls to zero.

Figure 1 shows clearly that the value of the guarantee has its greatest sensitivity to the fraction of benefits immunized when there is full funding. When the plan is 20 percent underfunded, the value of the guarantee is by far the largest, but it is less sensitive to the composition

TABLE 1   Risk-Based Premiums as a Function of Fraction Immunized and
Funding Ratio

Fraction of benefits immunized (percent)	Risk-based premium		
	20% underfunded	Fully funded	20% overfunded
0	21.18	7.98	2.14
10	20.83	7.20	1.59
20	20.53	6.40	1.11
30	20.29	5.60	0.69
40	20.13	4.80	0.37
50	20.04	4.00	0.15
60	20.01	3.20	0.03
70	20	2.40	0.00
80	20	1.60	0.00
90	20	0.80	0.00
100	20	0	0

Note: The value of the guarantee is computed using Merton's (1977) model. The risk-free interest rate is 10 percent per year compounded continuously. In the absence of immunization, the variance of the logarithmic change in pension fund net worth (σ^2) is .04 per year. The term of the guarantee is one year.

of the pension asset portfolio. The premium starts at 21 percent of guaranteed benefits when none of the liability is immunized, and it gradually falls to 20 percent as the proportion of benefits immunized rises to 100 percent. When the plan is overfunded by 20 percent, the premium, in the absence of any immunization, is just over 2 percent of the value of the guaranteed benefits. As the proportion of benefits immunized rises, the value of the guarantee gradually falls to zero. For the fully funded case, the value of the guarantee starts out at 8 percent of guaranteed benefits and declines approximately linearly to zero as the proportion of benefits immunized rises to 100 percent.

In reality, the majority of defined-benefit pension funds in the United States invest about half of their assets in equity securities. Ten percent is a rough estimate for the annualized standard deviation of the logarithmic change in net worth. In the calculations here, pension assets include the portion of corporate assets pledged to the guarantor. Under this definition of pension assets, the vast majority of real-world plans are more than 20 percent overfunded. If the plans were monitored once per year and those found to be underfunded were terminated and liquidated, then the actuarially fair risk-based premium for a 20 percent-overfunded plan would be .15 percent of guaranteed benefits (i.e., 15 basis points or 15 cents for every $100 of covered pension liabilities).[70]

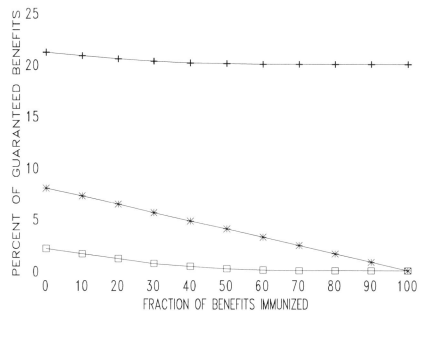

Figure 1. Risk-based premiums as a function of fraction immunized and funding ratio. The value of the guarantee is computed using Merton's (1977) model. The risk-free interest rate is 10 percent per year compounded continuously. In the absence of immunization, the variance of the logarithmic change in pension fund net worth (σ^2) is .04 per year. The term of the guarantee is one year.

Note that this scheme implies that the premiums are adequate to cover any funding deficits that are created *each year*. Thus consider a plan that this year is 50 percent immunized and 20 percent overfunded. It pays a premium equal to .15 percent of the present value of guaranteed benefits. If, as a result of a decline in the stock market, it becomes just fully funded, then next year's premium will be 4 percent of the present value of guaranteed benefits. If the sponsor cannot pay the new premium, then the plan is terminated.

If the PBGC were to monitor more frequently than once a year—

TABLE 2   Risk-Based Premiums as a Function of Term of Guarantee and Funding Ratio

Term of guarantee (years)	Risk-based premium		
	20% underfunded	Fully funded	20% overfunded
0	20	0	0
.01	20	0.80	0.00
.05	20	1.79	0.00
.10	20	2.53	0.00
.25	20.04	4.00	0.15
.50	20.31	5.65	0.72
.75	20.72	6.92	1.42
1	21.18	7.98	2.14
2	23.08	11.27	4.82
3	24.81	13.77	7.14
4	26.38	15.88	9.18
5	27.81	17.72	11.02
10	33.66	24.84	18.39

Note: The value of the guarantee is computed using Merton's (1977) model. The risk-free interest rate is 10 percent per year compounded continuously. The variance of the logarithmic change in pension fund net worth (σ^2) is .04 per year.

and it can do so at low cost—then the premiums can be lower. Table 2 and Figure 2 illustrate the tradeoff between the risk-based premium and the term of the guarantee for various levels of funding. This tradeoff is calculated using a variance of the pension fund net worth of .04 per year, which is approximately what it would be with no immunization.

The schemes just described rely primarily on adjusting the risk-based premiums at the end of each insurance period. Suppose, however, that the PBGC is constrained to charge a fixed premium—say 10 basis points or 10 cents per $100 of guaranteed benefits. In that case, the PBGC would have to rely exclusively on the other methods of managing the guarantee business: monitoring and asset restrictions. One approach is to require full funding and 100 percent immunization. In that case, minimal premiums required just equal the operating costs of monitoring compliance with the rules. However, if 100 percent immunization is undesirable, then the PBGC can allow a tradeoff between the funding ratio and the fraction of benefits immunized. If the term of the guarantee is fixed at one year, then the PBGC could set a required funding ratio to offset the risk in the pension asset portfolio—the higher the fraction of benefits immunized, the lower the required funding ratio.

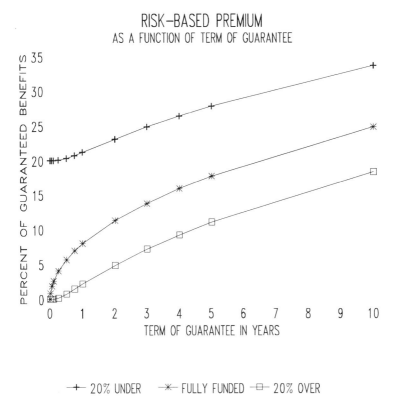

Figure 2. Risk-based premiums as a function of term of the guarantee and funding ratio. The value of the guarantee is computed using Merton's (1977) model. The risk-free interest rate is 10 percent per year compounded continuously. The variance of the logarithmic change in pension fund new worth (σ^2) is .04 per year.

VII. Indexation of Pension Benefits[71]

While Social Security benefits and pension benefits under some public plans are indexed to the cost of living, the vast majority of private-sector pension plans offer no automatic inflation protection. This is true regardless of whether the employer's plan is of the defined-benefit or defined-contribution type. Many plan sponsors have in the past offered ad hoc increases in payments to retired employees to help offset the effects of inflation.[72] However, to the extent that inflation protection of private-sector retirement benefits exists in the United States, it is not guaranteed.[73]

That real-world practice has pension annuities fixed in nominal rather than in real terms is incongrous with life-cycle models of household behavior. In that model, people are concerned about the purchasing power of their retirement income rather than its dollar amount. Nevertheless, in the United States, we find that it is nominal rather than real benefits that are promised by sponsors of defined-benefit plans and guaranteed by the PBGC.

Most people are probably aware of the fact that inflation will erode the real value of a money-fixed pension annuity. Many errors nevertheless occur because of failure to properly account for inflation effects. Even professional financial planners sometimes fall into the trap of treating pension annuities as if they were adjusted for inflation. For instance, a rule of thumb commonly used by financial planners and benefits specialists to judge the adequacy of retirement income is: add expected Social Security benefits and expected pension benefits together and compare their sum to pre-retirement income. If this so-called "replacement ratio" is greater than some target value such as 80 percent, then retirement income is judged adequate to maintain consumption based on preretirement wage or salary income.

The problem with this approach is that by ignoring the effect of inflation on pension benefits, it can lead to inadequate saving for retirement. For example, consider a 45-year-old employee who works for a firm that has a defined-benefit pension plan offering a benefit equal to 1.5 percent of final pay times the number of years of service. The employee's salary is currently $50,000 per year, and she expects it to grow at the rate of inflation. By retirement time, she will have worked for the company 40 years, and the pension benefit will therefore be 60 percent of her final salary or $30,000 per year in today's dollars. If Social Security is expected to provide a benefit of $10,000 per year, then her expected combined retirement income is $40,000, and the replacement ratio is 80 percent. Suppose that the inflation rate is 5 percent per year. The Social Security benefit has a COLA (cost-of-living adjustment), so the benefit increases in parallel with inflation. But the employee's private-pension benefit does not. After 14 years, the $30,000 of pension income will have only about half of its original purchasing power. If the employee is fortunate enough to survive 28 years beyond the retirement age, her pension benefit will be worth only one quarter of its original value in real terms.

Short of offering automatic inflation adjustment of pension benefits, what can plan sponsors do to help plan participants cope with the problem of inflation? The first and perhaps most important thing is to increase employee awareness of the impact of inflation on pension benefits. An effective way to accomplish this would be to quote expected pension benefits on a "social-security-equivalent" basis. Pension benefits expressed this way would reflect the reduced starting level of benefits under a hypothetical retirement benefit option with a COLA that the employer could offer at the time of retirement at no additional cost. In a typical example, the COLA annuity option might be 60 percent of the starting value of the conventional pension benefit.[74] Even if the employer did not offer such an option, and even if no employee would want to choose it, the quoted number would give a more accurate pension-benefit figure to use in computations of expected income replacement rates. Employees would have a more appropriate target to use in deciding how much to contribute to supplementary retirement savings plans offered by either their employers or other providers such as mutual funds and insurance companies.

The supplementary voluntary retirement savings plans now offered by many employers can be used to provide some inflation protection after retirement.[75] These supplementary plans usually provide several investment options and often participation is encouraged by matching contributions from the employer. Employers could advise their employees to target their supplementary retirement savings plans to match the provision of a COLA. Employers could offer further guidance by computing the additional contribution rate required and offering an additional inflation-hedge investment option. Employers could of course offer outright inflation insurance of retirement benefits. To lower the cost of this inflation insurance, a deductible or a cap could be introduced.[76]

We believe that the government has a positive and perhaps unique role to play in providing innovations that improve the efficiency of risk bearing in life-cycle allocations. Over the years, a number of economists have considered it desirable, if not essential, for the U.S. government to issue inflation-linked bonds in order to lay the foundation for private inflation insurance. Indeed, Nobel laureate economists, Milton Friedman, Franco Modigliani, and James Tobin, who often hold very different opinions on other issues, are united in their enthusiastic support for the idea of the U.S. Treasury's issuing CPI-linked bonds. The government is commonly seen as the only institution that could credibly guarantee default-free inflation insurance on a large scale, without the benefit of a traded CPI-linked instrument that could be purchased as a hedging asset.

An alternative to indexing retirement annuities to the cost of living is to index them to aggregate per capita consumption.[77] The idea motivating this proposal is that it is *standard-of-living* protection rather than *cost-of-living* protection which is of prime concern to most individuals. With a cost-of-living-linked annuity, the benefit is fixed in real terms regardless of what happens to the standard of living in the economy.

Individuals receiving only a cost-of-living annuity over a long period of retirement may experience a substantial decline in their *relative* standard of living compared to the rest of the population. According to this alternative proposal, however, pensioners would receive a benefit that changes with per capita consumption, thus maintaining their relative standard of living.

Note that with indexation to aggregate per capita consumption, there is no need to distinguish between the inflation and the real-per-capita-consumption components of the change. The benefits are simultaneously protected against both. By linking the benefits to per capita consumption rather than the consumer price index, the pension scheme is made more consistent both with finance theory and common sense. As with CPI-indexing, there is also a potential role for the government as a financial innovator in making this type of product possible by providing consumption-indexed bonds that are free of default risk. In particular, the government could perfectly hedge its exposure on these bonds by instituting a consumption tax.

VIII. Conclusions

The retirement-income system in the United States employs a complex mixture of government and private-sector guarantees of retirement income. One can view a mixed public-private system of providing retirement-income as a way of reducing the risks of each separate component through diversification across providers. Government can change the law to reduce promised benefit levels on public-sector pension plans. Private-sector pension-plan sponsors are committed by law (and perhaps reputation) to pay promised benefits, but they may default. To insure against this, the PBGC provides guarantees against default.

Some in government have come to see the PBGC as defender of the defined-benefit form of pension plan in the face of contrary trends in the provision of retirement income. A positive role for government as ultimate provider of guarantees against default risk of retirement annuities is less controversial than the use of such guarantees to encourage defined-benefit plans over defined-contribution plans. Both plan types have advantages and disadvantages, and there is no clear economic reason (or official public-policy decision) to favor one type over the other.[78] Moreover, we know of no apparent reason to use pension guarantees to subsidize firms or workers in distressed industries. Indeed, whatever the general merits of using government subsidies to help distressed industries, there are good reasons *not* to use "cheap" pension guarantees as the form for such subsidies. Subsidies provided by underpriced guarantees are less visible to the public than other subsidies; for that very reason, they can lead to large and unintended distortions in resource allocation, and they can result in a socially undesirable redistribution of income. We need do no more than mention "deposit insurance" to underscore the enormous costs that can be generated by the mismanagement of government liability-guarantee programs.

Notes

1. For a discussion of the rationale and methodology of functional analysis in finance, see Merton (1993) and Merton and Bodie (1992a).

2. There are other important functions served by pension plans. Pension plans are often used as an incentive device in labor contracts to influence employee turnover, work effort, and the timing of retirement. Key public finance issues surrounding pension plans are government guarantees of private pension benefits, the use of these plans to reduce or defer taxes, the effect of these plans on aggregate private saving, and the role of these plans as part of the social insurance "safety net." Corporate pension-funding and asset-allocation policies are also an important element in corporate financial management. For further details, see Bodie (1990a).

3. Indeed, in the United States, the part of the Social Security system that relates to this function is called Old-Age, Survivors, and Disability Insurance (OASDI).

4. For a comparison of sources of retirement income in 20 different countries, see the study by the pension-consulting firm Towers Perrin Inc. (1991). Achdut and Tamir (1985) present a more complete comparison of the various sources of income of the elderly in seven different countries; Clark (1990) covers Japan.

5. See, for example, Atkinson (1991), Diamond (1977), McGill (1977), Wachter (1988, chapters 2 and 8) and Merton (1983a, b).

6. See Rothschild and Stiglitz (1976) for an analysis of insurance company equilibrium with adverse selection. At least one study of the private annuities market seems to confirm the theory that private annuities are priced unattractively for the average individual. See Friedman and Warshawsky (1988).

7. The base to support the system was expanded by requiring more employees to join. The present value of benefits was reduced by gradually raising the age at which full benefits are payable. See Myers (1991).

8. Prior to the passage of the Employee Retirement Income Security Act (ERISA) in 1974, private defined-benefit obligations in the United States had a somewhat ambiguous legal status. ERISA, however, clearly established them as corporate liabilities.

9. See Merton, Bodie, and Marcus (1987) for a more complete development of this idea. Myers (1977) presents a similar argument.

10. Much the same point applied to deposit insurance in the 1980s: no one doubted that the government would cover all insured deposits even if the government insurance agencies, FSLIC and FDIC, ran out of funds.

11. Under certain conditions depending on both the age of the beneficiary and the size of the benefit, there is an additional tax surcharge above the

ordinary earned-income tax rate. Distributions to the employer as part of a reversion of excess assets are also subject to a surcharge.

12. See Dailey and Turner (1992).

13. See Clark and McDermed (1990) and Gustman and Steinmeier (1990).

14. For a detailed description of an interesting variant of the cash balance account called a multivalue pension plan, see Paul (1988).

15. For further details, see Bodie (1989).

16. For a survey of pension funding practices in various countries around the world, see Bodie (1990b).

17. This section of the paper draws heavily on Bodie (1990a; c, section 6).

18. See Clark, Allen, and Sumner (1983) for a discussion of these ad hoc increases.

19. See, for example, Cohn and Modigliani (1985) or Ippolito (1986).

20. A benefit is vested if the employee is entitled to it even after terminating employment. Most employers require employees to work for some minimum number of years before their benefits are vested.

21. That this wage-indexation increment to the pension benefit can be achieved only through continued employment is well understood by plan participants facing the retirement decision. They will often delay the date of retirement if they anticipate inflation in the immediate future, in order to raise the salary base for computing their pension benefit.

22. In contrast to the situation in the United States, current law in the United Kingdom requires pension sponsors to index accrued pension benefits for inflation to the age of retirement, subject to a cap of 5 percent per year. Thus even a terminated employee has indexation for general inflation up to retirement age, as long as the benefit is vested. Therefore, under the UK system, the PBO is the appropriate measure of the sponsor's liability.

23. This section is adapted from a more general discussion of the role of guarantees in Merton and Bodie (1993).

24. For an alternative view, see Ippolito (1986, Ch. 10). Ippolito argues that when workers are represented by a union they accept default risk of the sponsoring firm (through the pension plan) as a way of binding the union to bargain more cooperatively with management. Under his assumptions, therefore, a defined-benefit plan with default risk is efficient.

25. Note that the risk exposure is especially large for a lifetime employee of a single firm. Even if the employee is willing to bear risk, we know from portfolio theory that efficient risk bearing calls for broad diversification across various firms and asset classes. Here the employee's entire pension benefit is tied to the fortunes of a single firm.

26. Should employees want to invest in the securities of their firm, they typically can do so through a variety of special employee stock ownership programs. These investment programs are usually voluntary. By contrast, participation in an employer's defined-benefit plan is usually a condition of employment.

27. For a more detailed description of how the United States pension-termination insurance system works, see McGill and Grubbs (1989, Ch. 24) or Allen et al. (1988). For a detailed description of the PBGC's brief history, see Ippolito (1989) and Utgoff (1991). Much of the factual information in this section was taken from the PBGC's 1991 *Annual Report* (USGAO, 1991).

28. Finland, Germany, Japan, and Sweden also have government pension-insurance schemes, although the rules are somewhat different.

29. The ceiling in 1992 is roughly $28,000 per year in the single-employer program.

30. There are no such requirements, however, for pension plans sponsored by state and local governments.

31. In customary accounting terms, the PBGC's *loss* corresponds to an entry in the income statement and its *deficit* to an entry on the balance sheet.

32. By contrast, the PBGC's multi-employer program shows an operating profit and a surplus of assets over liabilities. The main reason for the difference appears to be that the PBGC's multi-employer program relies primarily on mutual insurance among sponsoring employers in the insured group. It is similar in structure to the state-sponsored insurance-company guaranty funds, with the PBGC serving as insurer of last resort. If one employer defaults, most of the cost of a bailout is borne by the others. An employer who leaves the plan has a "withdrawal liability" equal to its proportionate share of the plan's un-funded liability. For further details, see Utgoff (1991, p. 6).

33. This premium structure is frequently called "risk related." However, as will be shown in the next section, relating the premium to the level of under-funding is not adequate for a true "risk-based" pricing system. The risk of the pension fund's asset mix must also be considered.

34. To avoid paying insurance premiums to the PBGC for employees whose benefits are insured by an insurance company, the plan sponsor must tech-nically terminate the participation of such employees in the sponsor's plan. Under U.S. pension law, the Department of Labor sets the standards that determine which insurance companies qualify to offer these annuities.

35. The U.S. General Accounting Office stated in the PBGC 1991 *Annual Report*: ". . . the Corporation had not yet developed the documentation and support for the techniques and assumptions used to estimate its reported $7.8 billion liability for future benefits nor had it assessed the completeness and ac-curacy of the data used by each estimating technique. . . . We continue to cau-tion users that the Corporation's financial statements have limited reliability."

36. Recently the Office of Management and Budget has estimated the PBGC's deficit to be $43 billion using a model developed by Marcus (1987). (See USOMB, Budget of the U.S. Government for 1993, Part One, p. 277). We agree with the general contingent-claim methodology used for valuation in the Marcus model, but we do not agree with its specific measure of the pension liabilities. As discussed, only those pension benefits already earned by workers as a result of past service should be taken into account; no account should be taken of future contributions to the pension fund or of future premiums to be paid to the PBGC. The Marcus model for computing pension liabilities, how-ever, includes pension benefits to be earned in the future, expected future contributions of the firm to the pension fund, and future premiums to be paid to the PBGC.

37. This section is drawn from Bodie (1992).

38. In a study published a few years before the creation of the PBGC, McGill (1970) warns about some of those potential side effects.

39. Moreover, the current structure can create incentives for extreme risk-taking that would not occur in the absence of government insurance. See the papers by Sharpe (1976), Treynor (1977), and Harrison and Sharpe (1983).

40. For an extensive discussion of the S&L crisis, see Benston, Carhill, and Olasov (1991), Benston and Kaufman (1990), Kane (1990), Mayer (1990), Merton and Bodie (1992b, 1993, section VI), and White (1991).

41. Although many have expressed this view off the record, it has been presented rather forcefully on the record by one of the key architects of ERISA, Michael S. Gordon. He maintains that the actuarial soundness of the PBGC was deliberately sacrificed at its inception in order to gain political support for passage of ERISA. In his "Dissenting Comments" on Ippolito's *The Economics of Pension Insurance* (1989), Gordon writes: "The supposition that Congress was prepared to accept loss of jobs and further industrial decline in return for sound insurance principles is preposterous and is why, even today, there will be stiff resistance to redesigning pension insurance along the lines he [Ippolito] proposes."

42. Utgoff (1991, footnote 14) writes: "In 1987, I calculated that the termination of the Wheeling-Pittsburgh Plans reduced funding costs by enough to allow a permanent wage increase of $3 per hour."

43. Utgoff (1991, footnote 16) writes: "One little known aspect of the Chrysler bailout is that the company received funding waivers in addition to a government loan."

44. The inside cover of the PBGC's 1991 *Annual Report* states: "To fulfill its mission, PBGC has established a long-term goal of building a service-oriented, well-managed, and financially sound insurance company to provide a strong safety net for a healthy defined benefit pension system."

James Lockhart, then Executive Director of PBGC, in referring to the growth in the premiums charged by the PBGC said in a 1991 speech before the National Employee Benefit Institute: "We have to slow this growth, or we stand a good chance of killing the very thing we were created to protect—the defined benefit pension system."

Of course, this opposition to the trend towards defined-contribution plans may be primarily a reaction to seeing the PBGC's premium base deteriorate.

45. PBGC experience shows that plan funding deteriorates substantially as it approaches termination. Typically, a plan is 40 percent funded when it terminates but had been reporting 60 to 80 percent funding five years before.

46. See the PBGC 1991 *Annual Report*, pp. 14–15.

47. We do not know the range of *politically* feasible ones.

48. Merton and Bodie (1992b, 1993).

49. As discussed in Merton and Bodie (1992b, 1993 section I), lenders whose loans are not guaranteed are themselves guarantors. Hence, the management alternatives described here for guarantors also apply to lenders generally.

50. ERISA also gives the PBGC a priority claim on 30 percent of the firm's net worth. But in the case of a bankruptcy the firm's net worth is typically negligible.

51. See Esty and Baldwin (1991).

52. For example, suppose that a sponsor buys an illiquid asset at an asked price of $100 when the bid price is $50. Suppose that the price subsequently drops to $75 asked and $25 bid. If this decline triggers a violation of the minimum cushion requirement and the asset is liquidated, the total loss in value is $100 − $25 = $75, even though the average of the bid and asked price has declined by only $25.

53. Thus Bodie, Light, Morck, and Taggart (1985, Table A1) report that the interest rate used by sponsors of large corporate defined-benefit plans in valuing their pension liabilities in 1980 ranged from a low of 4 percent to a high of 13 percent.

54. See Bader and Leibowitz (1987) for an analysis showing the enormous

distortions in the reported under- and overfunding of pensions caused by the pre-FASB 87 rules.

55. See the PBGC 1991 *Annual Report*, p. 15.

56. Employees with a claim to pension benefits exceeding the limits guaranteed by the government are in the position of subordinated debtholders. Thus, by taking a lump-sum settlement instead of a life annuity, the highly paid employees of Republic Steel accelerated their claims at the expense of the guarantor. This is similar to the action bondholders would take if they had a put option. In general, the PBGC has found that in the period before a firm goes bankrupt, its pension plan's funded status deteriorates very rapidly. Thus, if the PBGC waits to seize the pension assets until the firm actually declares bankruptcy, there may not be much left.

57. Section 4042 of ERISA gives the PBGC the right to terminate an underfunded plan before bankruptcy, but this provision has rarely been used. In a recent case of its use, the PBGC's right to terminate the underfunded plans of Pan American Airlines has been challenged in the courts by Pan Am's other creditors.

58. See the auditor's opinion in the PBGC 1991 *Annual Report*, pp. 53–58.

59. As is well known in the finance literature, the guarantee provided by the PBGC is analogous to a put option. Using this analogy, one can use the known response of the value of a put option to a change in the risk characteristics of the underlying asset to gain insight into the sensitivity of the PBGC guarantee's value to the pension fund asset mix.

60. See Leibowitz (1986 and 1992, pp. 695–994) for a complete development of immunization procedures.

61. Unlike mortality risk, prepayment risk is systematically related to the level of interest rates, which affects all fixed-income security prices. Therefore diversification across different kinds of fixed-income instruments with different issuers will not eliminate or even significantly reduce this risk exposure. Many of the innovations in the U.S. fixed-income securities markets in the 1980s (such as collateralized mortgage obligations or CMOs) have been driven by the desire of pension funds and other intermediaries with long-term annuity liabilities to hedge the prepayment risk of mortgages. See Bodie (1990b).

62. See Bodie (1991a).

63. For a discussion and analysis of this moral-hazard problem for the PBGC, see Harrison and Sharpe (1983).

64. This is the approximate annualized variance of the logarithmic change in net worth (at market value) of a typical U.S. pension fund that invests 100 percent of its assets in common stocks and equity real estate.

65. Thus pension assets as defined here includes 30 percent of the sponsoring firm's net worth *plus* a general claim against the rest of the firm's net worth.

66. The specific model used here is derived in Merton (1977). However, there is an extensive literature on using contingent-claim type models to estimate the value of deposit, loan and asset-value guarantees. See, for example, Acharya and Dreyfus (1989), Crouhy and Galai (1991), Cummins (1988), Jones and Mason (1980), Marcus and Shaked (1984), Merton (1977, 1978, 1990, 1992), Osborne and Mishra (1989), Pennacchi (1987a, 1987b), Ronn and Verma (1986), Selby, Franks, and Karki (1988), Sharpe (1978), Sosin (1980), and Thomson (1987), and the September 1991 issue of the *Journal of Banking and Finance*.

67. Note that a negative NPV does not necessarily imply that it will run out of

money. As with other insurance processes, good fortune might permit the situation to go on for many years even though the guarantor is actuarily insolvent.

68. This assumes that the pension plan rather than the guarantor bears all operating costs, including the cost of audits.

69. Remember that full funding here means that conventional pension assets *plus* 30 percent of the sponsoring firm's net worth *plus* a general claim against the rest of the sponsor's net worth equals the present value of the benefits guaranteed by the PBGC. By this definition, the vast majority of plans are currently overfunded.

70. As a reference point, we made a very rough calculation of the PBGC's current ratio of total premium income to total guaranteed benefits based on figures presented in the PBGC's 1991 *Annual Report*. The ratio was about 10 cents per $100 of covered pension liabilities.

71. This section is based on Bodie (1990c).

72. See Clark, Allen, and Sumner (1983) for a discussion of these ad hoc increases.

73. Full cost-of-living adjustment of private pension benefits is more common in Europe. See Clark (1990).

74. TIAA-CREF's "graded benefit method" of computing expected retirement benefits is an example of one organization's attempt to move partially in this direction.

75. These plans are known as 401(k) or 403(b) plans, depending on which provision of the IRS code is applicable.

76. For a discussion of the feasibility of such inflation insurance, see Bodie (1990d). One problem under current law hindering organizations such as TIAA-CREF in providing investment advice is the danger of being sued by retirees if the results turn out poorly.

77. This section is based on Merton (1983b).

78. For a discussion of those advantages and disadvantages see Bodie, Marcus, and Merton (1988) and Bodie (1989).

References

Acharya, Sankarshan and Jean-François Dreyfus. 1989. "Optimal Bank Reorganization Policies and the Pricing of Federal Deposit Insurance." *Journal of Finance* 44 (December): 1313–33.

Achdut, L. and J. Tamir. 1985. "Retirement and Well-Being Among the Elderly." Paper presented at the first Luxemburg Study Conference.

Allen, Everett T., Joseph J. Melone, Jerry S. Rosenbloom, and Jack L. VanDerhei. 1988. *Pension Planning*, sixth ed. Homewood, IL: R.D. Irwin.

Atkinson, Anthony B. 1991. "Social Insurance." *Geneva Papers on Risk and Insurance Theory* 16, 2 (December).

Bader, Lawrence N. and Martin L. Leibowitz. 1987. "Pension Settlements Under FASB 87 and 88: Recognizing the Pension Surplus in Corporate Financial Statements." New York: Salomon Brothers, Inc., October.

Benston, George J. and George G. Kaufman. 1990. "Understanding the S&L Debacle." *Public Interest* (Spring): 79–95.

Benston, George J., Mike Carhill, and Brian Olasov. 1991. "The Failure and Survival of Thrifts: Evidence from the Southeast." In *Financial Markets and*

Financial Crises, ed. R. Glenn Hubbard. Chicago: University of Chicago Press.

Bodie, Zvi. 1989. "Enhancing the Efficiency of Pension Plans." In *What is the Future for Defined Benefit Pension Plans?* Washington, DC: EBRI.

———. 1990a. "Pensions as Retirement Income Insurance." *Journal of Economic Literature* 28 (March): 28–49.

———. 1990b. "Inflation Protection for Pension Plans." *Compensation and Benefits Management* (Winter): 105–110.

———. 1990c. "Managing Pension and Retirement Assets." *Journal of Financial Services Research* 4 (December): 419–60.

———. 1990d. "Inflation Insurance." *Journal of Risk and Insurance* LVII, 4 (December): 634–45.

———. 1991a. "Shortfall Risk and Pension Asset Allocation." *Financial Analysts Journal* 47 (May/June): 57–61.

———. 1991b. "Pension Funding Policy in Five Countries." Chapter 5 in Turner and Dailey (1991).

———. 1992. "Is the PBGC the FSLIC of the 1990s?" *Contingencies* (March/April).

Bodie, Zvi, Jay O. Light, Randall Morck, and Robert A. Taggart, Jr. 1985. "Corporate Pension Policy: An Empirical Investigation." *Financial Analysts Journal* 41 (September/October). Also Chapter 2 in Bodie et al. (1987).

Bodie, Zvi, Alan J. Marcus, and Robert C. Merton. 1988. "Defined-Benefit vs. Defined-Contribution Pension Plans: What Are the Real Tradeoffs?" Chapter 5 in Bodie et al. (1988).

Bodie, Zvi and Alicia H. Munnell, eds. 1992. *Pensions and the Economy: Sources, Uses, and Limitations of Data*. Philadelphia: PRC and University of Pennsylvania Press.

Bodie, Zvi and John Shoven, eds. 1983. *Financial Aspects of the U.S. Pension System*. Chicago: University of Chicago Press.

Bodie, Zvi, John B. Shoven, and David A. Wise, eds. 1987. *Issues in Pension Economics*. Chicago: University of Chicago Press.

———. 1988. *Pensions in the U.S. Economy*. Chicago: University of Chicago Press.

Clark, Robert L. 1990. "Cost of Living Adjustments in International Perspective." In *Pension Policy: An International Perspective*, ed. J.A. Turner. Washington, DC: U.S. Government Printing Office.

Clark, Robert L., Steven G. Allen, and Daniel A. Sumner. 1983. "Inflation and Pension Benefits." Final report to the U.S. Department of Labor, contract J-9-P-1-0074.

Clark, Robert L. and Ann A. McDermed. 1990. *The Choice of Pension Plans in a Changing Regulatory Environment*. Washington, DC: American Enterprise Institute.

Cohn, Richard A. and Franco Modigliani. 1985. "Inflation and Corporate Financial Management." Chapter 13 in *Recent Advances in Corporate Finance*, ed. Edward I. Altman and Marti G. Subrahmanyan. Homewood, IL: R.D. Irwin.

Crouhy, Michel and Dan Galai. 1991. "A Contingent Claim Analysis of a Regulated Depository Institution." *Journal of Banking and Finance* 15 (February): 73–90.

Cummins, J. David. 1988. "Risk-Based Premiums for Insurance Guaranty Funds." *Journal of Finance* 43 (September): 823–39.

Dailey, Lorna M. and John A. Turner. 1992. "U.S. Pensions in World Perspective." Chapter 6 in Bodie and Munnell (1992).

Diamond, Peter A. 1977. "A Framework for Social Security Analysis." *Journal of Public Economics* 8: 275–98.

Esty, Benjamin and Carliss Baldwin. 1991. "Market Discipline in the Thrift Industry." Harvard Graduate School of Business Working Paper 93-029, October.

Friedman, Benjamin M. and Mark Warshawsky. 1988. "Annuity Prices and Saving Behavior in the United States." Chapter 2 in Bodie et al. (1988).

Gustman, Alan L. and Thomas L. Steinmeier. 1990. "The Stampede Toward Defined-Contribution Pension Plans: Fact or Fiction?" Unpublished working paper, Economics Department, Dartmouth College.

Harrison, M.J. and William F. Sharpe. 1983. "Optimal Funding and Asset Allocation Rules for Defined Benefit Pension Plans." Chapter 4 in Bodie and Shoven (1983).

Ippolito, Richard A. 1986. *Pensions, Economics and Public Policy*. Homewood, IL: PRC and Dow Jones-Irwin.

———. 1989. *The Economics of Pension Insurance*. Homewood, IL: PRC and R.D. Irwin.

Jones, E. Philip and Scott P. Mason. 1980. "Valuation of Loan Guarantees." *Journal of Banking and Finance* 4 (March): 89–107.

Kane, Edward J. 1990. *The S&L Mess: How Did It Happen?* Washington, DC: Urban Institute Press.

Leibowitz, Martin L. 1986. "The Dedicated Bond Portfolio in Pension Funds." *Financial Analysts Journal* 42, 1–2 (Jan/Feb, Mar/April): 68–75, 47–57.

———. 1992. *Investing: The Collected Work of Martin L. Leibowitz*, ed. Frank J. Fabozzi. Chicago: Probus.

Lockhart, James B., III. 1991a. "The Making of a Sound PBGC." Speech before the National Employee Benefit Institute. Washington, DC, September.

———. 1991b. Testimony before U.S. House of Representatives Budget Committee Task Force on Urgent Fiscal Issues. October 24.

Marcus, Alan J. 1987. "Corporate Pension Policy and the Value of PBGC Insurance." Chapter 3 in Bodie et al. (1987).

Marcus, Alan J. and Israel Shaked. 1984. "The Valuation of FDIC Deposit Insurance Using Option-Pricing Estimates." *Journal of Money, Credit and Banking* 16 (November): 446–60.

Mayer, Martin. 1990. *The Greatest-Ever Bank Robbery: The Collapse of the Savings and Loan Industry*. New York: Scribners.

McGill, Dan M. 1970. *Guaranty Fund for Private Pension Obligations*. Homewood, IL: R.D. Irwin.

———, ed. 1977. *Social Security and Private Pensions: Competitive or Complementary?* Homewood, IL: PRC and R.D. Irwin.

McGill, Dan M. and Donald S. Grubbs. 1989. *Fundamentals of Private Pensions*. Sixth edition. Homewood, IL: R.D. Irwin.

Merton, Robert C. 1977. "An Analytic Derivation of the Cost of Deposit Insurance and Loan Guarantees: An Application of Modern Option Pricing Theory." *Journal of Banking and Finance* 1 (June): 3–11.

———. 1978. "On the Cost of Deposit Insurance When There Are Surveillance Costs." *Journal of Business* 51 (July): 439–52.

———. 1983a. "On the Role of Social Security as a Means for Efficient Risk-

Bearing in an Economy Where Human Capital Is Not Tradeable." Chapter 9 in Bodie and Shoven (1983).

———. 1983b. "On Consumption-Indexed Public Pension Plans." Chapter 10 in Bodie and Shoven (1983).

———. 1990. "The Financial System and Economic Performance." *Journal of Financial Services Research* 4 (December): 263–300.

———. 1992. *Continuous-Time Finance*. Revised ed. Oxford: Basil Blackwell.

———. 1993. "Operation and Regulation of Financial Intermediaries: A Functional Perspective." In *Operational Regulation of Financial Markets*, ed. Peter Englund. Stockholm: The Economic Council.

Merton, Robert C. and Zvi Bodie. 1992a. "A Framework for Analyzing the Financial System." Harvard Graduate School of Business Working Paper.

———. 1992b. "On the Management of Deposit Insurance and Other Guarantees." Harvard Graduate School of Business Working Paper 92-081, May.

———. 1993. "On the Management of Financial Guarantes." *Financial Management* 21 (Winter): 87–109.

Merton, Robert C., Zvi Bodie, and Alan J. Marcus. 1987. "Pension Plan Integration as Insurance Against Social Security Risk." Chapter 6 in Bodie et al. (1987).

Munnell, Alicia H. 1982. "Guaranteeing Private Pension Benefits." *New England Economic Review* (March/April).

Myers, Robert J. 1977. "Concepts of Balance Between OASDI and Private Pension Benefits." Chapter 7 in McGill (1977).

———. 1991. "Summary of the Provisions of the Old-Age, Survivors, and Disability Insurance System." Unpublished Manuscript, Temple University, January.

Osborne, D. and C. Mishra. 1989. "Deposit Insurance as an Exchange Option, Public or Private." Unpublished manuscript, School of Management, University of Texas at Dallas, Richardson TX, November.

Paul, Robert D. 1988. "A Pension Plan for the Competitive 1990s." *Compensation and Benefits Management* (Summer).

Pennacchi, George. 1987a. "Alternative Forms of Deposit Insurance: Pricing and Bank Incentive Issues." *Journal of Banking and Finance* 11 (June): 291–312.

———. 1987b. "A Reexamination of the Over- (or Under-) Pricing of Deposit Insurance." *Journal of Money, Credit and Banking* 19 (August): 340–60.

Ronn, Ehud I. and Avinash K. Verma. 1986. "Pricing Risk-Adjusted Deposit Insurance: An Option-Based Model." *Journal of Finance* 41 (September): 871–95.

Rothschild, Michael and Joseph E. Stiglitz. 1976. "Equilibrium in Competitive Insurance Markets: An Essay on the Economics of Imperfect Information." *Quarterly Journal of Economics* 90 (November): 629–49.

Selby, Michael J. P., Julian R. Franks, and J. P. Karki. 1988. "Loan Guarantees, Wealth Transfers and Incentives to Invest." *Journal of Industrial Economics* 37 (September): 47–65.

Sharpe, William F. 1976. "Corporate Pension Funding Policy." *Journal of Financial Economics* 3 (June): 183–93.

———. 1978. "Bank Capital Adequacy, Deposit Insurance, and Security Values." *Journal of Financial and Quantitative Analysis* 13 (November): 701–18.

Smalhout, James. 1991. Unpublished study prepared for the National Taxpayers Union.

Sosin, Howard. 1980. "On the Valuation of Federal Loan Guarantees to Corporations." *Journal of Finance* 35 (December): 1209–21.

Thomson, James B. 1987. "The Use of Market Information in Pricing Deposit Insurance." *Journal of Money, Credit and Banking* 19 (November): 528–37.

Towers Perrin, Inc. 1991. "Retirement Income Throughout the World." Management report, New York: Towers Perrin, Inc.

Treynor, Jack L. 1977. "The Principles of Corporation Pension Finance." *Journal of Finance* 32 (May): 627–38.

Turner, John A. and Lorna M. Dailey, eds. 1991. *Pension Policy: An International Perspective*. Washington, DC: U.S. Government Printing Office.

U.S. General Accounting Office. Pension Benefit Guaranty Corporation. 1991. *Annual Report 1991*. Washington, DC: U.S. Government Printing Office.

U.S. Office of Management and Budget. 1992. *Budget of the U.S. Government, 1993*. Washington, DC: OMB.

Utgoff, Katherine P. 1991. "The PBGC: A Costly Lesson in the Economics of Federal Insurance." Paper presented at a conference of the Federal Reserve Bank of Cleveland.

VanDerhei, Jack. 1990. "An Empirical Analysis of Risk-Related Insurance Premiums for the PBGC." *Journal of Risk and Insurance* 57 (June): 240–59.

Wachter, Susan M. 1988. *Social Security and Private Pensions: Providing for Retirement in the 21st Century*. Lexington, MA: Lexington Books.

White, Lawrence J. 1991. *The S&L Debacle: Public Policy Lessons for Bank and Thrift Regulation*. New York and Oxford: Oxford University Press.

Comments by James B. Lockhart III

Bodie's and Merton's paper provides a good justification for a government guarantee of pensions. It makes the case that the largely non-diversifiable risk of an underfunded defined benefit plan does present a serious exposure to individuals. This exposure is compounded by 401(k) plans invested in company stock, unfunded retiree health benefits and, ultimately, the risk of job loss. The "government guarantee" provided by the Pension Benefit Guaranty Corporation (PBGC) does reduce and diversify a worker's risk.

The problem, of course, is that the presence of the cheap guarantee encourages companies to underfund their pension plans. As a result, as the authors say, pension guarantees "subsidize firms or workers in distressed industries." Certainly the steel and airline industries spring to mind. The Canadians have cited PBGC guarantees as a steel industry subsidy and recently the chairman of a major airline has complained about the subsidy of his failing competitors. I agree with the authors' conclusion that the pension guarantee subsidies "are less visible to the public than other subsidies; they can lead to serious distortions in resource allocation and they can result in a socially undesirable redistribution of income." In effect, well-run, successful companies are subsidizing poorly-run, unsuccessful companies.

FSLIC Comparison

PBGC shares this problem of a guarantee subsidy with any unsound government (and even some non-government) insurance programs including the Federal Savings and Loan Insurance Corporation (FSLIC). We also share the four similarities with FSLIC that the authors mention. Some of these similarities are legislated, but where they are within our control, we are taking steps to lessen their impact. Despite these steps and some of the differences with FSLIC, these similarities do put PBGC at risk.

1. Multiple and conflicting goals

PBGC's missions, as spelled out in ERISA, are to encourage the growth of private pension plans (the Single Employer Pension Plan Amendments Act of 1986 narrowed this to defined benefit plans), to ensure the timely payment of benefits, and to keep premiums at the lowest possible level. These are not necessarily conflicting goals. Encouraging the growth of defined benefit plans produces a stable premium base that will help ensure financial strength. Likewise, a stable program would reassure sponsors of well-funded plans that they are not going to be asked to subsidize poorly run companies if they stay in this voluntary system. The desire to retain a stable premium base does not mean that any individual plan would not be terminated if its termination minimizes long-term cost to premium payers. However, as interpreted by some individuals, PBGC's goals can be seen to be conflicting. This is especially true if that interpretation concludes that one of our missions is to subsidize distressed industries. Others have suggested that a goal is to encourage defined benefit growth no matter what assets are backing those promises. That is a misreading of the three real missions. We have summarized these missions as a long-term goal of building a service-oriented, well-managed, and financially sound insurance company to provide a strong safety net for a healthy defined benefit pension system.

2. Failure to fully recognize or disclose the true costs, benefits, and incentives of the program

Unfortunately, many observers have been fooled by cash flow accounting into believing that there is no PBGC problem. Similar accounting was used by FSLIC. PBGC has made major efforts in its financial statements, congressional testimony, and public communications to better expose its true position. The booking of large probable losses and the footnoting of reasonably possible losses ($13 billion in 1991) are examples. PBGC puts out a 10-year forecast extrapolating past results. We have also worked closely with the Office of Management and Budget (OMB) on its model and are continuing to develop our modeling capabilities. The proposal to shift from misleading cash budgeting accounting to accrual accounting will show Congress the true costs of PBGC's actions. As shown in Figure 1, cash flow accounting shows a surplus while accrual shows a deficit of $2.5 billion. And

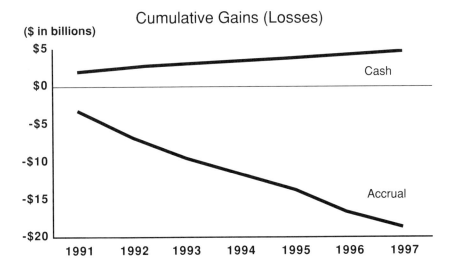

Figure 1. Cash accounting versus accrual accounting.

the OMB model produces a PBGC deficit of $18 billion in 1997, while the cash flow surplus continues to grow.

3. Interpreting losses as abuses rather than as a predictable response to the incentives built into the system

It is easy to slip into abuse language. I have even talked about steel industry "steeling" and "the great plane robberies," but the truth of the matter is that the system does not have the proper incentives. A perverse incentive, analogous to savers' willingness to invest in the highest paying guaranteed certificate of deposit available without regard to the S&L's financial condition, is the willingness of workers and unions to accept the empty promise of benefit increases because they are insured. The goal of PBGC's legislative proposals is to build the proper incentives into the system to encourage companies to fund rather than terminate their plans. Ideally, the incentives should be market based rather than totally legislated. Tax deductibility is one such incentive. Another might include changing the attitude of investors and creditors toward underfunded plans.

4. Failure to act promptly because of fragmentation and conflict of interests within the government regulatory apparatus

Under present leadership, the fragmentation is more theoretical than real. PBGC and the Internal Revenue Service (IRS) work very closely on waivers. Very few waivers are granted now and those that are granted are secured. There is a very real tension between higher pension funding to protect the PBGC and the resulting loss of tax revenues from higher corporate deductions. The adoption of accrual budgeting would eliminate the tension because the long-term benefits of these reforms to PBGC would be scored as a revenue gainer. In the case of the Department of Labor, we coordinate weekly. PBGC also takes a proactive role in monitoring companies. We concentrate on the financial health of the sponsor and its pension liabilities rather than pension assets, which seems to be the main concern of the authors. However, our ability to be too proactive is constrained by the legislative framework of Title IV. A very real tension exists that causes circum-spection by PBGC because a pension termination may force a company into bankruptcy and potentially into liquidation. If done unnecessarily, termination could harm the very people the program is designed to protect by causing the loss of nonguaranteed pension benefits, retiree health benefits, and even jobs. If not managed properly, the "back door industrial policy" that PBGC is sometimes accused of creating could become a "front door de-industrial policy."

Social Insurance

Some critics of the analogy to the FSLIC mess and PBGC's actions and proposals to prevent recurrences have suggested that PBGC was de-signed to provide subsidies to some plans. As the vast majority of the underfunded plans are flat benefit union negotiated plans in industries undergoing restructuring, the subsidy is to them from the final pay salaried plans of growing industries. The Employee Benefit Research Institute (EBRI) has suggested, in a forthcoming paper, that PBGC was designed to be a transfer agent from well-funded to underfunded plans. I am not sure the Congressional record supports that. But more important, the framers of ERISA would be appalled by the fallout: $40 billion in underfunded plans after almost 18 years, a rapidly growing federal bureaucracy serving 400,000 participants in 1700 plans, the potential of a government agency owning large equity positions in major U.S. companies, and a 19- to 72-fold increase in the premium.

In the EBRI paper a distinction is made between a social insurance company and a commercial one. It is suggested that Congress wanted a social insurance program and that the Bush administration and I want a commercial insurance company. The distinction is not useful, as PBGC is an insurance program that serves a desirable social purpose. I would suggest that a transfer agent is a social welfare program, not a social insurance program. That reasoning leads to the suggestion that the solution to PBGC's problems is to have a large one-time assessment on well-funded plans. Of course, as Bodie has pointed out previously, that would not solve the problem of a fundamentally unsound insurance program.

As Bodie and Merton so aptly put it in this paper: "Among the possible side effects in the case of the PBGC is the prospect that overcharging sponsors of well-funded plans in order to subsidize the underfunded plans of financially distressed firms might cause financially healthy sponsors to terminate their defined benefit plans. Ultimately, the United States could be left only with bankrupt defined benefit plans with the benefits financed directly by taxpayers" (p. 208).

Obviously, PBGC wants to avoid that fate. Therefore, the question is not whether we should be a social welfare agency, but how far to go in strengthening the underlying insurance principles supporting the program. In this post-FSLIC age, Congress is framing the debate on that basis as well.

Insurance Model

At PBGC we have used functional analysis as a methodology for improving the program as suggested by the authors. However, we have looked at a property and casualty insurance company model to develop ways to strengthen the program. It is similar to the authors' three areas of functional analysis, but has a different emphasis that produces different legislative proposals. The objective of both approaches is to produce the right incentives to reduce the risk and the size of losses from terminations.

The model (a pictorial view is shown in Figure 2) is very simple. The insured (in this case a factory owner) has to reduce the exposure to loss (fire) by putting in more sprinklers or (1) face higher premiums to reflect the risk of loss, (2) face a reduction or elimination of coverage, or (3) pay for a larger part of a loss if it occurs through coinsurance and/or deductibles.

Applying this insurance underwriting model to PBGC shows that losses occur when two things happen: a plan sponsor gets into severe financial difficulty and the plan is underfunded. The financial condition of the sponsor is largely outside the scope of the insurance program, but there are aspects that are designed to protect PBGC against a

Insurance

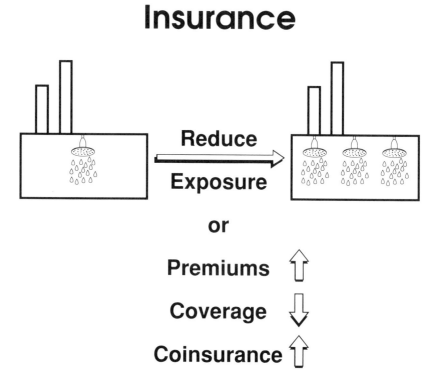

Reduce

Exposure

or

Premiums ⇧

Coverage ⇩

Coinsurance ⇧

Figure 2. Property and casualty insurance model.

controlled group restructuring, which leaves a weak sponsor with the unfunded plans by breaking up the controlled group (Section 4069). Another protection is the involuntary termination test, which allows PBGC to terminate a plan if there is an unreasonable risk of an unreasonable loss. PBGC has stepped up its monitoring of companies to review their financial conditions.

The key reason for underfunding is that required contributions are not high enough. The exposure often grows because of benefit increases in underfunded plans or large early retirement programs. There is a five-year phase-in for benefit increases to be fully guaranteed and there are requirements that do provide security in severely underfunded plans to back up this increase, but they are very weak. Also, poor investment performance that does not correlate to the effect of interest rates on liabilities can increase underfunding. However, the fiduciary rules of Title I of ERISA and the ensuing general practices do provide protection on the asset side.

These two loss tests are not entirely independent. Sometimes the size of the underfunding can drag a company into bankruptcy such as in the LTV situation. Of course, there are steps companies can take to minimize PBGC's risk of loss. For instance, in the auto industry firms have been raising equity and putting more than the minimum required into their pension plans.

Premiums are charged to all sponsors and they are related to one aspect of risk—the underfunding. PBGC does not have the flexibility of a normal insurance underwriter in that the premiums are dictated by Congress. Although it is not part of the present legislative package, in the longer term the kind of pricing flexibility given to the FDIC should be considered.

Coverage includes the policy limits (approximately $28,000 per year at age 65 for 1992) and conditions (insurance of only basic pension benefits). However, one questionable benefit is included—"shutdown benefits." They are heavily subsidized, non-prefunded, early retirement benefits that kick in when a factory is shut down. One dramatic difference from a commercial underwriter is that PBGC does not have the ability to refuse to cover our "uninsurable" risk.

Coinsurance includes many stakeholders of a corporation—workers, retirees, shareholders, suppliers, and creditors. The concept behind coinsurance is simply that if the insured share some of the risk of the loss they will work harder at preventing it. Coinsurance with shareholders, creditors, and suppliers is achieved by our claims in bankruptcy. The higher our recoveries the more incentive they have to push for better funding and the less incentive they have to push for termination. On average 80 to 90 percent of retirees receive their full benefit if an underfunded plan terminates. Of course, they lose the possibility of any future benefit increases. For the remainder, whose old and future accruals will be cut off, there is significant coinsurance. Coinsurance was the underlying principle of PBGC's successful battle against "abusive follow-on plans" in the LTV Supreme Court case.

Coinsurance in its broadest sense includes all premium payers. Those 80 percent of the sponsors with well-funded plans are mutually insuring or, unfortunately, subsidizing the underfunded plans through their higher premiums. The coinsurance factor gives the well-funded sponsor the incentive to create a sounder insurance program by supporting the PBGC reforms.

Functional Analysis

This paper's approach to functional analysis is that of a lender. It proposes three methods to manage the business: (1) monitoring, (2) restricting collateral, and (3) setting premiums. PBGC has used all three, but I take issue with how the analysis is applied to PBGC. There is an overemphasis on the pension plan itself and an underemphasis on the other part of the loss test—the financial health of the sponsor.

Although PBGC has increased its monitoring capability, at best we can only monitor 50 to 100 companies plus several hundred plans in the process of terminating out of the 85,000 we insure. For most of the rest we have to rely on the tax and insurance incentives. The monitoring emphasis is on the sponsor's financial condition and pension liabilities. Pension assets are considered secondary because they are usually significantly less than liabilities, easier to price, and generally well diversified.

Rather than terminate a plan as soon as a payment is missed, as the authors suggest, we place a lien against the controlled group's assets after sixty days. Just like a lender, we negotiate with the sponsor to try to prevent seizure of the assets (termination), which normally leads to bankruptcy. In a distressing number of cases Chapter 11 bankruptcies are turning into liquidations after a large wasting of the assets. PBGC's experience has been that it is often better to work with a sponsor of an ongoing plan rather than to terminate it and try to recover the underfunding from the bankrupt estate. Therefore, PBGC (as are lenders) is often faced with the dilemma of whether it is better to move quickly or use our leverage to achieve better protection for an ongoing plan with the result of no losses to PBGC and participants.

Another point should be made on monitoring. Despite what the authors write, PBGC's accounting problems have no impact on our monitoring capability as the accounting problems are related to measuring the liabilities of already terminated plans. We do take control of plan assets as soon as a plan terminates.

PBGC has not ignored the impact of asset mix on our exposure, but does not believe any action is necessary. As is well known, PBGC immunized its own liability structure through a dollar duration matching strategy. We choose to keep 25 percent of our assets in equities, with an upper limit of 35 percent. The argument that led us to keep some equity percentage applies even more to pension plans that do not have our contingent liability exposure to equities. Over the long term, equities perform better than fixed income securities. As only 0.1 percent of the plans PBGC insures terminate in distress in a year, long term is the proper perspective.

Removing from sponsors the added return of equities by charging them for it could cause them to rethink the advantages of sponsoring a defined benefit plan. It could significantly hasten the day that only underfunded plans remain in the system. Only underfunded plans cannot leave this system on a voluntary basis. It is my belief that the benefit to the PBGC, if any, of forcing immunization would be far outweighed by the impact on equity markets and the sponsorship of defined benefit plans.

PBGC must refine its risk-based premium in the future. Asset mix could be considered for larger underfunded plans. There is certainly the risk in recession that bankruptcies increase while pension liabilities grow as interest rates fall, early retirements increase, and pension assets shrink as equities fall. Historically, that has not occurred to any significant extent. The authors' model seems to overcompensate for these risks. The model includes, as part of pension assets, our priority claim for 30 percent of the sponsoring firm's net worth plus a general unsecured claim against the rest. The measurement of the value of these claims in an ongoing company would be complex, especially given the large uncertainty about the present priority and size of PBGC's claims. Over the last five years recoveries have averaged only 7.5 percent of benefit liabilities. An annual 20 percent premium for a 20 percent underfunded plan (with 7.5 percent of the assets assumed to be recoveries) seems extremely high unless there were an immediate risk of termination. PBGC roughly estimates that there is a total of $180 billion in liabilities in underfunded pension plans. If one assumes that average underfunding is 80 percent including recoveries, the suggested premiums would raise $36 billion in one year from these plans, which would cover the net present value of all our future expected losses. This result occurs because the other prong of our loss test (corporate financial distress) should play a significant part in risk-based pricing.

A different approach would be to define underfunding in the traditional manner and apply a premium to only the underfunding, based on the spread between Treasury bonds and the corporations' unsecured long-term borrowing rate. That could then be added to a base rate that might reflect the pension asset mix. This approach would only be practical for larger plans and would have to account for the large swings in quality yield spreads over time. Certainly, at present spreads it would produce a premium much lower than the authors' model.

PBGC Legislative Proposals

Some have questioned whether an insurance model is appropriate for PBGC, as we are required to insure all plans. It is true that we have no underwriting discretion and that the mammoth risks presented by large underfunded plans sponsored by financially troubled companies cannot be reinsured.

Legislative reforms have to address these large plans. The $2.5 billion deficit of PBGC's single-employer program can be traced to only seven companies. Another seven may determine the fate of the PBGC. The flip side of this analysis is that the rest of the program is insurable with some strengthening of the underlying insurance principles.

The three reforms included in the Pension Security Act of 1992, coupled with the move to accrual accounting, does create a sounder insurance program based on three of the four features of the insurance model. Only premiums are not addressed. There is no premium proposal because we have to know the terms of the insurance policy before we can price it. Without Congressional action on the reforms, pricing will continue to be a function of how far the subsidy from well-funded plans can be pushed before they desert the system. Risk-based pricing will require a better underwriting model. The model should include corporate risk as well as asset mix and the amount of underfunding. Certainly, over time, the three reforms should reduce this latter risk. They are:

1. Stricter funding rules

Despite the pension reforms of 1987 (Pension Protection Act) and the strong investment markets, pension underfunding is *not* decreasing. The minimum requirements are too weak. As Figure 3 shows, under present rules a typical 60 percent flat benefit plan would take 15 years to get 75 percent funded. The Bush administration's proposal would have plans fully funded in a 10 to 20 year period. The three alternative minimum funding rules are designed to force both growing and shrinking companies with underfunded plans to pay more. The rules require phase-ins because some companies with underfunded plans are so underfunded that too tight a funding schedule might cause a bankruptcy. Higher funding is analogous to more sprinklers, as it is the most direct way to reduce both participants' and PBGC's exposure to losses.

2. Restrict the growth in guarantees

In union negotiations companies often give benefit increases they cannot afford in lieu of a wage increase. Unions accept them because benefits are insured, albeit with a phase-in. The practice reached the ultimate perversity in the Continental and TWA bankruptcies when pension benefits were increased because the creditors said the airlines could not afford a wage increase. To combat exposure to these empty promises, the administration is proposing that no new benefit in-

FUNDING RATIO

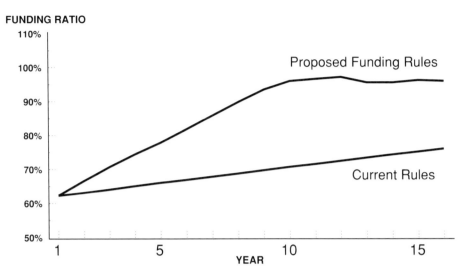

Figure 3. Funding ratios with and without funding reform for typical plan presenting exposure to the PBGC.

creases, including newly created shutdown benefits, be guaranteed if a plan is underfunded. Once the plan gets funded, those past benefit increases would be guaranteed. This reform places a limit on coverage, but it also has a coinsurance feature. Participants at risk of losing non-guaranteed pension benefits if a plan terminates will push for better funding.

3. Clarify and increase PBGC's bankruptcy recoveries

PBGC's recoveries in bankruptcy are primarily from general unsecured claims. As such, they are small (14 percent of underfunding on average). Included in the small recoveries are priority claims for missed contributions and for underfunding up to 30 percent of the net worth. Because the net worth test ignores pension underfunding and is calculated subsidiary by subsidiary, with negative net worth counting as zero, there is often some net worth. Unfortunately, the creditors and the courts are ignoring these priorities because they are acknowledged only in ERISA and the Tax Code. The administration's proposals seek to clarify these priorities by putting them in the Bankruptcy Code and then building on them by allowing an alternative for the underfunding priority—a percentage that gradually increases—as well as a priority for shutdown benefits triggered within three years of termination.

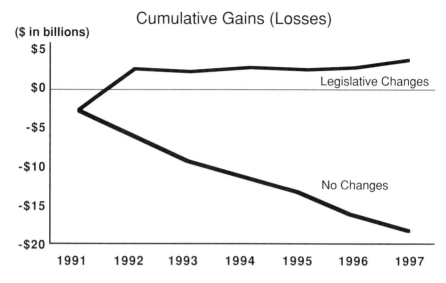

Figure 4. Impact of legislative proposals on PBGC's financial status.

Higher recoveries will obviously reduce the level of losses. They will also act as an important coinsurance feature since creditors' and shareholders' losses will rise if a plan terminates. Therefore they will put pressure on corporate management to better fund these plans and not to terminate them in bankruptcy.

If enacted, these three reforms would have an important impact on the program by basing it on sound insurance principles. As seen in Figure 4, they will turn PBGC's large deficit into a small surplus based on the OMB model. That would then give us the opportunity seriously to reconsider the structure and size of PBGC's premiums.

Chapter 6
Estimating the Current Exposure of the Pension Benefit Guaranty Corporation to Single-Employer Pension Plan Terminations

Christopher M. Lewis and
Richard L. Cooperstein

The Pension Benefit Guaranty Corporation (PBGC) was established as a federal corporation in the Employment Retirement Income Security Act of 1974 (ERISA) as a vehicle for insuring pension benefit payments of private retirees. The PBGC was designed to promote the growth of private pension plans by guaranteeing pension benefit payments. Over the past 15 years, the PBGC has been successful in this mission: the number of insured single-employer private pension plan participants has grown from 30 million to 32 million; single-employer pension plan assets have grown from $166 billion in 1975 to a level of $1.3 trillion in 1990; and PBGC insured benefits have risen from $195 billion to just over $800 billion by the end of 1990 (Turner, 1989).

As PBGC insured single-employer benefits have grown, however, so has the exposure of the PBGC to pension plan claims. For fiscal year 1991, the PBGC recorded terminated pension plan claims of just over $1 billion, with an additional $800 million in probable terminations. Since 1982, the accumulated deficit of the PBGC has increased roughly eightfold to $2.5 billion. This surge in PBGC claims follows a period of low interest rates and strong asset returns in the stock market—developments that should have boosted pension funding. Meanwhile federal pension insurance and federal funding rules in the tax code have allowed many corporations to underfund their pension plans to an extent that would have been unacceptable in a strictly private labor market. Currently, the PBGC insures underfunded single-employer defined benefit pension plans with over $33 billion of unfunded liabilities. Another $8–$10 billion in underfunding exists in multi-employer plans, although this exposure is not addressed in this paper (PBGC, 1991).

Although these measures raise concern over PBGC's current funding position, they do not reflect PBGC's exposure to currently active plans. In addition, the current budgetary treatment of the PBGC, by focusing only on cash flow, greatly understates the potential exposure of the agency, and ultimately the federal government, to plan termination claims. It also obscures the rising potential for a large scale federal "bailout" of the pension insurance system in the future.

A better approach for assessing the solvency of the PBGC is to estimate the value of expected pension claims over a long-term horizon. Fortunately, the finance literature and, specifically, the options pricing literature offers a well-developed method for estimating this type of contingent claim. The options pricing approach has long been accepted as a method for analyzing contingent claims (Merton, 1973), and has been useful in estimating potential costs of deposit insurance (Merton, 1977, 1978; Marcus and Shaked, 1982; Pennacchi, 1987); mortgages (Foster and Van Order, 1984, 1985; Cooperstein, Redburn, and Meyers, 1992); international interest guarantees (Borensztein and Pennacchi 1990); and pension insurance (Treynor, 1977; Langetieg, Findlay, and da Motta, 1982; Marcus, 1989).

In an options pricing framework, pension insurance is analogous to an indefinite maturity American put option, with the value of the pension assets representing the underlying asset, the value of pension liabilities representing the exercise or strike price, and the maturity determined by the expected life of the sponsoring firm. Expressing pension insurance as an option is complicated further, however, by the legal constraint that permits firms to exercise their put option only in the case of firm bankruptcy. In order for the PBGC to experience a pension claim, two simultaneous events must occur: a firm must file for bankruptcy and its pension plan must be underfunded. Thus the central problem of assessing the value (options price) of pension insurance is relating the failure probability of the sponsoring firms to their respective level of pension underfunding.

This paper estimates the current contingent liability of the PBGC to pension claims using an options pricing approach. A simplified closed-form options pricing model used in conjunction with a Monte Carlo simulation was used to provide a reasonable basis on which to construct these estimates. We are moving, however, toward a more flexible options pricing model for deriving future liability estimates. Section I extends the closed-form bankruptcy-only options pricing model of pension insurance first developed by Marcus, and incorporates the model into a Monte Carlo simulation framework. Section II specifies the assumptions used in evaluating 1,792 single-employer defined benefit pension plans currently insured by the PBGC. Section III presents a comparative static analysis of the sensitivity of the options pricing equation to the assumptions developed in Section II. Finally, Section IV presents the results of our comparative dynamics analysis of PBGC's current exposure under current law assumptions, as well PBGC's contingent liability under several policy simulations. An analysis of the PBGC's current reform proposals before Congress also is presented in Section IV.

I. Pension Insurance Model

A. Marcus's Bankruptcy-Only Options Pricing Formula

In estimating the present value of expected pension claims to the PBGC over the next thirty years, we extend Marcus's closed-form bankruptcy-only options pricing model. Like Marcus, we assume that pension assets, pension liabilities, firm assets, and firm liabilities all follow a stochastic differential based upon a Wiener process.[1] Specifically, the annual movements in pension assets (F_t), pension liabilities (A_t), firm assets (V_t), and firm liabilities (D_t) are assumed to be lognormally distributed with a mean rate of growth $(\alpha. + C_{.t})$ and a historical variance $(\sigma.)$ $(dz$ is the stochastic term).

(1) $$dF_t = (\alpha_F + C_{Ft}) F_t dt + \sigma_F F_t dz_F,$$

(2) $$dA_t = (\alpha_A + C_{At}) A_t dt + \sigma_A A_t dz_A,$$

(3) $$dV_t = (\alpha_v) V_t dt + \sigma_v V_t dz_v,$$

(4) $$dD_t = (\alpha_D) D_t dt + \sigma_D D_t dz_D,$$

where

C_{ft} = expected growth rate in pension assets (firm contributions),
C_{at} = expected growth rate in accrued benefits,
α_f = normal expected return in pension assets,
α_a = normal expected growth in pension benefits,
α_V = normal expected growth in firm assets,
α_d = normal expected growth in firm debt,
$\sigma.$ = standard deviation.

We compute the market value of assets by adding firm book liabilities to market equity, which was derived from end-of-year stock market values. While offering a substantial improvement over book asset values, this approach presents a simultaneity problem in the valuation of pension insurance. As Marcus and Shaked (1984) show for deposit insurance, stockholders incorporate the value of federal guarantees in their calculation of expected future earnings, and hence, into the stock price used to calculate market assets. If underfunded pension plans did not have a PBGC guarantee, future cash earnings of the firm would be required to fund up the pension plan. This cash drain on future earnings would lower equity holders' valuation of the firm and, hence, the stock price. Thus, without the PBGC guarantee, firm stock prices would be discounted for pension underfunding, resulting in lower estimates of the market value of firm assets.

To properly value firm equity in calculating the option value of pension insurance, we follow the analysis used by Marcus and Shaked and deduct the dollar value of the pension guarantee from our calculation of market equity (E_t), and hence, market assets. We then iteratively solve for both the options price (P_t) and the market value of firm assets (V_t) until the change in the options price with respect to firm assets is less than 1 percent in absolute value.

$$(5) \qquad V_t = D_t + E_t - P_t,$$

$$(6) \qquad P_t = P_t(v_t, FR_t, C_{ft}, C_{at}, R_t; \sigma, \rho)$$

$$\text{for} \quad \frac{\partial P_t}{\partial V_t} \leq |.01|.$$

We then express the position of the firm as a ratio of the adjusted market value of assets over the value of firm liabilities, denoted as the firm ratio $(v_t = V_t/D_t)$.

In this bankruptcy-only termination model, firm insolvency occurs when $v_t \leq 1$ or when $V_t \leq D_t$. The limiting assumption in this model is that the firm puts the pension plan to the PBGC as soon as market equity is zero and $v_t = 1$. Thus, in terms of the model, v_t never theoretically falls below unity. When $v_t = 1$, the firm will put the plan to the PBGC in an amount equal to the underfunding at time of plan termination. Since the probability of termination in this case is 1, growth rate and variance assumptions are no longer important in determining the exposure to the PBGC, which is known with certainty to be the level of underfunding at time of bankruptcy; $(A_t - F_t)$ if underfunded and zero otherwise.

Using Ito's lemma[2] and assuming $C_{\cdot t}$ and α_t are constant, Marcus solves this system of stochastic differential equations for a closed-form solution of the options value of pension insurance. For simplicity, in estimating the value of this insurance for each firm, we calculate the firm's funding ratio ($FR_t = A_t/F_t$) and, normalizing pension liabilities to one, use the funding ratio as a measure of pension assets. Assuming constant growth rates for pension assets (C_{ft}) and liabilities (C_{at}) and adjusting for PBGC recoveries on claims ($1 - R_t$), the options pricing function can be expressed as in equation (7):

(7)
$$P_t = (1 - R_t) \times [v_t^{-\phi} - FR_t v_t^{-\theta}],$$

where

$$\theta = \left(\frac{K}{M}\right) + \left[\left(\frac{K}{M}\right)^2 - \left(\frac{2C_{ft}}{M}\right)\right]^{1/2},$$

$$\phi = \left(\frac{L}{M}\right) + \left[\left(\frac{L}{M}\right)^2 - \left(\frac{2C_{at}}{M}\right)\right]^{1/2},$$

$$K = -\tfrac{1}{2}\sigma_V^2 + \tfrac{1}{2}\sigma_D^2 - \rho_{DF} + \rho_{VF},$$

$$L = -\tfrac{1}{2}\sigma_V^2 + \tfrac{1}{2}\sigma_D^2 - \rho_{DA} + \rho_{VA},$$

$$M = \sigma_V^2 + \sigma_D^2 - 2\rho_{DV},$$

$$FR_t = \frac{F_t}{A_t},$$

P_t = options price (dollar value) of pension insurance in period t,
R_t = PBGC's expected recovery rate on pension claims in period t,
v_t = ratio of firm assets to liabilities in period t,
$\sigma_{\cdot}^2$ = variance,
$\rho_{\cdot\cdot}$ = covariance.

The variance and covariance estimates for pension and firm assets and liabilities used in the options price and presented later in Table 1 represent historical averages over the past 10–15 years. The variance in firm assets and firm liabilities reflect the 20 percent historical standard deviation in firm equity, as measured by the S&P 500 index over the past 20 years. The closed-form options pricing approach assumes that these historical variances and covariances are known with certainty in the pension market.

TABLE 1   Historical Growth Rates and Variances for Pension and Firm
Assets and Liabilities (percents)

	1986–1990 growth rates	Model growth rate assumptions	Model* variance assumptions
Pension assets			
Overfunded plans	5.3	5.0	4.0
Underfunded plans	2.6	Eq. (13)†	4.0
Pension liabilities			
Overfunded plans	8.5	5.0	1.0
Underfunded plans	3.3	3.0	1.0
Market value of firm assets	6.7	6.0	4.0
Book value of firm liabilities	6.7	6.0	1.0

Source: Marcus (1985).
*Estimates represent Marcus's original variance assumptions. The variance assumptions for firm assets and firm liabilities assume that the variance in firm equity corresponds to the 4.6% variance in the S&P500.

B. Monte Carlo Simulation

Using an options pricing valuation approach for PBGC's contingent claims from pension terminations provides a reasonable estimate of PBGC's future losses based upon the initial conditions and expectations existing in any one period—the current value of the option. This option value represents a one-time payment that the PBGC would need to collect to secure the value of its perpetual pension guarantee. However, this one-time payment cannot measure annual budgeting costs, or the effect and timing of changes in federal policy. Budgeting for annual costs requires not only projections of current exposure, but also of fluctuations in aggregate exposure and claims over the budget period arising from changes in federal policy or in the economy. Therefore, we incorporated the options pricing formulation into a Monte Carlo simulation framework, based upon the same Wiener process assumptions used to derive the options price. Using the options pricing approach within a Monte Carlo framework allows us to simulate movements in pension assets and liabilities, and firm assets and liabilities over time, recalculating the options price each period.

In the Monte Carlo, we atomize our sample of 1,792 firms into 5,000 equally-sized anonymous firm-units, with each unit bearing the characteristics of its parent firm. This atomization process is valuable for two reasons. First, in budgeting for future claims to the PBGC, the primary concern is with projecting claims from the industry as a whole, not for specific firms. The atomization process removes the sensitivities involved in dealing with firm-specific estimates. Second, atomizing the sample generates a probability distribution of firm insolvency and pension terminations, avoiding lumpiness problems in the timing of pension terminations. This process produces a smooth profile of claims and obviates the need to conduct continual runs of the model to yield average per annum claim estimates.

The number of firm-units generated by the Monte Carlo for each parent firm (N_k) is proportional to the parent firm's market share of total liabilities (D_k) in our sample:

$$(8) \qquad N_k = 5000 \times \left(\frac{D_k}{D} \right) .$$

This allows us to normalize pension liabilities to one, because the firm's total pension liabilities are reflected in the market share of firm-units generated by the model relative to the overall size in industry liabilities. Each of the N_k units, representing one actual pension plan, behaves independently according to the variances in pension assets, pension liabilities, firm assets, and firm liabilities. Thus, the options price, P_t, has a diffusion process over time.

The stochastic dynamics used in the Monte Carlo simulation are based on the same Brownian motion used to derive the options pricing formula. Accordingly, the $(t+1)$-period values of pension assets (F_{t+1}), pension liabilities (A_{t+1}), firm assets (V_{t+1}), and firm liabilities (D_{t+1}) are calculated as follows:

$$(9) \qquad F_{(t+1)} = F_t + dF_t ,$$

$$(10) \qquad A_{(t+1)} = A_t + dA_t ,$$

$$(11) \qquad V_{(t+1)} = V_t + dV_t ,$$

$$(12) \qquad D_{(t+1)} = D_t + dD_t ,$$

with dF_t, dA_t, dV_t, and dD_t defined in equations (1)–(4). Once the value of these variables are recalculated at the beginning of year $(t+1)$, we compute a new corresponding firm equity ratio $v_{(t+1)}$ and funding ratio (FR_{t+1}) to estimate the contingent liability for the new period: $P_{(t+1)}$. The Monte Carlo simulation also allows us to forecast the trend in critical variables under different economic and financial scenarios, adding richness to our assumptions about firm behavior as it approaches insolvency.[3]

The Monte Carlo simulation is also used to enrich our assumptions governing the timing of firm bankruptcy, firm behavior as it approaches insolvency, and the rate at which new pension plans replace terminated plans. The Marcus closed-form solution relies on a simple bankruptcy rule trigged when $v_t \leq 1$, with v_t following a Wiener process. Our simulation results, however, suggest that one or both of these assumptions may be violated. Many insolvent firms remain open for several years before filing for bankruptcy (or recovering). Part of this increase in firm longevity may be directly attributable to the role the pension option has in boosting firm equity. The more insolvent a firm with an underfunded pension plan becomes, the higher the value of the option in the shareholder evaluation of firm net worth. Hence, the increasing value of the pension option partially offsets declines in real firm equity.

Take, for example, a hypothetical firm with $42,000 in assets, $39,500 in liabilities ($v_t = 1.06$), $5,000 in pension assets, and $9,000 in pension liabilities ($FR_t = 55\%$). Firm equity before removing the value of the pension option is about 6 percent—weak, but solvent. Jointly solving for the value of the pension option and adjusted equity (reported equity less the value of the option) shows that the pension contract is worth $3,000 and firm equity less the value of the pension option is actually negative. Thus the value of the pension guarantee increases reported firm equity, permitting an otherwise insolvent firm to remain in business. Bankruptcy transaction costs may also affect the decision to exit the industry. These costs along with high earning variances may lower the firm's hurdle rate used in deciding whether or not to exit the industry during periods of negative profits (Dixit, 1991). It may, therefore, make economic sense for firms facing negative earnings streams to delay making an exit decision from the industry. In addition, if creditors refrain from liquidation because of the loss of value that coincides with bankruptcy, and instead, hope for firm resurrection, stockholder equity will be higher, if for no other reason than the additional dividend earnings they will receive (Merton, 1990).

Thus, in determining the annual stream of pension plan terminations, we define a closure rule for insolvent firms that generates a realistic stream of bankruptcies based upon three years of PBGC termination data. According to this closure rule, one out of every three insolvent firms actually becomes bankrupt[4]. The remaining two insolvent firms are given 1 percent equity and retained in our sample with a negative 3 percent drift in equity. Hence, near-insolvent but non-bankrupt firms may bounce along the bankruptcy boundary for several years before failing (or recovering). This assumption is intended to reflect the realities of bankruptcy, where although 85 percent of firms filing for chapter 11 never recover, they often remain open for several years before actually failing. Simulating bankruptcy rates and specifying the appropriate bankruptcy rule in the closed-form options pricing equation is an area which requires further study.

Another behavioral reality that we have tried to incorporate into the Monte Carlo simulation is the difference in pension funding status on a going-concern basis versus a date of pension termination (DOPT) basis. As a firm approaches insolvency or bankruptcy, it experiences severe employment declines, as early retirement programs, layoffs, and attrition reduce the number of active workers. Thus, during the period immediately preceding bankruptcy, firms experience a dramatic increase in the ratio of retired workers to active workers and an equally dramatic decrease in the expected retirement age. By the time a pension claim is registered at the PBGC, these two factors combine to increase the expected present value of pension liabilities by as much as 20 percent. Since the Marcus version of the closed-form solution is expressed on a going-concerns basis, this "DOPT differential" is not incorporated into the options pricing formula. Therefore, the options pricing estimate of the closure cost for any one firm, ceterus paribus, should underestimate the actual cost of failure. In the budget, we account for this additional cost in the closure cost stream produced using the Monte Carlo simulation for terminating plans. Alternatively, this additional cost could be incorporated directly into the closed-form solution of the pension option.

We also specify a replacement rule in the Monte Carlo process for terminating plans, which creates a new pension plan for every two pension plans that terminate. This 1 : 2 replacement rule assumes shrinkage in the defined benefit pension plan population, as defined contribution plans capture a larger and larger share of the industry. In the model, the newly created pension plan is given the mean ratio of firm assets to firm liabilities (1.35) and a funding status of 10 percent overfunded or underfunded depending upon the funding status of the plan it replaced.

II. Assumptions

The value of the PBGC guarantee is estimated using Compustat data for 1,792 publicly traded firms reporting single-employer pension plan information. Total pension liabilities reported in this sample were $570 billion, approximately 95 percent of the single-employer pension liabilities insured by the PBGC.

The present value of pension liabilities reported in the Compustat data set includes firm assumptions for interest rates, retirement age, and mortality rates. Although unable to adjust for retirement age and mortality assumptions, we did adjust liabilities based upon their reported interest rate assumption. Multiplying reported pension liabilities by the ratio of the 30-year Treasury bond rate to the reported long-term rate assumed for each plan places pension liabilities on a more consistent basis from which to draw cost comparisons. The long-term interest rate assumption is consistent with the 1992 30-year T-bond yield assumed in the President's 1993 Budget (7.32%). Adjusting for the variance in mortality and retirement age assumptions, which are equally important, is a subject for future research.

The baseline simulation reflects current behavior and legal constraints governing single-employer private pension plans. Since almost all overfunded plans are final salary plans and almost all underfunded plans are flat benefit plans, we classify them as such. Hence, mean growth rates in pension liabilities and pension assets are based upon the expected growth in final salary plans and flat benefit plans.

The future growth rate assumptions for both overfunded and underfunded pension liabilities, presented in Table 1, reflect the average annual growth rate in over/underfunded pension assets and pension liabilities during the 1986–1990 period. (Disaggregated pension data were not available prior to 1986.) Thus, overfunded pension liabilities grow 5 percent annually and underfunded pension liabilities grow 3 percent. In addition, we assume that overfunded pension asset growth matches the growth in overfunded pension liabilities, a 5% annual rate. For underfunded pension assets, however, the mean rate of growth was derived as a function of last period's funding ratio (FR_t), the expected growth rate in underfunded pension liabilities ($\alpha_a + C_{at}$), and current funding rules (L).

(13) $$C_f = C_f\,(FR_t,\,(\alpha_t + C_{at}),\,L).$$

Under baseline assumptions, we assume that the Pension Protection Act (1987) would force firms with underfunded pension plans to increase the mean growth rate of contributions such that their funding ratio would rise by one-half of a percentage point per year over the next thirty years, or until the funding ratio reaches 90 percent. (Note that one of the main caveats of this closed-form solution is the constant growth rate assumptions. While the contribution rate for each plan is a function of its current funding status, this rate is assumed to hold for the expected option term, potentially overstating the increase in funding for underfunded plans.)

The market value of firms' assets, as well as their liabilities, grew at a 6.7 percent annual rate over the 1980–1990 period. This was almost identical to the 6.8 percent annual rate of growth in nominal Gross Domestic Product over the same period. Thus, in projecting firm assets and liabilities into the future, we used 6.0 percent—the same rate as the long run growth assumed for GDP in the President's 1993 Budget.

Recoveries in the baseline are assumed to remain constant at 14 percent of pension claims (unfunded pension liabilities put to the PBGC). This assumption is consistent with PBGC estimates of the long-term rate of recoveries under current law. However, if the September 1991 Southern District Court of New York's ruling in the LTV case, which denied priority status for PBGC claims in bankruptcy court, is upheld in the courts, PBGC estimates that its recovery rate could fall to almost 5 percent, drastically increasing PBGC's exposure.

III. Comparative Statics

Based on the specification of the options pricing formula and the assumptions outlined above, we analyze the sensitivity of the model to pension funding, firm equity, and the estimated variance parameters. Figures 1 and 2 present the relationship between the option value of the PBGC insurance contract and firm equity for firms which are 25 percent overfunded and underfunded respectively. In both figures, the value of the pension insurance is a one-time payment expressed as a percentage of pension liabilities, analogous to a "fair premium" fee.

Figure 1 shows that the value of the pension insurance for overfunded pension plans is primarily an increasing function of firm equity. As equity rises, the expected term of the option grows and firms have a longer period over which asset volatility and/or falling contributions can decrease the level of funding. Figure 1 reflects this risk, showing that the option value generally rises as firm equity rises.

The exception is a plan with future contributions expected to substantially exceed pension liability growth. For example, if pension assets grow at a 7 percent annual rate while pension liabilities grow at a 5 percent rate, the extra contributions overcome the increased risk associated with rising firm equity. Note also that lower growth rates and variances in pension assets and pension liabilities partially offset the increased risk associated with rising firm equity.[5] Figure 1 clearly demonstrates how valuable the pension guarantee is even for substantially overfunded pensions.

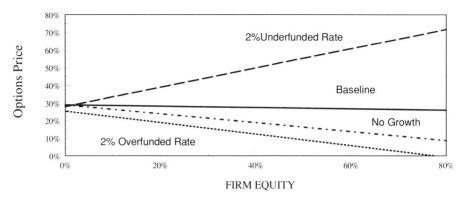

BASELINE: 5% GROWTH PENSION ASSETS & LIABILITIES;
4% ASSET VARIANCES; 1% LIABILITY VARIANCES

Figure 1. Option value for a 25-percent overfunded plan.

Figure 2 shows how differently the option value responds to firm equity when the pension plan is underfunded. In this case, the value of pension insurance is often a decreasing function of the sponsoring firm's equity—as pension asset variances and time provide an opportunity for the funding position to improve. This negative relationship between firm equity and the value of the option for underfunded plans is especially true under our assumption that underfunded plans will increase pension contributions to meet the higher funding regulations specified by 1987 Pension Protection Act. However, if the expected growth rate in pension assets is below the expected growth rate in liabilities, Figure 2 shows that option value is an increasing function of equity. Increases in variance (omitted) and growth have the same effect as in the case of overfunded plans—increasing the option value. For underfunded plans, this positive relationship between variances and the option value is easily understood when recalling that the option value of the pension insurance to the PBGC is limited to down-side risk.

IV. Comparative Dynamics

A. Industry Results: Baseline

Using the baseline assumptions presented in Section II, the option value of pension insurance is estimated from two distinct approaches: currently guaranteed pension liabilities, and current and expected future guaranteed liabilities. The options price specified in equation (7)

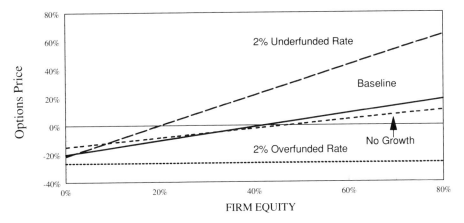

BASELINE: 5% GROWTH PENSION ASSETS & LIABILITIES
VARIANCES; ASSETS = 4%, LIABILITIES = 1%;

Figure 2. Option value for a 25-percent underfunded plan.

addresses this second approach. By providing a point-in-time estimate of the option value of pension insurance based upon the expected future growth rate in the value of PBGC insurance, this formulation reflects the full value of the option to the firm and to contributing workers. Hence, for the government and the PBGC, incorporating future growth rate assumptions into the current value of the pension option is appropriate for calculating the "fair" premium charge necessary to secure the insurance contract. Option value estimates derived using this approach were used in the President's 1993 Budget in budgeting for both the current level and future changes in PBGC's exposure over time.

An alternative way of analyzing PBGC's exposure involves setting the expected growth rates in pension assets ($\alpha_f + C_{ft}$) and liabilities ($\alpha_a + C_{at}$) to zero and estimating the value of pension insurance from just currently insured pension plans.[6] Examining only the currently guaranteed stock of pension benefits answers the question: what volume of PBGC claims can we expect to see from only those benefits that are presently insured. That is, if the PBGC froze all guarantees today, what exposure would still exist for the federal government? While addressing slightly different questions, both approaches provide meaningful information on the current exposure of PBGC.

Table 2 presents estimates for PBGC's contingent claims exposure, the volume of terminated liabilities, and the expected closure costs at the PBGC for both approaches. Although the actual data for 1989 and

TABLE 2   PBGC Contingent Claims Exposure Baseline

Year	Total pension liabilities	Current and future guaranteed plans			Currently guaranteed plans only		
		Contingent claim exposure	Terminated liabilities	Closure costs	Contingent claim exposure	Terminated liabilities	Closure costs
1989	405.7	22.3	2.9	0.2	20.4	3.6	0.3
1990	532.5	31.1	4.6	0.4	23.4	5.3	0.5
1991	567.1	46.7	8.4	0.9	38.6	7.2	0.9
1992	588.0	42.8	12.9	1.4	34.8	12.9	1.2
1993	607.0	44.5	12.0	1.0	35.8	15.2	1.4
1994	624.3	46.6	16.4	1.5	36.1	14.1	1.0
1995	642.7	47.6	15.5	0.9	36.9	14.9	1.6
1996	659.3	48.4	14.6	1.2	37.1	16.4	1.3
1997	677.0	49.6	16.8	0.9	37.5	15.3	1.1
1998	695.9	51.0	16.0	1.5	37.4	17.0	0.8
1999	714.0	51.5	16.6	1.0	38.8	19.5	1.1
2000	733.4	52.2	15.5	0.8	39.4	19.6	1.2
2001	753.0	53.6	19.2	0.8	40.0	18.7	0.9
2002	773.0	54.8	17.5	0.6	40.8	16.8	0.5

Source: Contingent claim exposure, terminated liabilities, and closure cost estimates for 1989–1991 were based on actual Compustat data. Terminated liabilities represent the total amount of guaranteed benefits residing in pension plans that terminate during each year. Closure costs represent the net costs of terminating pension plans in each year: pension underfunding at termination net of expected recoveries.

1990 project a dramatic increase in the option value for pension insurance, rising from $22 billion to $31 billion for current and future guarantees, most of this increase is attributable to the 31 percent jump in plan liabilities reported in our 1990 sample. In fact, expressed as a percentage of pension liabilities, the option value of pension insurance was 5 percent in both years. The subsequent rise in the option value in 1991, however, was caused by a real fall in pension funding—as reduced contributions and depressed stock market values during the January 1990 reporting period for pension funding combined to lower pension asset growth. (Moving forward in our simulations from the 1991 base, we compensate for the depressed stock market valuation of pension assets, assuming a 5 percent rebound in funding during 1991.)

Including future growth in pension guarantees, the option value, or outstanding accrued liability, in 1991 was $47 billion, with $8 billion in terminated pension liabilities and $0.9 billion in closure costs. This compares with actual PBGC closure costs in 1991 of approximately $1.0 billion (PBGC, 1992). Assuming the 5 percent increase in funding during 1991 to compensate for the depressed stock market values for

1990, PBGC's accrued liability fell in 1992 to $43 billion, with closure costs of approximately $1.4 billion. Our assumptions on the growth in pension assets and liabilities subsequently increase the accrued liability of the PBGC at a 3 percent annual rate to a level of $50 billion in 1997. In 1992 dollars, however, the accrued liability actually falls 19 percent to $35 billion by 1997. This decline in the real option value of pension insurance reflects the modest increase in pension funding under the baseline scenario attributable to the Pension Protection Act, as well as slower growth in pension liabilities. PBGC's accrued liability as a percent of total pension liabilities, however, stayed relatively constant at just over 7% during this period.

If we examine just the currently guaranteed value of pension funds, PBGC's expected claims were $20 billion in 1989, jumping to $35 billion by 1992, and then, rising at a 1.5 percent annual rate to $38 in 1997. In 1992 dollars, the accrued liability falls nearly 25 percent to $26 billion by 1997, again with most of the decrease attributable to increased pension funding.

Tables 3A and 3B provide a breakdown of PBGC's accrued liability by funding status. These tables show that although underfunded pension plans (flat benefit plans) represent only 20 percent of the current outstanding pension benefits ($118 billion) insured by the PBGC in 1991, these plans constitute 62 percent of the currently guaranteed exposure ($24 billion). If we include future growth in the insured pension pool, underfunded plans still constitute 55 percent of the current and future exposure ($26 billion). This translates into a one-time premium in the range of 20–30 percent on pension liabilities for underfunded plans (flat benefit plans) compared with a 4 percent charge for overfunded plans (final salary plans).

Figures 3 and 4 show PBGC's contingent liability exposure by industry. Figure 3 presents the breakdown of PBGC's 1991 contingent liability by the Standard Industrial Classification (SIC) codes reported by each firm in our sample. Because 88 percent of PBGC's exposure is concentrated in the manufacturing sector, we present a subdivision of manufacturing in Figure 4. Decomposing PBGC's contingent liability by industry highlights several concentrated areas of exposure. As reported by PBGC, two of the largest areas of PBGC's contingent liability reside in the transportation equipment ($14.9 billion) and the primary metals ($3.3 billion) industries. However, Figure 4 shows several other areas of exposure, including the petroleum industry ($7.7 billion), the industrial machinery industry ($4.8 billion), and the chemical industry ($4.5 billion). When expressed as a percentage of guaranteed liabilities, however, PBGC's exposure to these industries (8%) is considerably less than in transportation equipment or primary metal production (12%).

TABLE 3A   PBGC Contingent Claims Exposure, Current and Future Guaranteed Plans

	Overfunded plans				Underfunded plans			
Year	Total pension liabilities	Contingent claim exposure	Terminated liabilities	Closure costs	Total pension liabilities	Contingent claim exposure	Terminated liabilities	Closure costs
1989	341.4	8.3	1.9	0.0	64.3	14.0	1.0	0.2
1990	432.8	13.0	2.8	0.0	99.7	18.1	1.8	0.4
1991	448.8	20.5	4.4	0.0	118.3	25.8	3.7	0.2
1992	471.2	19.6	5.9	0.1	116.8	22.3	5.3	1.2
1993	492.3	22.5	8.0	0.1	114.7	21.3	5.4	1.1
1994	513.6	25.3	8.3	0.2	110.7	20.2	5.2	0.9
1995	534.9	27.3	9.8	0.3	107.8	19.4	5.4	0.9
1996	557.0	29.1	11.4	0.3	102.3	18.6	5.8	0.9
1997	579.3	31.2	11.5	0.2	97.7	17.9	4.4	0.7
1998	601.8	32.6	13.8	0.2	94.1	17.2	4.8	0.7
1999	625.4	34.4	11.6	0.0	88.6	16.8	4.9	0.5
2000	648.6	36.3	9.5	0.4	84.8	16.4	4.0	0.5
2001	674.3	38.1	15.6	0.3	78.7	16.0	3.9	0.4
2002	702.3	40.2	13.1	0.2	70.7	15.6	3.8	0.4

Source: See Table 2.

TABLE 3B PBGC Contingent Claims Exposure, Currently Guaranteed Plans Only

Year	Overfunded plans				Underfunded plans			
	Total pension liabilities	Contingent claim exposure	Terminated liabilities	Closure costs	Total pension liabilities	Contingent claim exposure	Terminated liabilities	Closure costs
1989	341.4	5.6	2.1	0.0	64.3	14.8	1.5	0.3
1990	432.8	8.3	2.8	0.0	99.7	15.1	2.5	0.5
1991	448.8	14.9	4.8	0.1	118.3	23.9	3.9	1.0
1992	471.2	13.6	7.9	0.2	116.8	20.5	5.0	1.1
1993	492.3	15.0	8.2	0.2	114.7	19.5	5.1	1.0
1994	513.6	16.2	11.0	0.2	110.7	18.8	4.9	0.9
1995	534.9	17.7	10.0	0.3	107.8	18.0	5.3	1.0
1996	557.0	18.8	9.4	0.1	102.3	17.3	4.6	0.8
1997	579.3	19.7	11.8	0.2	97.7	16.7	5.0	0.8
1998	601.8	20.7	14.2	0.3	94.1	16.1	4.8	0.7
1999	625.4	22.2	15.0	0.2	88.6	15.5	4.5	0.7
2000	648.6	23.2	14.7	0.2	84.8	14.9	4.0	0.6
2001	674.3	24.5	16.3	0.3	78.7	14.6	3.5	0.5
2002	702.3	25.7	14.7	0.1	70.7	14.2	4.1	0.4

Source: See Table 2.

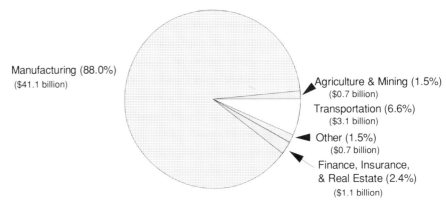

(Total 1991 Contingent Liability = $46.7 Billion)

Manufacturing (88.0%)
($41.1 billion)

Agriculture & Mining (1.5%)
($0.7 billion)

Transportation (6.6%)
($3.1 billion)

Other (1.5%)
($0.7 billion)

Finance, Insurance,
& Real Estate (2.4%)
($1.1 billion)

Note: "Other" includes Wholesale Trade ($300 million),
    Retail Trade ($200 million), and Services ($200 million)

Figure 3. 1991 contingent liability by industry.

In addition, the comparative statics presented earlier show that as firms approach insolvency, the implicit life of the firm shortens and the contingent liability exposure of the PBGC approaches the funding level of the firm's pension plan. Thus, most of the contingent liability of industries experiencing financial difficulties, like the automobile industry, is attributable to current underfunding. On the other hand, for profitable industries, like the oil industry, most of the contingent liability reflects the risk of a future deterioration in the industry and in the pension fund, resulting in future pension termination claims. (For every firm, there exists a nontrivial probability that under some state of the world the firm's pension plan will become underfunded and the sponsoring firm will file for bankruptcy.)

For all firms, the contingent liability, as measured by the option value, is the one-time premium charge necessary to cover PBGC's risk of future pension termination claims. In translating this one-time charge into annual premiums, however, the solvency of the firm or industry is important. Since the expected life of firms nearing insolvency is short, the annual premiums required to pay for PBGC's exposure will have to be high and front loaded so that the full premium charge can be collected before the firm files for bankruptcy. For solvent firms, on the other hand, the premium can be spread over a longer

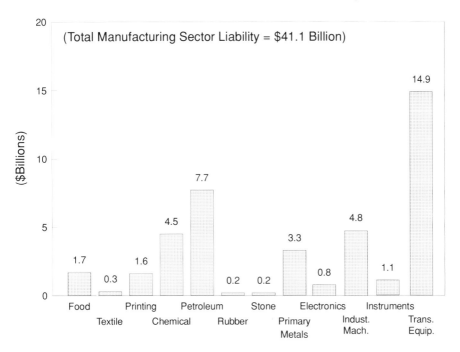

Figure 4. 1991 contingent liability in manufacturing.

time frame, resulting in a much smaller annual premium charge. Thus, the costs of pension insurance for solvent firms is even lower on an annual basis relative to the costs for near insolvent firms. While the determination of the optimal premium structure for the PBGC goes beyond the scope of this paper, the relationships between PBGC's contingent liability and the expected life of the firm must be kept in mind when comparing the contingent liability of various firms or industries.

B. Policy Simulations

A distinct advantage in estimating PBGC's accrued liability within an options pricing model and Monte Carlo framework is the ability to estimate the effects on the pension option of various policy proposals and changes in the economy. In Tables 4–6, we present the effects of changes in several key economic parameters used in valuing the pension insurance option. This analysis is useful in testing the sensitivity of

TABLE 4   Sensitivity of Industry Exposure to Variance Estimates, Current
and Future Pension Guarantees

Firm asset variance

| | | | (Baseline) | | | |
| | Variance = 5% | | Variance = 4% | | Variance = 3% | |
Fiscal year	Contingent liability	Closure costs	Contingent liability	Closure costs	Contingent liability	Closure costs
1991	43.4	1.2	46.7	0.9	51.8	0.6
1992	39.8	1.1	42.8	1.4	46.9	0.9
1993	41.3	1.6	44.5	1.0	48.5	0.9
1994	43.3	1.5	46.6	1.5	50.0	0.8
1995	44.5	1.8	47.6	0.9	51.9	0.8
1996	44.9	1.2	48.4	1.2	53.3	1.1
1997	45.8	1.4	49.6	0.9	54.4	0.8

Firm liability variance

| | | | (Baseline) | | | |
| | Variance = 2% | | Variance = 1% | | Variance = 0.5% | |
Fiscal year	Contingent liability	Closure costs	Contingent liability	Closure costs	Contingent liability	Closure costs
1991	48.2	0.4	46.7	0.9	44.3	1.5
1992	44.0	0.6	42.8	1.4	40.3	1.4
1993	46.8	0.9	44.5	1.0	42.0	1.6
1994	48.5	0.5	46.6	1.5	43.0	1.8
1995	50.6	0.9	47.6	0.9	43.8	1.4
1996	51.8	0.9	48.4	1.2	44.5	1.7
1997	53.8	0.8	49.6	0.9	44.7	1.4

Pension asset variance

| | | | (Baseline) | | | |
| | Variance = 5% | | Variance = 4% | | Variance = 3% | |
Fiscal year	Contingent liability	Closure costs	Contingent liability	Closure costs	Contingent liability	Closure costs
1991	51.6	1.3	46.7	0.9	42.1	1.0
1992	46.4	1.4	42.8	1.4	38.3	1.2
1993	48.9	1.3	44.5	1.0	40.3	1.4
1994	49.8	1.3	46.6	1.5	41.6	1.4
1995	50.7	0.9	47.6	0.9	42.6	1.0
1996	51.7	0.9	48.4	1.2	43.8	1.2
1997	53.4	1.3	49.6	0.9	45.5	0.9

TABLE 4   *Continued*

Pension liability variance

Fiscal year	Variance = 2%		(Baseline) Variance = 1%		Variance = 0.5%	
	Contingent liability	Closure costs	Contingent liability	Closure costs	Contingent liability	Closure costs
1991	52.8	0.8	46.7	0.9	42.5	1.1
1992	49.2	0.8	42.8	1.4	38.2	1.5
1993	51.8	1.1	44.5	1.0	39.3	1.7
1994	53.0	0.6	46.6	1.5	40.4	1.6
1995	54.8	0.9	47.6	0.9	41.3	1.7
1996	55.0	0.9	48.4	1.2	42.3	1.3
1997	56.7	1.1	49.6	0.9	43.0	1.5

Source: See Table 2.

the model to multi-period changes in economic and policy variables, as well as identifying some of the dynamic relationships between pension funding and the value of the guarantee.

Given the difficulty in estimating instantaneous variances for movements in pension assets and liabilities and firm assets and liabilities, we follow Marcus in assuming variance rates based upon stock market returns. However, in Tables 4 and 5, we present PBGC's contingent claims exposure under different variance assumptions in firm assets and liabilities, and pension assets and liabilities. Note that the variance in pension asset returns and pension liability growth is positively related to the growth of PBGC's expected future claims as demonstrated in the comparative statics section. In addition, the variance in firm assets is inversely related to expected future claims in our sample data base. In Section III we suggested that this inverse relationship between firm asset variance and the value of the pension option was especially true for overfunded pension plans. Our result for the entire industry is not surprising, therefore, because over 80 percent of our sample pension liabilities reside in overfunded plans.

In addition to variance and covariance assumptions, key determinants of the options value are the growth rate assumptions in pension funding. In Table 6, we simulate the affects of raising the rate of pension funding in both overfunded and underfunded pension plans, starting in the year 1992. For underfunded pension plans, we examine scenarios where strong (weak) pension funding results in a 100 basis point annual improvement (reduction) in the baseline trend in pension

TABLE 5   Sensitivity of Industry Exposure to Variance Estimates Current
Pension Guarantees Only

Firm asset variance

| Fiscal year | (Baseline) | | | | | |
| | Variance = 5% | | Variance = 4% | | Variance = 3% | |
	Contingent liability	Closure costs	Contingent liability	Closure costs	Contingent liability	Closure costs
1991	37.9	0.9	38.6	0.9	39.9	0.4
1992	34.2	1.9	34.8	1.2	35.7	1.3
1993	34.4	1.8	35.8	1.4	36.3	0.9
1994	34.6	1.7	36.1	1.0	37.3	1.3
1995	35.4	1.5	36.9	1.6	37.8	1.1
1996	35.8	1.4	37.1	1.3	38.5	1.5
1997	36.2	1.3	37.5	1.1	38.7	0.7

Firm liability variance

| Fiscal year | (Baseline) | | | | | |
| | Variance = 2% | | Variance = 1% | | Variance = 0.5% | |
	Contingent liability	Closure costs	Contingent liability	Closure costs	Contingent liability	Closure costs
1991	39.4	0.6	38.6	0.9	37.8	1.1
1992	35.7	0.9	34.8	1.2	33.7	1.3
1993	36.7	0.6	35.8	1.4	34.6	1.5
1994	38.5	0.9	36.1	1.0	34.8	1.4
1995	39.4	0.7	36.9	1.6	35.1	1.2
1996	40.4	0.8	37.1	1.3	35.1	1.0
1997	41.9	0.8	37.5	1.1	35.9	1.2

Pension asset variance

| Fiscal year | (Baseline) | | | | | |
| | Variance = 5% | | Variance = 4% | | Variance = 3% | |
	Contingent liability	Closure costs	Contingent liability	Closure costs	Contingent liability	Closure costs
1991	41.7	1.0	38.6	0.9	36.0	0.9
1992	37.4	1.1	34.8	1.2	32.2	1.3
1993	38.9	1.2	35.8	1.4	33.5	1.2
1994	39.7	1.3	36.1	1.0	34.2	1.1
1995	40.7	1.5	36.9	1.6	34.6	1.1
1996	41.1	1.6	37.1	1.3	35.3	1.1
1997	41.2	1.0	37.5	1.1	36.2	1.2

Table 5 *Continued*

Pension liability variance

Fiscal year	(Baseline) Variance = 2%		Variance = 1%		Variance = 0.5%	
	Contingent liability	Closure costs	Contingent liability	Closure costs	Contingent liability	Closure costs
1991	43.2	0.7	38.6	0.9	36.1	1.0
1992	39.3	1.2	34.8	1.2	32.3	1.8
1993	40.0	1.2	35.8	1.4	32.7	1.9
1994	41.0	1.0	36.1	1.0	33.0	1.3
1995	42.2	0.9	36.9	1.6	33.7	1.2
1996	42.8	0.6	37.1	1.3	34.1	1.3
1997	43.4	0.8	37.5	1.1	34.8	0.9

Source: See Table 2.

funding. As shown in Table 6, the one percentage point increase in pension funding results in a $3.4 billion reduction in PBGC's expected future claims in 1992, while a similar decrease in funding resulting in a rise of $3.4 billion. This reduction in PBGC's expected future claims attributable to the increase in pension funding highlights the potential savings to the PBGC of encouraging flat benefit plans to fund up their pension plans.

Table 6 presents a similar analysis of funding for overfunded pension plans, assuming that pension asset growth falls short of (exceeds) the 5 percent growth rate in liabilities by 100 basis points. This increase (decrease) in overfunded plan funding results in a large $15 billion ($13 billion) drop (increase) in PBGC's expected future claims. The current funding rules governing final salary pension plans, however, make it unlikely that overfunded pension plans would consistently underfund (overfund) their pension plans by 100 basis points. Therefore, this simulation is just an illustrative example of the impact of pension funding.

In addition to changes in pension funding assumptions, Table 6 shows the sensitivity of PBGC's exposure to fluctuations in the discount rate used in valuing the pension option. (This does not address the simultaneous change in the value of reported pension benefits that would be associated with different long-term interest rates.) Interest rates were chosen to create a range around our baseline interest rate assumption of 7.32 percent.

TABLE 6   Sensitivity of Industry Exposure to Funding and Interest Rates
Current and Future Pension Guarantees

*Pension plan funding, underfunded plan contributions**

Fiscal year	1% point decrease		Baseline		1% point increase	
	Contingent liability	*Closure costs*	*Contingent liability*	*Closure costs*	*Contingent liability*	*Closure costs*
1991	46.7	0.9	46.7	0.9	46.7	0.9
1992	42.8	1.3	42.8	1.4	42.8	1.2
1993	46.3	1.4	44.5	1.0	41.1	1.3
1994	48.2	1.1	46.6	1.5	41.8	0.7
1995	50.1	1.5	47.6	0.9	41.9	1.2
1996	52.2	1.3	48.4	1.2	43.4	1.2
1997	53.9	1.4	49.6	0.9	43.4	0.5

Pension plan funding, overfunded plan contributions

Fiscal year	1% point decrease		Baseline		1% point increase	
	Contingent liability	*Closure costs*	*Contingent liability*	*Closure costs*	*Contingent liability*	*Closure costs*
1991	46.7	0.9	46.7	0.9	46.7	0.9
1992	42.8	1.3	42.8	1.4	42.8	1.2
1993	59.5	1.9	44.5	1.0	31.1	1.3
1994	60.3	1.4	46.6	1.5	32.0	1.2
1995	61.8	1.1	47.6	0.9	33.1	1.5
1996	62.8	1.2	48.4	1.2	33.7	1.4
1997	63.8	1.0	49.6	0.9	34.0	0.8

Long-term nominal interest rates

Fiscal year	6.32%		(Baseline) 7.32%		8.32%	
	Contingent liability	*Closure costs*	*Contingent liability*	*Closure costs*	*Contingent liability*	*Closure costs*
1991	48.1	1.0	46.7	0.9	43.9	0.7
1992	44.6	1.4	42.8	1.4	40.2	1.4
1993	46.4	1.3	44.5	1.0	41.6	1.5
1994	47.9	1.5	46.6	1.5	43.3	1.6
1995	48.5	1.0	47.6	0.9	44.5	1.1
1996	49.4	1.3	48.4	1.2	45.0	1.4
1997	50.1	0.9	49.6	0.9	46.8	1.1

Source: See Table 2.
*Funding changes were assumed to take effect in 1992.

TABLE 7   PBGC Contingent Claims Exposure Reform (incremental recovery rates)

Year	Current and future guaranteed plans			Currently guaranteed plans only		
	Contingent claim exposure	Terminated liabilities	Closure costs	Contingent claim exposure	Terminated liabilities	Closure costs
1991	46.7	8.4	0.9	38.6	7.2	0.9
1992	42.8	12.9	1.4	34.8	12.9	1.2
1993	36.9	15.1	1.4	32.1	11.2	1.3
1994	36.6	17.0	1.3	30.8	15.6	1.9
1995	35.7	15.1	0.7	29.5	15.0	0.9
1996	35.2	12.9	0.5	29.1	18.5	1.2
1997	35.2	14.0	0.7	28.6	19.6	1.3
1998	34.8	18.0	0.7	27.9	14.3	0.8
1999	33.8	18.0	0.5	27.1	17.4	1.0
2000	33.6	18.3	0.4	26.8	20.3	1.4
2001	33.0	18.6	0.5	25.9	16.3	1.1
2002	33.0	18.5	0.4	26.3	15.2	0.9

Source: See Table 2.

C. 1992 PBGC Reform Proposals

Based on the assumptions presented in Section II, Table 7 and Table 8 present PBGC's contingent liability exposure under one specific policy simulation; namely, the PBGC reform proposals presented in the 1993 Budget. Prompted by a rising balance sheet deficit and the estimated $43 billion in contingent claims exposure, the Bush administration proposed several reforms for the PBGC designed to bring expected claims back in line with expected premium revenue. These reforms would reduce PBGC's expected future claims by increasing pension funding requirements in underfunded pension plans (funding reform), limiting PBGC's future exposure to chronically underfunded pension plans (guarantee freeze), and raising PBGC's recoveries in bankruptcy court (bankruptcy reform).

Specifically, the Bush administration proposed to increase the minimum funding requirements under a new solvency maintenance rule and a revised underfunding reduction rule for underfunded pension plans. By taking the greater of the funding requirements under these funding rules, PBGC expects to raise the pension funding in underfunded plans at a rate which increases firm funding ratios by 2.25 percentage points per year until the funding ratio reaches 95 percent. The guarantee freeze effectively places a ceiling on plan amendments

TABLE 8   PBGC Contingent Claims Exposure Reform (weighted average recovery rates)

	Current and future guaranteed plans			Currently guaranteed plans only		
Year	Contingent claim exposure	Terminated liabilities	Closure costs	Contingent claim exposure	Terminated liabilities	Closure costs
1991	46.7	8.4	0.9	38.6	7.2	0.9
1992	42.8	12.9	1.4	34.8	12.9	1.2
1993	31.0	13.8	1.3	29.3	13.7	1.5
1994	30.5	15.7	1.2	28.4	15.8	1.4
1995	29.8	14.9	0.7	27.5	16.0	0.8
1996	29.4	16.5	0.9	27.2	13.7	0.8
1997	29.0	19.8	0.9	26.9	17.1	0.6
1998	27.7	14.7	0.5	26.6	14.8	0.6
1999	27.2	17.4	0.7	26.3	15.6	0.4
2000	27.1	18.3	0.4	26.3	17.6	0.7
2001	27.3	18.3	0.4	26.1	17.4	0.4
2002	26.8	17.0	0.3	26.0	15.4	0.2

Source: See Table 2.

increasing guaranteed benefits in chronically underfunded pension plans as of 1993. Such benefit increases in these plans would not be guaranteed by the PBGC until the plans become fully funded. The bankruptcy reform proposal would clarify and improve the status of PBGC's claims in bankruptcy court, as well as granting the PBGC the right to participate on the creditor's committees during bankruptcy court proceedings—effectively resulting in significantly higher PBGC recovery rates on terminated pension plans.

If all three reforms were enacted in 1992, using the current and future pension guarantees[7] in Table 7, the PBGC would have recognized an $8 to $9 billion reduction in its contingent claim exposure in 1992 and a present value savings of $18 to $20 billion over the 1992–97 period.[8] Assuming that premium revenues stay constant at a present value of $10 billion over the next 30 year period, the total impact of these reforms would have been to reduce PBGC's contingent claim exposure in 1992 dollars, net of premiums, from $33 billion in 1992 to $6 billion in 2002. Additional out-year bankruptcy savings would have reduced PBGC's exposure further, as would likely nominal increases in premium revenue.

Using the currently insured portfolio of pension benefits in Table 8, the total savings from the three reforms would have been $3 billion in 1992 and a present value savings of $12 billion over the 1992–97 period. The first year effect is relatively small because without future growth rates in the model, savings from the funding and guarantee freeze reforms are only recognized as firms actually increase funding in the insured pension plans in each period. However, assuming that the present value of expected premium receipts over a 30-year period remains constant at $10 billion, the long-run effect of the reforms would be to lower the exposure of the PBGC from $25 billion in 1992 to $3 billion ($1992) in 2002.

Table 8 presents the impact from the reforms when the bankruptcy reform effects are pulled forward using a schedule of weighted average recovery rates. In this case, PBGC would have recognized a present value savings of almost $12 ($7) billion in 1992 and a present value savings of over $19 ($14) billion over the 1993–97 period for current and future guaranteed plans (currently guaranteed plans only). This would have lowered PBGC's contingent claim exposure net of premiums from $32.8 billion in 1992 to approximately $3 billion ($1992) by 2002 under both scenarios.

V. Conclusion

In this paper we have applied the theory of options pricing to construct initial estimates of PBGC's contingent claims exposure to pension terminations. We have shown that the current exposure of the Pension Benefit Guaranty Corporation is almost $35 billion from current guarantees and an additional $8 billion from future guarantees, and that, without reform, this exposure is projected to rise to almost $50 billion by 1997. With a large portion of this exposure attributable to chronically underfunded single-employer pension plans, our analysis clearly identifies the need for substantial reforms in the pension funding regulations for flat benefit pension plans. This paper shows, however, that the PBGC reforms published in the 1993 Budget succeed in reducing this exposure over the next ten years through a series of funding reforms, bankruptcy reforms, and guarantee freezes on chronically underfunded plans. This paper also demonstrated the important relationships between pension funding, pension benefit growth, and firm equity with the options value of pension insurance. Understanding the interaction of these pension variables is vital not only in judging the effectiveness of pension reforms, but also in analyzing the impact of changing pension policy or economics.

Finally, by incorporating the options price approach into a Monte Carlo framework, this paper provides a basis for budgeting for contingent liabilities as they accrue, instead of as the cash outlays come due. By acknowledging these accruing costs in the federal budget, contingent claim pricing provides policy makers with time and the correct incentives to enact reforms to reduce the contingent liability before the option is exercised. Thus, this paper not only provides a framework for assessing the current exposure of the PBGC, but also establishes a foundation for budgeting for any contingent liability of the federal government.

The authors are economists with the Office of Management and Budget. The views expressed are their own and do not necessarily reflect official positions of the Office of Management and Budget. The cooperation of PBGC staff is gratefully acknowledged.

Notes

1. For a specific definition of a Wiener process see Malliaris and Brock (1982), 36–38.

2. Ito's lemma is the stochastic analogue for the chain rule in calculus. For a thorough discussion of Ito's lemma and stochastic calculus see Malliaris and Brock (1982).

3. For example, in aging our sample from end of year 1990 to end of year 1991, we assume an additional 5 percent improvement in pension funding for all firms. This assumption is based on the depressed stock market values on the January 1, 1991 reporting date for pension funding, and the subsequent sharp rise in the stock market during 1991. The presumption behind this funding increase is twofold:

- The subsequent 30 percent rise in the stock market will have greatly increased the return on pension assets during 1991, raising reported pension funding in all plans.
- The depressed pension asset values at the beginning of the year triggered above normal funding requirements for all underfunded plans for 1991.

Preliminary funding data reported to the PBGC support this hypothesis.

4. We could alternatively assume smaller variances for firms with lower levels of equity and generate fewer insolvencies. However, a preliminary analysis of the data does not appear to support this.

5. The elasticity of the option value with respect to variances and growth rates are essentially the same, so the simulations showing changing variances are omitted from Figures 1 and 2.

6. We thank Professor Zvi Bodie for suggesting this alternative specification.

7. Note, when examining both current and future guarantees, the bulk of the savings is recognized in the year in which the reforms are enacted. This upfront recognition of savings is a direct result of incorporating our long-run expectations of the increased pension funding (C_{ft}), slower liability growth (A_t), and higher recovery rate (R_t) into the assessment of PBGC's long run contingent claim exposure in the year in which the reforms are passed.

8. The reform savings shown here do not incorporate the tax revenue loss estimates associated with the funding reforms proposed by the PBGC. As of

January 31, 1992, the Treasury Department had estimated tax losses of $0 in 1992 and 1993, $300 million in 1994, $400 million in 1995, $600 million in 1996, and $800 million in all subsequent years.

References

Black, Fisher and Myron Scholes. 1972. "The Pricing of Options and Corporate Liabilities." *Journal of Political Economy* 81 (June): 637–54.

Bodie, Zvi. 1990. "Managing Pensions and Retirement Assets." International Competitiveness in Financial Services Conference Paper. Washington, DC: American Enterprise Institute. June.

Borensztein, Eduardo and George G. Pennacchi. 1990. "Valuation of Interest Payment Guarantees on Developing Country Debt." *IMF Staff Papers*, 37, 4: 806–24.

Cooperstein, Richard L., F. Stevens Redburn, and Harry G. Meyers. 1992. "Modelling Mortgage Terminations in Turbulent Times." *AREUEA Journal* (April).

Cooperstein, Richard L. and F. Stevens Redburn. 1992. "The Dynamics of Deposit Insurance: Using Options Pricing and a Stochastic Process." Report for U.S. Office of Management and Budget. Washington, DC: U.S. Government Printing Office.

Cox, John C. and Stephen A. Ross. 1976. "The Valuation of Options for Alternative Stochastic Processes." *Journal of Financial Economics* 3:145–66.

U.S. Department of Labor. 1983. *Estimates of Participant and Financial Characteristics of Private Pension Plans*. Washington, DC: U.S. Government Printing Office, p. 27.

Dixit, Avinash. 1992. "Investment and Hysteresis." *Journal of Economic Perspectives* 16, 1 (Winter): 107–32.

Executive Office of the President of the United States. 1992. *Budget of the United States Government: Fiscal Year 1993*, Washington, DC: U.S. Government Printing Office, pps. 267–79.

Foster, Chester and Robert Van Order. 1984. "An Option-Based Model of Mortgage Default." *Housing Finance Review* (October): 351–72.

———. 1985. "FHA Terminations: A Prelude to Rational Mortgage Pricing." *AREUEA Journal*: 273–91.

Hirtle, Beverly and Arturo Estrella. 1990. "Alternatives for Correcting the Funding Gap of the Pension Benefit Guaranty Corporation." New York: Federal Reserve Bank of New York, May.

Langetieg, T. C., M. C. Findlay, and L. F. J. da Motta. 1982. "Multiperiod Pension Plans and ERISA." *Journal of Financial and Quantitative Analysis* 17, 4 (November): 603–31.

Malliaris, A. G. and W. A. Brock. 1982. *Stochastic Methods in Economics and Finance*. New York: North-Holland Publishing Company.

Marcus, Alan J. 1985. "Corporate Pension Policy and the Value of PBGC Insurance." In *Issues in Pension Economics*, ed. Zvi Bodie, John B. Shoven, and David A. Wise. Chicago: University of Chicago Press, 49–76.

Marcus, Alan J. and Israel Shaked. 1984. "The Valuation of FDIC Deposit Insurance Using Option-Pricing Estimates." *Journal of Money, Credit, and Banking* 16, 4 (November, Part 1): 446–60.

Merton, Robert C. 1973. "The Theory of Rational Option Pricing." *Bell Journal of Economics and Management Science* 4, 1 (Spring): 141–83.

————. 1977. "An Analytical Derivation of the Cost of Deposit Insurance and Loan Guarantees: An Application of Modern Option Pricing Theory." *Journal of Banking and Finance* 1: 3–11.

————. 1978. "On the Cost of Deposit Insurance When There Are Surveillance Costs." *Journal of Business* 51, 3.

————. 1990. "The Financial System and Economic Performance." *Journal of Financial Services Research*: 263–300.

————. 1977. "An Analytical Derivation of the Cost of Deposit Insurance and Loan Guarantees: An Application of Modern Option Pricing Theory." *Journal of Banking and Finance* 1: 3–11.

Merton, Robert C. and Zvi Bodie. 1992. "A Framework for the Economic Analysis of Deposit Insurance and Other Guarantees." Harvard Business School Working Paper #92-063 (January).

Pennacchi, George G. 1987. "A Reexamination of the Over- (or Under-) Pricing of Deposit Insurance." *Journal of Money, Credit, and Banking* 19, 3 (August 1987): 340–60.

Pension Benefit Guaranty Corporation. Annual Report, 1991.

Pension Protection Act. Title IX, Subtitle D. Part II of the Omnibus Budget Reconciliation Act of 1987 (PL 100-203).

Redburn, F. Stevens, Richard L. Cooperstein, and George G. Pennacchi. 1993. "The Aggregate Cost of Deposit Insurance: A Multi-Period Analysis." Presented at a Conference of the Journal of Financial Intermediation, Northwestern University, May 1993.

Treynor, Jack L. 1977. "The Principles of Corporate Pension Finance." *Journal of Finance* 32, 2 (May): 627–38.

Turner, John. 1989. *Trends in Pensions*. Pension and Welfare Benefits Administration. Washington, DC: U.S. Government Printing Office.

Chapter 7
Panel Discussion: The Role of Regulation in Pension Policy

Ray Schmitt

I hope that yesterday's papers and discussion and today's discussion have provided everybody with a good backdrop for discussing the role of regulation in pension policy. I am sorry that not everybody was with us yesterday, but hopefully we can pick up where we left off and have a good basis to react to some of these major issues. Moderating the panel on pension regulation and questioning its role is Dallas Salisbury, President of the Employee Benefit Research Institute. I really appreciate Dallas's taking on this task. The panelists in today's discussion include Phyllis Borzi, who is the Counsel for Employee Benefits for the House Subcommittee on Labor-Management Relations. Filling in for Ann Combs is Richard Hinz from the Department of Labor. We also have Ed Hustead, Senior Vice President at Hay/Huggins; James Klein, Executive Director of the Association of Private Pension and Welfare Plans; Meredith Miller, Assistant Director of the AFL-CIO Employee Benefits Department; and Evelyn Petschek, who is Benefits Tax Counsel with the Treasury Department. We are going to give them the opportunity to provide brief remarks because we want to have time for you all to have an opportunity to ask questions, raise points, comments, observations, whatever. I would like to turn it over now to Dallas Salisbury.

Dallas Salisbury

Good morning. If each of us takes about nine minutes, we will end up with time for discussion.

Part of what came into my mind at many points in the discussion of the last day is an old course that I took in graduate school called

Administrative Law. The classic text in the administrative law field was that of Mr. Davis. The essence of the book is its focus on administrative discretion and judicial discretion. When you finish that course you realize that, when it comes to law and regulation, there is no such thing as absolute truth—even though at points during this meeting and the last session, sitting in the audience, you have had the feeling from the way something is presented that it's so irrefutably the truth, there is no room for any movement one side or the other.

This field is interesting to watch simply because of yesterday's and today's discussion of PBGC and issues of the role of government. Even when we go to the courts, if we look at abortion issues and others, we find that yesterday's truth may not be tomorrow's truth, based on who sits on the court and who has been appointed. This morning's paper points out even more vividly that it's worth having a mixed panel up here this morning on this topic. The only thing we are really missing to get some sense of alternative definitions of truth is the news that points out that in California, Colorado, and nationally Ross Perot would be president if the election were held today. We do not have anyone here to tell us what Ross Perot's definition and interpretations of the appropriate role of PBGC or other things would be. Hopefully, we'll be able to get a feel for that in the future. So there's more even in this election relevant than a Republican or Democratic view of the truth of PBGC or others. If we want to have a feel for the level of that ability to interpret broadly, differently, what truth is, we only need look to the issue of the Great Society and yesterday's introduction by the Democrats of a bill to put an additional, immediate $5 billion into Great Society programs to solve the problem in Los Angeles that the current President says was caused by the Great Society programs. So there's room for clear differences and clear judgmental differences.

Is PBGC purely a social agency or purely a casualty insurance company, or does the truth lie somewhere in between? Or is there no truth? Is it really dependent on who is running the agency or which administration is in power for what the approach is? What is the truth of this morning's modeling discussion and yesterday's session? With that as backdrop, my general view is that there are lots of shades of gray. We may well find that what some think is truth today will be redefined, if not tomorrow, maybe after November; if not after November, maybe four years hence; but someday.

Today the panel will be focusing on the questions that were on the initial outline agenda. What should be the role of regulation in pension policy? What *is* the role of regulation in pension policy? What do the panelists think are the purposes and the objectives of their organizations in pension policy? We might even touch on an issue related to the taxation of pensions and other areas, which as we know from yesterday, are also realms where there are multiple truths. Rather than getting complicated here, since I did not learn my alphabet well and did not take the time to alphabetize the names of the panel today, we are just going to go from right to left.

Evelyn A. Petschek

Dallas asked us to focus on where we sit and our perspective on the role of regulation in pension policy. Of course, I have to start out any delivery of remarks with the normal disclaimer that my views are my own and not necessarily shared by anyone else in the Office of Tax Policy or the Treasury Department. From where I sit, my emphasis is obviously on the tax policy aspects of pension policy. Our tax policy is very important in the regulation of pensions because our private pension system is a voluntary one, encouraged through a system of tax incentives. You notice, as we look at the federal tax expenditures on an annual basis, that the tax expenditure for pensions exceeds $50 billion a year. It's a substantial tax expenditure. As a result, one of the most important elements of tax policy as it applies to pensions is the existence of nondiscrimination and coverage rules to insure that private pension plans are not mainly tax shelters for the wealthy, that for the expenditure there is some delivery of benefits to the rank and file.

When Dallas and I spoke a couple of days ago, he suggested that we focus on a couple of examples as to how our perspectives on tax policy can be seen through the regulation of pensions. I thought I would focus on the nondiscrimination rules because of their importance. They initially came in 1942 on a very simplified and broad basis. When Congress was looking at pensions in 1974 with ERISA, there were a number of areas in the nondiscrimination and coverage areas where it tightened the rules to insure a broader coverage of low paid workers. We saw that trend continued in 1986 with one very important difference in the emphasis. Congress expressed, both in the legislative history and in the way in which some of the provisions were formulated, a concern with the preexisting nondiscrimination rules, which were by and large subjective. This led to employers basically being able to negotiate with the various IRS districts across the country as to what was and was not discrimination in a pension plan.

What we saw in the 1986 Act was an objective definition of "highly compensated," which of course is one of the cornerstones for the determination of what is and is not discriminatory. We saw in the coverage area that, while Congress retained the old subjective fair cross section standard, the standard was coupled with an objective average benefits percentage test. We also saw the addition of new nondiscrimination provisions, such as the minimum participation rules, which set absolute, objective standards. With that as the legislative backdrop of the 1986 Act, the agencies in implementing those changes made a call to move to more objective standards in our regulatory guidance under the nondiscrimination rules generally.

We, as I am sure anybody who knows and cares about pensions is aware, published our final set of nondiscrimination regulations back in September of 1991. In gauging the reaction that we have now had to those objective rules as employers themselves set to implement these regulations and redesign their plans to conform with the 1986 Act changes, we can see that there is necessarily an important balance to be struck between purely objective rules on the one hand and the subjective rules that we had before the 1986 Act on the other. Again, much of the underlying importance of nondiscrimination standards is to insure that our tax dollars are being well spent and that the distributional effects of the scheme set up in the tax code is broad based. It's important as we think about pensions to keep that in mind.

I will leave you with a very quick example of why tax policy is so important. Focusing on 401(k) plans, we see there a Congressionally permitted form of discrimination. The 401(k) rules permit higher paid employees to defer on average a greater percent than what the low paids defer on average. After those rules had been working for awhile and the tax expenditure attributable to those plans became greater, Congress in 1986 sought to limit the contributions that high-paid workers could put in by putting a cap on the contributions that individuals could make to a 401(k) plan. As those plans become increasingly more popular, and as there is a greater emphasis within the agencies, in the private sector, and in Congress to move toward greater simplification, there are a number of proposals that would permit design-based nondiscrimination rules as an option in the 401(k) area. From a tax policy perspective the concern for such an approach is that with a design-based test there is no real assurance that the low paid rank and file employees will in fact contribute and benefit from the tax expenditure to any particular extent. People pushing for this type of design-based safe harbor need to recognize if that type of provision comes in, and if 401(k) plans come to benefit disproportionately the higher paid employees, that is, if the rank and file do not participate in significant proportions, Congress will undoubtedly once again revisit the limits on 401(k) plans and the way the statutory scheme regulates those plans.

I guess I am hitting my time limit. Dallas should have recognized in putting together a panel of lawyers that it's very hard to keep lawyers talking under a half an hour about anything.

Dallas Salisbury

That's why the entire panel is not made up of lawyers. We are now going to take a quick switch from your left to the right.

Meredith Miller

I am going to take a part of my nine minutes with a little story. I think it's apropos to this discussion. This is about two parents—you have probably already heard this, so bear with me, if you have. Two parents have two children who are twins. One is an optimist; one is a pessimist. The parents are really interested in behavior modification. They are tired, really tired of the children "acting out," as we say. So they put the pessimist in a room with really great toys and, of course, that child complains about how the toys are broken, and they put the optimist in a room with a lot of manure and she says, "Hey, but you know, I know there's a pony in here somewhere." I feel like I am looking for that pony. If you all had been there, they would probably switch rooms every half hour. Anyway, Dallas did ask us to speak about both regulation and legislation and to speak from where we sit, so I will go ahead and do that.

Organized labor has really believed that the role of government regulation and legislation should be an activist one: a role that really furthers specific pension goals, such as preservation, security, and enhancement, but also one that would have the government be an equalizer. We expect the government to take into consideration the multiple roles—and I underscore, multiple are the roles—that workers and funds have in the pension area. The kinds of legislative efforts we have seen recently involve a balancing act that requires considering not only plan participants' rights or interests, but the effect the enhancements of those rights may have on the fund itself. We in labor recognize that many workers who are not under collective bargaining agreements are not afforded the kinds of grievance mechanisms and the kinds of legal aid that workers who are covered have, and are really left to their own devices. We understand that that's a very important gap, but in our estimation many of the legislative and regulatory efforts to try to empower plan participants' rights need to go hand in hand with the building of the legal and technical infrastructure of this country, much like the legal aid system that we had in the 1980s that was gutted by the Reagan administration. I think the interest in the ADR (Alternative Dispute Resolution) efforts are really interesting and important, but they need to be very far-reaching to build this infrastructure. The balancing act of the government is also evident on the state level when corporate takeover and governance laws struggle with the issues of company fiduciary responsibility, which could embrace, as many of you know, as many parties as shareholders, workers, and the local community itself.

The SEC is currently reviewing a new set of rules that would liberalize the issues and methods that shareholders can use to communicate among themselves and to exert leverage on companies. As unionists, we have an interest in these kinds of legislative and regulatory developments, both as shareholders and as workers of those companies. We also expect the government to appreciate the multiple interests that pension funds and their participants have. In the AFL-CIO pension investment guidelines, we define the long term, best economic interest of plan participants to include a balancing of such factors as appropriate financial rate of return relative to risk, continuous employment of plan participants, promotion of long term and local economic growth, corporate responsibility for the company's reinvestment, and job creation.

As many of you are aware, the recession has spawned increased interest in what we call economically targeted investments (ETI), investments that meet ERISA standards for prudence and at the same time provide an economic benefit that translates into jobs, causing business growth. There is a wave of public-private pension fund partnerships occurring across the country. Some, as you may have noticed, the President also has his eye on as well. Some proponents are looking at a clarification of ERISA—whether under current law ETI investments are permissible—and some even seek new funding arrangements involving federal subsidies to promote these interests.

We also look to the government to have a vantage point and a political strong arm that individual funds or trade associations cannot leverage. In this regard we expect the government to recognize that pensions play a significant role in the emerging global economy. As of March of 1991, international investment managers were handling $11.7 billion in assets for U.S. tax-exempt institutions. The impact this flight of capital may have on domestic companies and the job base is an important factor to filter into the pension equation and a necessary component of any national retirement income policy.

With respect to issues of preservation and expanded access, we would envision a stronger federal role than currently exists. We are at a crossroads where we must deliberate tough decisions about whether we are going to maintain and build upon an employment based system or instead beef up Social Security. At a minimum we have to raise two serious concerns. The first is the lack of study of empirical data on the proposed changes to expand access. The spillover of small market reform efforts in health care to pension policy has not gone unnoticed.

The masquerade of tax favored pension plans for legitimate retirement plans is just bad pension policy. As policy makers we are doing a
terrible disservice to the plan participants if we convince them that
their overly conservative investment practices will provide adequate
income down the road. No longitudinal studies based on future workforce demographics and their investment patterns have been conducted that I am aware of, and yet this is the pension system of the
future which has bipartisan support.

Equally mind-boggling is the chameleon-like identity of the PBGC.
We can't figure out whether the agency, before we discuss this ad
nauseam, truly wants to be converted into an insurance company or
become a pure social insurance program so it can be carried on the
budget with liabilities and shortfalls shifted to taxpayers. Our other
concern for the PBGC is that without hearings for questioning numbers, the agency in our mind has declared unadulterated war on the
flat benefit plans in collectively bargained agreements.

In closing I would remark that government regulation in the pension area should reflect political reality. It is no wonder that our message to Congress is fractured. It has been a long time since we have had
issue unanimity or an issue among the different interest groups sitting
here finally put to rest. After a decade-or-so-long babble over who
owns pension fund assets, it is our hope that we can at least now move
beyond those kinds of differences and harness some of the power of
pensions to correct the course we have taken and to set us down the
road of long-term productivity and security. I want to close with a quote
from John Kennedy, which is either a very popular reference from the
1960s or really a death knell of a statement. It is from his 1962 State of
the Union address. He said, "Finally, a strong America cannot neglect
the aspirations of its citizens—the welfare of the needy, the health care
of the elderly, the education of the young. For we are not developing
the Nation's wealth for its own sake. Wealth is the means—and people
are the ends. All our material riches will avail us little if we do not use
them to expand the opportunities of our people."

James A. Klein

I feel a little bit like the fellow whose name I now forget, but whose
name I knew in high school, who had the difficult task of delivering
remarks at Gettysburg after Lincoln. [Editor's note: Edward Everett,
who gave a two-hour oration *before* Lincoln spoke.] After a day and a
half of presentations, I have the feeling that just about everything that
needs to be said has been said rather eloquently, but nonetheless I will
try to add my own gloss to it. Dallas did ask us to speak from our own

perspectives, so I should tell you, those who are not aware, the perspective of the Association of Private Pension and Welfare Plans of which I am the director. Our members are principally plan sponsors, mostly large plan sponsors, though some small ones. Other members are financial institutions, insurance companies that provide the product to the plan sponsors, as well as actuaries, consultants, accountants, and anyone else who services the plan. So we like to think of ourselves as representing most of the benefits community.

My Association has certainly been over the years, and I believe justifiably so, often critical of the lawmakers and folks within the Executive Branch who provide us with the regulations which we must comply with. But I think it's important in a forum of this type to make one point that is not often noted, and particularly in terms of the agency people in this regard, that they are in fact faced with a very difficult job. For both good and bad reasons, Congress often leaves to the regulatory agencies the rather messy task of filling in the gaps of what are generally vague or sometimes structurally complex legislation. It is bad, of course, because we all know that benefits legislation typically is the product of a number of different committees with different agendas. It is often put together in haste and often appendaged to some larger budget or tax bill, at least that has been the case over the past decade or so. It is not always easy, I think, for the folks at the Treasury Department or the Department of Labor, or wherever they may be, to pick up the pieces. Congress though also leaves the details to them for good reasons. Congress in its wisdom recognizes that there are often a number of things that cannot be set forth with specificity in the legislation itself and therefore leaves it to the more thoughtful approach of the agencies to put further gloss or finality to it. So for both those reasons, I tend to have a great deal of sympathy for people like Evelyn and Richard, notwithstanding the criticism that I sometimes feel compelled to launch their way.

Having said all that, I have to say, notwithstanding the sympathy, that several hundred pages of 401(a)(4) nondiscrimination rules to implement a few lines of statutory restatement is by any objective measure regulatory overkill. I think that if in the preamble to the separate lines of business rule the IRS acknowledges up front that it anticipates that fewer than 700 companies in the entire country will be able to use those rules, we are justified in questioning whether the agency has thwarted the will of the Congress in establishing that legislative standard. When the Department of Labor seeks to add stricter auditing requirements, asking the plan sponsors to be the auditors of the plans, to look for the things that perhaps the Department of Labor itself should be looking for and report those things to the Department, we question whether the burden has been shifted inappropriately.

Why has it evolved to this point? I think that President Bush may have put it best, although he was speaking in an entirely different context. In his January 1992 State of the Union address, he was talking about capital gains, I think, when he said that "A Puritan is one who stays up all night worried sick that somebody out there may be having a good time." I think that we have evolved to the point where our lawmakers and regulators have adopted a puritanical approach to legislating and regulating in the pension area. They seem to have become so inordinately worried about every theoretical opportunity for plan sponsors to discriminate or breach their fiduciary duty that the system as a whole has been overly burdened, both good plan sponsors and bad ones alike.

In our APPWP Report entitled "Gridlock," which sets forth some of the causes of some of this complexity, and more importantly, lays out twenty-nine specific recommendations for how it might be simplified, we attribute this mind-set to what we think are two misconceptions held by those who legislate and regulate these areas. The introduction to this report is included in your conference materials. The first misconception is something that we somewhat humorously call "evil plan myopia," and that is the apparent belief on the part of those who regulate in this area that the principal objective of too many plan sponsors is somehow to cheat the participants in their plans and not to provide them with adequate benefits. How that really philosophically parses with the voluntary system we have, when no one is compelling employers to provide the program in the first place, is something that I have never completely understood. The second misconception is something that we call "computer omnipotence," and that is the equally misunderstood belief that new rules, new requirements, new compliance burdens can be placed upon the system and that somehow employer plan sponsors can magically press a button and comply with all the data and compilation requirements that are necessary to deal with these tests that are put forth.

By the way, it goes without saying that none of these comments are at all directed toward individuals. In fact I would have to say parenthetically that Evelyn has been a breath of fresh air since coming to the Treasury in this regard. But I do think that this is a mind-set that has evolved and that we have had to deal with it in dealing with people in the Department of Labor and other regulatory agencies as we have seen the burden get greater.

The bottom line of all of this is that we seem to have lost any kind of connection to a cost-benefit analysis with respect to this system. Many have spoken at this conference about the $50 billion tax expenditure for pensions, but what about the billions that are wasted, tax deductible billions that are wasted, in terms of employers having to spend money to essentially prove that circles are round. What is the sense of putting plan sponsors through excruciating pain for some perhaps marginal increase.

Not to repeat the excellent data that has been presented, I would just cite the very good Hay/Huggins study (1990) that was done for PBGC on the administrative burden and conclude with these three thoughts. We have fundamentally three problems—and, until we address them, we will not be able to restore a vibrant system. The first one is that we are going to hear more and more that, "You know, these rules, they're understandable once you get into them. You really can work them out, and you know, plans can pass these tests." I think that misses the point. I do not think that there's been a rational explanation for why plan sponsors must go through this exercise. Why has the burden shifted from government to plan sponsors to prove that plans are not discriminatory, for example? The second point is that we as benefits professionals have not understood ourselves, and certainly have not therefore communicated to our policy makers, that pensions are not just an expense but rather a tremendous investment. I do not just mean investment in terms of delivering retirement income but also in terms of national savings. I would cite particularly Syl Schieber's excellent work with respect to the equitable distribution of the pension system. Finally, since I cited President Bush, I should cite a Democrat as well, with what I call the Richard Gephardt message. When he ran for president four years ago, his campaign theme was "It's Your Fight Too." I think that's right. Ultimately, this system does not exist for me or my members, who are really only the conduits for delivering retirement income security, but really for people that Meredith and the retiree advocacy groups represent. I do not understand why it is just the business community that is always complaining about the complexity of the system and its direction. It seems to me that it's the other group's plight as well to join us helping to make this system simpler. Even though to do so in a direct and immediate sense would of course be relieving burdens on plan sponsors, they, after all, are the ones who have to make the decision to sponsor the plans. I fear that if we do not address those things, the prophecy that Ron Keller made yesterday here in the discussion group would become true in terms of the trend toward nonqualified plans. What an ironic and bitter twist that would be, if in the name of greater equity, we ended up diminishing employers' support for the tax qualified system. Thank you.

Phyllis C. Borzi

Let me start by issuing my disclaimer as Evelyn did. Anyone who knows me knows that I never speak in anything but a personal capacity. I am clearly not speaking for the Committee on Labor-Management Relations or any member or official of the Committeee. My perspective is formed from my thirteen-plus years as a Congressional staffer, my work in the private sector before then, and the daily interaction I have with members of Congress, their constituents, other policy makers, and regular, ordinary people who often drop in, because my office happens to be located on the first floor of the Cannon Building, right near the guard's desk, and says, "Labor-Management Relations." So all these things are what inform my comments on what I think the role of Congress is in the development of pension policy.

The first thing people ought to think about is that members of Congress are usually elected as problem solvers. Because of the unpredictability in this election coming up, maybe this year problem solvers will not be elected. Probably the people who will be elected to Congress are people who run on the platform, "There are no problems. I have no intention of solving any problem that exists or creating any others," and so we may have different philosophies. But up to this point, members of Congress of all political stripes are elected because they see problems and they convince the voters in their districts, whether it be for a state or local office or a Congressional seat, that they are in a position to create change and apply that creativity and change to the problems. So when they begin problem solving, politicians believe that they can identify the problems and, with the assistance of their constituents and other outsiders, sometimes euphemistically called "special interests," can craft fairly well-targeted solutions.

Now the one thing you know after you spend more than five minutes looking at the legislative problems and the nature of the issues that Congress faces, certainly in the employee benefits area, and perhaps even in a broader context, is that it's not so easy to figure out what the problems are. And it's even more difficult to figure out what the solutions are, assuming that you do not want to create more problems than those you are purporting to solve. So the role of the Congress is, I think, to move through problem solving activities in a judicious fashion, not breakneck, not hectic, not constantly responding to crisis. Yet I would be silly and unrealistic if I told you that in fact, that is what Congress does. Congress is responding most often to a crisis, real or perceived, and trying to develop policy in a way that balances the interests of the affected parties.

Sometimes Congress is successful and sometimes not. When the framers of ERISA enacted that statute in 1974, they thought they were providing protection for plan participants. They thought they were establishing minimum standards that would protect plan participants, but they recognized that Congress cannot just write laws and then go off into the sunset for the next forty, fifty, sixty years. What you need to do is write standards and then figure out a way to make people obey those standards. There are many different ways to go about it. One fairly extreme way would be to slap people in jail or restore capital punishment, even if they violated some technical rule. On the other hand, you could set up a system like the framers of ERISA did, which I think is a sensible scheme. It creates a balance between government enforcement of these rules and private sector enforcement, self-help, which some of you are very fond of talking about now in other contexts. That's the scheme that Congress set up in ERISA. Now fast forward to where we are today, and say to yourself, "Well, did ERISA fulfill the vision that its framers had for it? Is this a balanced statute? Is it enforced? Are there basic rules? Do people know what those rules are and do they obey the rules?" I think the answer is not clear. It's a matter of whether you think the glass is half full or half empty.

One major reason that we are all here today talking about pension policy and these various issues, many bemoaning the complexity of the statute, bemoaning the complexity of regulations, is that when Congress enacted ERISA there was a fundamental difference of opinion, a schizophrenia, if you will, about what the critical nature of the minimum standard was to be. Congress sets the basic rules but, as Jim said, "Who gets to fill in the gaps?" This is what over the years I have called the problem of the "Doublemint Twins statute." ERISA is like the Doublemint Twins commercial we used to see on television; it is a labor statute and it is a tax statute. It was developed as a labor statute, and the people who wrote the basic rules came from the Labor Committee in Congress and had a labor background. Yet in the past ten years or so most of the changes in the minimum standards have been accomplished through the tax law. That has had a significant impact. As I looked over the participant list, I did not see many labor lawyers. For those of you who are not labor lawyers, you should realize that the way labor laws are written and enforced is fundamentally different from the way the tax laws are written and enforced. Labor laws are broadbrush principles, and the gaps in those principles are filled in, not by federal regulatory agencies, but by the courts. These broad-brush principles set out goals, objectives, some rules; and employers and unions, employers and their employee representatives, employers and workers operate in that context, in some sense at their peril. If Section 89, the hated Section 89 of the Internal Revenue Code, had been a labor statute, it would have simply said, "Thou must not discriminate in favor of high paid workers in providing health benefits." Period. It would not have had 422 bright line tests and 67 safe harbors and all that other detail that eventually caused Congress to repeal it. A Section 89, written as a labor law, might have had a couple more lines, but not 800 pages of regulations. In designing a plan an employer would have had to make basic policy decisions on how to structure the plan in a way not to violate the basic nondiscrimination principle, because, if challenged, the employer would not be able to say, "I met the third safe harbor under the sixth alternative rule." The employer would simply have to demonstrate on a facts and circumstances basis that the plan did not discriminate.

Since ERISA was passed, we have moved away from the labor approach of broad-brush principles into a highly technical tax statute, and to a great extent the complexity we see in the statute is because it has taken on the aura of a tax statute. For a couple of years I have taught a course on the contemporary legal environment of employee benefit plans as part of the joint program developed by Wharton and the International Foundation of Employee Benefit Plans leading to the professional designation of Certified Employee Benefits Specialist. One of the early lessons focused on the constitutional principles that underpin the benefits system. If you focus on the constitutional difference between a remedial statute, which is what labor laws are, and a punitive statute, which is what our tax laws are, you can begin to see the problem. In interpreting a remedial statute, any ambiguities are resolved in favor of participants, since they are the group Congress was trying to protect. In contrast, when a punitive statute is being examined, the approach is much more narrow. In order to hold the taxpayer liable, you must write a rule in which the taxpayers' conduct is clearly within the four corners of the rule. To the extent that Congress has moved away from a labor protection law and over the past few years focused on the tax law, complexity was inevitable. This focus occurred in part because the deficit was driving the issues, not pension policy. With tax law, the answer to the question of who fills in the gaps has to be the agencies. It does not need to be so. We could step back from that, but it has been the path that Congress has chosen to follow recently. One serious and troubling result of that choice has been inordinate complexity.

The final observation I want to make here is that we really are talking about a form of policy or regulatory quicksand. To the extent that you begin spending a whole lot of time regulating every last detail, prescribing every last rule, you are almost bound to continue down that path. If the role of Congress in enacting legislation and the federal agencies in interpreting those laws is to think about every theoretical possibility where a rule could be violated, and then writing a rule to cover it, that makes a strong statement about the failure of the enforcement structure that Congress first set out. To the extent that you must have a complicated and constantly changing regulatory structure, you are as much as admitting that the law can not be enforced. We know that the government agencies are incapable of enforcing ERISA, which is not really a commentary on their competence or willingness to do the job. It's just a fact of life. I always say that even if you gave each ERISA agency Casper Weinberger's wish list of resources times ten, there still wouldn't be enough resources for the agencies. From a Congressional point of view, we need to go back to first principles. We need to figure out a way to let participants enforce their rights themselves, because the agencies are looking at broader issues, not individual participants' rights. We need to move back toward reestablishment of fundamental labor law principles and broad-brush goals and objectives and not continue to be bogged down in the detail that inevitably results when you approach ERISA as a tax statute, not as a labor law. Thank you.

Edwin C. Hustead

Now I can understand all of that and all of the reasons why we need involved regulations; nevertheless, the outcome of all of it is going to be to continue the trend toward the defined benefit plan dying off. I think it should be clear from data like ours, Professor Clark's, and everybody else's that we have here in the corner. Defined benefit plans are now dropping throughout the sizes, medium and larger employers as well. They were over 90 percent at the beginning of the 1980s, and after the flurry of regulations, laws, accounting rules, and court decisions, we are now down to under 70 percent of medium and large employer plan sponsors having defined benefit plans. How far that will go, I do not know. I would guess it's going to go at least down to as low as 50 percent; maybe as little as 25 percent. The result is going to be, given the current structure, and I know there are those who will say, "Well, you actuaries should be helping employers and sponsors design better plans," but it does not work that way. The result is going to be, given the typical 401(k) plan, that the amount of money produced from employer-sponsored retirement plans in the next generation is going to be substantially lower than it is now. When that occurs, then Congress and the Administration are going to look around and say, "What should we do? Should we accept that this generation of retirees should have less income, or should we raise Social Security?" We will not be able to go back then and reinvent the present system.

Now I am not arguing, and I would not say, that defined benefit plans are inherently better than defined contribution plans. I would simply say they are very different plans. They do very different things as far as the distribution of income, and in their current structures certainly, defined contribution plans produce much more income for current consumption and much less for retirement than do defined benefit plans. I would agree, and I think that other people would agree, with the intent of most of the changes. I was one of the advocates of what became the *Norris* decision, and with that we can see, at best, I am very disturbed by certain members of my own profession who are helping doctors and lawyers squirrel away what monies they possibly can by using what are incorrect actuarial assumptions among other things. There has to be discrimination in regulation. Nevertheless the result of all this, in the way it has taken, is to create the trend we see today.

The immediate problem is that no one sat down in 1980 and said, "We are going to take a series of actions that will tilt the playing field toward defined contribution and away from defined benefit plans." There probably needs to be a new decision at some level, a new direction, because you cannot make minor changes to the current law and level the playing field. So they have to decide, first, whether the playing field should be level, and then take some action. I think that during the next, certainly three or four years, the focus is going to be very much on health care for both the employers, and the legislature and the administration.

Let me leave you with an example of perhaps the other extreme of the current legislation and regulation, and that is the recent decision by the European Community. The European Community, in planning for 1993 and later, and with their authority to have laws that extend throughout the twelve nations, looked at a plethora of social security systems and plans. They range all the way from pay-as-you-go funding to full reserve funding in some countries; from requirements in some countries for full inflation protection to no requirements in other countries. Some allow some discrimination; some do not have any rules on it. They asked themselves, "So what should we do?" They said, "What you have is twelve different systems. They are very much driven by their twelve different cultures. It would be a mistake for us to try to have legislation at the European Community level that would affect these systems. Let's let them run the way they are, because otherwise, we will create quite a problem." And so I think defined benefit plans, which have been growing quite a bit throughout Europe as social programs get cut back, will now continue to prosper there under that scenario. Thank you.

Richard Hinz

Dallas has given me a rather difficult task in that I did not learn until I walked in here this morning that I would be expected to speak, and then to place me last, behind such a distinguished and thoughtful panel, it leaves very little to be added to the discussion. I will offer you a few observations of a career civil servant who does not speak for his agency or would ever presume to. It seems to me that the fundamental issue in the role of regulation, particularly that of the Department of Labor, is this balancing act that Phyllis describes, or in more simple terms, the choice between equity and efficiency. To define it a little differently, the Department of Labor tries to find a balance between a rational and efficient system and one that has compassion for the participants. That's always the balance that we seem to be trying to strike as we approach these sort of issues.

Superimposed on that general framework there's an additional consideration best described with a historical analogy. Dallas introduced this as somewhat of a discussion of the history of regulation. As we seem to stick with these metaphors and clever sayings through these presentations, there's one that I have found particularly apropos given yesterday's discussion describing this conference as a wake for the defined benefit system, or perhaps a memorial service. Looking back at one of the earliest forms of government regulation, which interestingly enough is that of the funeral industry, it seems to me that our role in acting as fiduciary regulators has some similarities. Generally, the beneficiary of the investment decision is rarely in a position to participate in that decision and never in a position to complain too much about the outcome. So we also have superimposed on this equity and efficiency balancing act an agency problem. Our role in the Department of Labor is to fulfill this agency function, to represent the participant where he cannot be represented adequately.

These general principles extend to many of the broad issues that have been discussed over the last couple of days. We continue to concern ourselves with the equity of discrimination testing, balanced against the efficiency of broader incentives for sponsors to provide plans. We concern ourselves with the compassion and equity issues of providing broad insurance coverage to all defined benefit participants by the PBGC with the efficiency problems of distortions in capital markets, if that may be the result, moral hazard problems, and the whole construct of providing what amounts to a free "put" of the liabilities. Likewise, we have the discussion of taxation and the compassion issue of providing incentives for universal coverage balanced against the efficiency problem of treating all forms of capital equally and providing the optimal environment for economic growth. It seems to me that this is really the fundamental problem that we all face in different permutations.

The problem for the regulators, it appears from my limited perspective not having spent a great number of years in this business, is that there's a fine line between harmonious balance and stalemate, and that we are always trying to draw that line between the harmony and the stalemate. To judge from the observations of practitioners over the last several days, we have varying interpretations as to whether we have gone too far in the equity side, or too far in the compassion side, and have paid too little attention to economic efficiency. Nevertheless, we seem to continue to look to regulation and legislation to solve these problems. A cynic might interpret this in a similar way to Samuel Johnson's description of second marriages: "the triumph of hope over experience."

I can leave you with one final observation, that's somewhat a reflection of my own personal experience. Spending some time in China and being married to a Chinese woman and having been imbued deeply with the culture, it seems to me that the regulatory process is a balancing act that is very similar to the Eastern concept of balancing yin and yang and never being able to proceed forward until there's a harmonious balance between the two. Yin and yang are not the Western concepts of good and evil, but the concept that in all of life we face two different and complementary objectives and can only achieve success when we achieve harmony. So, the next time that you get new regulations and wonder what those yin yangs in Washington came up with, you should realize that we consider that high praise indeed!

Dallas Salisbury

In an effort to be at least somewhat upbeat as we end this meeting, I would like to mention that one of the statistics in the Schieber paper which was not noted yesterday was that in 1978, only 25 percent of defined benefit plans were sufficiently funded on a termination basis. That number is now nearing three-quarters, if not higher than three-quarters. I underline 1978. It was worse in 1974. So, as one statistic, that simply says things at least seem on some measures to be getting better. That does not mean the markets cannot go straight down and affect it, but that's tomorrow. Ross Perot will solve that. Second, on the statistical point, I hate to leave it with quite as dreary a notion of the future of defined benefit plans as Ed did. We are seeing fundamental change, but a huge proportion of those companies that pay premiums to the PBGC are in fact staying with defined benefit plans, frequently modifying them, as I briefly mentioned yesterday, to cash balance defined benefit plans. I note that the consulting firm data indicates that in the Fortune 500, nearly one hundred, or nearly 20 percent, have now in fact moved to at least partial cash balance versus getting out of the defined benefit business. Major employers like Xerox, that previously never had a defined benefit plan, have very recently moved to a cash balance plan and have become for the first time in their history premium payers to the PBGC. So there's reason to wonder, especially given demographics. A recent mover into the large company category of more than 10,000 employees is Microsoft Corporation, which has adopted the defined contribution approach, and one has to question that, if Microsoft someday hits a point where the average age of its workforce is 44 or 45, compared to today's 24 1/2, will it have a different attitude about these things? So the fact that companies like Microsoft are moving into the large plan category and bringing down the proportional statistics—should that be taken as a statement of anything to do with the issue of defined benefits' strength or weakness? I think it's too early in the life of Microsoft to be able to make flat statements like that.

Finally, as a comment on the statistics of yesterday's debate on tax expenditures relative to these last discussions and comments, one of the things we have developed over the last few years to do tax expenditure estimates is a mimic model of the Treasury and Joint Tax Committee models. It is not unique other than that it has far more comprehensive data on employee benefits than do any of the government models. One of the things that we have used it for just as a curiosity factor is to take the pension system tax expenditures and break them into their relative components. As a footnote to the politics of this, we have heard that public and federal plans are not subject to nondiscrimination criteria. Our data on the demographics of the public sector workforce would contradict what you are suggesting, Evelyn, that they are very similar to the bulk of the private sector. And I would just note, of the amount of money in the last budget for tax expenditures, $3 billion is attributable to public sector defined contribution plans, $23 billion to public sector defined benefit pension plans, $19 billion to private sector defined contribution plans, and $8 billion to private sector defined benefit plans. So, in terms of looking at the politics and looking at the issues of this, I think it's worth at least putting these numbers in the back of our minds. As tax expenditures are presented today in the federal budget, more of that revenue loss is attributable to public employees than it is to the whole of private employees. More than twice as much is attributable to private defined contribution plans than private defined benefit plans. Underline as the government currently calculates it.

We talked about whether or not the pension system will lose its tax treatment. Public employees probably would not find it very attractive, given that they are the ones from whom most of the money would come. So let me put a few statistics on the table in closing that to me say that there will be a pension system here. It will be regulated, because it will have tax preferences. It is in fact growing in the strength of its fundedness. It is growing in the strength of benefit delivery, and albeit the theoretical models that it implied, I am at least one American taxpayer who has never lost a minute's sleep and never will, or even momentarily believes that any of my taxes will have to help pay any liability for the Pension Benefit Guaranty Corporation. And I will not suggest to my nieces and nephews or their eventual children that they worry about it either. With that, this panel I think has been a very good one. I think that we have met the goal of brief presentations, and I would like you to join me in thanking the panel.

References

Arizona Governing Committee v. Norris, 463 U.S. 1073 (1983).

Association of Private Pension and Welfare Plans. 1991. "Gridlock on the Road Toward Pension Simplification, Revisited." September.

Hay/Huggins Company, Inc. 1990. *Pension Plan Study for the Pension Benefit Guaranty Corporation*. September.

Contributors

EMILY S. ANDREWS, a senior economist in the Washington D.C. office of Mathematica Policy Research, Inc., specializes in employee benefit and pension policy issues. Her previous experience includes client work at Fu Associates and free-lance consulting. Prior to that, she was associate professor at the University of Rhode Island's Labor Research Center and research director at the Employee Benefit Research Institute. Dr. Andrews has held policy-research positions at the Social Security Administration, the U.S. Department of Labor, and the President's Commission on Pension Policy. Her publications include *Pension Policy and Small Employers: At What Price Coverage*. She holds a Ph.D. in economics from the University of Pennsylvania.

DWIGHT K. BARTLETT, III is currently Principal of Bartlett Consulting Services, Inc. He previously was Associate Director of the Pension Research Council and Visiting Executive Professor in the Department of Insurance and Risk Management of the Wharton School. He has been Senior Vice President and Chief Actuary, Monumental Life Insurance Company, Baltimore; Chief Actuary, Social Security Administration (1979–1981), and President, Mutual of America Life Insurance Company. Mr. Bartlett, a past president of the Society of Actuaries, is a graduate of Harvard College and holds a M.S. in management science from The Johns Hopkins University. He has spoken and written extensively on employee benefit and insurance topics.

ZVI BODIE is Professor of Finance and Economics at Boston University School of Management. He holds a Ph.D. in economics from the Massachusetts Institute of Technology and has served on the finance faculty at MIT's Sloan School of Management. Dr. Bodie's areas of specialization are pension finance and investment management. He was co-director of the National Bureau of Economic Research Project on the Economics of the U.S. Pension System from 1979 to 1985. Since 1985 he has been a member of the Pension Research Council. Dr. Bodie has written over twenty articles and book chapters on pensions and has co-edited four books on the subject. The latest of these is *Pensions and the Economy: Sources, Uses, and Limitations of Data,* published by the University of Pennsylvania Press in 1992 (co-editor, Alicia H. Munnell). He is also co-author of *Investments*, a college textbook on portfolio management and security analysis, and a member of the Financial Accounting Standards Board Task Force on Interest Methods. He has consulted on pension finance for the U.S. Department of Labor, the State of Israel, and

Batterymarch Financial Management, a pension investment management firm.

PHYLLIS C. BORZI is Pension and Employee Benefits Counsel to the Labor-Management Relations Subcommittee of the House Committee on Education and Labor. She provides professional legal advice to members of Congress and their staff with respect to pension and welfare plans sponsored by private employers and state and local governments. After earning a M.A. degree from Syracuse University and teaching English to senior high school students in New York, Ms. Borzi received her law degree from Catholic University Law School, where she was Editor-in-Chief of the Law Review. She was in private law practice prior to joining the staff of the Committee in 1979. A frequent speaker on pension and health issues, Ms. Borzi is also actively involved in bar association and other professional organizations. In 1986 she was the recipient of *Pension World's* Outstanding Achievement Award in the area of public policy.

ANGELA CHANG received a Ph.D. in economics from the Massachusetts Institute of Technology in 1993. Her dissertation topic is "Moral Hazard Problems Associated with the PBGC Insurance." Recently she wrote a Congressional Research Service report for Congress, "Explanations for the Trend Away from Defined Benefit Pension Plans." She earned her A.B. in economics from Princeton University.

ROBERT L. CLARK has been on the faculty of North Carolina State University since 1975 and is Professor and Interim Dean of the College of Management. Concurrently, he serves as Senior Fellow at the Center for the Study of Aging and Human Development at Duke University and as Senior Research Fellow at the Center for Demographic Studies at Duke University. Dr. Clark is the author of numerous articles, papers, and monographs on retirement and pension policies, economic responses to demographic change, and the economics of aging. Some of his books include: *Economics of Individual and Population Aging*; *Retirement Policy in an Aging Society*; *Reversing the Trend Toward Early Retirement*; *Retirement Systems in Japan*; *Inflation and the Economic Well-Being of the Elderly*; and *The Choice of Pension Plans in a Changing Regulatory Environment*. Dr. Clark is a member of the American Economic Association, the Gerontological Society of America, the International Union for Scientific Study of Population, and the National Academy of Social Insurance. He earned a B.A. from Millsaps College and M.A. and Ph.D. degrees from Duke University.

RICHARD L. COOPERSTEIN is a senior economist at the Federal Home Loan Mortgage Corporation, where he prices options embedded in mortgage securities. In his previous position at the Office of Economic Policy, Office of Management and Budget (OMB), he analyzed the risks in federal credit and insurance programs. He co-authored OMB's 1991 report to Congress on *Budgeting for Federal Deposit Insurance*. He also helped to develop the accounting structure and budget estimates for the federal costs of deposit insurance, pension guarantees, and federal credit programs. Much of his work both on quantifying federal financial risk and on housing issues has been presented at academic conferences or published in professional journals. Before coming to OMB, Dr. Cooperstein spent five years at the General Accounting Office evaluating federal domestic programs. He received his Ph.D. in economics from the University of Maryland at College Park in 1985.

GORDON P. GOODFELLOW is consultant to The Wyatt Company's Research and

Information Center. During his professional career he has specialized in the analysis of Social Security policy and private defined contribution plans. Prior to joining the Wyatt Company, he was with the Office of the Assistant Secretary for Planning and Evaluation as a senior policy analyst and project manager of the Panel Study of Income Dynamics.

DONALD S. GRUBBS, JR. is President of Grubbs and Company, Inc., a consulting firm specializing in both single-employer and multi-employer pension plans. He is a Fellow of the Society of Actuaries, a Fellow of the Conference of Actuaries in Public Practice, and a member of the Pension Research Council. Mr. Grubbs is the co-author with Dan M. McGill of *Fundamentals of Private Pensions, Sixth edition* and is the co-author with George B. Johnson of *The Variable Annuity.* He has been published in a variety of journals. Mr. Grubbs was the first Director of the Actuarial Division of the Internal Revenue Service and Chairman of the Joint Board for Enrollment of Actuaries. Prior to joining the IRS, he was Vice President and Chief Actuary for the National Health and Welfare Retirement Association. He has been retained as a consultant by numerous governmental bodies. Mr. Grubbs graduated from Texas A&M University and Georgetown University Law Center, and has done graduate studies at several other institutions. He is a member of the District of Columbia bar and formerly was an Adjunct Professor of Law at Georgetown University.

ALAN L. GUSTMAN is Loren M. Berry Professor of Economics at Dartmouth College, which he joined in 1969. He is a Research Associate at the National Bureau of Economic Research and a member of the National Academy of Social Insurance. Dr. Gustman serves on advisory panels to the Unviersity of Michigan for the design of its Health and Retirement Survey and to the Bureau of Labor Statistics for its National Longitudinal Survey. From 1976 to 1977 he served as Special Assistant for Economic Affairs for the U.S. Department of Labor. He holds a Ph.D. in economics from the University of Michigan and a B.A. from the City College of New York. His areas of research are labor economics and the economics of aging.

GARY D. HENDRICKS joined the American Academy of Actuaries staff as Chief Economist and Director of Government Information in 1989, after completing a nine-year stint at the U.S. Department of Labor. During his first three years at the department he was the chief advisor to the Assistant Secretary for Policy on issues relating to private pensions and Social Security. He then became director of the Office of Policy and Legislative Analysis for the Pension and Welfare Benefits Administration (PWBA), and finally served as PWBA's chief economist and director of the Office of Research and Economic Analysis. During his last three years at the Department he worked extensively with congressional labor and tax committee staff while acting as the Department of Labor's representative during budget reconciliation and pension reform negotiations. In addition, he established a health research program at the Department of Labor that is focusing primarily on employer-sponsored retiree health benefits and the potential impact of mandated health benefits on workers, employers, and the health care system. Prior to working at the Department of Labor, Mr. Hendricks spent nine years at the Urban Institute, where he directed the development of microsimulation models for estimating the cost and distributional impacts of government tax and transfer programs and conducted private pensions and social security studies.

RICHARD HINZ is the Director of the Office of Research and Economic Analysis of the Pension and Welfare Benefits Administration (PWBA) of the U.S. Department of Labor. Under the regulatory and enforcement responsibilities assigned to the Department of Labor by the Employee Retirement Income Security Act (ERISA), Mr. Hinz administers the Pension and Welfare Benefits Administration's policy research program which includes the maintenance of comprehensive statistics on private employee benefit plans. Mr. Hinz has been with the Department of Labor for nine years in various capacities and assumed his current position in 1990. He is a graduate of Tufts University, has a MPA from Columbia University, and is a Chartered Financial Analyst (CFA).

EDWIN C. HUSTEAD joined Hay/Huggins in 1980 and is Senior Vice President and Actuary in charge of governmental actuarial and benefits consulting. His work with the federal government includes an impressive list of health insurance and retirement income projects for the executive and legislative branches. For example, he is the manager of a series of projects analyzing and reporting on possible strategies for reform of the health care system. Previously, Mr. Hustead was Chief Actuary for the United States Office of Personnel Management. He has appeared many times before federal and state legislative committees, has testified in court cases on actuarial issues, and has been widely quoted in the press.

JAMES A. KLEIN is the Executive Director of the Association of Private Pension and Welfare Plans (APPWP). Previously, he was the Deputy Executive Director of the association. Prior to joining the APPWP, Mr. Klein has served as Manager of Pension and Health Care Policy for the U.S. Chamber of Commerce, as an associate in a Washington, D.C. law firm specializing in employee benefits, and as a legislative assistant for Congressman John J. LaFalce (D-NY). He is the author of *AIDS: An Employer's Guidebook*. He graduated from Tufts University with a degree in bioethics and from the National Law Center-George Washington University and is a member of the District of Columbia bar.

CHRISTOPHER M. LEWIS is an economist in the Office of Economic Policy, Office of Management and Budget (OMB). For the past two years, he has been developing risk assessments for major federal credit and insurance programs, including international loans and guarantees, small business loans, deposit insurance, and overseas private investment insurance. He received his M.A. in economics from the University of Connecticut in 1989.

DAVID C. LINDEMAN is Director of the Corporate Policy and Research Department of the Pension Benefit Guaranty Corporation (PBGC). Mr. Lindeman advises PBGC officials on various policy matters including legislation, regulations, and research projects to protect the pension insurance program and the retirement security of American workers. Before joining the PBGC, he was a principal analyst in the Tax Division of the Congressional Budget Office (CBO) and served as Acting General Counsel. At CBO, he authored papers and studies on tax policy, pension funding, and social security. Previously, he was a senior policy analyst in the Office of Management and Budget where he worked on policies related to private pensions. He also directed a program and policy analysis division in the Department of Health and Human Services (HHS) Office of Planning and Evaluation. At HHS, he supervised the legislative agenda on social security and managed research and analysis of retirement income policy. Mr. Lindeman earned a B.A. in government from Columbia College. He received his J.D. degree from Columbia Law School and is a member of the District of Columbia bar.

JAMES B. LOCKHART, III is Managing Director of Smith Barney, Harris Upham & Company. He served as the Executive Director of the Pension Benefit Guaranty Corporation (PBGC) from 1989–1993. From 1983 until his appointment as the top executive officer of the PBGC, he was Vice President and Treasurer of Alexander & Alexander Services, New York. He served as Chairman of Alexander & Alexander's finance company and of its pension investment committee. Previously, Mr. Lockhart was Assistant Treasurer of Gulf Oil Corporation, with responsibility for Gulf's financing, investments and cash management. He also was Chief Financial Officer for Gulf operations in Belgium, Luxemburg, Germany and France and an Assistant Treasurer for their European operations based in London. Mr. Lockhart received his B.A. degree from Yale University and M.B.A. from Harvard Graduate School of Business Administration.

ANN A. MCDERMED is an aassociate professor in the Department of Business Management at North Carolina State University. Her research focuses on pensions and other forms of employee benefits with an emphasis on women and job mobility. She received a B.A. in general science from Oregon State University and an M.E. and Ph.D. in economics from North Carolina State University.

DAN M. MCGILL founded the Pension Research Council in 1952 and directed its affairs until 1990. In 1959 he was appointed to the first endowed chair in the Wharton School, the Frederick H. Ecker Professorship of Life Insurance. He served as Chairman of the Wharton School Insurance Department for 24 years, stepping down from that post on July 1, 1989. He was Executive Director of the S.S. Huebner Foundation from 1954 to 1988 and continues as Chairman of the Administrative Board and Corporate Secretary of that organization. Dr. McGill is the author of eight books, co-author of several more, and editor of many others. His best known book is *Fundamentals of Private Pensions*, now in its sixth edition. His *Guaranty Fund for Private Pension Obligations*, published in 1970, was a precursor of Title IV of ERISA. He was the first Chairman of the Presidentially appointed Advisory Committee of the Pension Benefit Guaranty Corporation and has been a consultant to many government agencies and corporations. He holds a Ph.D. in economics from the University of Pennsylvania.

ROBERT C. MERTON is the George Fisher Baker Professor of Business Administration at the Harvard Business School. He joined the faculty of the Harvard Business School in 1988 and currently teaches finance in the doctoral program. Previously he was the J. C. Penney Professor of Management in the finance area of MIT's Sloan School of Management. Dr. Merton is a Research Associate of the National Bureau of Economic Research and a trustee of College Retirement Equities Fund, and he serves on the advisory and editorial boards of many professional publications. His research focuses on developing finance theory in the areas of capital markets and financial institutions; his book, *Continuous-Time Finance*, was published by Basil Blackwell, Inc. in 1990. Dr. Merton has served as a director and as the President of the American Finance Association. He received the Distinguished Scholar Award from the Eastern Finance Association in 1989 and the Leo Melamed Prize from the University of Chicago in 1983. He was twice awarded first prize by the Institute of Quantitative Research in Finance in its Roger

Murray Prize Competition. He is a fellow of both the American Academy of Arts and Sciences and the Econometric Society. He received a B.S. in engineering mathematics from Columbia University in 1966, a M.S. in applied mathematics from California Institute of Technology in 1987, and a Ph.D. in economics from Massachusetts Institute of Technology in 1970. He has received two honorary degrees, a M.A. from Harvard University in 1989 and a Doctor of Laws (LL.D.) from the University of Chicago in 1991.

MEREDITH MILLER is an Assistant Director with the Department of Employee Benefits of the American Federation of Labor and Congress of Industrial Organizations (AFL-CIO), Washington, D.C. Her responsibilities include coordination of the AFL-CIO affiliate unions' activities on pension and health policy issues. Primary among her responsibilities is her work with affiliates to forge new pension policy on investments and shareholder issues as well as to track federal legislative developments. Ms. Miller also works with affiliates on the AFL-CIO National Health Care Reform Campaign and on benefit issues as they relate to collective bargaining. Ms. Miller is currently a member of the Department of Labor ERISA Advisory Council, the National Managed Health Care Council, and the National Academy of Social Insurance. Prior to joining the AFL-CIO, Ms. Miller was Assistant Director of Research for Employee Benefits for the Service Employees International Union. In this capacity she spent a great deal of time in the field assisting Service Employee locals with bargaining over health and pension benefits. Prior to the Service Employees Union position, she taught labor relations courses at Hobart and William Smith Colleges, Geneva, New York. She holds a M.SC. in labor relations from the London School of Economics and a B.A. from Hampshire College.

OLIVIA S. MITCHELL is a Professor of Labor Economics at Cornell University's Industrial and Labor Relations School, where she specializes in labor economics, evaluation analysis, and public finance. She is co-author of *Retirement, Pensions, and Social Security* and many other published studies on the economic impact of the baby boom, pensions and health insurance, and labor market regulation. She is concurrently an Associate Editor of the *Industrial and Labor Relations Review*, a member of the Pension Research Council, and a Research Associate at the National Bureau of Economic Research. Dr. Mitchell has been a member of the ERISA Advisory Council to the Secretary of Labor representing the public and a visiting scholar at Harvard University's Department of Economics; she has also served as a consultant to corporations, unions, government and non-profit organizations. She has testified before Congress and lectured widely within the United States and abroad. Dr. Mitchell holds a B.S. degree (1974) in economics from Harvard University, and M.A. and Ph.D. degrees in economics from the University of Wisconsin-Madison.

ALICIA H. MUNNELL is currently Assistant Secretary Designate in the Office of Economic Policy of the U.S. Department of the Treasury. She previously served as Senior Vice President and Director of Research for the Federal Reserve Bank of Boston. In addition to her responsibilities as director, Dr. Munnell conducted research in the areas of tax policy, social security, public and private pensions, and public capital spending. The author of many articles on these topics, she has also written numerous books, including *The Economics of Private Pensions* and *The Future of Social Security*. Most recently, she has edited three conference volumes: *Is There a Shortfall in Public Capital*

Investment (Federal Reserve Bank of Boston); *Retirement and Public Policy* (National Academy of Social Insurance); and *Pensions and the Economy: Sources, Uses, and Limitations of Data* (Pension Research Council). Among many other affiliations, Dr. Munnell is co-founder and served as the first president of the National Academy of Social Insurance. She is a member of the Institute of Medicine, the National Academy of Public Administration, the Pension Research Council, the Economic Policy Institute's Research Advisory Board, and the Pension Rights Center's Board of Directors. She received her Ph.D. in economics from Harvard University in 1973 and joined the Federal Reserve Bank of Boston shortly thereafter.

EVELYN A. PETSCHEK currently serves as Benefits Tax Counsel with the Treasury Department's Office of Benefits Tax Counsel. Ms. Petschek joined the Treasury in July 1990, as Deputy Benefits Tax Counsel shortly after the Office of Benefits Tax Counsel was formed under the Assistant Secretary of the Treasury for Tax Policy. The Office of Benefits Tax Counsel is the principal legal advisor to the Assistant Secretary and the Secretary of the Treasury on all legislative and regulatory matters relating to employee benefits, including qualified and nonqualified plans, welfare benefits, fringe benefits and executive compensation. Prior to joining the Treasury Department, Ms. Petschek had been in private practice in the employee benefits field for over twelve years and was a partner in the law firm of Patterson, Belknap, Webb & Tyler, with offices in Washington, D.C. and New York City. She holds a J.D. and LL.M. (in taxation) degrees from New York University School of Law and an A.B. degree from Smith College. She is a frequent lecturer on employee benefits matters and an active member of a number of professional organizations, including the American Bar Association, the District of Columbia bar and the New York State Bar Association.

ANNA M. RAPPAPORT is a Managing Director of William M. Mercer, Inc. and serves as a consultant to major clients of the firm. Her practice includes all areas of benefits with particular emphasis on retirement plans, retiree medical benefits, flexible benefits, and benefits planning and strategy. For the last few years, she has specialized in strategic issues relating to retiree medical benefits. Ms. Rappaport has taught graduate and undergraduate courses at the College of Insurance in New York, spoken at many professional meetings, and written many articles and papers. She is both co-editor of and contributor to the forthcoming Pension Research Council symposium volume, *Demography and Retirement: The Twenty-First Century,* and she was a recipient of the ACME award for Literary Excellence in 1987. Ms. Rappaport holds a M.B.A. from the University of Chicago and is a Fellow of the Society of Actuaries, a member of the American Academy of Actuaries, and an Enrolled Actuary. She previously served as Vice President of the Society of Actuaries, three years as Treasurer, and six years as an elected Board member.

DALLAS SALISBURY is president of the Employee Benefit Research Institute (EBRI). He helped found EBRI in 1978 as its first employee and has been building the organization since. Mr. Salisbury is presently a member of the Health Reform Assessment Committee of the National Academy of Social Insurance; the Board of Directors of the Health Project; the Institute of Medicine's Committee on Employer-based Health Benefits; the National Academy on Aging's National Advisory Board; the National Coordinating Committee on Worksite Health Promotion; and on the Editorial Advisory

Boards of *Employee Benefit News, Journal of Total Compensation, Benefits Quarterly* and *Employee Benefits Journal*. Prior to joining EBRI, Mr. Salisbury served as Assistant Executive Director for Policy at the Pension Benefit Guaranty Corporation (PBGC) and as Assistant Administrator for Policy and Research of the Pension and Welfare Benefit Programs Administration, U.S. Department of Labor. He has also served on the Secretary of Labor's ERISA Advisory Council, the Presidentially appointed PBGC Advisory Council, and as a consultant to numerous government agencies and private organizations. He attended the University of Washington and the Maxwell Graduate School in Syracuse, New York.

SYLVESTER J. SCHIEBER is a Vice President of The Wyatt Comapny and the Director of its Research and Information Center in Washington, D.C. He received a Ph.D. in economics from the University of Notre Dame in 1974. He has specialized in the analysis of public and private retirement policy and health policy issues and has developed a number of special ongoing survey programs focusing on these issues. Prior to joining The Wyatt Company in 1983, he served as the first Research Director of the Employee Benefit Research Institute. Before that, he served as the Deputy Director, Office of Policy Analysis, Social Security Administration, and Deputy Research Director, Universal Social Security Coverage Study, Department of Health and Human Services. Dr. Schieber has given numerous presentations before trade associations and professional groups and has testified before several Congressional Committees on employee benefit issues. Dr. Schieber is the author of two books and many journal articles and policy analysis papers. He is co-editor of and a contributor to a forthcoming Pension Research Council symposium volume, *Demography and Retirement: The Twenty-First Century.*

RAY SCHMITT, a Specialist in Social Legislation at the Congressional Research Service, Library of Congress, examines pensions and employee benefit issues. For over twenty years Mr. Schmitt has been the ERISA expert at the Congressional Research Service where he works exclusively for the Congress conducting research, analyzing legislative proposals and issues, and providing information and personal briefings at the request of committees, members, and their staffs. Previously he was a Supervisory Auditor at the U.S. General Accounting Office. He is a Certified Public Accountant (CPA) and member of the Pension Research Council. He holds a B.S. in Business Administration from Waynesburg College.

BRUCE D. SCHOBEL is currently Corporate Vice President and Actuary at New York Life Inusrance Company, where he is responsible for actuarial aspects of various company and policyholder tax matters. During 1989–90, he was Principal in William M. Mercer, Inc.'s Social Security and Medicare Information Services unit. During 1979–88, Mr. Schoebel held various positions in the U.S. Social Security Administration, including Senior Advisor for Policy to the Commissioner, and Staff Actuary to the National Commission on Social Security Reform. Mr. Schobel is a Fellow of the Society of Actuaries and the Conference of Consulting Actuaries, a member of the American Academy of Actuaries, a Chartered Life Underwriter, and a Certified Employee Benefit Specialist. He is also a Founding Member of the National Academy of Social Insurance. He received a B.S. from the Massachusetts Institute of Technology in 1974.

MICHELLE WHITE TRAWICK holds a B.A. in economics from Western Kentucky University. She received a M.A. and is a candidate for a Ph.D. in economics from North Carolina State University. Her current research interests are firm structure and total compensation as well as the effect of government regulations on benefits such as pensions and health insurance. Ms. Trawick is a National Institute on Aging Trainee in the Economics of Aging. She plans to complete her degree in early 1994.

MARC M. TWINNEY is the Director of the Pension Department of the Ford Motor Company. He holds a B.A. in mathematics from Yale University and a M.B.A. in finance from Harvard Business School, and is a Fellow of the Society of Actuaries. He has been a member of many professional groups, including the Conference of Actuaries in Public Practice; the Washington Pension Report Group (predecessor to ERIC); Enrolled Actuary, U.S. Treasury; consultant to the U.S. Civil Service system (1977–1978); Committee on Pension Actuarial Principles and Practices (1979–1981); Board of Directors, American Academy of Actuaries (1982–1984); and the Pension Research Council (1985 to present). He was the member sponsor for the 1989 Pension Research Council symposium, Corporate Book Reserving for Postretirement Healthcare Benefits, and a contributor to the 1991 symposium volume, *Demography and Retirement: The Twenty-First Century.*

Index

Aaron, Henry J., 182
Account based plans, 70
Accrual accounting, xxxiii, 206, 236, 238, 244
Accumulated benefit obligations (ABO), xxviii, 174, 201, 202
Actual deferral percentage (ADP), 166, 174, 176
Administrative costs, 66–67, 77, 111
Advisory Council on Social Security, 16
Age: and pension demand, 74; and pension participation, xxiv, 158; and poverty rates, 13
Airline industry, 235
American Federation of Labor-Congress of Industrial Organizations (AFL-CIO), xxxiv–xxxv, 282
Andrews, Emily S., xiii–xv, xvi
Asset income (investment income): microsimulation projections, 20–21; minorities and, 14; and poverty rates, 15; as retirement income source, xvi, 3, 8–9, 14, 29n.10, 44
Asset restrictions, xxix, xxx, 211, 215–16
Association of Private Pension and Welfare Plans (APPWP), 284, 285
Automobile industry, 241, 264
Average indexed monthly earnings (AIME), 176

Baby boom generation: earnings, 73–74; and government retirement programs, 80, 150; pension plan participation rates, xxiv, 74, 158; retirement income projections, 20, 21, 23; women's retirement income, xiv, 15–16

Bangladesh, 38
Bankruptcy: bankruptcy-only options pricing formula, 249–51, 254–55; PBGC claims on assets in, 210, 214, 243, 245–46, 248, 257, 272, 273; and pension coverage rates, 77; pension termination and, xxxii, 69, 229n.57, 238, 242, 254; pension underfunding and, 241, 243; personal, defined contribution pensions in, 67; put options in, xxxiii, 248
Bodie, Zvi, xxviii–xxxi, xxxii
Bond prices, 207
Borzi, Phyllis C., xxxv, 277
Boskin, Michael J., 28–29n.8, 132
Bureau of Labor Statistics (BLS), 6
Bureau of the Census, 8, 18, 154
Burkhauser, Richard V., 13
Bush, George, xxxiii, 133, 285
Bush administration: PBGC policy, 238–39, 244, 271; proposed 1993 budget, xxiii, 133
Business conditions, 53, 77, 83
Business Week, 142

Canada, 25, 184
Capital gains tax, 182, 188
Carter Commission. *See* President's Commission on Pension Policy
Cash-balance plans, xxxvi, 70, 83, 199, 294
Cash-flow accounting, xxvii, xxxiii, 189, 236
Cash-flow tax, 184
Chang, Angela, xx–xxi, 102, 117
Charles D. Spencer and Associates, 69

Chrysler Corporation, 207
Church Plan rules, 65
Civil service, 65, 150
Civil Service Retirement System (CSRS), 128
Clark, Robert L., xxi, 102, 111, 112
Companies: choice of pension plan designs, xx–xxi, 107, 111, 112–13, 115–16; corporate culture, 77; corporate downsizing, 55, 69, 74, 77, 98–99; corporate income tax, 129; firm equity, xxxiii, 251, 254, 257, 258, 273; firm size, 75–76, 117–18, 121–23; pension liability measures, 201–2; pension termination and bankruptcy, xxxii, 69, 229n.57, 238, 242, 254; profitability, 55, 83. *See also* Employers
Conable, Barber, 134
Congressional Budget Act of 1974, xxiii, 130, 148, 172
Consumer Expenditure Survey, 6
Consumer price index (CPI), 137; CPI-linked bonds, 223, 224
Consumption: benefit indexation for, 224; consumption theory, 93; deferred, 143–47; replacement rates, 5–6
Consumption tax, xxvii, 143, 181, 182, 187, 224
Continental Airlines, 244
Contingent workers, 78
Contribution waivers, 209
Cooperstein, Richard L., xxxiii–xxxiv
Cost-of-living adjustments (COLA), 134, 137, 201, 222–23
Courts, 210, 288
Current Population Survey (CPS), 154, 155, 183, 190

Danziger, Sheldon, 4, 12
Default risk: employee assumption of, xxix, 203–5, 226nn.24 and 25; federal insurance against, xxviii, xxxi, 194, 207, 208, 224; protection of guarantor against, 212
Deficit Reduction Act of 1984, 174
Defined benefit (DB) plans, 73; annuity payments, 54, 83, 165–66; benefit formulas, 55, 199, 201; combined with defined contribution coverage, 63; compared with defined contribution plans, 55–61; coverage rates, xx, 55–56, 108, 111; declining use in favor of defined contribution, xv, 36, 66, 81, 95, 102, 293–94; employee understanding of, 60; employer costs of, xxi–xxii, 66–67, 109; employer liabilities under, xxxii, 200–201, 206; employer size and choice of, xxi, 63, 77, 99, 105, 117–20, 121–23; firm-preference/employment-shift explanations for decline of, xx–xxi, 66, 103–10, 111–13, 115–25; funding rules, 174, 199–200; income replacement rates, 5, 62–63; innovations in plan design, 67–70, 83, 199; investment income, 60–61, 218; investment risks, xix–xx, xxviii, 83, 99, 113, 199, 203, 204; labor unions and, 54, 75, 111, 226n.24; lump-sum distributions, 36, 83; manufacturing preference for, xx, 98, 111; nondiscrimination regulations and, 68–69, 79; PBGC insurance of, xxviii, 194, 195, 205; PBGC preservation function, xxxi, 209, 224, 228n.44, 236; preferred as labor management tool, xix–xx, 56, 69–70, 76, 98–99; public policy and, 82, 87; public sector coverage, 65; regulatory explanation for decline of, xx, xxxv–xxxvi, 67, 69, 82, 95, 111, 290–92; supporting factors for, xviii, 56, 203; Tax Reform Act regulations, 67–68; termination of plans, 69, 74–75, 87
Defined contribution (DC) plans, 76; combined with defined benefit coverage, 63; compared with defined benefit plans, 55–61; contribution formulas, 198; coverage rates, xxi, 56; demand for, xii; employee understanding of, 60; employer contributions to, 44, 71; employer costs of, xix–xx, 66–67, 109, 111; employer size and choice of, xxi, 63, 77, 99, 105, 117–20, 121–23; firm-preference/employment-shift explanations for increase in, xx–xxi, 66, 103–10, 111–13, 115–25; funding levels, 200; income replacement rates, 43, 52, 291; increasing use over defined benefit, xv, 36, 66, 81, 95, 102, 293–94; inflation risk, 87; innovations in plan design, 70–73; investment choices, 60–61, 71–73, 82–83, 198–99; investment income, 61; investment risk, 87, 199;

lump-sum distributions, xv, 25, 36, 61–62, 71, 83, 85–87; nondiscrimination rules, 67, 71, 79; nonprofit organizations and, 64–65; personal bankruptcy and, 67; portability of, 43, 52, 60, 85; public policy and, 82, 87; public sector coverage, 65; regulatory explanation for increase in, 70–71, 79, 82, 291; service industry preference for, 111; supporting factors for, 56, 81; tax expenditures of, 295

Demographic changes, xi, 20, 196

Dexter, Michael K., 6

Disemployment effects, xiv, 26

DYNASIM microsimulation model, xiv, 1, 16–23, 29n.11, 36, 41–43, 46

Early retirement: pension incentives for, 55, 69, 76, 93; Social Security benefits, xxii, 48; Tax Reform Act and, 173–74; trends in, 82, 83–85, 86

Early-withdrawal restrictions, 71

Earnings: defined benefit replacement formulas, 62–63; effects on pension coverage, xii, 73–74, 159–61, 163–64, 190; microsimulation projections, 19; relation to poverty, 15; replacement in retirement, 2–3, 6, 10–11; as retirement income source, 8, 9, 15, 29n.10; Social Security replacement formulas, 135, 139, 175–77; tax-preference inequity, xii, 135, 163–64, 170–74, 175, 190, 191, 192. *See also* Income; Replacement rates; Wage growth

Economically targeted investments (ETI), 282

Economy: economic growth, xi, 19; structural changes, and defined benefit coverage, xxi, 104, 105, 106, 116–17, 120, 123, 124, 125, 185

Elderly: asset income, 15, 20, 21; health insurance coverage, xv, 32; income inequalities, 7, 12; income levels, xiii, 1, 3, 4–5, 10; income needs, 5, 12, 29n.9; income and poverty projections, 22; income sources, 9, 15; labor force participation, 24; living standards, xi, xiii, 1, 5, 9–10; minorities, 14–15; noncash benefits, 7–8; poverty among, xv–xvi, 12–15, 23, 26, 27, 35; SSI eligibility, 27; unmarried, 9, 13–14, 24, 28n.4

Employee Benefit Research Institute (EBRI), 238–39

Employee Benefit Survey, 62, 63, 65

Employee Retirement Income Security Act of 1974 (ERISA): and corporate liabilities, 225n.8; creation of PBGC, 129, 205, 228n.41, 247; encouragement of private pensions, 109, 129, 209, 236; funding requirements, 129, 133, 173, 240, 245, 282; labor law/tax law tension, xxxv, 287–88, 290; nondiscrimination rules, xxxiv, 279; vesting requirements, 85

Employees: and default risk, xxix, 203–5, 226nn.24 and 25; demand for pensions, xviii, xix, 53–54, 73–75, 92–93; inflation protection and, 223; influences of pensions on, xix, 54–55, 56, 68, 98; investment choices, 71, 73, 82–83, 198–99; investment risk, xxviii, 199, 203; retirement decision, xviii, 85; Social Security contributions, 136, 181; understanding of pensions, 60, 68; voluntary 401(k) participation, 25–26

Employee stock ownership plans (ESOP), 55, 61, 62, 226n.26

Employers: defined benefit pension liabilities, xxxii, 200–201, 206; employer size and choice of plan type, xxi, 62–66, 76–77, 99, 105, 117–20, 121–23; firm preference in plan choice, xx–xxi, 66, 103–10, 111–13, 115–25; human resource management incentive, xix, 25, 54–55, 69, 76, 77; investment risks, 199; mandated pension provision, xvi, 38, 44, 100–101; nondiscrimination rules and, xxxiv, 68, 79, 279; pension contributions, xvi, 44, 71; pension costs, xviii, xix–xx, 66–67, 77, 109, 111; pension tax incentives for, xxii, 130, 170–71, 174, 195; and pension termination, 69; regulatory complexity and, 83; retirement trusts, 129; Social Security contributions, 136, 181; willingness to offer pensions, xix, 75–78, 81, 93–94. *See also* Companies

Employment: part-time and temporary, 128, 155–58; structural shift in, and defined benefit use, xx–xxi, 66, 103–10, 111–13, 115–25; termination, and pension eligibility, 99

Equal opportunity programs, 28
Equipment trusts, 200
Equity securities, 218
European Community, 291–92
Excise tax, xxvi, 25, 183, 184
Executive Life, 71

Families: dual income, 74; income levels,
    3–4, 7, 10; pension coverage rates, 154;
    single-person, 50
Feaster, Daniel, 13
Federal Deposit Insurance Corporation
    (FDIC), 225n.10, 241
Federal Home Loan Banks, 212
Federal Savings and Loan Insurance Cor-
    poration (FSLIC), 225n.10; compared
    to PBGC, xxxi, 208, 235, 236, 238
Ferrara, Peter J., 134
Financial Accounting Standards Board
    (FASB), 201, 214
Financial industry, 67
First Executive Life, 198
"Floor" plans, 199
Food consumption, 4
Food stamps, 7–8, 173
Ford Motor Company, 100, 107
Form 5500 data, 112, 115, 124
Fortune 500 companies, xxxvi, 294
401(k) plans: actual deferral percentage
    tests, 174, 176; benefit levels, xxxv, 290;
    employee investment choices, 60–61;
    employer costs of, 66–67, 71; growth in
    use of, 25, 70, 82, 95; lump-sum dis-
    tributions, 25; nondiscrimination rules
    and, 280; PBGC guarantee of, 235; vol-
    untary participation in, 25–26; Wyatt
    Company data, 165, 166
Fox, Alan, 11–12, 34, 51
Friedman, Milton, 223

Galper, Harvey, 182
General Accounting Office (GAO), 214,
    227n.35
Gephardt, Richard A., 286
Gini coefficient, 7, 12, 23, 51
Goodfellow, Gordon P., xxii–xxvi, 139
Gordon, Michael S., 228n.41
Government: commitment to retirement
    income security, xxii, 126–27, 128, 130;
    deposit insurance, 225n.10; federal
    budget deficits, xi, xxxv, 130–31, 142,

171, 174–75, 289; home loan guaran-
    tees, 212; and inflation indexing, xii,
    177, 223; legislative power of, 197, 224;
    mandated pension coverage, 196; pen-
    sion benefit guarantees, xxviii, xxxi,
    xxxiii, 195, 198, 205, 207–9, 235, 248;
    regulatory role of, xxix, xxxiv–xxxv, 79,
    281–82, 290; state, 206. *See also* Public
    sector pensions
Grad, Susan, 8, 10–11, 12, 13, 16, 21–22,
    34
Gross Domestic Product, 257
Grubbs, Donald S., Jr., xv–xvi
Gustman, Alan L., xviii–xix, 29n.12, 42,
    111, 112–13

Hardy, C. Colburn, 132
Hardy, Dorcas R., 132
Hay/Huggins Company, Inc., xxi, 95,
    108, 111, 286
Health care costs: long-term care, 3, 8;
    Medicare coverage, 33; and pension
    coverage, 75, 76, 87; and retirement in-
    come adequacy, xv, 32
Health insurance, 101; elderly coverage
    levels, xv, 32–33; employer-provided,
    63–64, 70, 71, 75, 80, 83; national,
    xviii, 80; and retirement decision, xviii,
    85; and retirement income adequacy, 3,
    32, 33, 63
Hendricks, Gary D., xvi
Hinz, Richard, xxxvi, 277
Holden, Karen C., 13
Housing, 4, 21, 74
Human resource policies, 54, 69, 76, 77
Hurd, Michael D., 9, 10, 14
Hustead, Edwin C., xxi–xxii, xxxv–xxxvi,
    102, 277

Iacocca, Lee, 46
ICF/Lewin, Inc., xiv, 1, 16, 22
Immunization, xxx–xxxi, xxxii, 215, 220,
    243
Income: family, 3–4; income inequality,
    xiii, 1, 7, 12, 22–24, 27–28, 43; mea-
    sures of, 3, 143, 181. *See also* Earnings;
    Replacement rates; Retirement income
Income tax: application to pension assets,
    xxvii, 144–45, 148, 151, 187, 191–92;
    application to pension benefits, 148,
    149–50, 153; application to Social Se-

curity benefits, xv, 27, 137, 141–42, 149–50, 181; capital-gains deferral, 182, 188; "comprehensive" system, xxvii, 144–45, 148, 187, 192; corporate, 129; employer-sponsored pension preferences, 128–29, 143, 145, 148, 180; subsidization of Social Security benefits, 136; treatment of married couples, 161. *See also* Payroll tax

Individual retirement accounts (IRA), 25, 130, 184

Inflation: adjustment of Social Security benefits for, 34, 137, 192, 222; declines in retirement income from, 35, 51, 52, 63, 177, 222; erosion of investments, 34–35; pension benefits not adjusted for, 34, 98, 134–35, 177, 201, 203, 221–24; and pension portability, 201; retiree health insurance as protection against, 63; returns to assets from, in tax expenditure measurements, xxiii–xxiv, xxvii, 144–48, 153–54, 188–89; risk under defined contribution plans, 87; United Kingdom, benefit indexation in, 226n.22

Insurance companies, 76–77; contracting for pension liabilities, 205, 206, 227n.34

Insurance industry, 67

Interest income, xxiii, 148

Interest rates, 145, 215, 243

Internal Revenue Code, 68, 129, 130, 288–89

Internal Revenue Service (IRS): and nondiscrimination rules, xxxiv, 279, 284; pension funding regulation, xxix, xxxii, 209, 238

Investment choice, 71, 73, 82–83, 198–99

Investment income: defined benefit plans, 61, 218; inflationary erosion of, 34–35; tax exemption, 185. *See also* Asset income

Investment risk: in defined benefit plans, xix–xx, xxviii, 83, 99, 113, 199, 203, 204; in defined contribution plans, 87, 199; pension benefit guarantees and, 196

Ippolito, Richard A., 95, 111, 112–13

Ito's lemma, 251, 274n.2

Job training programs, 28

Junk bonds, 207

Keith, Hastings, 134–35

Keller, Ron, 286

Kennedy, John F., 283

Keogh plans, 130

Klein, James A., xxxv, 277

Labor costs, 76, 80, 202

Labor force: aging of, 74; unionization rates, 54

Labor force participation: and pension coverage rates, 20, 74, 149, 158; in retirement, 24; and retirement income adequacy, 19, 26; and wage growth, 43; of women, 15, 19, 43, 74, 149, 155–56, 157, 158

Labor law, xxxv, 288–89, 290

Labor market: role of pensions in, 96; structural shifts in, xx, xxi, 82, 111

Labor mobility: effects on pension coverage, xi–xii, xv, 24, 36; effects of pensions on, 20, 25, 29n.12, 42, 54–55, 85–87; Social Security and, 192

Labor unions: and defined benefit plans, 54, 75, 111, 226n.24; and government regulation, xxxiv, 281; in manufacturing, xvii; and pension benefit increases, 244; and pension coverage rates, 54, 64, 65, 75; public sector, 65

Large businesses: early retirement incentives, 69; pension design choice, xxi, 62–63, 99, 108, 121–22; willingness to offer pensions, 75–76, 77, 105

Leveraged buyouts (LBO), 69, 75

Lewis, Christopher M., xxxiii–xxxiv

Life expectancy, 195

Lindeman, David C., xxvi

Living standards: elderly compared with nonelderly, 5, 9–10, 35, 50–51; elderly's expectations of, 5; income replacement rates and, xiii, 5, 10–12, 22, 34, 45; indexation of annuities to, 223–24; postretirement reductions in, xiv, 1, 23, 24, 46; preretirement, maintenance of, xiii, xv–xvi, 1, 2, 40, 45–46

Lockhart, James B., III, xxxi–xxxiii, 228n.44

LTV Corporation, 210, 214, 241, 257

Lump-sum cash distributions, 99–100; in defined benefit plans, 36, 83; in defined contribution plans, xv, 25, 36, 61–62, 71, 83, 85–87; tax penalties on, 78–79; United Kingdom plans and, 101

McDermed, Ann A., 111, 112
Manufacturing: contingent liability in, 265; employment declines in, xx, 53, 75, 99, 111, 117; and pensions as retirement incentive, xix, 98; unionization in, xvii
Marcus, Alan J., 248–49, 250, 251, 254, 255, 267
Married couples: income replacement rates, 34; income sources, 8–9, 29n.10; income taxation, 161; pension coverage rates, xiv, 18; poverty rates, 13, 15, 23; retirement income projections, 18, 19, 22, 23; Social Security spousal benefits, xiv, 37–38, 49–50, 142
Medicaid, 8, 33
Medicare: financial troubles of, 47, 80, 133; and retirement income adequacy, 7–8, 32, 33
Men: income replacement rates, 11; labor force participation, 19, 155–56; pension coverage rates, 28n.5, 158; poverty among, 13, 23; retirement income projections, 18, 22; Social Security benefits, 139
Merton, Robert C., xxviii–xxxi, xxxii
Microsimulation models, xiv, xv, xvi, 1–2, 16, 20, 41–43, 46–47. *See also* DYNASIM; PRISM
Microsoft Corporation, 294
Military pensions, 150
Miller, Meredith, xxxiv–xxxv, 277
Minimum Universal Pension System (MUPS), xiv
Minorities, poverty among, xi, xiii, xiv, 1, 14–15, 21, 23, 26
Mitchell, Olivia S., xvii–xix, 92
Modigliani, Franco, 223
Monitoring, xxix–xxx, xxxii, 211–15, 219–20, 240, 241–42
Monte Carlo simulation, xxxiii, 248–49, 252–55, 265, 273
Mortality risk, 215, 229n.61
Multi-employer plans, 64, 85, 227n.32, 248
Munnell, Alicia H., xxvi–xxviii, 131, 135, 143, 144, 151, 153, 154
Mutual Benefit Life, 71

Near-poverty, xvi, 13, 14, 23, 35
New Beneficiary Survey (NBS), 10

New England Economic Review, 131
Non-cash benefits, 7
Nondiscrimination regulations, 85; and defined benefit plans, 68, 70–71, 79; and defined contribution plans, 67, 79; ERISA and, xxxiv, 279; excessive complexity of, xxxv, 68, 82, 284–86, 289; Labor Department and, xxxvi, 284–85; origin of, xxxiv, 279; Tax Reform Act and, xxxiv, 71, 279–80
Nonmarried individuals, 28nn.4 and 5; income sources, 9, 29n.10; poverty among, xiii, 1, 7, 13–14, 15, 21, 26; retirement income adequacy, 24; retirement income projections, 22; women, poverty among, xi, xiv, 13–14, 23
Nonprofit employers, 64–65, 150–51
Non-tax-qualified plans, 68, 77, 85

Office of Management and Budget (OMB), xxxi–xxxii, 227n.36, 236
Oil industry, 264
Omnibus Budget Reconciliation Act of 1987 (OBRA), 153, 174, 183, 201, 209–10
Options pricing model, xxxiii, 248–51, 252, 255, 257–65, 273
Orshansky, Mollie, 4

Palmer, Bruce A., xiii, 6–7, 22, 34, 51
Pan American Airlines, 229n.57
Part-time employment, 155–57, 159, 161
Payroll tax, Social Security, 80, 131–32, 136, 137, 181, 196–97; payments compared with benefits, xxii, 127, 139–42, 163, 180–81, 185, 191
"Peace dividend," 174–75
Pellechio, Anthony, 139
Pension assets, 198, 200; asset choice restrictions, xxix, xxx, 211, 215–16; income taxation on, xxvii, 144–45, 148, 151, 187, 191–92; inflationary returns on, xxiii–xxiv, xxvii, 144–48, 153–54, 188–89; monitoring and seizure of, xxix–xxx, 211–15, 240, 242; and national saving, 187; and PBGC premiums, 217–18; in pension insurance valuation, xxxiii, 200, 238, 243, 248; total funds, 247. *See also* Pension funding
Pension Benefit Guaranty Corporation

(PBGC), xii; accounting practices, xxxiii, 206, 214, 227n.35, 236, 244, 273–74; asset choice restrictions, xxix, xxx, 211, 215–16, 242; asset monitoring and seizure, xxix–xxx, xxxii, 211–15, 219–20, 240; bankruptcy claims of, 210, 214, 243, 245–46, 248, 257, 272, 273; benefit guarantees, xxviii–xxix, 70, 133–34, 204, 222, 235, 247–48, 295; and benefit increases, xxxiii, 237, 240, 244–45, 273; creation of, 129, 205, 228n.41, 247; deficits, 205, 206–7, 210, 227n.36, 236, 244, 247; defined benefit preservation function, xxxi, 209, 224, 228n.44, 236; insurance model of, xxxii, 239–41; multi-employer program, 205, 227n.32; options-pricing value of insurance, xxxiii–xxxiv, 248–69, 273; premiums, xxxvi, 205–6, 241, 244, 294; profits and losses, xxxi–xxxii, 205, 208; reform proposals, xxix–xxxi, xxxii–xxxiii, 210–11, 241–42, 243–46, 271–73; regulatory role of, xxix, xxxii, 209–10, 238, 278, 283; risk-based premiums, xxix, xxx, 216–21, 243, 244; similarities to FSLIC, xxix, xxxi, 207–8, 235–38; single-employer program, 205, 206, 244, 247; social insurance function, 238–39; subsidization of employer costs, xxxi, 208–9, 236
Pension benefits, 83–85; accrual formulas, 55, 199, 201; accumulated benefit obligations (ABO), xxviii, 174, 201, 202; forms of payment, 54, 83, 198; and funding levels, 200; income taxation of, 148, 149–50, 153; increases, PBGC insurance and, xxxiii, 237, 240, 244–45, 273; inflation indexing, 34, 98, 134–35, 177, 201, 203, 221–24, 226n.22; integration with Social Security, 68, 83, 84; maximum-level restrictions, 68, 151, 173–74; PBGC guarantees, xxviii–xxix, 70, 133–34, 204, 222, 235, 247–48, 295; projected benefit obligations (PBO), xxviii, 174, 201–2, 203; recipiency rates, 14, 18, 19–20, 161; role of guarantees, 203–5; vesting rules, 54–55
Pension coverage (participation): demographic measures of, 8, 9, 14, 18, 158; earnings levels and, xii, 73–74, 159–61,

163–64, 190; employee demand for, xviii, xix, 53–54, 73–75, 92–93; employer willingness to offer, xix, 75–78, 81, 93–94; influences on employees, xix, 54–55, 56, 68, 98; influences of labor mobility on, xi–xii, xv, 24, 36; influences on labor mobility, 20, 25, 29n.12, 42, 54–55, 85–87; mandated, xiv, xvi, 26, 38, 100–101, 196; microsimulation projections, xiv, xv, xvi, 18, 19–20, 36, 42; lifetime measures of, xxiv–xxv, 149, 154–55, 158, 161–63, 190–91; part-time employment and, 157–58; PBGC and, 247; supporting and depressing factors, xviii, 36, 81; and tax expenditures, 164, 167–70, 173, 183, 187–88; of women, 28n.5, 149, 158
Pension funding, xxxvi, 198, 199–200, 274n.3; accounting treatments, 174; ERISA requirements, 129, 133, 173, 240, 245, 282; IRS regulation of, xxix, xxxii, 209, 238; maximum-level restrictions, 209–10; OBRA requirements, 209–10; and options value of pension insurance, xxxiii, 256–58, 260–61, 267–69, 273; overfunding, 200, 212, 256, 261, 267, 269; PBGC claims in bankruptcy, 210, 211, 272; PBGC monitoring of, xxix–xxx, 211–15; PBGC reforms, 211, 244–45, 271–73, 274–75n.8; Pension Protection Act and, 244, 256, 258, 261; plan termination and, 228n.45, 236, 241, 247, 255; public sector pensions, 65, 71, 78, 82; and risk-based premiums, xxx, 217–18, 220, 243; underfunding, 200, 240–41, 247–48, 250, 256, 261, 264, 267. *See also* Pension assets
Pension liabilities, 200–201; accumulated benefit obligations (ABO), xxviii, 174, 201, 202; default risk, xxix, 203–5; immunization of, xxx–xxxi, xxxii, 215–16, 220, 243; and options value of pension insurance, xxxiii, 248, 249, 253, 256, 258–59, 267; PBGC insurance of, 247–48; PBGC monitoring of, xxxii, 238; projected benefit obligations (PBO), xxviii, 174, 201–2, 203; underfunding and, 243
Pension participation. *See* Pension coverage

Pension portability: defined contribution plans, 43, 52, 60, 85; and income replacement rates, 24; and labor mobility, 24–25, 29n.12, 85, 201
Pension Protection Act of 1987, 244, 256, 258, 261
Pension Security Act of 1992, 244
Pensions and Welfare Benefits Administration, 209
Pension termination, 87; as cause of bankruptcy, xxxii, 69, 229n.57, 238, 242, 254; claims, PBGC exposure to, xxxiii, 247, 248, 252, 264, 273; regulations and, 76; relation to funding levels, 228n.45, 236, 241, 247, 255
Perot, H. Ross, 278, 293
Pestieau, Pierre, 185
Petschek, Evelyn A., xxxiv, 277
Poverty, 38; elderly in, xv–xvi, 12–15, 23, 26, 27, 35; eradication of, xv–xvi, 2, 35–36, 37, 40; married couples in, 13, 15, 23; measures of, 7–8; men in, 13, 23; minorities in, xi, xiii, xiv, 1, 14–15, 21, 23, 26; nonmarried in, xiii, 1, 7, 13–14, 15, 21, 26; projected rates of, 21, 22, 23, 36–37; Social Security taxation and, 27; women in, xi, xiv, 13–14, 23, 26
Poverty-line index, 4, 5, 7, 10, 12, 35
Prepayment risk, 229n.61
President's Commission on Pension Policy, xiv, 6, 26, 34, 51
President's Tax Proposals to the Congress for Fairness, Growth, and Simplicity (Treasury Department), 188
Primary insurance amount (PIA), 176
PRISM microsimulation model, xiv, 1, 16–23, 36, 41, 46
Profit sharing plans, 55, 63, 71
Projected benefit obligations (PBO), xxviii, 174, 201–2, 203
Public sector pensions, 65–66; funding levels, 65, 71, 78, 82; governmental power over, 197, 224; inflation indexing, 134–35; state and local, 65, 78; tax expenditures, xxxvi, 150–53, 294–95
Put options, xxxiii, 248

Radner, Daniel, 10, 51
Rappaport, Anna M., xvii–xix
Reagan administration, 281

Regulation, 95, 100–101, 104–5, 277; Congress and, xxxiv, xxxv, 68, 284, 287–90; and defined benefit plans, xx, xxxv–xxxvi, 67, 69, 82, 95, 111, 290–92; and defined contribution plans, 70–71, 79, 82, 291; Department of Labor and, xxix, xxxii, xxxvi, 67, 284–85, 292–93; nondiscrimination rules, xxxiv, xxxv, 68–69, 71, 79, 82, 279–80, 284–86; and non-tax-qualified plans, 68, 77; organized labor and, xxxiv–xxxv, 281–83; and plan termination, 76; tax policy and, xxxv, 279, 288–89; Tax Reform Act, 67–68, 71, 78, 279–80; United Kingdom, xx, 101
Replacement rates: defined benefit plans, 5, 63; defined contribution plans, 43, 52, 291; and maintenance of living standards, xiii, 5, 10, 22, 24, 25; microsimulation projections, 21–22; preretirement earnings levels and, xiii, 6, 10–12, 34; public sector pensions, 65; and retirement income adequacy, xiii–xiv, 5–7, 45–46, 51, 222; Social Security, xiv, xvi–xviii, 26, 47–48, 49–50, 51–52
Republic Steel, 210, 229n.56
Retirement, 48–49; definitions of, 2; employment in, 24; health insurance coverage and, xviii, 32–33; incentives, xx; independent living in, 7; poverty in, 26. *See also* Early retirement; Retirement income
Retirement age, 32, 82; definitions of, 2; Social Security law, xvii, 24, 47, 48, 52
Retirement Equity Act of 1984, 161
Retirement History Survey, 14
Retirement income: adequacy, xiii, 2, 32, 45–46, 222; compared with poverty, xiii, 7–8, 12–15, 35–36; compared with preretirement income, xiii, 5–7, 10–12, 34; compared with working population, xiii, xvi, 3–5, 9–10, 35; definitions of, 1, 2–3; government commitment to security of, xxii, xxviii, 126–27, 128, 130, 134, 135; health care costs and, xv, 32–33; inequalities, xiii, 7, 12, 27–28; inflation and, 34–35, 51, 52, 63, 177, 222; measurements of, 8–9, 40–41; microsimulation projections, xiv, xv, xvi, 1, 16–23, 36–37, 41–43, 46–47; mini-

mum, 45; policy, budget deficits and, xviii, xxxv, 82, 289; policy, tax policy and, xii, 288–89; policy options for improvement of, xiv–xvi, 23–28, 37–38, 44, 175; and preretirement living standards, xiii, 9–12, 24–25, 40, 45–46; replacement rates, xiii–xiv, 5–7, 10–12, 21–22, 45–46, 222; Social Security portion, xvi–xvii, 47–48; sources of, 2, 3, 8–9, 15, 194–95

Retirement Income Survey, 28–29n.8
Retirement trusts, 129
Revenue Act: (1921): 128–29; (1926), 129; (1938), 129; (1942), xxxiv, 129
Revolutionary War, 128
Risk-based premiums, xxix, xxx, xxxii, 211, 216, 217–21, 243, 244
Risk-sharing, 87
Robertson, A. Haeworth, 131–32
Roosevelt, Franklin D., 137
Rudman, Warren B., 130–31
Ruggles, Patricia, 4

Salisbury, Dallas, xxxiv, xxxvi, 277
Savings: defined contribution plans and, 82–83; demand for, 74; and demand for pensions, 93; income inequalities and, 12; inflationary erosion of, 34–35, 145; investment of, 34–35, 83, 196; maintenance of living standards and, xiv, 2; national, pension tax-deferral and, xxvii, 187; personal, pattern of decrease in, xvii, 50, 80, 87; as retirement income source, 15, 37, 38, 194–95, 223; Social Security subsidization of, 127–28, 191; taxation of gains on, 147, 149; tax deferrals, 25, 148–49, 176, 185; U.S. rates of, 20
Savings and loan associations (S&L), xii, xxix, 208, 210, 237
Schieber, Sylvester J., xxii–xxvi, 286, 293
Schobel, Bruce D., xvi–xvii
Securities and Exchange Commission (SEC), 282
Self-employment, 195
Service industries, xx, 111
Shaked, Israel, 250
Shoven, John B., 28–29n.8
Single Employer Pension Plan Amendments Act 1986, 236
Smalhout, James, 207

Small businesses: growth of, xxi, 108, 110; mandated pension provision, xiv, 26; pension administrative costs, 66–67; pension design choice, xxi, 63–64, 66, 110, 121–22; pension regulations and, 79; willingness to offer pensions, 77, 80, 105
Smolensky, Eugene, 4, 10, 12, 50
Social Insecurity (Hardy and Hardy), 132
Social Security, 282; benefit formulas, xiv, xvi–xvii, 14, 27, 197; benefit reductions for higher earners, xxv–xxvii, 128, 175–76, 177, 192; benefits, compared with tax payments, xxii, 127, 139–42, 163, 180–81, 185, 191; benefits, future instability of, xxii–xxiii, 80, 127, 132–33, 137–39, 197; benefits, future stability of, xvi–xvii, 47–48; benefits, income replacement rates, xvii, 37, 47, 48, 49–50, 51–52, 183; benefits, inflation indexing, 34, 137, 192, 222; benefits, taxation of, xv, 27, 137, 141–42, 149–50, 181; combined with pensions, tax effects of, xxiv, xxv, 127–28, 150, 163–70, 188, 191; creation of, 129, 135–37; disability benefits, 52; early retirement benefits, xxii, 48; and eradication of poverty, xvi, 26, 37–38; income adequacy/equity conflict, 134, 135–36, 171; integration of pension benefits with, 68, 83, 84; "money's worth" analysis, xxv–xxvi, 141–42, 181, 183; Old Age, Survivors, and Disability Insurance (OASDI), xvi–xvii, 24, 47, 132–33, 137–38, 139–40; payroll tax, 80, 131–32, 136, 137, 181, 196–97; retirement age, xvii, 2, 48, 52; as retirement income source, 2, 8, 9, 14, 15, 48, 194–95; spousal benefits, xiv, 37–38, 49–50, 142; survivor's benefits, 14; Trustees Reports, 19, 21, 36, 47–48, 137–39; underfunding of, 127, 128, 133, 139, 142; wage growth assumptions, xv, 19, 36, 191; women beneficiaries, xiv, 14, 15–16, 51–52, 142; work disincentives, 24
Social Security Act of 1935, 129
Social Security Administration, xv, 5, 14, 46
Social Security Amendments: (1939), 136, 137; (1972), 137; (1977), 47, 137; (1983), xxii–xxiii, 24, 48, 132, 137–38, 139, 181

Somalia, 38
Spouses, 26; Social Security benefits, xiv,
    37–38, 49–50, 142
States, 206, 281–82
Steel industry, 235
Steinmeier, Thomas L., 29n.12, 92, 95,
    111, 112–13
Stock market values, 274n.3
Supplemental Security Income (SSI), 8, 9,
    26–27, 29n.18; underutilized eligibility,
    xiv–xv, 27, 173
Survey of Consumer Finances (SCF), 20
Survey of Income and Program Participa-
    tion (SIPP), 20, 29n.12

Taxation. *See* Excise tax; Income tax;
    Payroll tax; Tax expenditures; Tax law;
    Tax preferences
Tax Equity and Fiscal Responsibility Act
    of 1982 (TEFRA), 174
Tax-exempt employers, xxiv, 150, 151
Tax expenditures: cash-flow measures,
    xxvii, 189; Congressional Budget Act
    and, xxiii, 130, 148, 172; cost estimates
    of, xi, xxiii, xxvii–xxviii, 130, 151–53,
    189, 279; on 401(k) plans, 280; infla-
    tion adjustment measures, xxiii–xxiv,
    145–48, 151–52, 154, 188–89; on in-
    vestment income, 185; measurement
    of, 143–54, 189–90; negative tax ex-
    penditure, xxiii, 148; PBGC funding
    levels and, xxxii, 274–75n.8; on public
    sector plans, xxxvi, 150–53, 294–95;
    Tax Reform Act and, 150–51
Tax incentives. *See* Tax expenditures; Tax
    preferences
Tax law, 54; contrasted to labor law, xxxv,
    288–89, 290; exemptions from, 151;
    inflation indexing, xxvii, 188–89; reg-
    ulatory implementation, xxxv; and so-
    cial welfare goals, 184
Tax penalty, xxiii, 148
Tax policy, xii, 142–43, 174–75, 190, 280
Tax preferences: and employee demand
    for pensions, 92–93; and federal bud-
    get deficits, 130–31, 171, 174–75; his-
    tory of, 128–29; incentive to employ-
    ers, xxii, 54, 93, 130, 195, 237; inequity
    to lower-income workers, xii, 135, 163–
    64, 170–74, 175, 190, 191, 192; limita-
    tions on, xxvi, 78–79; Social Security

interactions, xxv–xxvi, 164–70, 175–
    77, 181–82, 183, 191. *See also* Tax
    expenditures
Tax Reform Act of 1986 (TRA), 184; de-
    lays in implementing regulations, 67–
    68, 78; maximum benefit limits, 68,
    150–51, 173–74; nondiscrimination
    rules, xxxiv, 71, 279–80; and pension
    integration, 83; and retirement income
    adequacy, 6
*Tax Reform for Fairness, Simplicity, and Eco-
    nomic Growth* (Treasury Department),
    188
Tobin, James, 223
Too Many Promises (Boskin), 132
"Total quality management," 54
Trans World Airlines (TWA), 244
Twinney, Marc M., Jr., xix–xx

Unemployment, 128
United Kingdom, xx, 101, 226n.22
United States, 38; federal budget deficits,
    xi, xxxv, 130–31, 142, 171, 174–75,
    289; and mandated private pensions,
    xx, 100–101; savings rates, 20
United States Congress, 81; and annuity
    guarantees, 198; approach to regula-
    tory agencies, xxxiv, xxxv, 284, 287–90;
    and budget deficits, xi, 131, 289;
    changes in Social Security rules, 197;
    and defined benefit plans, 67; enact-
    ment of ERISA, 173, 279, 287–88; en-
    actment of Tax Reform Act, 67, 68,
    173–74, 279–80; exemptions from
    maximum-benefit reductions, 151;
    limits on pension tax prefer-
    ences, xxvi, 68, 78–79; and lump-sum
    distributions, 83, 85–87; and non-
    discrimination rules, xxxiv, 279–80,
    284, 288–89; and PBGC, 205, 214,
    238–39, 241; and pension liabilities,
    201; and public sector pensions, 82;
    and regulatory simplification, 68–69;
    and tax law, 187, 192, 288–89
United States Constitution, 172
United States Department of Agriculture,
    4
United States Department of Labor, 103,
    227n.34; Employee Benefit Survey, 62,
    63, 65; and employee investment
    choice, 67; and LTV bankruptcy, 210;

and PBGC, 205, 209, 238; regulatory role of, xxix, xxxii, xxxvi, 67, 284–85, 292–93. *See also* Bureau of Labor Statistics; Bureau of the Census

United States Department of the Treasury, 187, 223; and nondiscrimination rules, xxxiv; regulatory role of, xxix, 284; and taxation of inflationary gains, 188; tax expenditure estimates, xxiii–xxiv, 130, 148, 149, 150, 151, 153, 189, 274–75n.8; and Tax Reform Act regulations, 67–68

Universities, 64

Urban Institute, xiv, 1, 16

Van der Gaag, Jacques, 4, 10, 12, 50

Vaughan, Denton R., 4

Vesting, 16, 20, 52, 54–55, 85, 226n.20

Wage growth, 73, 191, 202; microsimulation projections, xvi, 36–37, 38, 42–43; Social Security assumptions, xv, 19, 36, 191

Welfare benefits, xiv–xv, 8, 27, 194

Wiener process, 249, 252, 254

Wise, David A., 14

Women, 28n.4; income replacement rates, 11, 51–52; labor force participation, 15, 19, 43, 74, 149, 155–56, 157, 158; pension coverage rates, 28n.5, 149, 158; poverty among, xi, xiv, 13–14, 23, 26; retirement income projections, 18, 22; Social Security benefits, xiv, 14, 15–16, 51–52, 142; widows, 13–14, 26, 142

Wyatt Company, 140–41, 165–66

Xerox Corporation, 294

Zedlewski, Sheila R., 20, 22, 52

Pension Research Council Publications

Concepts of Actuarial Soundness in Pension Plans. Dorrance C. Bronson. 1957.

Continuing Care Retirement Communities: An Empirical, Financial and Legal Analysis. Howard E. Winklevoss and Alwyn V. Powell, in collaboration with David L. Cohen and Ann Trueblood-Raper. 1983.

Corporate Book Reserving for Postretirement Healthcare Benefits. Edited by Dwight K. Bartlett. 1990.

Demography and Retirement: The Twenty-First Century. Edited by Anna M. Rappaport and Sylvester J. Schieber. 1993.

An Economic Appraisal of Pension Tax Policy in the United States. Richard A. Ippolito. 1990.

The Economics of Pension Insurance. Richard A. Ippolito. 1989.

Employer Accounting for Pensions: Analysis of the Financial Accounting Standards Board's Preliminary Views and Exposure Draft. E. L. Hicks and C. L. Trowbridge. 1985.

Fundamentals of Private Pensions, Sixth Edition. Dan M. McGill and Donald S. Grubbs. 1988.

The Future of Pensions in the United States. Edited by Ray Schmitt. 1993.

Inflation and Pensions. Susan M. Wachter. 1987.

It's My Retirement Money, Take Good Care of It: The TIAA-CREF Story. William C. Greenough. 1990.

Joint Trust Pension Plans: Understanding and Administering Collectively Bargained Multiemployer Plans under ERISA. Daniel F. McGinn. 1977.

Pension Asset Management: An International Perspective. Edited by Leslie Hannah. 1988.

Pension Mathematics with Numerical Illustrations. Second Edition. Howard E. Winklevoss, 1993.

Pensions and the Economy: Sources, Uses, and Limitations of Data. Edited by Zvi Bodie and Alicia H. Munnell. 1992.

Pensions, Economics and Public Policy. Richard A. Ippolito. 1985.

Proxy Voting of Pension Plan Equity Securities. Planned and edited by Dan M. McGill. 1989.

Retirement Systems for Public Employees. Thomas P. Bleakney. 1972.

Retirement Systems in Japan. Robert L. Clark. 1990.

Search for a National Retirement Income Policy. Edited by Jack L. VanDerhei. 1987.

Social Investing. Edited by Dan M. McGill. 1984.

Social Security. Fourth Edition. Robert J. Myers. 1993.

Social Security and Private Pensions: Competitive or Complementary. Planned and edited by Dan M. McGill. 1977.